take
your kids
to europe

eighth edition

how to travel safely (and sanely) in
europe with your children

cynthia w. harriman

Guilford, Connecticut

The information in this guidebook was confirmed at press time. We recommend, however, that you contact establishments before traveling to obtain current information.

To buy books in quantity for corporate use or incentives, call **(800) 962–0973** or e-mail **premiums@GlobePequot.com.**

Text design by Nancy Freeborn
Text illustrations by Bob Nilson

ISSN 1535-8062
ISBN 978-0-7627-4563-0

Printed in the United States of America
Eighth Edition/First Printing

contents

before you go

on the road

home base

the totally biased guide
to what to see and do

acknowledgments

I want to express my greatest thanks to my children, Libby and Sam Harriman, for making it possible for me to see Europe through the eyes of a child.

Sam kept a vivid and creatively spelled "jernle" that captured the excitement of so many firsts—a "roman coleceam with a statue of Uguestis Seser," "a very diffrent toylet flusher," "black liquish flavord gum," and eating "octapus tenticals." His original words kept the wide-eyed discoveries of our trip alive as I wrote this book.

Libby read and annotated the original manuscript for *Take Your Kids to Europe*. As the book's most demanding critic, she was responsible for making sure the kids' perspective came through whenever possible. Working with Libby gave us both a chance to relive the trip one more time and to be amazed at how differently we viewed the same events. I thank her for her valuable advice.

My nieces, Hannah and Emma Rausch, have since traveled to Europe with me, reminding me how each child and each family sees the world differently. We discovered Windsor Castle and the rooftop of Notre Dame Cathedral together and thoroughly enjoyed getting to know one another better through travel.

I'd like to thank my mother, Arline K. Wills, for her painstaking copyediting of the first edition. I'd also like to express my appreciation to Candice Richard for the time and encouragement she gave me by editing the first draft of *Take Your Kids to Europe*. My friends Betsy Bolton, Maddy Tourville, and Max Feintuch were invaluable in helping with updates of later editions.

Special thanks also to all the readers who wrote in and shared their experiences for the newest edition of the book. We hope their contributions will encourage all of you out there to drop us a line at cynthia@takeyourkidsto europe.com.

introduction

this is not your usual travel guide

It does not list thirty-seven good hotels in Paris or the best restaurants in Madrid. It will not tell you how to apply for your passport or what shots you need to visit Greece. It does not include a handy chart that converts centigrade to Fahrenheit, nor does it give the European equivalent for every American shoe size.

What does that leave? Simply everything the average family needs to know to survive—and get the most from—a trip to Europe. Who else will tell you where to find a chocolate factory in Switzerland, or why to avoid the Changing of the Guard at Buckingham Palace? What other book explains the best way to get your kids interested in art museums or how to deal with late-night dinnertimes in Spain?

We wrote *Take Your Kids to Europe* with the goal of including all the information we wish we had known before *we* took *our* kids to Europe. Then we've augmented our experience with that of more than two dozen other families, whose contributions appear throughout the book. Does that mean this book includes everything there is to know? Of course not. Our goal here is not to tell you exactly where to go or what to do. Instead, our aim is to show you enough of what works and what doesn't work so that you can call your own shots and start up where we left off, with the benefit of our collective experience—knowing everything anyone would know after weeks of family travel on the Continent, with children of different ages.

In short, our approach is to teach you how to fish rather than simply hand you page after page of "fish." Sure, we throw in lots of recommendations—it seems a shame to waste the "fish" we've caught. But you'll want your family travels in Europe to be unique. So consider *Take Your Kids to Europe* as a practice outing. Read the whole book—then leave it at home, and take with you only the attitudes and experiences from within its covers so you can chart out your own special voyage of discovery.

who is this book for?

We wrote this book for all open-minded families who would like to share an unforgettable experience with their children. Even though all families can get something from this book, we've made a few assumptions about our target audience.

First of all, we're assuming that your kids are school age. All the activities and experiences we discuss are aimed at kids from roughly six to sixteen.

You'll know your kids are old enough when they can carry all their own luggage, don't need naps, and can be counted on not to wet the bed. (Traveling with babies, toddlers, and preschoolers can be great, too, especially if you stay in rented homes and forgo on-the-road travel as much as possible. But it's a very different experience from what we're recommending here.)

Second, we're assuming you're not made of money. For most families, a trip like this will entail a huge financial sacrifice. I'm not writing for the well-off. After all, if things don't turn out as they expected, they can always try again next summer. For us normal folks, this is a once-in-a-lifetime splurge. Therefore, all our advice is offered with the assumption that you want to stretch your traveling dollar as far as possible. (Those of you with the means to do so will have to figure out how to spend more money all on your own.)

tell us about your trip

We'd like future editions of *Take Your Kids to Europe* to incorporate the experiences of as many families as possible. Please help other families by sending in your tips and reflections, such as:

- Additional places to visit and why families might like them
- Tried-and-true ideas for saving money
- Useful resources—books, Web sites, agencies, etc.
- Anything else you'd like to share

Send an e-mail to cynthia@takeyourkidstoeurope.com, or write to Cynthia Harriman, Box 6547, Portsmouth, NH 03802. Our family loves to hear from other families.

the harriman family

We turned our lives upside down and took our kids to Europe when Sam was ten and his sister Libby thirteen. Our trip lasted four wonderful months: one each in rented houses in England, France, and Spain, and another month of traveling.

This trip was the culmination of two years of saving and planning and a decade of dreaming. My husband, Lew, had spent a year at a small Catholic school in the Spanish Pyrenees at age fourteen and had since credited that experience—attending classes in an unknown language, competing in local ski races, and living away from his family—with giving him self-confidence and the ability to look at any situation from another point of view. We wanted to pass those strengths on to our own kids, and slowly the idea grew to travel together in Europe for as long as our savings would hold out.

Nothing is ever the same after an experience like this. All of us became infected by the travel bug and resolved to find ways to see more of the world.

Libby returned to Spain on her own the following summer, then traded her last two years of high school for a year studying Mandarin in Beijing. She's since traveled around the world by boat, spent five months in Vietnam and southern China, and lived in Korea.

Sam discovered a school in Switzerland that mixed intensive academics and skiing and spent a term of his sixth-grade year in the Alps on scholarship. Two years later he attended ski-racing camp on a French glacier and navigated his way home alone by bus, TGV train, cab, and plane. Lew has found occasional consulting work with a Swedish conglomerate, and I was fortunate enough to find a new job that required me to attend several European trade shows each year.

Our couch sags, and it's been years since we bought a new car, but we're happy using every penny we can find for that next travel opportunity. We hope your family gets hooked on the world as we did!

about the author

Cynthia Harriman is the author of five books, including *Take Your Kids to Europe*, now in its eighth edition. Her travel articles have appeared in the *San Francisco Examiner*, the *Washington Post*, and the *Chicago Sun-Times*. A passionate advocate of the gifts and growth that can be discovered through traveling with your children, she is also family travel editor of *Transitions Abroad*. Cynthia's personal and family travels have taken her to more than two dozen countries, including most of Europe, along with Ghana, Japan, Thailand, Korea, and China.

In addition to her travel writing, Cynthia works for Oldways Preservation Trust, a Boston food issues think tank dedicated to helping people enjoy delicious, healthy food. She lives with her husband, Lew, in Portsmouth, New

The Harrimans enjoy "central" heating in Spain.

Hampshire, where her favorite leisure activity is singing in a local folk chorus with 200 other women.

about the illustrator

According to his family, Bob Nilson was born with an ingrown pencil. Originally right-handed, he taught his left hand to draw and now draws with both hands at once, which—you guessed it—is twice as fast. Bob's work has appeared in *Esquire, Playboy,* and the *New Yorker,* and he has illustrated textbooks on speech, psychology, and mathematics. He also published a cartoon book, *The Hanging Book,* with a foreword by Ogden Nash. Bob was raised aboard the Chinese junk *Amoy* on the waters of Long Island Sound. He currently resides in Portsmouth, New Hampshire, where he retired from teaching math and psychology.

about the contributing editors

Dan and Wendy Hallinan contributed volumes of valuable information to the first edition of *Take Your Kids to Europe,* especially on the subject of camping and on Italy, Greece, and Switzerland. The Hallinans have traveled extensively throughout the world with their three children, Nathaniel, Morghan, and Kate. Their favorite European trip lasted five months and took them to England, France, Luxembourg, Germany, Switzerland, Italy, and Greece by camper and in rented homes.

Jodi Tripp helped bring a fresh perspective to the eighth edition. Jodi spent six months in Europe while her husband, Tom, was a visiting professor in Switzerland. With kids Chloe (age five) and Charlie (four), the Tripps traveled extensively in Switzerland and made side jaunts to France, Spain, Italy, Greece, and England, all by rail and boat. At their home base, Chloe attended Swiss kindergarten, while Tom taught and Jodi surfed the Internet, planning each new adventure. Hooked on travel, the Tripps were heading for New Zealand as this edition went to press.

Whenever possible, our contributing editors' names appear along with information they provided.

why take your kids to europe?

Even a good school is by definition a limited place. When we left for Europe, we were convinced that a class of four with the world as its teacher could acquire more knowledge in a few months than a class of twenty-five with a single certified instructor. We itched to remove ten-year-old Sam from an environment where an overt interest in knowledge wasn't "cool." We knew Libby, at thirteen, could learn more Spanish buying penny candy in Salamanca than she had reciting dialogues in a classroom in New Hampshire.

Some of the reasons for taking our kids to Europe were obvious before we left. Others we realized only by looking back after our return. In this chapter we'll discuss all the reasons that might help you overcome your inertia, get your in-laws to donate to your travel fund, or justify the trip to your school system.

We're proposing four different things in this book:

- travel with your kids . . .
- outside of the States . . .
- specifically to Europe . . .
- for as long as possible . . .

Let's take a look at them one at a time, starting with a few reasons for taking the kids along *anywhere*.

why take the kids?

Wouldn't it make more sense to leave the kids at Grandma's and spend the money on a second honeymoon? Why shouldn't you just go by yourselves? After all, the children won't appreciate the Louvre or that Tudor inn in England.

You're not the first one to think those very logical thoughts. Surprisingly though, most parents we've talked to said that in retrospect they appreciated the slower pace of traveling with children. The typical adult trip too often races from one well-known sight to the next, a victim of the ten-countries-in-eight-days syndrome. The best family travel involves staying put, taking it slowly, learning more about everyday life. Leave the kids behind, and you're on vacation in Europe. Take them along, and you're temporarily *living* in Europe.

Better communication is another reason to travel with kids. Part of growing up is learning to separate yourself from your parents. This is a positive step, yet the way it is implemented is often negative. Some kids dye their hair pink. Others experiment with drugs or alcohol. Others do nothing worse than mope in their rooms with the doors locked.

As it turns out, traveling with your kids may be a great way to bypass several years of adolescent wrangling. When we left for Europe, Libby, at thirteen, was just beginning to spend more and more time behind a closed door. But for the four months of our trip, she often had no room of her own, let alone a door. Unable to avoid one another when we had our differences, we learned to talk them out in reasonably productive ways.

Although this meant that we all weathered some nasty storms in the middle of our "idyllic" trip (see chapter 15, Homestay Survival), the price we paid was worth it. These positive communication patterns persist, a lasting legacy of our travels.

Even a short trip of a week or two can jolt your relationship with your kids out of its ruts, as you come to see one another in a different light.

Traveling to Europe made me see that my kids are more self-sufficient than I realized. Reading signs and maps . . . knowing where to stand on train platforms . . . I won't worry about them getting lost in a city, now that I've seen how quickly they caught on. That was a real eye-opener for me.

—Martha Rausch, Rowley, MA

---

why leave the states?

Whatever happened to "See America First"? Couldn't these same benefits be gained by taking the kids cross-country? Why not pack up the van and set out to discover America? If you can afford the time and money to do this kind of thing more than once, you should certainly consider a Stateside trip, too. But there are indeed some compelling reasons to leave the country.

Traveling overseas exposes your family to different points of view. Americans can be very parochial about their lives. So can teenagers. Put them together and you get the American teenager, convinced that there's only one way to dress, speak, or act. Nothing can counteract this tendency quite so well as a trip outside the country. Your kids will look at the burden of school differently when they realize summer vacation starts in late July in England, and the schoolday goes till after 4:00 P.M. in France. They may develop a new tolerance for their siblings when they see Spanish brothers and sisters playing in mixed groups of six- to fourteen-year-olds.

One incident during our trip made it especially clear that our kids were thoroughly rearranging their assumptions. It came on a spring afternoon in the Dordogne region of France, as we drove back to our hotel from a day of exploration. The kids were unusually quiet in the backseat, till Sam broke the silence to announce, "I always thought the United States was the freest country on earth. But when you come right down to it, we're not really." He sighed as he finished, obviously perplexed by his realization.

We pressed him to explain how he'd arrived at that conclusion. "The French didn't even mind that we climbed all over that ruined castle today. Back home there would have been railings and DO NOT ENTER signs everywhere—they would have been so afraid of being sued." He paused, dredging up another example from his experience. "And in Germany they don't even have speed limits. It's like over here they trust you more."

The longer your trip, the more pieces your kids can put together to arrive at a new worldview. But even on a short trip, it's almost impossible to avoid noticing that people in different countries eat differently and dress differently than we do, yet still survive to see the next day.

Overseas travel can give everyone a better sense of time. Children by definition live for the moment, with little regard for the past or the future. Part of growing up is learning to see ourselves as links in a chain that stretches into the past and can, with our help, extend into the future. In a country as young as the United States, though, it's not often easy to make that connection.

Traveling in countries with a more obvious past can help. Early in our trip we visited our first Roman ruins, the immense amphitheater at Orange, France. This stop recalibrated the kids' internal calendars almost instantly. As Sam mused, "I used to think that the *Little House on the Prairie* stuff was really old. But that's only like a hundred years old. That's *nothing*."

With their scales reset to Roman times, your kids can better assimilate everything else they see, from Norman churches half as old as the Roman remnants to prehistoric caves nine times older than Caesar's theater. It's almost impossible to learn from isolated events of history until you have some way to link them in your mind as part of a continuing pattern.

Traveling also gives you a sense of ownership toward every place you've ever visited. Spend a week in Germany, and that item about the German elections on the evening news suddenly seems more interesting. Stop in Morocco for even a day, and you'll be more curious about Muslim issues. That automatic filter we all have—the one that screens out information that's "unrelated" to us—will filter out less and less, the more countries you visit.

This holds true for both adults and kids. For us as grown-ups, owning the world means that we'll read some articles in *Time* magazine that we might otherwise skip over or that we'll be more fascinated by that new novel that takes place in Brittany. For kids, though, owning the world could well mean a quantum difference in school success after their return. All the history, geography, and current events they'll study from now on will sink in much more easily.

why europe?

The reasons for traveling overseas apply just as well to areas other than Europe—perhaps even more so. Yet at the same time there are compelling reasons to visit the Continent as a first lesson in international awareness.

The obvious one is Europe's place as the seat of Western culture. Both for better and for worse, much of our American society is based on European precedents. Understanding the history of Europe is important to understanding the history of our own country—even though Asia, Africa, and South America may better define our future.

Europe is the best living museum of history, an unparalleled opportunity to understand the big picture of the past. Traveling to Europe can help your whole family realize how individuals banded together into tribes, tribes into villages, villages into cities, cities into states, and states into countries.

It's not that Europe is more historic than any other continent. It's just that its history is so accessible—so ubiquitous, so well preserved, and so well presented. In the space of just a few days, you and your children can visit Cro-Magnon caves, Roman ruins, medieval fortresses, Renaissance palaces, and Dickensian factories. That makes the contrasts between eras so much more striking.

The rise and fall of societies was a constant revelation to us. The Moors had held sway over all of Spain, building fabulous palaces and mosques, but now Morocco was so poor. Spain had colonized much of the Americas and was now so self-contained. Tiny England had a global empire in the past, but now Napoleon's description of England as a "nation of shopkeepers" seemed totally apt. All our lives and all our children's lives we'd been told the United States was the greatest, a perennial world leader. Traveling in Europe reminded us that leadership comes automatically to no one; it must constantly be earned.

why stay longer?

All the above benefits can be found whether your trip is for two weeks or two years. But the longer trip, of a month or more, offers its own special benefits in personal and family growth.

Our recommendation of long trips bewilders some of our readers and exasperates others. "Do you know how hard it is to get away for even ten days?" parents e-mail me. "Your book is unrealistic!" I plead guilty as charged. It is very difficult to carve out a longer trip. If your circumstances just *won't* allow a long trip, skip the chapter on long-term stays, and accept my apologies. Scores of families contact us every year for advice on longer trips, however, so I will continue to tout the benefits of an extended stay abroad if at all possible.

One big benefit of the longer trip is the creation of a powerful, shared family culture. Years after you return, your family will hold a solid core of private jokes, food preferences, and memories in common, tying all of you together securely. At home, parents and kids may barely see each other. Dinner is rushed, with some family members already at play rehearsal or PTA, others not yet back from work or basketball practice. On weekends the kids sleep till noon, and no one can ever agree on a family outing. Only a drastic departure from daily routine lets you build a collection of shared experiences.

When people ask me what was the best part [of my husband's temporary military duty in Germany], I tell them "Two months in a two-room apartment with no English-speaking TV and no toys." . . . It was fantastic for our marriage, for our kids, and for our family as a whole to draw together and count on each other. So many "inside jokes" since we've gotten back . . . lots of neat memories that we're hoping to move back to Europe and expand on.

—Ellen Manuel, Bellevue, NE

One of the best shared experiences that come out of an extended trip can be discussions. At home, school and work suck up time and the phone rings at just the wrong times. Yet we had all the time in the world to answer when, a week into our trip, Sam suddenly asked us to explain "How come Jesus was so important that everyone built so many churches to him?" Or a month later, in Morocco, when he wanted to know what made some people rich and other people poor.

Discussion isn't something you can force. Don't for a moment picture yourselves climbing off your transatlantic flight, hopping in your car, and driving away into the sunset discussing politics. Give it time. The longer your trip and the less hectically scheduled it is, the more discussion opportunities will arise. Thrown together in a car for days on end, or sitting around in a TV-less, phoneless rental home, the art of conversation will eventually be reborn.

Staying longer also gives your kids valuable coping skills. Travel is not always a day in the park. And there's a lot that kids (and adults) can learn from coping with the ups and downs of foreign travel.

"Take a trip like ours and you'll be subjected to so much that you can stand anything." Libby's words sum up one of the most lasting benefits of taking an extended trip outside of the country. If you take a week's vacation and stay in luxury hotels, your kids won't learn to cope with anything but jet lag. Stay a bit longer and live like the locals, and you'll all inevitably learn something about flexibility.

Coping means learning to eat new foods when you're hungry and there's nothing familiar on the menu. Coping means putting on extra sweaters and blankets when there's no central heat. It means taking showers down the hall in a strange hotel and figuring out how to use awkward stand-up toilets.

Is there anything more important you can teach your children—anything that could be more useful to their future than learning how to make the most of any situation? Start planning now, and make your dreams happen. What's your excuse for not taking your kids to Europe?

My father suffered a very damaging stroke at age forty-nine. Much of his right side was paralyzed, he couldn't talk, and he could barely walk. He decided to take my mother and all five of us kids (ranging from age fifteen down to twins age five) to Europe. We were there for three months, through seventeen countries, on a bare-bones, low-budget trek financed by a loan on his life insurance. Well, he lived for thirty-five years after they said he'd soon be gone, and that trip was the source of literally decades of wonderful shared family memories. The lesson here is to take the trip whenever you can and let no obstacles stand in your path.

—Thomas Zoss, South Bend, IN

---

planning

Before we left for Europe, a well-traveled friend of Sam's warned him not to let us drag him into every cathedral in Europe. But how do you introduce your kids to the history and culture of another continent without making the whole thing boring and "too educational"? It can be done, and planning can be a fun part of the process. Definitely start six months to a year ahead.

planning your itinerary

Involving your kids in planning can be a challenge. If you ask most kids what they'd like to see in Europe, they'll say "Stonehenge" or "the Eiffel Tower" or "the Leaning Tower of Pisa." They're not going to say, "Oh, I'm just dying to see the most exquisite little Tuscan hill town I read about in the paper last week." It's only predictable: Your average kid just hasn't heard of anything but the most stereotyped sights on the Continent.

Not yet anyway. Start by exposing the kids to as many possibilities as you can. Library books, television specials, the latest issue of *National Geographic*—all become part of stage one in planning an itinerary. Use the books in chapter 22, Resources, especially the kids' guidebooks, for inspiration.

It also helps to enlist the aid of relatives and neighbors who've been to Europe. Invite them to dinner and a show-and-tell session about their trip. (Most people hesitate to bore others with their travel stories. Make it clear that you *want* them to tell you everything!)

pushpin planning

What can you do with all these great recommendations? One method that works rather well is to hang a large map of Europe on the wall of some heavily trafficked room in your house. Use spray adhesive to mount the map on foam board or thick corrugated cardboard so that you can mark interesting sites with colored pushpins.

We used this approach with an enormous map on our dining-room wall, regularly recording intriguing places we'd read about or seen on televison. A friend sent Sam a *Smithsonian* article about Legoland (the amusement park devoted to the bumpy plastic blocks so many kids love so well), and he immediately pushed a pin into the middle of Denmark. Libby read about Morocco in a guidebook we'd bought and staked out her interest in Tangier.

Reach out beyond your family for suggestions. For six months before we left, we invited every guest in our home to mark a favorite location with a numbered pin, then scribble a description marked with the corresponding number in a nearby notebook.

The book started to fill with tempting ideas:

Brighton, England. Delightful town—have a friend, Margaret Marinko, who will show you around.

Morron de la Frontera, Spain. Gypsy music capital.

Wiesbaden, Germany. Gaststätte zum Schwejk—restaurant that serves the original Budweiser.

Bruges, Belgium. Swans, great old atmosphere.

Bergen and Hardanger fjords, Norway. Great prototypical Norwegian fjords.

Oslo, Norway. Great camping and Viking Museum with jumbo boats.

Everyone contributed: a favorite free-spirit aunt, the neighbor who came to borrow a paint scraper, our Federal Express agent. People we thought we knew well excavated unexpected memories of a week spent in a commune in Scotland and stories about the plumbing in Amsterdam and shared them with us so vividly that we felt we'd already left home. Our map was quickly covered with so many red pins that it seemed to have caught chicken pox. We swallowed and digested European geography with every meal.

If your friends are like ours, many of their suggestions will be on the fringes of Europe, in locations you'll never come close to. Others will be out of your price range—an old English inn from someone's twenty-fifth anniversary trip, or a five-star dinner in Paris. A few more, sadly, will be in areas with possible security issues. But some suggestions will actually be useful, and the process will help all of you learn more about the endless possibilities you face in your travels.

what kids want to see

Most kids want to see things that fall into four different categories: namebrand sites and cities, active things, gory things, and kids' things.

name brands

If your child has ever begged for Reeboks or Nikes instead of Kmart sneakers, you know perfectly well the hold that name brands have on kids, thanks to television ads and peer pressure. You'll find this brand consciousness extends to travel, too. It's almost useless to buck the tide.

Our sixteen-year-old surfed the Net and found pictures of the places we would visit. She printed each picture twice, laminated them, and made three matching games called "Rome Memory," "Florence Memory," and "Paris Memory." She gave them to the four-year-old twins for Christmas. Every night after dinner we played a game of memory from one of the cities. Worked great!

—Tim Ramstad, Gresham, OR

My daughters are eleven, eight, and six, and one thing that gets them psyched about a trip is to find children's movies set in those various places. My middle daughter wanted to visit Rome and the Trevi Fountain because of The Lizzie McGuire Movie. Harry Potter, Mary Poppins, The Hunchback of Notre Dame, Gladiator . . . *the younger children want to reenact the story, which is a great way to "see" the city.*

—Mira Radujkovic, Belgrade, Serbia (three-year stay)

Libby explained a kid's perspective on this shortly after we visited Stonehenge. There's not much to Stonehenge. The few stones remaining upright are cordoned off from visitors, who circle the ancient site on asphalt paths, elbowing and jostling with half the population of Japan and Germany. As we left, Libby commented to me, "It wasn't terrible, but it was no big deal—just a few stones."

Stonehenge contrasted sharply with France's leading megalithic site at Carnac, in southern Brittany. There the ancient stones were smaller, but the mystic impact greater, with hundreds of stones marching in straight rows across rolling fields of grass. On our first visit to Carnac, in fact, it was still possible to wander freely among the stones, with no paths, no restraining ropes, and far fewer tourists.

Yet when I asked Libby which I should recommend to other kids in this book, she replied without hesitation, "Stonehenge. If you say, 'I went to Carnac,' people say, 'Oh, that's nice.' But if you say, 'I've been to Stonehenge,' they say, 'Oh really? What's it like? It must be great.' After all, there must be something to it if it got so famous. You have to go see for yourself."

Her reply points out both sides of the name-brand coin for kids: the importance of impressing other people, and the importance of putting in your own two cents against accepted adult wisdom. *All the experts used to say Stonehenge was wonderful. Now they call places like this tourist traps—I'm going to make up my own mind,* many kids will decide.

This fascination/skepticism extends to name-brand cities, too. Paris, London, and Rome are the big three in this area, with Paris being perhaps the biggest magnet of all. Even though big cities are the hardest places to travel with kids (see chapter 6, Sightseeing Survival), your kids will want to go there—and their friends are sure to ask them if they've been after they return.

active things

Anything that involves physical movement is more attractive to kids than anything that does not. Three-dimensional museums, where kids can run around freely, are better than traditional museums, where everything is in flat little glass cases. A climb to the top of the bell tower makes Mom and Dad's cathedral visit palatable. The more senses an activity involves, the more fun it is for kids (and for adults, too, by the way).

Our teenagers loved roller-tobogganing, hiking, paddleboats. Once near Reutte, Austria, we stopped at the ruins of an old fortress. It was a long hike up, but when you got there, you could jump in and out of the big stone windows and pretend you were Robin Hood, so they loved it.

—Maya D'Anjou, Morgan Hill, CA

Despite all the landmarks we visited, the activities our kids rated highest included sliding down the highest sand dune in Europe, hiking in underground caves, and renting bikes for a day. Make sure to alternate "traditional" tourist attractions with offbeat, active ones like these. The longer your trip, the more important these breaks become.

gory things

Dungeons, haunted castles, torture chambers—all of these hold a strange attraction for kids. Guidebook entries like "used as a prison during the Inquisition—don't come here on a full stomach" or "forty-minute tour of sinister dungeons—be glad you're only a visitor" will draw most kids with uncanny magnetism.

Our typical kids carried their blood lust through several empty and unevocative dungeons, only to lose all interest in torture after it was made very real and graphic at a museum in Amsterdam. This special exhibit featured scores of drawings, descriptions, and actual relics from torture through the medieval and Renaissance periods, all laid out on black backgrounds in dark rooms. The effect was not spooky—it was simply disgusting.

Was it the knowledge that this wasn't simply a movie? Was it because we had visited Anne Frank's house that day, and the kids had just been reminded that horror is often more than a fantasy? I don't know, but gory things no longer held any attraction for the kids.

I'm not recommending that you scurry over to a torture museum to cure your kids of their fascination for blood and guts. First of all, I don't think these feelings are abnormal; most kids like to feel a little shivery-scared from time to time. But it will help you plan your sightseeing ventures to know this attraction exists.

kids' things

The same kids who lust after dark dungeons will be equally interested in amusement parks of all sorts. After all, they know this is a vacation. They know your wallet's open, and you're a little more lax about junk food and bedtimes than usual, so it's a great time to try to convince you to waste money at the midway. Don't categorically refuse, but keep your eye out for cheaper alternatives.

My kids give rave reviews to the three-story indoor amusement park in Blackpool. [But] frankly, they're just as enthralled by street performers. In San Gemignano, Italy, we stayed almost an hour watching a man playing a harpsichord, which echoed beautifully under the arcaded buildings. They also love mimes and marionettes.

—Dave Fittante, Würzburg, Germany

If the kids insist and you can afford a splurge, visit and compare. How does Disneyland Paris compare to Orlando? Visit neighborhood fairs and local carnivals especially. We had a lot of fun one day at an elementary-school fund-raiser in France. Sam could compare everything to his own school's "lawn fête"—and enjoy the similarities and differences. (*His* school doesn't serve hot dogs in a hollowed-out length of French bread—or offer béarnaise sauce instead of ketchup.)

Elementary-age kids will want to look around every toy store on the Continent. Usually this doesn't mean they expect to buy anything—just that they want to compare what they know best to the European counterparts of those things. It's really a lot of inexpensive fun, better than many museums. (The adult equivalent—hardware stores—can be fun, too. Did you know flyswatters in France are very different from ours?)

One caution, though. In some countries, small, local stores are not used to self-serve browsers. Normal American toy-store behavior of trying out the various trucks, dolls, and games may make the staff in such stores very nervous. Be sensitive to this difference.

what you'll want the kids to see

Your sightseeing goals will likely be different from the kids'. You'll see an appreciation of art and history as a major reason for taking your kids to Europe. Put that fact to them bluntly, though, and they're bound to roll their eyes. Try a less direct approach. Let the cultural treasures of Europe seep in as you go about everyday activities, and don't limit your ideas solely to the past. Some of the pointers below might help.

art—and getting the most out of museums

Left to their own devices, most kids would put art museums on the bottom of their priority lists. Luckily, art isn't found only in museums. Try focusing on architecture instead with your kids. Wander around a Dutch village and challenge the kids to find five different styles of roof gables. Count the angels in a baroque chapel, or start a photo collection of gargoyles. Anything you can do to make your kids notice their surroundings in detail will help them appreciate Europe's artistic past.

As we walked through the Louvre, Mary [age five] suddenly exclaimed, "I know that painting!" She recognized it from one of our art books. What a thrill to see the original work! At the Musée d'Orsay, she was mesmerized by the art students sitting on the gallery floors attempting to copy the great masters.

—Jennifer and Tim Woods, Chicago

Don't rule out museums, though. We made the mistake of rushing through the Louvre in reaction to what we perceived as immense boredom on our kids' parts. Later they told us they had wanted more time there. From this and subsequent experiences, we evolved the following tips for getting the most from museums:

- Do some homework before your trip. *The History of Art for Young People* by Anthony Jansen is an excellent book to buy or borrow before you go. Browse through the pictures. You may be surprised to find your kids gravitating toward a specific style or period that they'd like to see "in person."

- When you arrive at a museum, start at the gift shop. Flip through the postcards and let each child buy three or four favorites. Then you can set out to find each person's "own" pictures and sculptures.

- Go to museums early, when everyone is rested and museums are less crowded. Limit your visit to a few hours, followed by lunch and some sort of physical activity in the afternoon.

- Ask if the museum has special children's guides. Many museums have checklists that encourage kids to take an organized treasure hunt of the collections. Even in another language, these can be fun for kids.
- Create your own children's guide if no official one exists. *Mona Winks: Self-Guided Tours of Europe's Top Museums* by Rick Steves and Gene Openshaw is an excellent source of ideas (and a good way to avoid the expense of buying guides at each museum). Browse through *Mona Winks* the night before your visit, and make an informal checklist with choices such as "Find the painting of Noah's Ark" or "What color stones are in the king's crown?"

Use your imagination and think up other games, too. The goal is to make sure museum trips consist of more than aimless wandering. One game we played in the Louvre, after the kids were underwhelmed by the *Mona Lisa,* was to pick a painting we each thought more worthy of Mona's fame. The search led us to more than an hour of close inspection of a wide variety of paintings.

history

Naturally, history will be of major interest on any trip to Europe. The challenge is to help your kids get a sense of time and a sense of the major changing points of history, without anybody—kids or adults—getting bored.

Museums may not bore your kids as much as you suppose.

European history museums, in general, are not interesting to most children. While American museums often make an effort to draw television-spoiled visitors in with audiovisual extravaganzas and colorful displays, European ones more frequently fill their cases with artifacts labeled in small type in the local language. Read your guidebook carefully to see whether any museum you contemplate visiting is one of the few recently redesigned ones. One exception to this is folk museums. These often feature furnished rooms you can walk through, or colorful costumes and everyday utensils from hundreds of years of history. If your guidebook mentions several museums, choose the folk museum.

But the best historic sites for kids are those that are large and/or located out of doors, where it's not necessary to be quiet and orderly. Fortunately, Europeans are much less anxious about liability issues than Americans are, so it's possible for your kids to run around a Roman amphitheater or climb the walls of a crumbling medieval castle without anyone getting upset.

Of course, there's no point in looking at something just because it's old. You want the whole family to learn and grow from your experiences, to integrate new information into what you already know. That's why we like to fit historic sites into three themes:

Mystical past. All of us are intrigued by places so old that no one's really sure why they were built or what they mean. Skip Europe's prehistory museums with their dry, boring rows of bones, arrowheads, and beads, and instead visit tangible *places* that reek of the distant past. A few examples (described in chapters 17–21) include:

- Prehistoric caves, Les Eyzies, France
- Carnac Alignements, Carnac, France
- Avebury stone circle, Avebury, England

War and conflict. The study of history is all too often the story of battles and conquests. Help your kids realize the pervasive extent of the Roman Empire. Let them ponder the contrast between Morocco today and the glories of Moorish architecture in Spain. Explore the lingering evidence of Hitler's mad march across Europe. No child is too young to learn the tragic consequences of settling disputes through aggression—and the magnificent legacies of cultural sharing. A few examples:

- Roman ruins at Orange, France; Bath, England; Hadrian's Wall, England; Mérida, Spain
- Moorish architecture in Spain in Sevilla, Córdoba, and Granada
- Viking museums in Denmark and England
- World War II museums in London, Normandy, Berlin, and the Ardennes

Time line. Learning history is useless if you can't put the information in context. Young children start off dividing everything into "now" and "then." The challenge is to help them develop a continuum that places the cathedrals halfway between now and the Romans, so that they can begin to tell the difference between the fortress castles of the Middle Ages and the palace castles of the Renaissance.

Before we traveled we bought a World History Chart and stretched it 7 feet down our hallway (see chapter 22, Resources, to learn where you can get one). It reminds us that Hammurabi wrote his laws about the same time Stonehenge was built and that the Mayan temples date from the fall of Rome to the Vandals. When we returned we amazed the kids by adding 9 feet of yarn to the beginning of the chart to show how much further back the Les Eyzies cave paintings are thought to date.

Try to see sites from a variety of periods, then build your own time line on a piece of paper (like the one in chapter 18), including, for example:

- Prehistoric caves (12,000 B.C.)
- Roman ruins (A.D. 100)
- Gothic cathedrals (A.D. 1200)
- Loire châteaus (A.D. 1500)
- Industrial Revolution (A.D. 1850)
- World Wars (1914–1918 and 1939–1945)

science and technology

Europe has a present and a future as well as a past. Those who see a European trip only in terms of art and history will miss some fun and interesting sites. Our American pride leads us to think that no one—except perhaps the Japanese—eclipses us in state-of-the-art technology. In our travels we've found lots of evidence to dispel that theory, from high-tech vegetable scales to coin-operated toilet kiosks and credit-card toll booths. France, especially, cultivates a high-tech image, and deservedly so. Your kids will enjoy visiting hands-on science museums and factories as well as engineering marvels like the Thames Barrier and the English Channel Tunnel.

natural world

Kids love nature, and so do Europeans. Many European countries are very environmentally conscious. Germany, for instance, has a nationwide recycling system funded by manufacturers. You'll see the *Grüne Punkt,* or Green Dot, on almost everything sold, testifying that the maker has paid a few cents into a central fund to pay for recycling the packaging. Build an appreciation of the natural world into your trip. Draw your kids' attention to the squat green bottle-recycling receptacles on French streets and the manicured appearance of German forests. Venture into areas formerly behind the Iron Curtain, and compare the landscape to that in the West. Enjoy visiting zoos and nature parks as part of your travels, and keep your eyes open for the myriad wine caves, cheese-ripening caves, and underground grottoes all over the Continent.

Our kids loved visiting a mushroom cave near Saumur, France. It was just a little roadside place, real low key; whenever enough people showed up, they gave a tour. The caves were cool and dark, reaching deep into the earth, and the tour, which demonstrated all the different stages of mushroom growing, was all in French. But our kids were utterly fascinated. Nine-year-old Dan wrote in his journal, "It's always neat to go in a cave, and you never get to see a whole bunch of mushrooms growing together."

—Lisa Geibel and Doug Alexander, Austin, TX

---

stereotypes

Are stereotypes real or imagined? The Dutch don't wear wooden shoes anymore, but many Bavarians actually sport lederhosen. The Swiss still make lots of cheese and chocolate, and older Greek women almost always wear black. Investigating these perpetual images is a lot of fun and overlaps with kids' desire for "name-brand" experiences, so here's one area where you'll all agree. In the last few chapters of the book, we'll tell you where you can see windmills in Holland, how to make the best of London's Changing of the Guard and Paris's Eiffel Tower, and where to find a watch museum in Switzerland, among other great ideas.

The best way to plan your itinerary is to take the general principles outlined in this chapter and figure things out for yourself. How you involve your kids in the decision process can be even more important than where you go.

However, if you'd like a few more concrete suggestions, or if you're curious about our kids' (and our readers') reactions to several different sites in Europe, check out "The Totally Biased Guide to What to See and Do" section at the end of this book (chapters 17–21). It's organized by countries and regions to help you get the most out of your travels.

planes, trains, boats, and cars

Airplane tickets, trains, car rental, and ferries can account for a huge proportion of your budget. Although the available discounts change almost daily, our experiences could help you save thousands of dollars.

airfares

Most people assume that the longer you stay and the further ahead you purchase your ticket, the less you'll pay to fly. In fact, special rates are usually good for stays of ninety days or less. If you're planning an extended trip to Europe, you may pay more. And some excellent deals are available at the last minute.

There's really no alternative to spending hours on the phone or the Web researching possibilities. Don't resent the time you'll spend: It could easily save you many hundreds of dollars. And don't simply take the cheapest offer the first day you start looking.

Finding the best fare isn't easy. Airlines these days practice yield management, which works something like this: Flight 1000 starts off with twenty-five seats earmarked as SuperSaver seats, with a fare of $625. You call on Tuesday, and they're all sold out. They offer you the Vacation Fling fare of $987 instead, but you decline and call back or check the Web each day. A week later the airline checks ticket sales and finds there's a good chance that several seats on flight 1000 will be unsold when the plane takes off. They decide to offer twenty-five more seats at the SuperSaver fare. When you check that day, your tickets are booked at $625 each. You've saved more than $1,400 for your family of four by investing in a few hours on hold or online.

Use our list of Web sites in chapter 22, Resources, to look for fares online. Start at a Web site that serves several airlines, such as Orbitz or Expedia (www.orbitz.com, www.expedia.com), or two of our new favorites, FareCompare and Bootsnall (www.FareCompare.com and www.bootsnall.com), to get a general idea of fares. When you find a flight you like, check out that airline's own site to book. You may find a better price, and making any changes to your ticket may be easier and cheaper. FareCompare lets you see the history of ticket prices for your route. If you know the price is on the low side of its trajectory, you can buy now. Otherwise wait: FareCompare will send you automatic alerts of low fares on your route.

Now that most travel agents work for a set fee per ticket (often around $25) instead of a percent commission, they're much more interested in booking budget airfares. If you know a good travel agent, consider letting him or her do the work, especially if you have a complex itinerary.

A final caution: Make sure all taxes and fees are included when you compare airfare prices. These can come to a few hundred dollars on some overseas flights!

trains versus cars

How will you travel once you arrive in Europe? When we first started contemplating our trip, I imagined that we would ride the trains. I remembered college friends roaming Europe cheaply for weeks on a Eurailpass, oblivious to the high cost of European gasoline. I was sure that Europeans always use trains, and I was determined not to play the part of the typical American, born with wheels where his or her feet should be.

But when we checked out the facts, we got a car. The Tripps, on the other hand, opted for the train. Our different experiences point up the pros and cons you should consider in making the choice that's best for *your* family.

advantages of trains

Most younger kids are happier on trains than in cars, because trains offer:

- **Freedom of movement.** Trains have big, comfortable seats, and you can even get up and walk around.
- **Bathrooms.** Trains have 'em. When you gotta go . . . you don't have to stop. Very important with little kids.
- **More to do.** On a train you can read without getting carsick, or watch movies, or simply see out the windows more easily. Many trains have tables between two rows of facing seats, allowing families to play cards or enjoy Legos, play dough, or coloring books more easily.
- **Food.** Long-distance trains usually have restaurant cars, and most trains at least have snack carts that roll through offering sandwiches and beverages. Local trains generally don't offer food.
- **New friends.** Jodi Tripp's kids would often start playing with other kids on trains. You can't do that in a car! "Train travel immerses you in a culture, while car travel makes you a mere observer of the countryside," she reports. "Watching the interactions of other parents and kids can teach you a lot about the place you are visiting."

Using trains also means you don't have to haul car seats around Europe. You—and your preteen kids who use regular seatbelts at home—may be surprised to learn that new EC rules require the use of booster seats for all kids under the age of twelve or until they're 4 foot 11 inches (150 cm) tall.

tips for trains

Start by visiting www.raileurope.com or www.ricksteves.com for pointers about deciding on passes vs. individual tickets, for help buying the right passes, or simply to learn how trains work: how to buy tickets, find your seats, locate the right track, etc. There's a lot to learn, but once you've taken your first few trains, you'll start to feel comfortable. Don't be daunted.

Rail passes bought in the United States are generally cheaper. The best deals can usually be had when you know which countries you'll be visiting and when; the go-anywhere-anytime passes are more expensive. If you're buying individual tickets, you'll usually save money by buying them in Europe.

The pass vs. tickets decision is very important. It's easier to just buy one pass and be done with it, but experienced train travelers find that, unless you're traveling almost constantly, it's far cheaper to get individual tickets for the few days you actually travel.

Most countries and big cities have Web sites where you can check train schedules and purchase tickets (see chapter 22, Resources). Before your trip, explore these Web sites from home so that you can navigate them quickly on the road to price and compare fares. If you have printer access while traveling,

Train travel may mean trudging for blocks with luggage.

you can even buy online; if not, write down the date, times, train number, price, and service class, and take the information to the station with you.

No computer access? Carry a copy of the *Thomas Cook European Timetable*, which lists schedules for all trains and ferries in Europe. Monthly editions are available at www.travelbookstore.com and seasonal ones at www.amazon .com. Or check schedules at the station, where arrivals are usually in white and departures are in yellow. With your train numbers and dates scribbled on a piece of paper, even a ticket clerk who speaks no English should be able to understand your needs.

Except on high-speed trains, reservations are not usually required, and they cost extra. *But* they guarantee you a specific seat in a specific car—it's printed on your ticket. Ask the conductor to help you find the right seats. Without a reservation, your family may not be able to sit together. You may board a train without reservations and see lots of empty seats. Beware: Seats marked with a slip of paper (or an LCD on newer trains) are reserved by some-one else, who will evict you in a few minutes or at a stop down the line, leav-ing you standing in the aisles. The Tripps easily found seats on Swiss trains without reservations, but found reservations essential in other countries (especially Italy).

Watch other passengers as you board. Many trains require you to validate your tickets before boarding, either in a machine or by train personnel stand-ing near the tracks.

advantages of cars

Unlike the Tripps, we opted to rent a car for three main reasons:

- **More flexibility.** "What if the only hotels near the train station don't have room for a family of four?" Lew asked me. "Will we spend half our time sit-ting in train stations? And can we even get to places like Les Eyzies and Legoland without a car?" We already had four conflicting sets of needs to juggle; dealing with trains would be like having a fifth person along.

- **Potential savings.** My college friends had traveled on their own, trading a single car for a single train pass. As a family we were comparing the cost of a single car to four train passes: A three-month all-inclusive Eurailpass and a one-month BritRail pass for each of us would have been prohibi-tively expensive. (Today the total is $6,758—though careful planning with flexpasses or individual tickets could cut that cost immensely.) And passes would have been just the start of our expenses, since we'd inevitably spend money on buses, taxis, and ferries to extend the reach of the trains.

- **Older kids.** Our kids, at ages ten and thirteen, were happier sitting still than the Tripps' preschoolers.

The age of your kids is the biggest factor in the trains vs. cars choice. Younger kids are free or half price on trains (depending on age and country) and need to move around—and use the bathroom—more often. Older kids don't need car seats in cars. So in the end the cost-benefit balance tips different ways for different families.

renting cars

Shopping around for a rental car is almost as important as shopping for airfare savings. Although European rentals have become less expensive in recent years, they still represent a large part of your trip cost.

A Web search of major agencies in early 2007 found that weekly rates for a four-door midsize car—including value-added tax (VAT) but *not* insurance—ranged from $219 to $720 per week, depending on the country and on the agency.

Is there one best agency? No. The firm that's lowest in one country may be highest—or may not even do business—in another. And rates change daily. Call around or check Web sites, using the list in chapter 22.

Is there one best country? It's not that cut and dry, but here's a rough grouping of countries starting with the least expensive:

1. Belgium, Germany, Luxembourg, the Netherlands, Ireland

2. England, Spain, Switzerland, France

3. Austria, Greece, Portugal

4. Norway, Denmark, Sweden, Italy

Rates in Italy almost always top the pack, as CDW (collision damage waiver) is now mandatory there no matter what other insurance you may have, there's a 14 percent airport surcharge, and VAT is 20 percent. You'd pay $559 per week in Rome for the same car that costs $219 in Britain. So if your itinerary is flexible, pick up your car in a cheap-rents country. When you compare rates, ask if VAT is included. VAT (a sort of national sales tax) on rental cars is stiff: a full 25 percent in Sweden and Denmark, and around 15 to 20 percent in most other European countries. Make sure you know what's included in your quoted rate. Some agencies quote two rates: basic (without VAT or collision damage waiver insurance) and inclusive (which still may not include some local taxes).

Check insurance costs carefully; they can add another $50 to $150 per week. Although your regular car insurance may cover you for rentals at home, it's unlikely to extend overseas. Many gold and platinum VISAs or Master-Cards include CDW coverage, but not for all countries and only for a limited time, usually thirty days for VISA and fifteen for most MasterCards. Call your insurance and credit-card companies and bring a copy of your coverage, or you may be coerced into buying unneeded insurance when you pick up your car. As we said above, Italy requires CDW for all rental drivers.

shifting gears

Another way to save a lot of money is to rent a manual car. Most Europeans drive a standard transmission; rental agencies stock only a limited number of automatics for American tourists. You'll pay $100 to $300 per week extra for an automatic—plus your insurance and gas will cost more. An automatic also screams, "I'm an American tourist," when you may want to blend in. If you haven't driven a manual in years, rent or borrow one for a day in the United States and reassure yourself that you remember how to shift gears. Then rake in the savings.

don't rent a car—buy it!

If you're staying in Europe for more than five weeks, don't rent a car—buy one! This option, known as a purchase/repurchase (P/R) plan, is often your best deal.

Here's how it works. Before you go you pay a set fee to buy the car of your choice. This fee depends on the car you choose and the length of time you'll be keeping it. At the same time you sign a promissory note for the remaining value of the car. When you land in Europe, a local auto dealer picks you up at the airport in your brand-new car. He shows you all the car's knobs and switches, then waves you off. For the rest of your trip, you act as if the car is yours: You get it serviced at the recommended intervals and perform any necessary repairs. When you're ready to return to the States, you drop the car at the nearest dealer (all prearranged), and your promissory note is destroyed.

When does a P/R deal make sense? You can compare at www.auto europe.com. Auto Europe rents and offers Peugeot's P/R plan. For a hypothetical one-month period in July 2007, the P/R with insurance was priced about the same as the rental without insurance. At two months the P/R deal saved more than $1,400 compared to the rental with insurance. If your credit card doesn't cover a collision-damage waiver and you plan to buy that coverage, the P/R deal might be cheaper even for two to three weeks (since insurance is included in tax-free P/Rs). Compare complete costs including insurance, VAT, and any airport tax on the rental, and then decide.

Only Peugeot and Renault continue to offer P/R programs. But we still recommend you look into them under four circumstances: (1) if you're planning a megatrip of two months or more; (2) if you have a large family, as the rates for vans and minibuses may save money even on a shorter trip; (3) if your itinerary includes ferries, since most rental agreements disallow ferry travel (or even the Chunnel); and (4) if one of your drivers is under twenty-five. Most rental companies don't allow people under age twenty-five to drive, but most P/R deals let drivers as young as eighteen operate your car. If you have a responsible young adult or a nanny in your group, this could be a real plus in added flexibility.

size does matter

We're focusing on cutting rental costs in this chapter, but it's worth pausing to consider when a savings becomes a false economy. You may routinely rent subcompacts on business trips, when you're driving alone from the airport to a downtown meeting and back. Or you may drive a compact at home. If you're planning to spend hours at a time in the car, however, with the kids in the backseat, please consider a midsize car. Common European midsize models include the Alfa Romeo 156, Renault Laguna, Peugeot 407, Opel Vectra, and VW Passat.

The larger car may cost you $60 to $100 more per week, but this comes to $14 a day or less additional. Especially if your kids are reaching long-legged, raging-hormones adolescence, seriously consider spending the extra money for a larger car.

A great tip for saving money is renting a car that runs on diesel. We found the fuel is cheaper and more available than regular gas—unlike in the USA. Also, if you rent a minivan, check the size. Generally they're a lot smaller than in the States. Our Citroen was a great car, but we have four kids and I ended up with some luggage on my lap all the time!

—Barbara Noyes, Blauvelt, NY

---

ferries and cruises

Your itinerary may take you across the English Channel, the North Sea, or the Mediterranean by ferry. Ferryboats range from rusty relics barely bigger than fishing boats to trim hovercraft or even giant floating casinos.

A great Web site where you can check schedules and prices for ferries throughout Europe is www.ocean24.de. These prices for a family of two adults and two kids traveling in July 2007 give you an idea of the costs for ferries:

Route	lasts	on foot	with car
Denmark to England (w/cabin)	17:45 hrs	€373	€493
Italy to Greece (w/cabin)	16:30 hrs	€391	€671
England to France	1:30 hrs	€72	€124
Spain to Morocco	1:10 hrs	€106	€195

Here are a few helpful pointers for ferries:

- Ferrying your car is fairly expensive, and reservations are almost always needed; ferrying on foot is much cheaper and does not usually require reservations.

- Hovercrafts are quicker and more comfortable than regular boats but are more often canceled by rough seas and high winds, and they are usually more costly than regular ferries.
- Even if you've never been seasick in coastal travel, you can become queasy on the open sea, or even in the English Channel. Try going up on deck. The fresh air helps many people.
- Get a cabin for longer trips (like the eighteen-hour passage we took from Esbjerg, Denmark, to England). It's worth it for the privacy and comfort.
- Check your car rental contract. Some do not allow you to take your car on ferries.

If you love ships, you might also consider a cruise. The Tripps included a one-week Mediterranean cruise in their itinerary and found it an ideal splurge for traveling with preschoolers. Tom Tripp describes cruising as "a floating hotel with built-in babysitting."

Every night your hotel floats to a new port while you sleep. In the morning you can check out the sights: While Jodi and Tom visited the Leaning Tower of Pisa, their kids, Chloe and Charlie, were back on ship enjoying activities more appropriate to their ages. You can also choose family outings like snorkeling, horseback riding, boat tours, and visits to ancient ruins from the list of available excursions.

Check out www.cruisesforfamilies.com to compare the options. Week-long cruises start at about $500 a day for a family of four, so they're well above the usual TYKE budget. But if your finances allow, it can be a great stress-free way to sample Europe.

Cabins are welcome on ferries in case anyone gets seasick.

what to bring

Travel books always tell you to pack light. The more imaginative ones tell you to lay out everything you plan to take, then put half of it away. Our rule is even simpler: Pack only what you can carry yourself.

By "carry" I don't mean what you can briefly raise off the ground with supreme effort. I mean what you can comfortably haul up three flights of stairs or across as many blocks. Don't kid yourself: Try it. Pack your suitcase and tote it around the block a few times. If gawking neighbors embarrass you, use the stair test instead. Go up and down your own stairs three times, then see how you feel.

These tests apply to everyone in the family. That's just one of the reasons we hesitate to recommend traveling with preschool kids: They can't carry all their own stuff. Family members should have a single suitcase each, filled with their own belongings, that they can carry totally by themselves.

suitcases

Good suitcases contribute surprisingly to the success of an extended family trip and don't cost much. For our four-month trip, each of us had one carry-on-size suitcase. This size varies from airline to airline, but a common limit is 45 inches total height, width, and length (for example, 20 by 15 by 10 inches). Within this size limit, look for the following:

- **Lots of zippered compartments.** When you're on the road, you can keep pajamas and toiletries in one section and avoid unpacking everything to get at a few crucial things. Or you can isolate dirty or wet items.

- **A good shoulder strap.** Does it have padding? Does it slip off your shoulder? How is it attached to the bag? A strap that simply clips to the top of the bag may tear out; better shoulder straps clip to continuous strapping sewn around the sides and bottom of the bag to distribute the strain of the strap. Make sure the shoulder strap is detachable so you can remove it at check-in.

- **Heavy-duty nylon or canvas.** Cordura nylon is especially good. Cheaper materials rip easily in the hands of baggage gorillas. Check for strong seams, too.
- **Sturdy zippers.** Test that they zip smoothly when the bag is full.

Get a different color bag for each member of the family so you can easily tell them apart at a glance.

Wheels are a mixed benefit. They're useless on cobblestones and stairs and often make a suitcase heavier when it must be carried. If you're packing light, wheels are unnecessary. A bag with built-in backpack straps like those sold by Europe Through the Back Door might be a better choice.

Your suitcases will fit more if you use compression storage bags. Put bulky clothes in these special plastic bags then roll up the bags to squeeze out the air, and presto! Everything fits in much less space. Target's Web site (www.target.com) has these for $12 for a set of three.

Our four personal suitcases were augmented by our day bags (personal tote bags or backpacks for each person), one small bag for books, Sam's skateboard (don't ask), and a camera bag for our technical gear. I've seen individuals take more for a two-week vacation than our entire family took for four months. And yet there were times when it still seemed awfully heavy!

clothes

Count on doing laundry about once a week, and don't worry about being a fashion plate. For each person on a spring, summer, or fall trip, we recommend the following:

Pack your suitcase and try toting it around the block.

8 pairs socks and underwear
4 or 5 bottom clothes (pants, skirts, shorts)
7 shirts (including 1 or 2 with long sleeves)
1 nice-restaurant outfit (jersey dresses are great for women)
1 bathing suit
1 towel (for hostels as well as for swimming)
1 washcloth, if you use them
1 sheet sack (see chapter 9, Youth Hostels)
2 pairs walking shoes
1 pair sandals or dress shoes
2 sweaters (1 light, 1 heavy)
1 raincoat or windbreaker

Cotton-poly blends in simple styles are best. Choose dark colors for pants, skirts, shorts, and sweaters, since those garments pick up the most dirt. Avoid blue jeans: They take forever to dry.

Plan for layering in spring and fall. If the weather is unusually cold, you may want to wear a turtleneck jersey and both sweaters under your jacket. For real winter weather, look into high-quality long underwear. Silk tops and bottoms or special high-tech materials keep you incredibly warm and roll up into a tiny corner of your suitcase. It's much easier than bringing an extra heavy coat.

This list did fine for Lew, Sam, and me. All bets were off for Lib: You can't tell a thirteen-year-old girl what clothes she should wear. She made her own decisions and made sure they fit in her suitcase. When she learned more about traveling, we bought her a pair of sneakers and a sweater in Spain.

family photos

Bring along a small collection of photos of your home and family. A little 4-by-6-inch album from the five-and-dime holds about twenty-two pictures—just enough to give people you meet an idea of what your hometown looks like.

Choosing representative photos can be a fun exercise with the kids before you leave. We shot a roll of film, including the kids' schools, downtown and mall stores, and our neighborhood. A few shots of friends and relatives can help alleviate homesickness, too.

presents

It's nice to bring small gifts for people you might befriend on your trip. If possible, pick something typically American. Are you from New England? Pack a few miniature tins of maple syrup or some small maple sugar candies. Florida? Perhaps some simple shell jewelry. Don't bring fruits, vegetables, or preserved meats, as they are not likely to be allowed through customs.

Keep it simple. For instance, we brought New Hampshire and USA patches and pins, which the kids gave out to friends they made in Spain.

reading books

One of the largest mistakes we made was not bringing a good selection of paperback books with us. We dismissed the idea before we left: Heavens, we're not going to Europe in order to sit inside, isolated from the world, and read.

The reality is that there are twenty-four hours in a day. Wherever you'll be staying, there will be a few hours a day when you want to unwind. (Keep in mind also that rental homes, budget hotels, and hostels often don't have televisions.) If reading is one way you enjoy relaxing at home, you'll want to have books with you overseas. One good bet is to bring used paperbacks. Our hometown has two stores that sell them for 50 cents each. Now we pack several and give them to hostels or hotels as we complete them. Or you could bring e-books on a laptop, a portable e-reader, or an iPod.

telephone cards and cell phones

Calling home can add up to a big expense if you don't plan ahead. Whatever you do, don't call through hotel switchboards! Hotels are notorious for high rates. Let's look at the options you might consider, using France as an example.

Pay phones in Europe use phone cards more often than coins these days. You buy these phone cards at local newsstands or tobacco shops. They're convenient, and rates are usually fair, but they're good only in a specific country and may require some language knowledge to use. In France a Ticket Téléphone International from France-Telecom costs €7.50 and provides 244 minutes to the United States for a cost of about 4 cents per minute.

More versatile but usually more expensive is an international phone card, good in all countries. Typically you dial a toll-free number from any overseas pay phone or landline, and English-speaking operators connect you. At press time, for example, MCI's World Traveler card cost about 24 cents per minute for calling from France to the United States. Once you're in Europe you can find cheap phone cards at newsstands, hostels, and Internet cafes. Rates are often as low as 5 to 10 cents per minute. Deals change daily, so simply ask for the best card for calling the States.

You might also consider bringing a cell phone. Your per-minute charge will be higher than with a phone card, but it's convenient to be reachable anywhere, especially if your itinerary is flexible. But your existing U.S. cell phone is unlikely to work in Europe, so here's what you need to know to buy or rent one that will.

More than 200 countries worldwide, including all of Europe, use a cell-phone standard called GSM (Global Services for Mobile) with two main frequencies, 900 MHz and 1800 MHz. In the States the prevailing standard is CDMA. Some U.S. carriers use GSM—but at different frequencies (850 MHz and 1900 MHz). For a U.S. phone to work in Europe, it must be a GSM phone that specifically works at 900 MHz; you'll get the widest coverage if it also works at 1900 MHz. Phones that work on three or four frequencies are called "triband" or "quad-band" respectively. If your phone qualifies—or you can trade up to one that does—ask about any plans and costs your carrier might have for using it in Europe. With T-Mobile, for example, you can activate its WorldClass service for free, then pay 99 cents per minute for calls made—or received—in France.

You may also be able to use your existing GSM phone at lower rates, bypassing your carrier. To do this, make sure your phone is "unlocked" so it can accept other SIM cards. (A SIM card is a removable chip on the back of a GSM phone that stores your phone number and account information.) Your carrier can unlock it for you, but if they won't cooperate, sites like www.thetravelinsider.info can help. We've also heard from some travelers who simply bought a used Euro-compatible GSM phone on eBay.

Once you have a phone, go online and buy an international SIM card, available from many companies. The widely sold "Passport" SIM, for instance, works in about ninety countries. It would give you free incoming calls in France, and all outgoing calls—whether next door or to the United States—would be 49 cents per minute (plus 25 cents per call). The Passport card costs about $49, including $10 of airtime, and gives you a phone number in the United Kingdom, a country that's affordable to call from the States on most long-distance calling plans. If you're staying in a single country, country-specific cards may offer even lower rates. Many SIM cards (like Passport) work via callback service: You place a call, then hang up and wait for the phone to ring, a ploy that contributes to reasonable per-minute rates. Good deals and reliable providers change by the moment, so check blogs at sites like www.ricksteves.com, www .bootsnall.com, or www.slowtalk.com for advice. HI-USA members (see chapter 9) might want to check out the phone deals at www.hiusa.ekit.com.

Renting a cell phone is your final option. Auto Europe and some other car rental firms also offer cell phones. Per-week rental rates seem reasonable compared to buying, but if you actually use the phone to make calls, you'll pay through the nose: Auto Europe charges $2.35 per minute for a call back home from France. Still, for a short trip with few phone calls, this may make sense.

internet access

Bring the necessary passwords and account names for accessing your e-mail accounts over the Web. There are three main ways to get your e-mail in Europe. First, some hotels have a computer in the lobby that's available on a pay-as-you-go basis, through a purchased card or a coin slot. Other hotels have Wi-Fi access for your laptop, which may be free but may require you to pay for a card with a password that's good for so many minutes. You can also find Wi-Fi access in cafes and other hotspots, but not nearly as widely as in the United States, so a pocket Wi-Fi detector comes in handy.

Internet cafes (which rarely have Wi-Fi) are widely available in cities and even small towns. You buy a timed card with a password and then find a free computer. Be forewarned—keyboard layouts vary from country to country. You'll have to hunt and peck, and the smallest chores can take much longer!

toys

Bring along a few toys, even for kids who may think they're too old for them. Sam, at ten, didn't even consider packing toys, then spent all of his carefully hoarded souvenir money on Legos. Remember that your kids may have neither television nor friends for much of your trip. What will they do to amuse themselves?

Bring something open ended, like Legos or some other small and versatile construction toy. We ended up buying some other toys along the way—a soccer ball for games on the patio in Spain, shovels for sand castles in France, and a bow and rubber-tipped arrows from Sherwood Forest.

journals and blogging

A year, five years, or ten years after your trip, you'll still have scores of wonderful memories and a whole different family dynamic that can be traced to your trip. Still, it's nice to have some written reminders of your once-in-a-lifetime outing in addition to the mental snapshots. And writing about your experiences, on paper or online, will help you savor them more fully.

Journals and blogs each have their advantages. Blogs make it easy for friends and family at home to vicariously share your fun—no need to send postcards! On the other hand, paper journals can be private and contemplative and can be enjoyed sitting under a tree, without any need to find an Internet cafe. Either way, do encourage your family to write.

We packed four blank notebooks, and each of us kept a journal during our big trip. As you might guess, our kids did not keep journals voluntarily. But keep them they did. We insisted for several reasons:

- The kids were missing an entire term of school. A daily writing session was one way to keep up their academic skills.

- We do not think American schools do a particularly good job of teaching writing. This was my chance, as a writer, to have an influence on their writing skills.

- We wanted the kids' point of view to be included in this book.

- We hoped that Libby and Sam would eventually find their journals an interesting record of their trip.

Lib, already a good writer, made entries for about half the trip without too much prodding. She never shared her journal with us but claims to have reread it about five times since we returned. She's voluntarily kept lively and insightful journals on subsequent trips to China and around the world.

Sam had to be dragged reluctantly to each daily entry. "But what can I write?" he'd complain, after a day of passing through London, crossing the English Channel, and eating his first snails. Over and over, I'd help him brainstorm and show him how to organize his thoughts. Eventually he did learn a bit about writing and now fondly enjoys looking back over the seventy-seven pages he worked so hard to produce.

If you want to encourage journaling, give the kids a little help in what to write. When "Write about your day" gets no response, pick one of the following ideas to jump-start their brains:

- What things did you notice today that are really different from what they are at home?

- Write down all the words you know in this language and what they mean.

- What are your favorite new foods? What tastes awful?

- What would you tell other kids who come here?

Don't correct your kids' grammar or spelling. Don't even read their journals unless invited. Simply be available to help them think about their experiences, and make sure there's a quiet time each day when it's easy for them to write in their journals. And set a good example by keeping one yourself. Who knows? Someday your journal may—as mine did—become the basis for a book.

We decided our kids would keep journals for our four-week trip. Dan, who had just finished third grade, wrote a page a day in a little composition book about what he had to eat, about the Tin-Tin books he was reading, about anything medioval. Laura was just out of kindergarten, so she drew a picture each day. Now they're really really happy they have their journals—they take them to school for show-and-tell.

—Doug Alexander and Lisa Geibel, Austin, TX

Today it's also easy to create your own online travelogue on a public blog site. Two that Jodi recommends are www.letterpop.com and www.realtravel.com. RealTravel is designed specifically for traveling. It creates a map of your trip and lets you post reviews and comments on the places you visit and stay. Just fill in the blanks and your adventures are beautifully chronicled. LetterPop is more free form, lending itself to any kind of newsletter, not just travel, so you can be more creative. Google's www.blogger.com is another good choice; it's especially suited to lots of photos, and works well with www.flickr.com (see "Cameras," below). Kids who already have a MySpace account might enjoy posting news of their trip there, for their friends. As always with MySpace and similar sites, supervise what they post for everyone's safety.

Sites like LetterPop, RealTravel, and Blogger allow you to create an e-mail blog list, so you can invite your friends to follow you around Europe. All three sites are free and easy, so try them out before you go. Picking a blog is like a pair of shoes: You need to try on several to see what fits you best.

Your experiences and those of your kids could contribute to *Take Your Kids to Europe*, so please share your travels with us. Perhaps the thought of seeing their names in the next edition of this book will be incentive enough to get your kids writing. E-mail your adventures to cynthia@takeyourkidsto europe.com—or add my e-mail address to your e-mail blog list!

cameras

Of course you'll bring a camera. The only question is, what kind? Kids feel grown-up with their own camera; it often helps them notice things they wouldn't otherwise see. Help them decide on a theme, such as collecting gargoyles or weird trucks, then get out of the way. Whatever you do, don't constantly nag or make suggestions about what to shoot or not shoot!

We gave our daughter [a camera] and told her she could take any pictures she wanted. She decided—on her own—to take pictures of every dog in France! And we don't even have a dog at home! Letting her have the [camera] and butting out of that decision was the best thing we did. It gave her a focus when there wasn't much else to do. She'd be bored, and suddenly we'd hear, "Wait, wait, I have to get a picture of that dog!"

—Louise Goldenberg, Eliot, ME

Digital cameras are wonderful, but don't forget about storage issues. Even if you edit carefully, at some point your memory card will fill up. You can bring extra memory cards: A 1G card costs only about $20 and holds hundreds of photos. Larger cards are better if you want to store the little "microvideos" your camera can take. You can also download your photos to your laptop (if you brought one) or even to some iPods. Just make sure you have the right cables and software, and check it all out before you go. Or find a camera shop that will dump the photos on your memory card onto a CD; they're starting to spring up in major European cities.

Another option (if you have high-speed Internet access) is to upload your photos to a photo-sharing site, where not only are they safely stored but friends and family back home can view them. It's easy to post your photos and then simply e-mail a link to everyone, rather than sending all those postcards home. A few sites that Jodi recommends are Shutterfly and Flickr. Shutterfly is free, easy to use, offers unlimited storage, and lets you order prints online. Flickr's main advantage is that it allows you—or your friends—to leave notes and comments on the photos. Flickr charges $24.95 a year for unlimited storage, but accounts are free for less than twenty photos per month.

A video camera can be a mixed blessing. The best thing about it is its immediacy. Take some shots and (as with digital still cameras) you can check them out right away. Video has the added advantage of capturing sound, giving your memories an extra dimension.

Be aware that you will not be able to play back your video footage on a European TV. U.S. camcorders are designed for televisions that use the NTSC standard. European ones use either PAL or SECAM, depending on the country. To edit or review during your trip, you'll be limited to using the camera's own viewfinder, so get one that makes this easy. You may also need a transformer and a plug adapter to use your recharger—all issues to look into before you go.

A final challenge with video is editing. When you come home with ten ninety-minute tapes, you'll be hard pressed to combine the highlights into one forty-five-minute presentation to show Aunt Mary. Desktop editing equipment has improved tremendously—and become much cheaper—in recent years, but it can still require a fair amount of time and money to achieve enjoyable results.

Compare this to still photos. With these, editing is easy. You take the bad ones and throw them in the trash (or hit Delete on a digital camera), and only the best of your trip remains. Our advice? Bring along the video camera if you're familiar with it, but don't travel with a new video camera. And bring along a still camera as well.

A video camera can be a mixed blessing.

optional gear

Should you bring a laptop? You'll do fine without one on a trip of a week or two, and it will do you good to get away from the keyboard. But on longer trips, a laptop may earn its keep by serving many functions. You can manage your bills long-distance through e-banking and make travel arrangements on the go. If you have high-speed Internet service, you can cut phone costs by using SKYPE or similar voice-over-Internet services to call family and friends. Even without Web access, a laptop serves many purposes: watching movies, editing and storing digital photos, listening to music, enjoying e-books, playing computer games, and electronic journaling.

A portable DVD player is another option. Jodi's kids watched DVD movies on long train trips, which kept them peaceful in the fairly quiet environment of European trains. She bought Disney's *Mickey's Seeing the World* DVD to show during the plane ride over, and three-year-old Charlie learned to distinguish several European flags—and even recognized the Colosseum when he arrived in Rome.

Apple's iPods are an even more compact way to provide many of the functions of larger gear in a pocket-size gadget. Smaller-capacity iPods are designed just for music, but the larger ones can be used for digital file storage (a convenient and necessary way to back up your digital photos), and for enjoying books and movies. You can also download free podcasts of walking tours around famous tourist sites. The downside of the iPod is that there's no way to connect to the Internet.

To avoid getting lost—which may be an adventure when you're alone, but a nightmare with small children—consider a portable GPS (Global Positioning System) receiver. It pinpoints your location with an accuracy of within 20 feet. Jodi used one to navigate through big cities. A hand-held one, such as the Garmin eTrex GPS Navigator, costs under $100. Alternatively, your PDA or Smartphone might already be GPS ready. You will need the appropriate mapping software for Europe, which may cost more than the unit.

Make sure you pack any cables and chargers that come with your equipment. It's also important to have adaptors and transformers for this type of gear. An *adaptor* lets your U.S. plug fit into a European outlet, while a *transformer* allows a U.S. device (designed to work on 110V current) to operate on Europe's 220V current without frying. Most laptops and some other electrical gadgets have international power supplies that can work with 110V or 220V power; they will need only an adaptor. Other devices—your battery chargers, for instance—may need both an adaptor and a transformer. Don't worry; it's not as bad as it sounds. Walkabout Travel Gear (www.walkabout travelgear.com) has an all-in-one Hi-Lo Combination Converter/Transformer Kit for about $35 that solves most of your voltage problems when traveling in Europe. This unit comes with the most common adaptors needed in Europe, and everything fits in its compact carrying case.

managing money

Used to be, when you got ready to go on vacation, you'd buy a stack of traveler's checks at the bank and head off into the sunset. Today the best choice for travel funds is a credit card—for several reasons.

In this short chapter we'll discuss money management on the road for vacations of any length. At the end of the next chapter, we'll add some extra tips that are especially important for handling finances on an extended trip overseas.

advantages of plastic

Today's plastic options (credit cards, debit cards, and ATM cards—we'll discuss the differences in a minute) offer advantages over traveler's checks:

- You don't have to worry about misestimating your needs. How do you know how many dollars' worth of traveler's checks to buy? What if you run out? With plastic there's no need to figure it out ahead. (Of course, this can mean that spending can easily get out of hand. Be careful—stick to that budget!)

- You can cover the unexpected. Face it: Even if you estimate normal expenses properly, how can you plan for that broken leg in Athens, the camper totaled on the German autobahn, or the unexpected chance to take polo lessons in England?

- You don't have to tie up your money. With traveler's checks the money leaves your bank account at the start of your trip. With plastic you pay only as you spend, or at the end of your trip. Your money stays safely in your bank, earning interest.

three kinds of plastic

We often call the plastic in our pockets "credit cards" indiscriminately. In fact, though, you have three kinds of bank cards from which to pick. Each has advantages and disadvantages.

credit cards

Credit cards include the obvious: VISA, MasterCard, American Express, Discover, Diner's Club. In our experience, VISA is the most widely accepted card in Europe, with MasterCard coming in second. Go ahead and bring your other credit or debit cards if you want, but American Express does not enjoy the universal status that VISA seems to enjoy, and Discover has not yet been widely discovered.

Credit cards are a great way to pay for many of your travel expenses. On top of that, you can get cash advances from ATM machines or bank tellers with a credit card. It's easy, and you'll get a much better exchange rate than you'd get cashing traveler's checks. The drawback is that you will usually pay a transaction fee and accrue interest on your cash advance from day one—even if you carry no other balance on your credit card.

atm cards

You're also fully familiar with ATM cards; you almost certainly use one regularly to withdraw cash from your checking or savings account at home.

You may not know, however, that your same bank ATM card can access your account from overseas. As in the United States, many European ATMs belong to either the CIRRUS or PLUS network. Look for the usual logos, stick in your card, enter your PIN, and you'll be issued funds in local currency.

The drawback of ATM cards is clear: You can't hand them to restaurant waiters or hotel clerks to pay your bills.

debit cards

A debit card is a hybrid of a credit card and an ATM card and may be your best bet for overseas travel. (Technically speaking, ATM cards are also debit cards, but I'll use the term here only to refer to a special type of VISA or Master-Card.) Like credit cards, debit cards can be used to charge expenses at stores, hotels, and restaurants. And like ATM cards, debit cards can usually be used to withdraw money from ATMs without any finance charges.

You can think of a debit card as a personal checking account that's recognized everywhere you travel. You put money in an account, and then when you charge something, the money is immediately deducted from your account.

While you don't get the "float" of a free month that comes with most credit cards, there are two big advantages to debit cards:

- There's no bill sent to you at the end of the month. You'll never have to worry about your bill arriving before your return and finance charges of 18 or 19 percent kicking in.

- Debit cards often have overdraft privileges: You get an automatic loan if you use up all the money in your account. Many stock brokerages offer this service. This can give you peace of mind in a financial emergency.

If you don't already have one, ask your bank or your broker for a VISA or MasterCard debit card tied to your savings or checking account.

three points to check

No matter which type of plastic you take to Europe, you'll want to check three important points before you leave:

- **What's my four-digit PIN?** Most European ATMs require a four-number PIN, entered on keypads without any letters. If your PIN is more than four digits, get a new one. If it uses letters, memorize the number equivalents on a U.S. keypad before you leave.

- **Is there a foreign-transaction fee?** In the past few years, many banks have started assessing a small conversion fee on all foreign transactions. AmEx charges 2 percent extra. Most VISAs and MasterCards charge a fee of 1 to 4 percent. Check with your issuing bank, and consider using another card if you'll be charged a hefty foreign-transaction fee.

- **What network is my card on?** Make sure your credit, debit, or ATM card belongs to one of the two widespread bank networks: CIRRUS (owned by MasterCard) or PLUS (owned by VISA). Which is better depends on where you're traveling. Britain and Spain offer lots of machines that take both cards. Italy and Belgium have both, but not as many machines. Germany has more PLUS ATMs that take VISA. We've found the best bet for all-around availability is to take a VISA/PLUS card.

Some rural areas only take local cards. I had just assumed we could use VISA anywhere, but this was not the case. A few times we skipped lunch or ate gas station food because we couldn't get cash. Next time I'd bring two different VISA cards, two MasterCards—one of each for me and my husband—plus more cash and traveler's checks.

—Nancy Fletcher, Portland, OR

When we travel, we use a VISA debit card from our stockbroker. We put our trip money—and some other savings—in a money-market fund earning good interest. Whenever we charge anything in Europe, the equivalent in dollars is deducted from our brokerage money-market account. There are no cash-advance or foreign-transaction fees. If our account runs out, our brokerage automatically lends us money at a preagreed interest rate.

When our cash in hand gets low, we simply look for a bank with a VISA decal and get about $200 in local currency. If the bank doesn't have an ATM, you can go inside and get cash. (It's logical. At stores you can buy stuff with a credit card; at banks you can buy cash the same way.) The transaction takes only a few minutes, and soon we're back on the street.

notify your bank

In an effort to protect honest cardholders from criminals, most banks maintain computer programs that keep an elaborate profile of your card use. Any usage out of that pattern, and the computer suspects fraud. This is what keeps your credit-card number from being copied when you buy gas in New Jersey and used tomorrow in Dakaar or New Delhi to buy stereo equipment.

Unfortunately, you may find yourself cut off when *you* are the one using the card to pay for a meal or hotel room in Bordeaux, Bremen, or Bristol—if your profile shows no history of travel. It's a good idea to call the customer service number on the back of your credit or debit card before you go, and tell them when and where you'll be traveling.

This is yet another reason to carry more than one card. I suddenly found one of my VISAs inoperable in England last year (my bank notified me of the temporary security measure in my next statement, when I arrived home—fat lot of good that would have done me if I hadn't had a second credit card!). The same thing can happen with phone calling cards (see chapter 3, What to Bring).

who accepts plastic?

You probably have a good idea of who accepts plastic at home and who doesn't. You may be surprised as you move from country to country in Europe. Don't jump to conclusions and be caught cashless!

In Spain, for instance, we were amazed to find that some gas stations wouldn't accept credit cards for $40 worth of gas—yet highway toll booths would take a card for a 40-cent toll! (These automated toll booths are great. You drive up, stick your credit card in the slot, then drive away seconds later with your card and a receipt. No need to even sign the slip.)

In France, England, Spain, and Italy, supermarkets readily accepted VISA for payment long before grocery stores in the United States. Yet most small family hotels and restaurants—the ones we recommend—do not accept credit cards of any kind. Taxis may or may not accept plastic.

Also be aware that in Germany, credit cards are not nearly as widely used as elsewhere, though this is changing rapidly. In smaller towns you may pass several storefronts in a busy commercial area before you see one credit-card decal on the door.

traveler's checks

With ready access to credit and cash, you probably won't need many traveler's checks. Still, you should bring some for emergencies. Who knows when there will be a bank strike or some other unexpected calamity? Bring a few plain dollar or euro traveler's checks, as they are readily accepted everywhere.

local cash and euros

Even though you'll count on your debit card for cash overseas, it's a good idea to have a small amount of cash in the local currency before you arrive. Change $50 at your home airport so you'll be prepared for a snack at your destination when you arrive famished or for that first taxi to collapse at your hotel.

But what is local currency? In 2002 most of Europe changed over to a new currency called the euro. As you're no doubt aware, all those pesos, deutschmarks, and French francs are now just a memory. As of 2007, thirteen countries are using the new currency (others may join later):

Austria	Greece	Portugal
Belgium	Ireland	Slovenia
Finland	Italy	Spain
France	Luxembourg	
Germany	the Netherlands	

You can't use euros *everywhere* in Europe. Western European exceptions still using their traditional currencies (as of 2007) include:

Denmark	(still using Danish kroner)
Great Britain	(still using British pounds)
Norway	(still using Norwegian kroner)
Sweden	(still using Swedish kroner)
Switzerland	(still using Swiss francs)

The symbol for the euro is €. There are seven euro notes (paper bills): €5, €10, €20, €50, €100, €200, and €500. Each euro is divided into 100 cents, giving us eight euro coins: 1 cent, 2 cents, 5 cents, 10 cents, 20 cents, 50 cents, €1 coin, and €2 coin.

Early in the euro's life, its value was very close to that of the U.S. dollar, making conversions a snap. But at press time you'd need to hand over about $1.36 to get a euro in return. It's still easier than learning a dozen different currencies, though.

protect yourself

A few commonsense safety tips will avoid money hassles during your trip.

- Ideally, carry both a VISA and a MasterCard—with one spouse pocketing one and the other the second. That way you're covered for both bank networks, and a pickpocket can't ruin your vacation.

- Use a money belt or neck pouch for valuables. Better to feel like a silly tourist than a poor one.

- The obvious (just as at home): Don't count money in public, and be careful at ATMs in the dark.

- Guys, don't keep your wallet in your back pocket. Women should use purses with a good flap or zipper (no open top) and a thick, tough-to-cut strap worn crosswise across your chest. These measures aren't as necessary out in the countryside. But chances are you'll spend more time in big cities on your trip than you're accustomed to at home. These are simply normal big-city cautions.

- Make sure you know how to report a stolen or lost card, and get a replacement quickly. It's so much easier to check this out in the States than to figure it out on a Sunday in Portugal, when you have only twenty-four euros in your pocket. To do this you need to have the correct phone number (*not* the U.S. 800 number) and copies of your credit-card numbers in a safe place—obviously not in the wallet that just got stolen.

That's about the size of it. You now know the best way to spend money in Europe. If you're also interested in the best ways to *save* money, don't forget to look at our budget estimator in chapter 16, Can We Afford This?

long-te...

One- and two-week vacations are routine in the United States of America. Lucky souls can sometimes scrape together three or four weeks' vacation.

Many of our readers, though, have decided to do as we did and take a longer trip of a lifetime, a carefully planned family educational odyssey of six weeks, ten weeks, or longer. Such a trip presents extra hurdles: How do you take the time off from work? How do you get the kids out of school? What will you do with your house? And what extra money issues can arise? This chapter takes a look at some possible solutions to problems like these.

You can skip this chapter if you're planning a more "normal" vacation—unless you want to start dreaming now for that next, longer family trip.

out of school

The easy and obvious solution to school conflicts is to travel in summer. Given the absurdly abbreviated U.S. school year, most families will find this the simplest way to proceed.

Summer travel has its disadvantages, though. Almost everything will be more expensive, from car and house rentals to airfares. And it's harder to experience local life in many places when those places are overrun with tourists.

If you decide, for whatever reason, to make your trip during the school year, you may have to argue your case with the local school board. Most school districts deal regularly with children who miss two weeks of school for a trip to Disneyland and have some procedure for parents who remove their children from the classroom entirely for homeschooling. What you're contemplating, however, is somewhere between these two extremes, and the average school board will have no system for dealing with your request.

You wouldn't be pulling your kids out of school if you weren't convinced that your trip will be far more educational than the corresponding time spent in school. Yet your school board has two valid concerns. The first is atten-

're required by state law to provide something close to 185 days
ing and to police all cases of truancy. What's more, most public
get state funding according to actual attendance, so the removal of a
le of warm bodies actually hits your local schools in the pocketbook.

The reaction of our public schools was typical. We decided to travel for
our months, from April to August. Our plan called for Libby to miss the last
quarter of eighth grade, while Sam would miss the end of fourth grade. We
notified the schools early (about a year ahead) of our plan to have the kids
miss a term. There was no standard policy. Our superintendent of schools
tossed our request back to the children's respective principals; the principals
in turn consulted the teachers.

No one was sure what to do. Some teachers wanted both kids to complete
all the classwork for the year on their own. Others opted to waive the last
term's work, since both kids had done very well up to that point. But even
these teachers felt uncomfortable giving the same final grade to our disappearing children as they might give to someone who worked hard—and
showed up—the whole year. The junior high principal finally solved the
dilemma by simply withdrawing them from school.

"Let's just say they moved," he decided. "Then they can move back into
town again in the fall." This solution avoided reporting to the state that those
Harriman kids were absent forty-three consecutive days.

If state aid is an issue, you may need to submit an independent study plan
to your school district. If your plan is approved, your school may continue to
get funding for your kids, even though they're not there.

The second valid concern of both schools and parents involves the actual
classwork that will be missed. Will my child fall behind next year because of
important basic concepts he's missing now? For good students at the elementary and junior high levels, the answer to this question is most likely no,
though most schools (like ours) will require kids to take along their math
books to complete the same pages as their classmates.

One reason our schools required very little makeup work from our kids
may have been my detailed description of the educational benefits of our trip.
I reminded everyone involved that my children would be getting language
and history lessons in the obvious ways, math from constant currency and
measurement conversions, and English from keeping a daily journal. It never
hurts to remind people you're planning more than a fun-and-games vacation.

off from work

Now that you've pulled the kids out of school, how do you pull yourself out
of work? Gainfully employed people fall roughly into three groups. The first
is educators, whose schedules may include enough vacations, summer breaks,
and sabbaticals that they need no advice in how to get away from it all.

self-employed people

Next come the self-employed, a group that includes both Lew and me. To most people with more traditional jobs, being self-employed means that you can take off whenever you want, without any concerns. In reality, though, the self-employed may face extra obstacles in escaping from work. If you run a one-person business, there are no coworkers to take over your work when you're not there; if a client needs you and you're not around, you may lose that client permanently.

If you're on your own, give your clients plenty of advance notice of your impending disappearance. Suggest other subcontractors or businesses that can fill in for you while you're gone. Help your clients schedule special projects for the period before or after your trip. Lew and I told our clients our plans months before we left. Some delayed projects until our return, while others worked with us on an accelerated schedule. The theory's simple: All you have to do is work double-time in the months before you leave, and you can take time off without any problems.

There's no easy solution if you run a small business with employees. Contributing editors Dan and Wendy Hallinan faced this; they ran a restaurant before their extended trip and had to sell it. (Any of you who have run such a demanding business will understand that running a restaurant was the reason they needed a five-month vacation.)

nine-to-five jobs

Those with traditional nine-to-five jobs face even tougher choices. Most of you get only two or three weeks' vacation, and that's just not enough for a once-in-a-lifetime trip. First, try for an unpaid leave of absence. More and more companies are awarding "sabbaticals" to faithful employees; if your company hasn't yet done this, there's still no reason the policy couldn't start with you.

Or, if your company has overseas branches, see if there's any way to transfer. This is what worked for Jodi's husband, Tom, who teaches management at Washington State University. His visiting professorship at WSU's partner school, the César Ritz University Centre of hotel and restaurant management, allowed the Tripps to spend the fall semester in Brig, Switzerland, with two months of pan-European travel en route.

One option that many have suggested is tacking a vacation onto a business trip. We tried this once, when Sam, at thirteen, was old enough to sightsee on his own while we worked at a trade show in Birmingham, England. He felt grown-up taking trains on his own, and we felt less like tourists as we headed off to work every day. After the show we traveled together for an extra week.

what about the house?

If you plan to be away for a month or more, what will you do with your house? You'd like to protect it from theft and plumbing leaks, and at the same time you'd like your house to help pay for your trip. You have the options of renting your house or exchanging homes.

rent or exchange?

Swapping homes with another family has much to recommend it, from saving money to making new friends. (See chapter 12, Renting and Exchanging Homes, for details.) Then why doesn't everyone simply exchange homes rather than rent? Usually, the reason is flexibility. In our case, for instance, with three "home bases" planned, exchange would have involved the long-distance coordination and supervision of three tenant changeovers at our own home. It seemed easier to rent our house out to one dependable tenant, pocket the money, and use it to rent overseas. Money was first invented so that people who had nothing to barter directly could easily transfer value from one place to another. If for any reason you don't care to arrange a home swap, you'll no doubt want to rent out your home for cold cash as we did.

how to find a tenant

Finding tenants is rarely an easy task. Unless you live in a desirable resort area at the height of the season, renting out your home will require more than simply putting an ad in the paper. Here are a few ideas you might try:

- **Contact a local university or college.** Educational institutions often have visiting professors on campus for a month or a term. Such a tenant would probably take good care of your home—and you'd have the university to turn to if there were any problems. Don't rent to students, though, as they can be tough on an unsupervised property.

- **Contact a local military base.** All military bases provide housing for visiting personnel. But these barracks usually don't include space for pets, spouses, and kids. An officer on temporary duty makes a great tenant. We rented our home to a lonely naval officer who wanted his wife and dog with him after two months of bachelor housing. As an added plus, we knew we could follow up with the navy if there had been any damage to our home. (There wasn't. They kept the house cleaner than we do and left dinner on the stove the day we returned.)

- **Contact a large local company.** Corporations have visiting executives or managers who arrive in a new community and want to rent for a few months before they buy a home. Find out if any company near you could use your home while you're gone.

- **Contact a hospital, museum, or other institution.** By now you probably get the idea: Anyplace that has a great number of professionals coming and going on temporary grants and assignments may be a good source for prospective tenants.

Make up a one-page flyer about your home, with a short description and a snapshot. Run off a few dozen copies, so that you'll have information to give to all the people you contact. (We left the street address off our flyer to avoid advertising our soon-to-be-empty house to potential thieves too explicitly.)

tenant agreement

Once you've found a tenant, of course you'll want to check two or three references to make sure you're leaving your property in good hands. Beyond that, your best protection is an informal agreement with your tenant making clear the responsibilities of both parties. A good agreement spells out which rooms the tenants can (and can't) use, who's paying for which utilities, and just how the finances will work.

Don't be concerned with creating a legalistic document. Everyone involved is best served by a simple paper written in clear, commonsense terms. The agreement we used looks something like this:

Rooms: All rooms are included except my office. We'll store our clothes there so that all bedroom closets and drawers will be empty for your use.

Kitchen: You're welcome to use any spices, staples, cleaning supplies, and other bits and pieces you find in the kitchen. You'll probably leave some things for us, too, so we'll come out even.

Computers: Computers aren't included in the deal. Sorry, but they've been promised to various friends for the duration.

Telephone: We have two lines. We'll put our business line on an answering machine so you can ignore it and give you our personal line. We will pay the regular monthly fee, and you will pay for all long-distance calls.

Cable TV/Internet and water: We'll pay both these for the entire period before we go. There will be no charge to you.

Electric and gas: We'll read the meter when you arrive and when you leave. You'll reimburse us for electricity and gas when we return.

Repairs: The house is in very good repair. But we will leave you the names of our plumber, electrician, and so on, in case you have an unexpected problem. We will reimburse you for any expense you must pay in the unlikely case this type of thing happens.

Mail: Thank you for handling our mail as part of the deal. Just throw out the supermarket flyers and other obvious junk, and toss the rest in a cardboard box in my office.

Rent: The rent will be $750 per month; the last (partial) month's rent will be $629. As described above, the rent includes local telephone, cable, and water; long-distance phone, electricity, and gas are extra. You can mail the rent to my parents [name and address included] by the tenth of each month.

Deposit: We require a $1,000 deposit to cover damages and as security against the extra utility charges. This amount should be paid by April 1. It will be completely refundable on our return, as soon as we have settled utility fees and made sure everything's in the same shape it was when we left.

Time: This agreement will be for the period of Saturday, April 8, through our return on Thursday, August 3.

Cynthia Harriman & Lew Harriman

owners' names	tenants' names

This agreement served us very well. About the only area that disappointed us on our return was the yard, which was somewhat overgrown.

It's no coincidence, I'm convinced, that yard work was the only area we neglected to mention in our agreement—and our only letdown. You'll do well if you keep to the commonsense philosophy of this agreement and simply adapt it to fit your property.

uncle sam wants to know

If you rent out your home, you must declare the rent money you receive as income. But you may also deduct all expenses that are connected with the rental. These expenses can include:

Mortgage interest
Utilities (gas, electric,
   water, cable, phone)
Legal fees
Cleaning and maintenance fees

Commissions to rental agencies
Repairs
Advertising expenses
Supplies
Insurance

Beyond this, you may also be able to deduct depreciation, a percentage of the overall value of your house. Check with a qualified tax preparer to be sure, and for help on depreciation calculations.

Keep receipts for all your income and expenses, and fill out Schedule E. Make sure to hold on to those receipts until you sell your house, since treating your home as rental property for even a short time can affect the way the eventual profits from your home are taxed.

long-term money management

One of the most difficult management challenges that comes with an extended absence from home is paying bills. How can you be sure your taxes and electric bills will be paid while you're gone? Who will make your car payment every month and make sure the mortgage gets sent in? It's possible to delegate these tasks to a friend or family member, but it's probably better just to do it all yourself before you leave, or use e-banking during your trip.

what must you pay?

First you need to draw up the definitive list of what your obligations will be while you're gone. Your check register is the best place to start. Obviously, all your regular monthly bills go on the list first. Then dig back a few more months in your checkbook and add the quarterly bills—maybe medical insurance or life insurance. Finally, you'll have the semiannual and annual bills, like your real-estate tax.

Here's a bill-paying checklist that might jog your memory:

Utilities
_____ Water
_____ Gas

_____ Electricity
_____ Cable

Taxes

_____ Real estate taxes
_____ State income taxes or estimated payments
_____ Federal income taxes or estimated payments

Telephone/Internet

_____ Land line   _____ Cell phone
_____ Internet service

Insurance

_____ Car insurance   _____ Life insurance
_____ Health insurance   _____ Property insurance
_____ Disability insurance

Housing

_____ Rent   _____ Condo fees
_____ Mortgage payment   _____ Lawn service
_____ Cleaning service   _____ Snow shoveling

Finances

_____ Credit-card payments   _____ IRA or 401(k) funding

Miscellaneous

_____ Car payment   _____ Child support or alimony
_____ Newspaper delivery   _____ Magazine subscriptions
_____ Club dues

how to pay

If you opt to pay in advance, call up and explain the situation to each company on your list. "Hello, this is _____. We're going to be out of the country for three months, and we'd like to pay our electric bill ahead. Could you please tell us how much we should pay so that there won't be any problem while we're gone?"

Record the name and phone number of the person you spoke with. Ask that person to make an entry in your record explaining the situation so that you won't return home to find your phone disconnected or your electricity shut off. When you send in your check, include a brief cover letter that references your conversation and explains that you will settle any balance due when you return on _____ (mention the specific date). By calling and sending a letter, you double the chance that information about your special situation will actually be recorded.

You can of course predict what you'll be paying for services with a set monthly fee (cable, mortgage, etc.). Where consumption determines the bill, most companies will look back over several previous months, or look to the same period in the previous year to quote you an estimated amount.

Today another viable option is e-banking, which allows you to manage your money from the far corners of the earth—as long as you have Internet access. The Tripps used Bank of America for e-banking from Switzerland and found that:

- Changing their bills to arrive electronically instead of on paper was easy.
- You can set a regular payment day and amount for recurring, fixed bills like mortgage or cable.
- For variable bills, you can select options: pay in full, pay minimum, or pay a specific dollar amount.

What's more, it was easy to transfer money from savings to checking as needed, and Bank of America did not charge any fees for these e-banking services. Many banks have built-in alerts to notify you (by e-mail) when money is direct deposited, when a preset low balance is reached, and so forth.

E-banking is safest if you're using a hardwired network, in private, on a site that starts with *https* instead of *http* (the "s" stands for *secure*). You may be at risk if you type passwords or account numbers on a public Wi-Fi network, as "sniffers" can snatch data passing through the airwaves. Secure sites (used by all reputable banks and e-commerce sites) encrypt your data, thwarting the sniffers, but whenever you're computing in public—whether on Wi-Fi or in an Internet cafe—your key data can still be picked up by thieves looking over your shoulder or watching with binoculars. Keep these cautions in mind if you use the Net to e-bank or purchase transportation, hotels, etc., while on the road.

Make sure to pay all your bills before you leave.

turning over accounts

For a very long stay (more than four months), it might make more sense to put utilities in your tenants' name and make them directly responsible for their own bills. This saves you the up-front expense of paying and puts the onus for payment squarely on the user.

Changing over accounts probably isn't worth the bother unless you'll be gone quite a long time. Most utilities charge a fee ($5 to $25) for changing the name on an account, and you'll have to pay again to change it back when you return. And since most of your bills—from health insurance to car payments—will still have to be paid ahead, you won't gain that much from eliminating just a few utility bills.

car insurance

If you'll be exchanging homes with another family, find out if your insurance policy will cover them when they drive your car. What about when *you* drive *their* car? This differs widely from company to company, so get the scoop from your own agent.

If you're renting your house, it's unlikely you'll allow your tenants to use your cars. Arrange to get them out of the way (your tenants will need your parking spaces), farmed out, perhaps, to friends' driveways in the suburbs. Again, ask your insurance company what kind of coverage you need while your car's not being used. With some policies you won't pay anything if your car's up on blocks or the battery's removed while you're gone.

If you do suspend your car insurance for the duration, make sure to reinstate it immediately on your return. It won't be the first thing on your mind as your plane lands. Bring your insurance company's phone number with you, and call from the airport while you wait for your baggage to come down. Unless you do, you may not be covered for any jet lag–induced mishaps on the way home from wherever you stashed your car.

expiration dates

One final task: Before you leave, check through your wallet and your files for other important documents that might expire during your extended absence. Some possibilities include:

_____ Passport	_____ Pet licenses
_____ Driver's license	_____ Club memberships
_____ Car registration	_____ Credit cards

Of course the passports, credit cards, and driver's licenses are the most important, as you'll be counting on using them during your trip! It's surprising how many people discover in the middle of a vacation that their VISA card just breathed its last. Don't let this happen to you.

sightseeing survival

In our first few weeks of travel, we evolved three basic rules for better sightseeing. We also picked up some special tips on collective family decision making. In this chapter we'll discuss all these things, then finish up with some ideas for sightseeing in cities, where the hurried pace and high expectations add a lot of extra tension.

rule 1: pick and choose your sites

Just as you'd hate to spoil your appetite on a corn dog just before the filet mignon is served, it's helpful to save room in your brain for the sights you really want to see.

We saw our first castle on our second day in Europe. In fact, it was probably nothing more than some minor count's summer cottage—a little ruin with a satisfyingly crenelated tower silhouetted on the horizon. Both kids leaned toward that side of the car and stared. When we got closer, we pulled to the shoulder of the road, grabbed our cameras, and shot the obligatory photos. This was Europe. No doubt about it. Castles and everything. Wow!

Four months later Lew's parents joined us for a week in England, and we planned an outing to Warwick Castle. "Do we have to?" the kids chorused. "It's just another *castle*."

Warwick Castle is a rather interesting place. It features jousting knights, the world's largest catapult, and wax figures from Madame Tussaud. It's got its own alleged ghost, a few good suits of armor, and a park full of screaming, glorious peacocks. If we had gone there the first week of our trip, the kids would have loved it. But several castles later, it hardly merited a glance.

The point here is that it's important to plan ahead and pick representative sights with a little care. If you screech to a halt at the first six Roman ruins you come to, you may have to *drag* your offspring through some really fine amphitheater later on.

On a shorter trip kids aren't likely to develop immunity to any specific category of sights. But if you're only able to travel for a few weeks, isn't it even more important to see the best sights? Be discriminating, no matter what the length of your trip.

rule 2: prepare to be your own guide

After you've picked the sights you want to see, put some thought into what kind of tour will work best for your gang.

There are just two basic types of tours: guided and self-guided. Guided tours are not the best choice with kids. They're only given at certain hours, so you may have to wait for one when you arrive. And they proceed at the guide's pace, not that of the average child. You'll be rushed on just when your kids get interested in something—and held back while your guide discusses some obscure point of religious symbolism at length.

Another difficulty with guided tours is that they're often given in the local language, especially during the off-season. Unless you are quite fluent in that language, you won't understand much as the tour guide's voice echoes off dungeon walls and you get shunted to the other end of your group.

Self-guided tours are often better for family travel. You'll be able to choose your own pace, and you won't have to worry if the kids act like kids—asking questions without whispering, ducking out to visit the bathroom, or hopping on the stairs.

It's up to you, or one of your kids, to act as tour guide.

We always try to stay away from guided tours with the kids, but at Mont St. Michel, that was the only way to see certain parts of the abbey. The tour took one-and-a-half boring, crowded hours. Afterward we decided it would have been better to start the tour but slide up into the previous group just as they left the room you were entering. You'd end up in six different language groups, but you could get access to all areas and keep moving before the kids got too bored!

—Sandy Perez, Paris (one-year stay)

But "self-guided tour" should not mean "wandering aimlessly." It's up to you, your spouse, or even one of your older kids to be an intelligent and informative guide.

The site you visit will help you do this in two ways. First, there'll be labels and signs. These are often available in several languages. Even if they haven't been translated, someone with basic language skills will find it easier to translate a few lines of written text than to keep up with simultaneous oral translations. Most sites also offer an English-language brochure you can carry around and read aloud.

It's still a good idea to do a little preparation. European tourist attractions aren't as geared to entertainment as American ones often are, so signs and brochures may be a little limited, if not downright cryptic. They may also assume an in-depth knowledge of European history that you may not have right at the tip of your tongue. Buy a few good guidebooks ahead or at the site, and bone up on the topic at hand.

rule 3: allow for family differences

Different members of a family view each museum or site differently, depending entirely on what each brings to that place.

Take a typical family's visit to a typical cathedral. Dad's a carpenter, and he wants to look closely at the way the structure was put together. Mom's hobby is needlework, and she'd like to spend hours studying the tapestries. Their fifteen-year-old son picks out names he recognizes from his history book in the brass tomb markers on the walls—then tries to strike up a conversation with some local girls selling ice cream out front. His nine-year-old sister listens to Dad talk about building for a little while, briefly enjoys the colored tapestries with Mom, and ultimately tries to climb the base of a flying buttress.

It's impossible for everyone in a family to come out even. And it's probably not a good idea to try: It's important for people to respect others' interests. Lew and I almost always wanted to spend longer at museums, while the kids couldn't be pried away from outdoor sites such as ruins.

Pick a meeting place before you start to tour: a park bench or a patch of grass under a shady tree. If your kids are old enough, anyone who's finished early can go there and rest, read a book, play with a toy, or snack. Make sure all family members bring whatever is necessary to amuse themselves for a while.

A few small items were helpful: a Hacky Sack for each child, great for whiling away time spent in a line, and dice in their pockets to play Bunco or any games they made up. Great on the courtyard cobblestones if Mom and Dad took too long looking at cathedral architecture!

—Ellen Manuel, Bellevue, NE

When you're staying in a town or city, try to pick a hotel or hostel that's near the interesting sites. Older kids can head back to their room when they're bored without having to wait for a ride.

family decision making

How do you as a family go about making decisions that involve everyone? We'd always thought our approach was pretty democratic, yet we ran aground a few times in our travels. Let's explore some different decision-making strategies, and find out why.

In the Jones family, Mrs. Jones stays up every night scouring the guidebooks and planning a careful agenda for the next day. She tries to pick sites everyone will enjoy. When a museum turns out to be closed, or a castle tour is utterly boring, she feels personally responsible—guilty, even—for wasting a day of the trip. The kids complain that she's deciding everything, so she suggests the whole family vote on where to eat dinner. Two hours later, cranky and tired, they finally settle on a mediocre pizza joint.

The Smiths, in contrast, have evolved a different system. Each day a different member of the family is in charge. On Tuesday Mr. Smith picks the science museum. The kids go along, even though it sounds suspiciously educational. On Wednesday nine-year-old Steve chooses to rent bicycles to the dismay of his parents, who haven't biked in years. Thursday, Mrs. Smith plans a trip to a cheese factory. And on Friday thirteen-year-old Beth calls for sleeping late, then visiting the flea market. All during the week, the leader-of-the-day makes the final pick on dinner, too.

daily leader system

We've tried both these systems, and the second works infinitely better for us. With reflection, here's why:

- **It avoids the lowest common denominator.** One person trying to second-guess everyone's tastes will pick safe choices that no one will hate—but no one will really like, either.

- **It exposes family members to new interests.** Who'd have thought that ball-bearing factory would be so interesting? Well, even if it doesn't turn out to be, you've at least tried something different. Tomorrow's choice may open new worlds to you.

- **It contributes to family harmony.** Individual worth takes a beating on a hectic trip where privacy is hard to come by. Letting each person be king or queen for a day helps a lot. This is especially important for kids. At home they have their own sphere of school and friends. On the road they're in your world, going by your rules day after day—unless you give them a break.

- **It encourages family members to contribute actively to the success of the trip.** No one person should carry the entire burden of whether the trip is a success. And it's important for everyone to know that a major trip like this isn't something someone else does to or for you. Each person in the family needs to put something in to get the most out.

- **It avoids the paralysis that comes from trying to reach constant consensus.** Harriman's Law says that the more people involved in a decision, the longer it will take—and the hungrier you'll get in the meantime. It's still okay for everyone to put in his or her two cents' worth. But each day there'll be one person who makes the final decision so things can move ahead.

We use the leader-of-the-day system any time we stay in an area for four days or more. But we adapt it for shorter stays, letting each of us lead for half a day or for an hour, or by letting each person have one choice in the day, without reference to time.

Perhaps the single most important idea we used on our trip to France was to rotate decision making among the group members so no one person had to do all the planning and be blamed for it! We even let four-year-old Claire choose from several options on "her day," and she loved it. We'll use that rule on all future trips anywhere with anyone!

—Lynn Barclay, Perry, KS

Families can, in the final analysis, be too considerate of each other. If you're constantly worrying about what the others want to do, you may have trouble seriously considering what you want to do. The leader-of-the-day system gives everyone a chance to honestly figure out his or her priorities.

One important point is worth noting: You'll need to help your children understand what the possibilities are in any given area. You can't simply drive into the Swiss Alps and say, "Okay kids, what do you want to do today?" Sit down with maps and guidebooks, and make a list of several options to give the leader some inspiration.

Your kids will get the hang of planning quickly. Sam, for instance, was still just ten one day in Chartres when it was his turn to pick dinner. He grabbed a map, studied it for a while, then pointed with his finger at the different parts. "Now if the pedestrian zone is *here,* there are probably some good restaurants around *there.* Let's park here, like we did this afternoon—'cause we know there are spaces—and walk from there."

the big picture

The daily leader system helps to avoid power wars and resentments once you've arrived in a particular location. But don't forget your kids when you're mapping your overall route, too. Even though you may need to make some decisions unilaterally—which route to take, when to start out, how many miles to cover in a given day—your kids will want to be brought into the planning process.

Don't be haphazard about this. Early on, Lew and I would make plans, mention them in passing, and then assume the kids were clued in. It took two heated discussions to realize that one child or the other had missed out on the plans and felt disenfranchised. We wised up and put our whole remaining itinerary on the table for open discussion. The kids surprised us by proposing a side trip to Loch Ness. They sensibly demolished all our arguments about it being too far, and we ended up with a very successful addition to the trip.

Since then we've made sure to discuss plans systematically, when all four of us are present—the oral equivalent of making sure everyone's signed off on a memo. "Okay, so tomorrow we're going to leave about nine and drive straight through to Legoland, right? Then we stay there two days and take the ferry to England."

no, no, and no

All the planning in the world is worth nothing when your kids have decided not to cooperate. Teenagers are among the worst. Adolescent kids are on average 50 percent sunny and pleasant, 25 percent neutral, and only 25 percent a pain in the neck. Don't get so wrapped up in that last 25 percent that you forget the other 75 percent.

One problem that arises is kids who say "no" to every possibility. Lib did this with us several times. Once, in Paris, it was her day to be in charge. But she had no ideas of her own and turned down every one we proposed. Later, Lew and I made a family rule that no one could veto a proposed plan unless they came up with an alternative. Once you do this, of course, you should be ready to drop whatever you may have planned if your child comes up with a suggestion of any kind. A little positive feedback goes a long way.

When things get particularly bad, decide what you'd do without your kids and just do it. Give the kids a chance to join in if they want. "We're going to the British Museum this afternoon. You can come along, or you can stay here at the hotel. Which do you choose?"

Parent-child relationships work (or don't work) in both directions. If one of your kids seems very negative, there's a good chance that what *you're* doing is hitting him or her as unproductive, too. Talk it out, though not in the car or at dinner with everyone present. Pick a quiet time over pastries or at the Laundromat, when one parent can talk to that one child privately.

special pointers for cities

All things being equal, I'd stay away from cities when traveling with kids. They're crowded and expensive and demand more than the usual quota of sit-down-and-be-quiet behavior. What's more, if you're concerned about security, cities are much likelier targets for crime and terrorism than rural areas. Cities are also more generically international in language, architecture, and culture than towns and villages, where you can soak in the flavor of a country more quickly.

But all things are not equal. The major cities of the world have a name-brand draw that both you and your kids will be unlikely to resist. Who can go to France without visiting Paris or to England without a stop in London?

Given, then, that you're bound to visit many cities on your trip, here are some pointers we've found useful.

save the city for last

Don't start your trip in a big city. It's like taking your final exam on the first day of classes! If you'll be in Italy for a month, for instance, visit Rome at the end of your trip, not the beginning. Once you know a few basic words of the language and the meaning of the most essential street signs, you'll be in much better shape to tackle a major city.

stay put

Don't try to "do" a city in a day trip. Instead, stay three or four days, at least. Let's take Paris as an example. In one day you can see the Eiffel Tower, climb up Montmartre, and visit Notre Dame. With four days you can do all that *and* spend time watching the skateboarders near Centre Pompidou, visit the flea markets on the north edge of the city, take a boat ride on the Seine, and plenty more things without being rushed.

By staying put you'll come to "own" the city. It takes only about two days to feel at home in "your" neighborhood: to know where the pastry shop is, for instance, or which bus route stops where. In three days you can get a pattern of the city in your head: Where's the river? What are the major squares? In four days you can do more than the tourist highlights, creating memories of a city that go beyond the usual clichés.

use public transportation

In cities, park your car in a safe spot as soon as you arrive, and use public transportation for the rest of your stay. Cars are an immense hassle in any city, but especially so in a foreign one. You don't want to bother with traffic jams, foreign-language street signs, and unknown parking customs.

Some cities now ban cars from the city center or charge tolls for access. Oslo was first, in 1990, and now London charges £8.00 per day (you pay ahead online or at local shops), with Stockholm joining the trend in July 2007.

Traffic in Madrid is a nightmare—I'll never drive within the city again. No parking except in sleazy garages. I'm fluent in Spanish, but I can't imagine a non-Spanish speaker surviving (except maybe somebody who could afford an expensive hotel with a garage attached!). It would have been much smarter to take a cab into the city and go back to the airport to rent a car at the end of our Madrid visit.

—Paul Heald, Athens, GA

Start with the subway, or metro as it's called in many countries. (Note: In London, ask for the Underground. A subway is a pedestrian underpass in England.) Subways are usually easy to figure out from large route maps posted in the stations. A good guidebook can tell you about special deals for tourists, such as the *carnet* (a set of ten tickets for the price of about six) in Paris. Subways in Europe are generally safe, too.

Subways can be part of the feel of a major city. In Milan it's fun to pick out the fashion models at the stations nearest the fairgrounds. In Paris singers and puppeteers ply their trade in the stations and even on the trains, adding an unmistakable Parisian air to traveling across town.

Once you get comfortable with the subway, try the buses. Ask at the tourist office or at major stations for a bus map, and find out how fares are paid (correct change? ticket? tourist pass?). Buses are a bit more confusing than subways. But what do you care if you get lost? You might even choose to get lost on purpose. In London, for instance, you can ride a traditional red bus until the scenery gets boring, then hop off and go in another direction. If you're armed with a good map and a guidebook, you can see a lot of the city for just the price of a cheap bus ticket. Then the next day, when you really want to go someplace, you'll know how the buses work.

Many cities offer tourist passes and "hop on-off" tourist buses, but these options are usually much more expensive. You'll save money using regular public transportation, and you'll be taking part in real life rather than a canned tourist experience.

On our recent trip to London, the kids had the most fun just hopping on a double-decker bus and then switching buses at the end of the line and heading somewhere else. We purchased a family travel pass, which was good after 9:30 A.M. on all London transportation modes, and boy was it worth the £5.50!

—Katy Wessel, U.S. Air Force, anywhere and everywhere

---

plan a mix of activities

In cities it's especially important to plan a mix of activities. One good way to start is by visiting a city or town's tourist office as soon as you arrive. Pick up a good map and as many free brochures as you can carry. Ask the tourist office staff:

- if any fairs and markets take place in town
- whether there's a hands-on science or children's museum
- which squares or plazas are known for their street artists
- where the biggest toy stores in town are located
- what other sites they'd especially recommend for children the ages of yours

Leave the bustle of the tourist office for a quiet park bench or a small cafe. Spread all the brochures out in front of you, discuss all the possibilities, and come up with a plan. Some of our worst times as a family came when we simply wandered aimlessly hoping to discover something interesting. The times we planned were always better—even though we often scrapped our plans for serendipitous discoveries!

As you plan, remember to balance active and passive pursuits. For instance, combine a museum morning with an afternoon picnic and tower climbing. Don't schedule too tightly; allow lots of time for ice-cream breaks or simply resting to counterbalance the hectic pace of cities. Check out our specific suggestions for cities like Paris (in chapter 18) and London (in chapter 17), the two cities most often visited by traveling families.

I think the most important thing for parents to keep in mind is that your children are unlikely to have any more stamina on your European trip than they do at home. If the kids reach "meltdown" after two hours walking in the local mall, don't expect them to last much longer than that on your museum tour. Frequent breaks for snacks (you must carry these, or go broke buying from local vendors!) and chasing pigeons are mandatory.

—Timothy Moody, Pullman, WA

restaurants

Eating out in another country can be a surprising minefield, especially if your kids are fussy eaters. Dinner hours may be vastly different, menus can be indecipherable—and even after you figure out what they say, there may be little that's familiar. It's all a bit of a challenge: How can you interest the kids in trying squid when there's a McDonald's around the corner? In the end your children will probably surprise you with the new tastes they acquire, but in the meantime a glance at some of the issues you might encounter may help.

trying out new foods

To many normal American kids, eating out is synonymous with pizza. And since pizza is on the menu throughout Europe, you can't avoid it simply by boycotting American fast-food restaurants. Then how can you encourage your kids to try the local foods?

It's probably best not to pressure the kids. Most kids eventually climb out of their pizza rut, often because the pizza is very different from what your kids are used to. Crusts in Europe are thin, and strange toppings are everywhere. Italian seafood pizzas, for example, routinely include clams and mussels, shells and all. Our kids avoided pizza for several weeks after a restaurant in Spain served Sam a pizza covered with red peppers as "pepperoni" and gave Libby one with two whole, fat, greasy sausages embedded in the middle for "sausage." Cheeses will be different, too: Will your child enjoy pizza with Gruyère or goat cheese?

risk-free experiments

One strategy that works is to offer your kids a few bites of whatever you're eating. Pork in Breton cider or salmon with dill sauce tastes good in the middle of a disappointing pizza. Given a few nonthreatening bites, most kids will expand their repertoire enough to try something new on their own before long.

When they do finally experiment, don't insist they clean their plates. Your goal should be to take the risk out of experimenting. Luckily, European restaurants conspire to make this easy. Most meals consist of more than one course, so no one will starve if a particular plate turns out to be disgusting. And you'll almost always be served bread and/or french fries—*frites*—with your meal, things that even the most finicky eaters can fill up on.

If you're like me and you don't like many foods, stick with the salads. They're usually pretty safe. And the pizza was pretty good most places. I never get sick of pizza.

Emma Rausch, Rowley, MA (age thirteen)

We quickly adopted a system of ordering two "safe" dishes and two adventurous ones, then sharing everything Chinese-restaurant-style. With this approach, Lew and I were in fact occasionally disappointed when the kids downed the new experiment and left us with something tried and true.

menu readers

Even if you have some command of the local language, you'll do well to have a menu reader with you when you travel. A menu reader is a little phrase guide that includes just the words you'll need to use to get a meal.

A menu reader is infinitely more useful than a dictionary because it lists typical dishes, not just individual words. A German dictionary will tell you that *Schweinefleische* is pork; a menu reader will tell you that *Mainzer Rippchen* is pork chop, *Jungfernbraten* is roast pork with bacon, and *Selchfleisch* is smoked pork. We even found our menu reader useful in Britain, when we came across foods like Scottish eggs, Bubble and Squeak, and Melton Mowbray pie.

the lure of fast food

No matter what you do, your kids are likely to clamor for at least an occasional visit to a familiar fast-food chain, especially when they're particularly homesick.

Don't categorically refuse. There are things to be learned about other cultures even at McDonald's. In Denmark, for instance, McDonald's workers are bilingual, they wear ties, and they come to your table to refresh your coffee cup—for free. In Spain Burger King sells beer as well as soft drinks. In Great Britain Pizza Hut offers tuna, prawns, sweet corn, and pineapple among its toppings.

Plan at least one American fast-food stop in each country you visit, and encourage the kids to look closely for differences in the familiar format. It's fun to collect paper place mats and take-out menus with the well-known logos to show the kids back home.

But make sure your offspring agree up front that these visits will be limited to specific times and places: "Okay. We'll go to Pizza Hut once between here and Paris, and no McDonald's till Amsterdam, right?" This sort of agreement avoids a nightly chorus of predictable suggestions when it's restaurant-choosing time.

finding good dinner restaurants

Once everyone's agreed to branch out from fast food, you'll need to find a good alternative. Guidebooks are little or no help. Fortunately, most European restaurants post their menus outside the door, making it easy to see the variety and price of the food—if not the quality—at a glance.

A three-step approach works well. First, check the menu displayed for prices. Then, if it's within your budget, make sure there's at least one thing each person would be willing to eat. This isn't a careful final decision—just a quick scan to make sure there's at least one possibility for each person. Libby, for instance, is a great lover of shrimp. She learned to recognize the appropriate words—*prawns* (England), *crevettes* (France), and *gambas* (Spain)—and would willingly enter any restaurant that offered some variation of the shellfish, though she'd often order something else after due deliberation.

Finally, make some effort to check the quality of the food. Many French restaurants have outdoor tables, making it easy to peek at the nearest patrons' plates. At others you might want to make a scouting trip inside, under cover of asking directions to some nearby landmark. You'll almost always be able to get a whiff of the food: If it's irresistible, don't resist. If it smells peculiar, it may taste so, too.

As the last part of your quality check, take a look at the number of patrons inside. Crowded restaurants are mobbed either because the locals think they're good or because some guidebook has told the tourists they're good. Listen to the accents inside, and try to find ones residents favor that are at least half full. Avoid empty restaurants: Our worst dining experiences came when we ignored common sense and gloried in a nice, empty restaurant where we could be seated immediately. There's usually a reason empty restaurants are empty, and it's not because they're undiscovered treasures. (*One exception:* In countries such as Spain and Italy, where people dine very late, many restaurants may be empty simply because it's too early.)

A final word on choosing restaurants: It's a law of nature that the length of time it takes to make a group decision is in direct proportion to the size of the group. You may wander for hours before you find a restaurant the whole family thinks is ideal ("I don't know, I kinda liked the one back there, it had better desserts"—"But I liked the one that had the veal in cream sauce—"). Try taking turns choosing (parents one night, kids the next, or even one at a time) to speed up the process and to give each member of the family a chance to be in charge.

eating well for less on the road

If it's important to you to keep your restaurant tab to a minimum, stop at restaurants only once a day when you're on the road.

This doesn't mean you should starve. Breakfast is often included in your hotel tab. If it isn't, pick up some pastries and juice. Most bakeries will have satisfying "savory" (as opposed to sweet) pastries with meat fillings or cheese, starting very early in the morning. Sometimes the bakery itself will also sell drinks; if not, you'll often find bottled fruit juice at the nearest bar.

Lunches can be picnics. You can buy bread when you pick up your breakfast pastries, then stop before noon for cheese, fruit, cold cuts, yogurt, chocolate—whatever interests you. (Just remember that in some countries, such as Italy and Spain, you must stock up on groceries before stores close for lunch break.) It should be possible, with this approach, to keep your breakfast and lunch costs under €15 total per person per day, and you'll often eat healthier meals.

The one thing that saved us a lot of money was picnic lunches every day. We tried all the different breads and cheeses and meats, and strange drinks. And I'd practice my French and German on the butchers. They were very nice when I kept forgetting the word for "sliced" in German.

—Maya D'Anjou, Morgan Hill, CA

Picnics leave a lot of leeway in the budget for dinner. But you won't need to spend much, even for your major meal in a restaurant. Without great difficulty, you can spend under €80 for dinner for four on the road—and this is for real, multicourse meals, not fast food. We found little correlation between our best meals and our most expensive ones, so go ahead and try the little local restaurant on the corner.

One simple way to save money is to drink tap water instead of bottled water or pricey sodas. In the most-visited areas of Western Europe, tap water standards are high, although those who have recently taken a course of antibiotics or very young children may be sensitive to any water with *different* microbes, even those microbes that aren't dangerous. Here's how you ask for tap water in four common European languages:

French	*un carafe d'eau* or *l'eau du robinet*
German	*Leitungswasser*
Spanish	*agua del grifo*
Italian	*acqua del rubinetto*

english restaurants

Because restaurants differ widely from country to country, let's take a look at a few of Europe's most-visited countries. Stereotypes about English food are largely true: It does tend to be unimaginative and at the same time expensive compared to continental food.

english money savers

Fixed-price, multicourse meals, a standard in many European countries, are rare in England. So, given England's overpriced and underinspiring dinners, you may do well to dine lightly on pub food. Pubs offer dishes that can be quite filling for little money: baked potatoes with cheese topping, thick stews, meat pasties, or a "ploughman's lunch" (usually consisting of bread, a chunk of good cheese, a pickled vegetable dish such as chutney, and a salad). For soft drinks, encourage the kids to try squash (usually a sort of noncarbonated orange drink) or lemonade (like Sprite or 7-Up) instead of sticking to Coke. Children are permitted in certain areas of many British pubs. Look for a room designated "family room," but check your watch: Family rooms often close by 8:00 P.M. Since kids aren't allowed in the bar, you can't count on pubs for a late family meal.

Another option for good flavor at a good price is ethnic restaurants. Indian and Chinese restaurants abound at relatively reasonable prices. (Indian restaurants are common in England because of Britain's colonial past. On the Continent, look for Chinese, Turkish, Greek, and other ethnic restaurants.)

Keep in mind that younger children often don't like heavily spiced food. Sam, for instance, met his match at an Indian tandoori restaurant in northern

England. Despite the fact that he had downed octopus, rabbit, pigeon, and several other exotic foods earlier in our travels, he was unable to stomach the Indian spices. It was his only complete "pass" on the whole trip, and I mention it to remind you that even the most game kid will eventually run into some cuisine—not necessarily the most exotic one—that he or she simply cannot stomach.

My mother's favorite trick when traveling with her eight kids was to frequent Chinese restaurants where we could eat relatively cheaply, get lots of vegetables, and usually rely on a Kids-R-Welcome atmosphere. By the time I was fifteen and the veteran of several summerlong family trips to Europe, I could get along in pidgin Chinese, play Chinese checkers, and handle chopsticks like a native. Twenty years later I still find this to be the case traveling with my children.

—Kari Beck, Tallahassee, FL

---

english favorites

Your kids' favorite American foods will likely be their favorite foods in England. If they insist on a hamburger fix, stick to McDonald's and Burger King, and stay away from Wimpy's, which our experience and that of several readers confirms as uniformly terrible. Fish-and-chips are a better bet for British fast food. The traditional custom of serving fish in a cone of newspaper has been abolished, since officials discovered newspaper ink could be toxic.

We found the much-storied British breakfasts—cereal (cold or hot), sausage, eggs, broiled tomatoes, and fried bread—disappointing. English sausages (*bangers*) are soft and greasy, with a great deal of cereal filler. And fried bread is just what its name implies: dry bread crisped in fat until it's like a giant flat crouton. Not the healthiest breakfast. Your kids may prefer cold cereal.

Your favorite foods may be hard to find, as many common foods go by different names in Britain (and in English translations of continental menus). Look for some of the following on the menu:

English Term	American Equivalent
bap	bun (like a hamburger bun)
chips	french fries
crisps	potato chips
biscuits	cookies
prawns	shrimp
pudding	dessert (of any sort)
salad cream	mayonnaise
tunny	tuna fish

english hours and service

Meal hours in England are quite similar to ours in the United States, but with the added bonus of teatime. Tea is a lovely institution. It's quite civilized, as visitors, to indulge in cakes and tea at the end of the afternoon, all in the name of cultural understanding. In many parts of England, you'll be offered "cream tea." Cream tea usually consists of a pot of tea, a few scones, Devonshire cream (not unlike whipped cream), and jelly. The end result is something like eating a jelly-cream doughnut with tea.

You may also hear the word *tea* used to describe any evening meal. English kids may ask, "What's for tea tonight, Mum?" in much the same way our kids will ask, "What're we having for supper?"

french restaurants

France's reputation for good food is justified: For a very reasonable price, you can get a generous quantity of good food almost anywhere in France. And French cuisine is renowned enough that many kids will overcome their new-foods hesitation to try some exotic dishes.

Sam decided early on that he was going to try frog legs or snails before we left France. On our last night, in Calais, he finally did; I will never forget him poking into the shells with the tiny snail fork, saying, "I know you're in there. Come on out!"

french money savers

French food does not have to be expensive. Most restaurants offer one or more fixed-price dinners called *le menu*. These dinners usually consist of an appetizer (called the *entrée*), main course (*le plat*), dessert, and wine. For each course you get to choose from perhaps three to five options. Except in Paris, you can find *menus* starting as low as 10 to 12 euros, service included. In Paris we've found that many restaurants offer a *menu enfant* or *menu junior* that's a great value. For around €7.50 you'll get a main dish, beverage, and dessert, often with a toy or prize.

If there are several fixed-price choices, you order your dinner according to price: *Le menu de douze,* for instance, tells the waiter you'd like the 12 euro menu. Remember that *le menu* means "the fixed-price dinner." If you want to look at a menu, you would tell the waiter, *"La carte, s'il vous plaît."*

The first time we went to Paris, we paid 17 euros just for three small Cokes, a lemonade, and a cup of coffee. We learned the hard way to always have at least water and sometimes cans of soda along with us. In most places you can't just get tap water; you get bubbly water, and my kids do not like it.

—Katy Wessel, U.S. Air Force, anywhere and everywhere

---

french favorites

A few common dishes—which could be called "French fast food"—are popular with the average kid. Most simple cafes serve a *croque monsieur*. This delicious open-face grilled cheese and ham sandwich is ubiquitous, inexpensive, and well loved by kids. Sometimes you'll also see a *croque madame*, which includes an egg and is not as popular with the junior crowd. Another good option for kids is the ready-made sandwiches available at many cafes and sidewalk stands. *Un sandwich jambon* is simply a ham sandwich, but with a definite French accent: a small, fresh, crusty baguette with butter and sliced ham.

At restaurants most dishes should be acceptable to all but the fussiest kids. Many French adore organ meats (my friend Elise gets ecstatic over veal head, *tête de veau*, as it conjures up fond memories of Sunday dinner at Grandma's). If you don't agree with Elise, watch out for *rognons* (kidneys), *langue* (tongue), *tripes* (stomach lining), and *cervelle* (brains).

french hours and service

Restaurants are generally open for lunch from noon to 2:00 or 3:00 P.M. and for dinner from about 7:00 to 10:00 P.M. You won't find a sit-down meal in the late afternoon.

Should you tip? Service is almost always included in your bill. Look for the words *service compris* on the bottom of the check. If service has been extra nice, leave a little change on the table, too. Service in France is very leisurely. Don't be offended: Just because the tip is included in your bill doesn't mean your waiter is taking advantage of you. The French believe food is meant to be savored, that dinner is an event that should take the whole evening. I find this attitude preferable to that in some American restaurants, where the staff seems overeager to recycle your table for the next diners. But if you have other plans after dinner or you're exhausted, tell the waiter you're in a rush. *Les enfants sont si fatigués*—the children are so tired—would do fine.

german restaurants

Germany offers some wonderful meals. I've dined on marvelous venison, rabbit, and wild boar in Bavaria, topped off with apple strudel in vanilla sauce. But those meals stand out in a sea of unremitting pork (*Schweinefleisch*), potatoes (*Kartoffeln*), and sausage (*Wurst*). It takes a little creativity in Germany to find green vegetables and variety on a bargain budget.

german money savers

German breakfasts are usually a hearty buffet of meats, cheeses, breads, and yogurt, served in your hotel or hostel. Enjoy, since it's almost always included in the hotel charge.

For lunch, bakeries sell *Brötchen* (sandwiches), and take-away bars sell *Wurst*. *Wurst* come in many varieties, almost all greasier and chewier than American hot dogs, making them a bit daunting to younger kids.

The *Tagesmenu* is the fixed-price menu of the day. There's often just one choice, so peruse it carefully. German menus often feature organ meats and other odd body parts. If you don't normally eat these cuts at home, you have two choices: Order in ignorant bliss and learn to like something new, or keep your dictionary handy and watch out. Key words include *Nieren* (kidneys), *Herz* (heart), *Leber* (liver), *Schweinefuß* (pig's knuckle), and *Zunge* (tongue).

German meals are heavy and filling, so you may want to order full dinners for the adults and just side dishes for the kids. For instance, you order the *Schweinebraten,* or roast pork, and order a plate of *Spätzle* (homemade noodles) and a salad for the kids. You'll get about three pigs' worth of pork in your entree, so you can share a bit with the kids, and you'll all eat well.

german favorites

The ubiquitous *Wiener Schnitzel,* a thin breaded-pork cutlet, is popular with most kids. If your kids like fish, salmon (*Lachs*) and trout (*Forelle*) are almost fail-safe alternatives to pork. Here and elsewhere in Europe, try to get your kids to try something really unusual. Dishes such as rabbit (*Kaninchen*) are different, but are usually mild and tasty.

If German cuisine strikes out with the kids, try Chinese and Italian restaurants. Pizza is the European variety, with thin crust, and often with "lumpy" toppings (e.g., whole sausages or mushrooms). Pastas like lasagna or spaghetti are another option at Italian restaurants, though, again, warn your kids that the flavors may differ from what they're used to.

german hours and service

German meal hours are similar to American ones; you shouldn't have trouble finding someplace to eat dinner at 6:30 P.M.

Most restaurants expect you to seat yourself, so don't stand in the doorway politely waiting to be seated. If a single person or a couple is sitting at the end of a large table, it's considered perfectly acceptable to ask them if you can have the rest of the table. Remind your kids to be considerate of the "neighbors" in this situation, though.

When you're done, "*Zahlen, bitte*" signals that you want to pay. Your server will scrawl your order illegibly on a small pad, present you with a bill that includes service and VAT (*Mehrwertstauer,* or MWST), and make change on the spot from a large black wallet. Credit cards are not often accepted at small family restaurants, so ask first if you're low on euros.

italian restaurants

It's no accident that Italian food is really popular with most kids. It's unlikely that you'll have trouble here with even the fussiest eaters.

italian money savers

Italy offers three main eating choices: the *pizzeria,* the *trattoria,* and the *ristorante.* Pizzerias routinely offer other dishes, but specialize in *pizze* (yes, that's the Italian plural of pizza!), usually featuring a wood-burning oven in full view of the patrons. Trattorias (*trattorie* in Italian) are usually less expensive than restaurants, with a simple, limited menu. (In Italian terms, this may mean only ten kinds of pasta and fifteen dishes, instead of the overwhelming array most restaurants offer.) Basically, these are the little local places where the residents eat. *Ristoranti* tend to be more expensive and often larger, though the food is just as good at both places.

Your kids may be surprised when they order Italian pizza.

Meal prices can add up quickly in Italy because of the many different courses offered: *antipasti* (hors d'oeuvres), *primi piatti* (soup, rice, or pasta dishes), and *secondi piatti* (meat, chicken, or fish dishes). You can also order *contorni* (side dishes of vegetables or salads), *frutti* (fruits), and *dolci* (sweets, or desserts).

Save money by ignoring the system. No one minds, for instance, if you choose two kinds of pasta and a salad and skip everything else. Some places may offer a *menù* or *menù turistico*. This is a fixed-price dinner, usually with three courses, and is often a good deal—*if* you were planning to eat more than one course anyway.

Some restaurants in Italy offer specials where children eat free, but these deals are rarely publicized. Look for any sign with the word *bambini* in it, then pull out your dictionary and translate. Failing that, try a simple phrase like *"Bambino? Quanto costa?"*

italian favorites

Italian pizza is wonderful but has little in common with American pizza. The crust is relatively thin and crisp from cooking on the floor of a wood-burning oven, and the toppings are very different. Almost anything's available, from eggplant to ricotta cheese, from squid to clams, from ham to salami. But these toppings are often in big chunks rather than chopped fine: whole clams in the shell, a mound of ricotta on one side of the pie, large slices of eggplant. This can surprise American kids, who think they know everything there is to know about pizza.

Most pizza menus include the name of the pizza and the ingredients used. Work through the list with your dictionary, and don't make assumptions: If some kind of cheese isn't listed, then your pizza won't have cheese. If you think that pizza without cheese is like apple pie without apples, ask your waiter to add it. *Con mozzarella* will do the trick. For a plain cheese pizza, simply order a *pizza Margharita*. In Italy and throughout Europe, this name is used to describe a basic pie with mozzarella, tomato sauce, and a few Italian spices. (If you want a more "American" pizza, fast-food restaurants offer run-of-the-mill slices cooked in a rotating gas or electric oven, or maybe even microwaved. But why on earth did you go to Italy if that's all you want?)

One good way to explore new choices in Italy is to order nothing but *antipasti*. Most Italian eateries (in all three categories) feature an *antipasto* bar not unlike the salad bars in American restaurants. There you'll be faced with a wide array of yesterday's leftovers: a big platter of cold lamb chops, seven kinds of cold pasta, roasted peppers, eggplant. In most places you'll be charged by the size plate you take, whereas others may charge by the item. Check first.

The *antipasto* bar represents your best chance to lure the kids away from pasta and pizza in Italy. It invites kids to explore, with its wide selection of visible choices. At the very least *you* can do the antipasto bar and let them pick from your plate at the table.

italian hours and service

Italian restaurants serve lunch from perhaps 1:00 to 3:00 P.M., and dinner rarely starts before 7:00 P.M. (much later in the south). Plan your snacking schedule so you won't be caught with cranky, hungry kids in the early evening.

Italian restaurants usually serve your food as soon as it's ready, with no attempt to coordinate meals for everyone at the table. This means that some dishes will come in ten minutes and others in forty. Luckily, pizza and pasta are often the quickest dishes, so the kids' dinner will probably get there first. Tell everyone to dig in as soon as their food arrives. Don't let it get cold while you stand on ceremony.

Italians love children. In almost any restaurant kids will get special treatment. Dan and Wendy fondly recall a typical example in Rome. They had been nervous at bringing three children to a formal Michelin-rated restaurant, but found the kids were the center of attention: The waiter served their water in aperitif glasses with a flourish, and the *maitre d'* chased them around the room and pretended to put them in the oven.

The tip (*servizio*) will usually be included in your tab, though it's customary to leave small change on the table, too. You'll also be assessed a cover charge for each person in your party. Look for the phrase "*pane e coperto*" on the menu. This charge is usually about €2.00 per person and bears no relation to how much bread (*pane*) you eat. Unfortunately, this unavoidable charge adds to the cost of eating out in Italy.

Restaurants by law are required to give you a receipt, and you're required to hang on to it until you're well away from the restaurant—part of a government effort to force under-the-table cash transactions into the taxable economy.

spanish restaurants

Spanish food is about the same price as French food, but the quality is not as consistently good. Still, you can eat wonderfully in Spain as long as you pay attention to the clock.

spanish money savers

Budget diners should look for two options: the *menú del dia* and *platos combinados.* The *menú* usually includes an appetizer or salad, a main dish, bread, beverage, and dessert (often *flan,* or custard) and is usually found at restaurants. *Platos combinados,* a staple of cafeterias, combine a main dish with a few side dishes and bread—perhaps pork loin, salad, and potatoes, or something similar—but don't usually include dessert or beverage.

spanish hours and service

Many Spanish eat four meals daily. Breakfast is typically continental—bread or sweet rolls with coffee or hot chocolate. Lunch is a large, hot meal served somewhere between 1:00 and 3:00 P.M. Around 5:00 or 6:00 P.M. many people will indulge in *merienda,* a late-afternoon snack, often a pastry. Dinner is commonly eaten at 10:00 P.M. or later.

When you're on the road, it's essential to be aware of this schedule. For lunch, many restaurants will have just one seating around 1:00 P.M. Getting a meal in popular tourist areas is then like a game of musical chairs: If you're not seated when the music stops, you're out of the game. And I mean out—grocery stores, fruit stores, pastry shops, and all other manner of stores close at 1:00 or 2:00 P.M., too, and stay closed for three hours.

Adjusting to the Spanish dinner hour can be difficult. A restaurant that opens as early as 8:00 P.M. is rare; a 9:00 or even 9:30 P.M. opening is not unusual. Groceries and other food shops are usually open from 5:00 to 8:00 P.M., so buy a snack to tide you over if necessary—or eat your big meal at lunch and then picnic at dinnertime.

spanish bars and cafeterias

If you haven't bought picnic groceries and the restaurants are full or closed, try a bar. Bars are open afternoons and Sunday when everything else is closed, and most sell sandwiches (*bocadillos*) and little hors d'oeuvres (*tapas*). Don't hesitate to take your kids into a bar. Bars in Spain are social gathering places where you'll see people of all ages, including babies in strollers.

Babies and children are common sights in Spanish bars.

One word of warning: You may have trouble convincing your kids it's okay to visit bars. Be prepared for some resistance, and don't forget you can simply take your sandwiches and juice out to the car if the kids feel too uncomfortable with the smoke-and-alcohol atmosphere of the bars. Keep your eyes open for bars with mothers and babies in them, and your kids will feel better.

Cafeterias are a low-cost alternative to full restaurants. The food at cafeterias is usually nothing to boast about, but they offer several advantages. First, they're usually cheap. Second, they're often open earlier than restaurants—sometimes as early as 6:30 or 7:00 P.M. for dinner. Third, they usually offer *platos combinados* and feature big color pictures of their offerings, making it easier for those who don't speak Spanish to know just what they're getting.

greek restaurants

Greek restaurants provide not just a meal but an experience. Be prepared: It's hard to eat in a Greek restaurant without getting *involved* in the meal!

greek menus

At restaurants (as anywhere in Greece) it helps to know the Greek alphabet. If you only know the sound that each of those funny squiggles makes, you can sound out many dishes on the menu. For example, φετα is feta, the well-known Greek cheese. And κοτολεττα means cutlet. If you plan to spend much of your vacation in Greece, make a game out of learning the Greek letters with your kids before you go.

Once you've got the hang of a few basic foods, it gets easier. Almost all Greek restaurants use a standard menu, preprinted with all the same foods, so you'll see the same dishes worded the same way over and over. It helps to understand that only those foods with prices entered next to them are actually available. Don't ask for unpriced items because you won't get them.

In many restaurants you won't even get a menu. Instead, the staff will invite your whole family into the kitchen, where you can point to whatever looks good. You'll still probably end up with some surprises if you don't speak Greek, but most kids find this tangible system of picking food very welcome.

The fact that we could speak no Greek hampered us not one bit in ordering a delightful Greek meal. The usual pattern appeared to be for the guest to be brought into the kitchen and choose the food stuffs himself right out of the cooking pot on the large wood-burning range. We had a little bit of everything, washed down with Coca-Cola and local beer, and everybody seemed to enjoy it.

—Ula Handschin, Bellevue, WA

---

greek favorites

Most Americans have experience with at least some typically French, Spanish, and German foods—to say nothing of Italian! Greek food, though, may seem different enough that a few suggestions that usually appeal to kids may be in order.

- Virtually all outdoor cafes serve pizza.

- At many restaurants, half a roast chicken and fries is good and inexpensive. If you're faced with a menu in Greek script, the word κοτοποθλο is chicken.

- Greek yogurt is wonderful: plain, sweet, and creamy. It's often served with fresh honey. *Tzatziki* is a cucumber-yogurt-garlic dip. You dunk pieces of bread into it—a goopy process that appeals to kids.

- Greek salads vary but usually contain things like lettuce, onions, tomatoes, peppers, and feta cheese. They're most often sprinkled with herbs and oil; vinegar is served on the side. σαλατα (*salata*) is the Greek word for salad.

- Seafood is excellent. Many places let you pick your own fish from the day's catch.

greek money savers

Of course exchange rates change daily, but in general Greek meals can be inexpensive compared to those in other European countries.

Avoid tourist restaurants, though. The food is no better, and the cost can be up to ten times that in other Greek restaurants. For example, Dan and Wendy gave in to their kids' burgermania one night in Greece and went to an Athenian restaurant called the Stagecoach. A guidebook had recommended it as "a must for children" and described its Wild West hitchin' post decor. The hamburgers *were* good, but it turned out to be very formal, with linen napkins and tuxedoed waiters at a cost five times that of any other Greek meal they had had.

Time to go back to the corner *taverna* for a far better meal at a much lower price!

budget hotels and bed-and-breakfast inns

philosophy

In America budget-conscious travelers have few choices aside from character-less, cheap chain motels—for $59 or more per double. In Europe, luckily, there are four other options: simple, clean family hotels; youth hostels; bed-and-breakfast (B&B) establishments; and campground bungalows.

Even if saving money is not your top priority, consider these alternatives. The more expensive your hotel, the more isolated you are from the sights, sounds, and flavors of the country you're visiting: A Paris hotel room becomes much like one in Chicago or Los Angeles. Family hotels, hostels, B&Bs, and bungalows put you in more direct contact with the people and places you came to see.

One night we found ourselves in Mestre, Italy, in a hotel with no air-conditioning on a stifling, humid September night. We sat on our balcony overlooking the multiple balconies of a six-story tenement heavily populated with working people and kids and festooned with drying laundry. Radios were blaring to a variety of stations, until a rich baritone voice emanated from one male balcony occupant. Soon the radios were turned down and we and our kids were treated to an hour or so of opera arias, Neapolitan melodies, and even an Ave Maria rendered by various male and female singers sprinkled among the balconies. I remember that scene far better than what I saw in Venice the next day.

—Dick Handschin, Bellevue, WA

In this chapter we'll discuss the pros and cons of each of these four types of lodging, then give you specifics on each option, including how much you'll pay, what you'll get for your money, and how to find the right one.

star system

In most European countries hotels are rated with a certain number of stars, depending on the amenities available. The official name of the hotel and the appropriate number of stars are usually displayed prominently on a plaque near the front door. Rating systems vary slightly from country to country.

The presence or absence of a restaurant, an elevator, or a swimming pool and the number of languages spoken by the staff can affect the number of stars granted—without affecting your comfort.

Beyond cleanliness and safety the most important issue for most Americans is the presence of private ("en suite") toilet and shower/bath facilities. In Germany, for example, all one-star rooms must have a shower and toilet. In France, by contrast, 20 percent of the rooms in a one-star must have a private toilet *or* (not *and!*) shower, while 40 percent of those in a two-star and 80 percent of those in a three-star must meet this standard. You might get one of the few en suite rooms in a clean, family-run French one-star and have a nicer stay for lots less money than if you got one of the few communal-toilet rooms in a shabby, badly run three-star hotel.

Stars do correlate closely with price, so before you even enter a hotel, you'll have some idea whether you can afford it or not. We tend to look for one or two stars, then check out the specific rooms available.

what do you get for your money?

A budget hotel is one that provides simple, clean rooms with no frills. A typical room we stayed in in Seville, for instance, had two single beds with clean sheets and blankets, a chair, one small lamp, a sink, and a mirror. It didn't have its own bath, shower, or toilet. It also didn't have a rug on the well-swept floor, bedspreads on the beds, pictures on the walls, or even a wastebasket. But it did have its own little balcony filled with plants, overlooking a quaint pedestrian street. Similar Seville hotels today cost €30 to €50.

Enjoying budget hotels is a matter of expectations, so the best way to avoid surprises is to keep track of what's considered a "frill" in Europe's small, simple hotels. Frills include the following:

space

Double rooms in Europe—even the more expensive ones—are tiny by U.S. standards. Budget rooms may fit little more than the beds. There will *not* be room for a rollaway in your room, and rollaways are not routinely available. That said, triple rooms and quads are often available at budget hotels and are perfect for families.

bed size

King beds are nonexistent and queens are exceedingly rare. In Northern European countries, however, a "double bed" may mean two separate twins pushed together (but with separate linens).

heat and air-conditioning

Your room will have plenty of blankets if the heat is sparse (by American standards): We were given four in some Spanish hotels in early spring. And you'll find that many older buildings handle hot weather better than modern, sealed skyscrapers. Your hotel is apt to have thick walls, awnings, shutters, or curtains that keep out summer's heat quite well. Today most two-stars and up have air-conditioning, but ask to be sure.

bathrooms

Virtually all rooms will include a sink with both hot and cold water. Toilets in a one-star hotel are almost invariably down the hall. Showers or bathtubs are also down the hall, and there may be an extra charge for bathing. Be warned that a "room with bath" in many parts of Europe means just that: a room with a shower or bathtub. The toilet's still down the hall. If you want your own toilet, ask for it by name. Two-star hotels usually (but not always) have private shower and toilet facilities.

lights

All rooms will include at least one light. But that may mean a single, twenty-watt bulb hanging from a wire in the center of the room. If you like to read in bed or apply makeup at the mirror, you may want to bring an extra light or flashlight.

elevators

Don't expect elevators in a budget hotel. In Paris, for instance, reaching our sixth-floor rooms required climbing endless stairs. If you have health problems that make stair climbing difficult or hazardous, stay in more luxurious places or request a ground-floor room. (Remember: First floor in Europe is what we'd call second floor.)

credit cards

Most small hotels take cash only (traveler's checks are usually okay). Don't count on paying with a credit card. In Germany, for instance, only three-star hotels and up are required to accept credit cards.

for example . . .

Despite their limitations, budget hotels can be wonderful. In Les Eyzies on the banks of the Vézere River in the Dordogne region, there's a little country inn with a half-dozen rooms, nicely renovated in an old stone barn. A two-room suite there starts with a large carpeted room with a double bed, brass wall sconces, and a big casement window looking down the valley. Separated from this room by a sliding door is a smaller room with a set of neat, enameled bunk beds for the kids. And beyond that is a private bath, with sink, toilet, and shower.

The inn was added in 1989 to an established campground that also features its own small restaurant with a large fieldstone fireplace and delicious regional food. The year we discovered it, the suite cost 200 francs (then about $32) per night and a three-course dinner of regional specialties for four people about the same. By 2007 the suite had increased to €49 (€55 in July and August). (So many readers have called to ask about this hotel! It's called Camping La Rivière, at www.lariviereleseyzies.com.)

On the other end of the scale was a run-down *pension* in Lerida, Spain, populated by truck drivers who clomped up and down the hall all night. Our two rooms had no heat and no windows, and a frigid early-April wind howled down the ventilation shaft and into every corner of the place. The communal bathroom down the hall was none too clean, and the mirror on the wall turned each of us a sickly, wavering green.

We would never stay there again and certainly don't recommend the place to you. But if your heart is ready to travel, you can get something out of almost any experience. Lew enjoyed the garrulous desk clerk there who told us at length how Spain's never been the same since Franco died, and we learned a bit about the lot of Spanish truck drivers. Where else can you get all that for €10 per person?

kids' expectations

If your kids have ever stayed in hotels in the States, they will be shocked by their first European budget hotel. What, no swimming pool? And no color television? Even if they've only stayed at Days Inns and Motel 6s at home, they'll expect such frills. Talk about the types of places you'll be staying so they'll be ready for that mismatched wallpaper or a bit of peeling paint and can then appreciate the positive aspects.

Be especially sensitive about teenage girls' expectations. The possible lack of private toilet and bath facilities can be traumatic for girls who haven't been away to summer camp or boarding school. If your daughter's also being asked to share a room with a sibling—especially a brother—she'll be heading for the bathroom to change clothes as well. Check out the facilities with this in mind when you stop for the night.

finding good budget hotels

If you want to reserve before you go, try finding listings online. Enter "discount hotel London" or some such into your search engine, and see what you find. Or try www.travellerspoint.com for suggestions. Even some very small, inexpensive hotels have an online presence. I'd recommend booking only after you've seen photos, though.

If your itinerary is fluid and you'd rather wait till you arrive to find a hotel, start by looking at a good map of the city. When traveling with kids it's a good idea to find a hotel within walking distance of the most interesting parts of town. We found that our kids weren't as enthralled as we were at wandering around strange cities: If they knew they could head back on their own when they got tired, they were much more likely to join us in exploring the town. Trips like this already entail enough togetherness. Don't make it necessary for everyone to pile back in the car again just to do a little local sightseeing.

Once you've targeted a desirable part of town, look for a hotel a block or two off the main drag. Hotels on major streets can be very noisy. If your best bet is on a major street, ask specifically for rooms in the back or on a courtyard. (Don't take this too far, though. Remember those awful windowless rooms in Lerida, Spain, that I mentioned earlier? We chose them specifically because our previous nights' lodgings had been noisy ones facing the street. In the end the claustrophobia and lightless morning weren't worth our sound sleep!)

let's go guidebooks

The *Let's Go* guidebooks put out by Harvard Student Agencies are an excellent source of low-cost hotel rooms. Listings are checked every year by hordes of traveling students, and recommendations are refreshingly brief, honest, and descriptive, such as "Decent rooms and polite management but tiny bathrooms" or "Clean as a whistle, with a touch of class and paper-thin walls."

The rooms described are never spacious and full of period antiques. But with honest descriptions, you can decide what's important to you and proceed accordingly.

Let's Go has country-specific and city-specific books for almost anywhere in Europe. Originally written to cater to backpacking groups, *Let's Go* hotel listings often include triples and quads, making them a great resource for families.

tourist offices

In virtually every town and city in Europe, there is a tourist office, easily found by following signs with a small **i**. Tourist offices maintain hotel lists, often including every licensed hotel in the city. These lists are usually divided into price categories (so you can start at the bottom, with the cheapest choices), and sometimes the actual cost of each one is marked. A map is often included, sometimes with each hotel marked on it.

These lists rarely have descriptions or recommendations, so you'll have to set out with your list, find specific hotels, and judge for yourself. A good system is to stop midafternoon at your destination town, check into the tourist office for hotel information and interesting brochures, then combine sightseeing and hotel seeking on foot.

Tourist offices are a great resource when it comes to finding reasonable hotel rooms, as we discovered in Austria. In Alpenzell the tourist office must have worked a good half hour to find us what we needed. In St. Wolfgang you find your own hotel by punching push buttons for your price range and type of lodging—B&B, hotel, etc. When you find one you like, you pick up the phone and it automatically connects you.

—Maya D'Anjou, Morgan Hill, CA

---

wandering aimlessly

Once in a while, you'll end up in a town not covered by *Let's Go*, when the tourist office is closed. Then you're on your own. Leave the luggage (and maybe the kids) in your car and explore on foot. French hotels are required by law to post room prices on a sign by the front door. If you're in another country, just barge in and ask for information, or ask to see a room. Don't hesitate to walk out if you don't like what you see. This is not the time to be timorous.

to reserve or not to reserve?

In years past, making reservations at small hotels was almost impossible. First off, you couldn't find them from the United States. Second, many mom-and-pop operations don't have someone by the phone all day to take reservations. And if you did get through, the chance of misunderstandings in a verbal exchange were huge.

Today, with the advent of the Web and e-mail, you can often find good small hotels before you go and book them by e-mail. You may wait a few days until the cousin who speaks English comes in and answers all the e-mails, but you'll get a reply and an eventual written confirmation. Yet sometimes you still may not want to bother with reservations because:

- Traveling without reservations is more flexible. If you find a charming town, you may want to quit early and stay the night; another day, everyone might want to drive for hours.

- In person, you know what you're getting. You can check out the cleanliness of the rooms, the location, and the plumbing before you take the room. Plus, if there's a language barrier, you can draw pictures or make gestures.

when you *must* reserve

Big cities and midsummer are the exceptions to the rule. In cities you don't need the flexibility—you're sure you don't want to miss Paris. Your hosts are more likely to speak English. And the hotels are more likely to take reservations and even to accept credit cards for confirmation.

Reservations are a good idea in places such as Paris, London, and Rome, especially at the height of the season. Major cities are tiresome places to wander aimlessly, and they seldom offer safe places where you can park your kids and your luggage while you check out likely hotels. Nail something down in writing before you go to such a city.

Even outside the cities, reservations are recommended in July and August. We once called fourteen hotels on a July weekend in England before finding a place to stay, due to a major music festival in the area. (Luckily this was on a business trip—without any tired, whiny kids in the backseat.) You'll end up paying more and often staying at bigger hotels with less local flavor (see reasons above), but you may have no choice. Yet another reason to travel anytime except July and August if at all humanly possible!

what can you expect?

Budget hotels in different countries have more similarities than differences. Yet some specifics from a sampling of countries may help set up your expectations realistically.

england

Many English hotels—and virtually all B&Bs—charge by the person instead of by the room. This means that the great bargains to be had in triples and quads in some countries are much scarcer in England. Still, some places charge less for children, so it always pays to ask.

If you're looking for a private bath, the term to use is "en suite." Also, be sure to check for a shower if one is important to you. The British far prefer baths to showers, so some small budget places may not even offer showers as an option.

The system in Britain supposedly works like this:

- **Bed-and-breakfasts,** as their name implies, offer only breakfast and have fewer than six rooms.

- **Guesthouses** are small, private hotels that lack some requirements for the star rating system. They sometimes include meals and must have a bathroom for at least every six bedrooms.

- **Hotels** use a star system similar to those on the Continent, with costs corresponding roughly to the number of stars; however, you won't see these ratings as prominently displayed here as you will in other countries.

In reality, these categories get blurred. The British think (probably rightly) that the term B&B attracts tourists, and they'll slap it on many places with more than six rooms. The good news, though, is that if you're confused, you can get all your questions settled easily—after all, you speak the language. Check the section below on B&Bs for more on lodging in Britain.

france

If you ask for a double room in France, you'll almost always be given a double bed. This does wonders for your married life but is not so popular with your kids, who would likely prefer to sleep in separate beds. You may have to pay to have an extra cot put in a "double" room in many French hotels—if one is even available. Make sure you ask for *deux lits* (two beds) when you want single beds and *un grand lit* (a big bed) when you want a double bed.

Double beds in France sometimes sport a single pillow—a hard, round cylinder called a *traversin*. If you can't sleep on such a pillow, ask for *un oreiller* and you'll be given a standard American bed pillow.

French hotels must post their "star" rating on a sign outside the hotel. Just remember that the system rates frills, not cleanliness. A one-star hotel is certainly inexpensive and will have few private baths but it could be clean, light, and airy.

French hotels are also required *by law* to post their prices in a public spot. Usually this sign can be seen from the street; sometimes it's inside the entry. There you'll find prices for all the various types of rooms available: with and without bath and/or toilet. In France charges are usually per room, not per person.

germany

German hotels can be expensive, often double those in bargain-basement Spain. *Gasthof* or *Gästehaus* usually denote cheaper lodgings. When you gasp at the cost, keep in mind that your room almost certainly includes a full breakfast, not just bread and coffee. Cheese, juice, eggs, meat, toast—the Germans spread a good table for breakfast. Just wander down and look for the *Frühstück* room.

Your bed will include individual pillows and will most likely be made up with just a stretchy knit undersheet and a down comforter. As soon as you leave your room in the morning, the staff will open all the windows wide and hang the bedding over the sill to air. If your room includes a shower, the plastic stall may be right in the corner of your bedroom.

Less costly than hotels are the B&Bs of Germany. You'll recognize them by the *Zimmer frei* (rooms free) sign hanging from the wall. A better translation would be "rooms vacant," as these rooms are far from free. Still, you'll save money over hotels and enjoy the added benefit of meeting a family.

Check out Familotels (www.familotel.de), an affiliation of twenty-four German and nine Austrian hotels, plus four in Italy, Switzerland, and Hungary, that caters especially to families. It's not a chain—they're all unique, with offerings from special kid decor to playrooms to babysitting.

spain

Double rooms in Spain are more likely to contain two single beds than a double bed. Make sure to check if you and your spouse prefer a double bed (*una cama doble*) instead of twins (*camas individuales*). If you choose a double bed, a single pillow may stretch the width of the bed—an obstacle for couples where one spouse sleeps with a pillow and one doesn't or if either of you is used to wadding your pillow up at strange angles.

Overnight lodgings in Spain go by lots of names. At the very top of the list are *paradors,* converted castles and historic sites that are very expensive. Those actually using the name *hotel* and sometimes *hotel-residencia* are next on the list. But anything with the word *hotel* in it is likely to be on the more expensive end of the scale. Budget travelers need to look for any of six different terms: *pension, fonda, hostal* (these first three all roughly mean budget hotel), *camas* (beds), *casa* (house—followed by the owner's name), and *casa de huespedes* (guesthouse).

switzerland

It shouldn't come as a shock to anyone that the Swiss Tourist Office is one of the best organized in the world. Go to their Web site (www.myswitzerland .com) and you can search online among 2,500 rated Swiss hotels by your choice of criteria. For instance, you could ask to see all the family hotels in a region that are wheelchair accessible and serve Kosher food.

To focus on less expensive rooms, click on "Affordable Swiss Hotels" on the Swiss Tourist Office Web site for a selection of 120 hotels. Or go to www .rooms.ch for 240 "Swiss Budget Hotels."

Don't take the word "budget" too much to heart. These hotels generally charge about $85 to $120 for a double; that's only budget when compared to other Swiss hotels. Hotels in Switzerland are rather expensive. But they are invariably clean and well run.

On the other hand, Switzerland also offers one of the least-expensive lodging options in Europe: *Schlaf im Stroh* (Sleep in the Straw), where you bunk in a farmer's hayloft in your sleeping bag. It's something of a cross between camping out and a B&B, for about $20 (adults) or $12 (kids), breakfast included. You get to meet a farm family and have a roof overhead, without carting tents. But it's pretty basic lodging. Ask the Swiss Tourist Office for their *Schlaf im Stroh* directory, or check it out online at www.abenteuer-stroh.ch.

If a hayloft is a bit too rough for you, about 80 percent of Swiss youth hostels have family rooms. Read the next chapter for more details.

hotel chains

Europe doesn't have many budget chains comparable to our Motel 6s or Days Inns. But the concept of predictable, spartan lodgings is starting to catch on. Will you want to stay there? Probably not, as most chains are located along the superhighways, while the old family hotels are in more interesting city-center locations. Learn about these chains at www.eurapart.com.

France seems to lead the way in these "sub-budget" lodgings, with several cinderblock chains located on major highways. Names include Fasthotel, Formule 1, Liberté, and Première Classe. Rooms are small, and prices run around €35 for a room. Many of these low-end chains offer a room featuring a double bed with a single bunkbed over it, making them best for three-person families. When quirky family hotels in town don't cost much more, there's not much attraction in choosing a cement cell along the superhighway.

In France about 3,000 hotels belong to an association called the Logis de France. Most of these are small, clean family hotels specializing in regional cuisine and priced around €40 to €60 for a double. Those designated "Logis Famille Enfants" have play areas and family rooms sleeping at least four people. Check out details at www.logis-de-france.fr Sister organizations in Belgium (www.logis.be) and in Italy (www.logis.it) include another 250 or so hotels.

Many reasonable hotels in Europe are owned by Accor (Formule1, ETAP, IBIS) or by Envergure (Campanile, Première Classe). Accor also has two mid-price chains, Novotel (almost 300 hotels in Europe) and Mercure (over 500). With rooms around €100 and up, these aren't budget accommodations, but rooms are large, breakfast is included, and in-town locations are common. Novotel lets two children under age sixteen share your room for free and usually has a play area (with Legos!) near the dining area, in case you want to linger over wine.

Europe is not very large-family friendly. Ibis, Formule 1, and ETAP will only accommodate three people in a room. In Auray, near Carnac, the Ibis we booked required me to get two rooms, even though I was traveling alone with three small children. Adjoining rooms, but still! In a London ETAP they let three of us squash into the queen-size bed, while one kid slept on the berth [upper bunk].

—Katy Wessel, U.S. Air Force, anywhere and everywhere

---

b&bs

It's impossible to mention lodgings, especially in England, without mentioning bed-and-breakfast establishments—or B&Bs. Before we went to Europe, we thought B&Bs were probably the cheapest places to stay. This is not necessarily true: B&Bs were among our most expensive lodgings.

In England—the country most associated with B&Bs—the cheapest rates start at about £25 per person; £30 is still considered reasonable. At current exchange rates, that's the equivalent of $50 to $60 per person, or $200 to $240 per night for a family of four. You'll do better at a hostel, for about £5 to £17 per person.

There are several reasons B&Bs are so expensive. First, these establishments thrive in northern Europe, where all types of lodging tend to be more expensive. Second, B&Bs virtually always charge a per-person rate, so there's no way to save by ganging up in one room. Third, B&Bs are usually nicer than some budget hotels; fourth, they do include a substantial breakfast.

This isn't to say you should categorically dismiss B&Bs. Sometimes the only available hotels in an area are full or too expensive, and a B&B will make sense. I only mention the issue so you'll have the right expectations, since many people equate B&Bs with low-cost lodging. It ain't necessarily so.

B&Bs may cost more, but you also get a chance to meet people.

One final point: B&Bs can be one of your best ways to interact with people when you're on the road. In Denmark, when we visited Legoland, we stayed at a B&B booked by the tourist office. For about half the cost of the least expensive hotel, we got clean, comfortable rooms with fresh sheets, plenty of hot water, and a huge breakfast—everything we could want except conversation. Our hosts, the Olsens, spoke almost no English. Mr. Olsen spoke a few key words, but mostly we relied on sign language and smiles. Even that was okay: We "talked" to the Olsens for almost an hour nonetheless. They showed us through their family photos, and in return we spread out our map and explained the entire itinerary of our trip.

campground bungalows

Your final budget-hotel option is the nearest campground, but not necessarily for camping out. Many European campgrounds rent out bungalows or cabins at a very reasonable price. (See chapter 10 for details. This is just a teaser in case reading our camping chapter wouldn't have occurred to you.)

The first time we went to Legoland we stayed at the official hotel. It was wonderful, but we wanted to save money this time, so we stayed in Billund DCU Camping. It's a very easy walk to the Legoland gate. Their cabins were great: four bunks, a table, chairs, pans, utensils, stove, refrigerator. We had our sleeping bags and used the modern, clean toilets and showers in the nearby bath/shower blocks. We also used the town swimming pool, a lovely indoor complex with a large hot tub.

—Nicky Hardenbergh, Manchester, MA

Paris's lovely Bois de Boulogne campground, on the banks of the Seine, has rows and rows of two-bedroom bungalows, arranged like a modest but neat mobile home park and renting for €64 to €90 in June and September 2007 (see www.campingparis.fr). An arrangement like this may be just what you need. Be aware, though, that campground bungalows are popular, and it's wise to reserve far ahead, especially in major cities such as Paris.

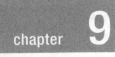

youth hostels

If you've even heard of youth hostels, you probably associate them with the college backpack crowd, not with family travel. It's a well-kept secret that many hostels offer family rooms in addition to single-sex dormitories and that hostels can be one of the cheapest, most pleasant options for overnight lodging.

how does it all work?

There are two types of hostels in Europe: private hostels and those of the HI—Hostelling International (formerly IYHF). Anyone can stay at private hostels; they're really just cheap hotels with dormitory accommodations in addition to, or instead of, private rooms. You must be a hostel member to stay at an HI hostel.

become an HI member

Get a membership from Hostelling International—USA (HI-USA) before you leave. HI-USA is part of the worldwide HI network and offers one-year adult memberships for $28 each; kids seventeen and under are free. All national associations honor reciprocal arrangements, so your HI-USA card is good in any country you'll be visiting. If for some reason you don't get a hostel card before you leave, many hostels will sell you a membership on the spot. (Always carry extra passport-size photos for things like this.)

Hostel membership carries an extra bonus, too. Your card entitles you to discounts at some attractions and on some transportation systems. The hostel guide details various discounts for each country, and it always pays to flash your card and look hopeful if you want a discount elsewhere.

a typical hostel

Hostels range from mountain huts to castles, so it's hard to describe a "typical" one. Some hostels have been built specifically for the purpose. Others are college dorms, pressed into service temporarily in the summer. Still others are mansions and private homes converted to hostels.

One of our favorites, at Esbjerg on Denmark's west coast, is more like an Ivy League dormitory. Housed in a large four-story brick building covered with vines, the hostel has a modern cafeteria and even an elevator. In this hostel the bunk beds are beautiful Scandinavian-modern wood, with individual reading lights. A carpeted floor, large wooden cupboards, and a private sink finished off our room. You can view this hostel for yourself at www.danhostel .dk/esbjerg.

In fact, if you want to sleep in a castle on a peasant's budget, there are at least nine hostels in Europe that are sited in castles. They include:

England	St. Briavels (on the Welsh border)
Scotland	Loch Lomond (not far from Glasgow)
	Carbisdale (in the Northern Highlands)
Germany	Stahleck Castle (about 60 km from Frankfurt)
	Schwaneck Castle (near Munich)
Netherlands	Kasteel Westhove (near Middelburg)
	Slot Assumburg (near Haarlem)
Switzerland	Marlastein-Rotberg (in the Basel area)
Italy	Finale Ligure Castle (near the French border)

Okay, okay, most hostels aren't castles. More often we've had a simple room with two iron bunks and a single, bare lightbulb. But today most hostels are visible on the Web at www.hihostels.com, so you can get some idea of what your choices are before you leave home.

Our favorite hostel was a twelfth-century castle in St. Briavels, Wales. It was filled with families (speaking English!), and our seven kids played chess and learned to juggle. We had five bunk beds in the top of a tower and loved it despite the two steep flights of winding stairs down to the toilet. Wished we could have stayed longer!

—Nancy Fletcher, Portland, OR

Despite these differences, there are common features in almost all hostels. You can expect dormitory/group sleeping accommodations, usually segregated by gender. You can expect some sort of common room, where people can gather to get acquainted, sing, or watch television. You can expect kitchen facilities, usually available for hostelers' use. And you can expect decent toilets and showers.

All of the above, though, wouldn't be enough to attract most families. The real plus of most hostels—and the most widely unknown factor—is family rooms: small, private dormitories of four to six beds that your family can have all to itself.

Family hostel rooms are simple, providing you with clean beds (almost always bunk beds) with mattresses, pillows, and blankets. Toilets and baths are down the hall, as in all hostel rooms. No furniture beyond beds is guaranteed, but many rooms have closets or lockers and even a sink. In Norway some family rooms are even suites, with a sitting room and a kitchenette!

But even when family rooms are spartan, they're clean and private. And there's usually no surcharge for using one: You're often charged the same per-person fee as the backpackers and other travelers sleeping among strangers in the dormitories—at worst case, a small additional charge. Hostels increasingly cater to families. Today over 80 percent of HI hostels have family rooms.

bring sheets and towels

Hostels have traditionally kept costs low by providing neither towels nor sheets. Although many now include linens or rent them for an extra fee, some still require you to bring your own *sheet sack,* a sort of sleeping bag made of sheet material. Regular sleeping bags are not allowed: No one wants the bag that lay in the mud last night at a campground to be on a hostel mattress tonight.

To make your own sheet sack, buy a double-bed sheet at a white sale. Simply fold the sheet in half, then sew across the bottom and about four feet up the side.

Also bring a towel and soap, as these are usually not provided.

reservations

Like budget hotels, hostels have a spotty reputation for taking reservations from individuals and families. In the past when families tried writing ahead for reservations, the hostels involved wrote back saying they had no idea whether there'd be space—guests should just show up. This even though these same hostels specified in the hostel guidebook that reservations were required for families!

This situation has improved, however. At most hostels, you can make reservations up to six months before you leave home, at www.hihostels.com, or you can book ahead from one hostel to the next when you're on the road. HI charges a small fee of a few euros for online bookings, but the peace of mind is worth it.

HI is aware of the uneven standards hostels have observed in the past when it comes to reservations, cleanliness, hours open, and lots of other variables. So now HI is promoting a program called Assured Standards, a list of requirements hostels must observe to be in the HI network. Among these is prompt response to reservation requests—so we urge you to try this reservation system.

finding a hostel

Finding a hostel is easy online. But on the road you may appreciate a hard copy of *The Hostelling International Official Guide*. This guide lists every HI hostel throughout the world.

The book is written largely in icons, so it can be read by travelers of any language. All this means, though, is that it's equally difficult to read in *any* language, until you get the hang of the icons. The fold-out English-language key in the front helps. You might not realize it if you're new to hosteling, but the guide's actually been simplified in recent years! A typical listing looks something like this:

This listing says that the Kasteel Westhove hostel in Domburg, Netherlands—one of the castle hostels we mentioned a few pages ago—is open year-round, twenty-four hours a day. It has 114 beds and costs €21 to €27 per person per night (linen and breakfast included), with a €2.50 discount for HI members. The castle's located 170 km from Schiphol airport and 100 km from the port of Rotterdam; the nearest train station is at Vlissingen and the nearest bus at Middelburg.

The icons at the end of the listing show that this hostel has family rooms, allows groups, and takes both reservations and credit cards. The hostel offers meals and has a cafe, Internet access for guests, a lounge, and tourist information. There are lockers (important for those staying in dormitories), parking, a garden, and a bike storage area. In the local area, hostelers may receive discounts and can take advantage of swimming, a beach, hiking, and sports. The only thing it doesn't say is that the hostel is a castle!

On the road all you'll have are the icons in the hostel guide, but at home, when you're planning your trip, you can also visit the Web site listed to learn more about each hostel. There's also a small detail map on the page, showing its street location. The icons may seem confusing at first, but they pack a lot of information into a small space.

Budget travel guides such as *Let's Go* also carry hostel listings—not only HI ones but also private hostels. Guidebook listings are less cryptic and often include more complete street directions. On the other hand, the official HI guide includes hundreds of hostels not mentioned in other guidebooks. Carry both if you plan to use hostels regularly.

pros and cons of hostels

They're cheap . . . they have family rooms . . . I don't have to cart sleeping bags all over Europe. . . . Gee, let's do it!

Hold on. There are still some pros and cons you should consider before you move ahead.

You can have a private family room at many youth hostels.

price

Hostels are inexpensive, often as low as €10 to €12 per person per night. And for that price, breakfast and linens are sometimes included.

The www.hihostels.com Web site shows the following country-by-country range of prices for hostels in these countries:

Country	Total hostels	Typical price	Top cities
England and Wales	214	£5–£17	£26.50 (London)
France	146	€4.80–€12.80	€22 (Paris)
Germany	562	€13–€16	€24 (Berlin)
Italy	121	€8–€17	€20 (Venice)
Spain	231	€11.50–€17.25	€27 (Barcelona)
Netherlands	30	€16–€24	€20 (Amsterdam)
Denmark	101	DKK 75–100	DKK 198 (Copenhagen)
Austria	108	€11.60–€15	€20 (Vienna)
Belgium	31	€13–€15	€17 (Brugge)
Scotland	66	€11–€15	€22 (Edinburgh)
Greece	7	€9.20–€10.90	€18 (Athens)
Ireland	25	€9–€25.50	€21 (Dublin)
Portugal	55	€7.50–€15	€16 (Lisbon)

As you can see from the table above, prices range wildly from country to country and from hostel to hostel. In our budget estimator in chapter 16, we allowed $18 (about €13) per person per day for hosteling.

Surprisingly, hostels sometimes are not your best deal. In France and Spain hotel rooms are relatively cheap, and you're charged by the room, whereas hostels always charge a per-person rate, even when you occupy a family room. Once in France, for instance, we had a choice between a bare hostel family room for about €10 per person or a two-room suite with private bath in a hotel for €49 total. We decided the private bath, double bed, clean sheets, and maid service were certainly worth the nine euros extra, and we stayed four nights.

interaction

We originally looked into hostels not just for possible savings but also for better interaction. Hotels can be isolating: Once you check into your room, you're unlikely to meet any other guests. Hostels, on the other hand, have common rooms where you can meet people from other countries.

We haven't met many other people this way—most other hostelers are college students rather than working adults or children—but a few times we got lucky. Once in France we spent a delightful evening with a group of Australian professionals, thirty-something, self-employed types like ourselves, who had traveled widely and avidly shared their experiences.

convenience and privacy

Hosteling is not all positive, and it's not for everyone. Most hostels shut their doors for part of the day: If you want to quit driving early and rest or read, you may not be able to get in until 5:00 P.M. Sometimes hostels are not in the best locations, either. Originally sited for hikers and bicyclists, hostels are often in small rural towns or on the outskirts of major cities. If you stay at a hostel, it may be hard for some of you to wander around while others rest.

Also—and perhaps most importantly—hostels mean togetherness. While many hostels have family rooms, virtually none have doubles. We found it best to stay in hostels for a few days, then splurge on a few doubles at a hotel to catch up on our privacy.

country-specific comments

Hostels in every country have their own flavor, run as they are by distinct national organizations. And, of course, within each country each hostel has a unique ambience traceable to the building and to its wardens. For traveling families, though, the most important question is whether a hostel has family rooms.

britain

Hostels in England are about equal in cost to any on the Continent—until you get to London, where fees are up to $50 per person per night. But given the cost of hotels in the British capital, hostels may still be an attractive option. Reservations are virtually essential in the busy London hostels and can be made online with VISA or MasterCard.

Many HI hostels in England have family rooms. The hostel guide states that you must make a reservation to get a family room, and certainly this helps cover your bets. But if an empty family room exists and you arrive without a reservation, no one's going to deny you the room.

Private hostels abound in England. When is a hotel a hostel? When oversize rooms are stuffed with extra beds to create a small dormitory, and strangers share your room. HI hostels in England tout their standards to differentiate themselves from the standardless private hostels. If you stay at a private hostel, just make sure to check out the rooms before you pay. Some are great, some are not, so go into them with your eyes open.

Hostels in Scotland are—well—very Scottish. This is the only country where we've encountered bed checks ("ye mun' use r-r-regulation sheet sacks"), mandatory lights out, and duties. What's a duty? It's a small chore required of everyone who stays at a hostel. Lew and I scrubbed the bathroom floors at one hostel while the kids swept the hall and emptied the trash. There's no escaping: Your hostel card won't be returned to you until you've done your duty. The housemother who made this clear to us explained that it was standard policy at all Scottish youth hostels. If you mention this ahead of time to your kids, they won't be as surprised as ours were the first time we hauled them back from the car to get to work.

france

France has a healthy number of hostels, many very nice, though some may be totally reserved by groups in midsummer or during school holidays. Many of the mountain hostels also run ski weeks in winter, when drop-ins aren't allowed.

In addition to HI hostels and a great many private hostels, France features something called *foyers*. *Foyers* are very much like hostels, though they were originally conceived in much the same spirit as our YMCAs—as places where young working people could get a clean, cheap room. Some, though by no means all, may allow families and those of us drifting past youth.

Foyers don't require an HI card, and they aren't listed in the HI guide. Look for them in *Let's Go* and other guides. Also look for them on the streets of any town you're visiting: You may see signs for *AJ* (*auberge de jeunesse,* or youth hostel) or *Foyer,* with an arrow pointing the way.

Another type of accommodation you may encounter in France is the *gîte d'étape,* which means, roughly, way station. These rather rudimentary hostels are meant only for those on foot or on bicycle, but they sometimes may admit families in cars if space is available.

One of our favorite French hostels is the Family Home hostel in Bayeux, which occupies a seventeenth-century abbey. There we enjoyed a two-room suite under the eaves, overlooking the cathedral. An optional family-style dinner was also available, which introduced us to a number of interesting fellow travelers. In 2007, this hostel charged €19 per adult for overnight lodging and €10 for dinner, including wine.

germany

Hosteling's big in Germany—not surprising, since the world's first youth hostel was built there in 1908. The country has almost 600 hostels, a tenth of those available worldwide, and nearly 90 percent of these have family rooms. Still, there are a few caveats to be aware of:

- Hostels in Bavaria only accept guests up to age twenty-six, but families with children under this age are welcome.

- Hostels in East Germany are in a state of flux, with many of them closed, turned into hotels, or reclaimed by those who owned them before the socialist takeover of private property.

- German hostels have a reputation as being among the noisiest in the world.

Several *Take Your Kids* readers have corroborated our experience with Germany's hostels or *Jugendherbergen:* They're wonderfully inexpensive and clean but are often overrun with noisy mobs of German kids. Our experience in Lüneburg, Germany, was typical. Our visit coincided with that of a large group of German schoolboys about eleven or twelve years old. At first this delighted us. Sam, using fluent body language, played ball and shared his skateboard with the boys.

Later that night we were not so pleased. The German kids ran up and down the halls, yelling and throwing balls until 3:00 A.M., with no adult supervision in evidence. In place of a solid door, our family hostel room had only swinging Old West–saloon-style louvers that kept out none of the noise and light and afforded us little privacy. The hostel manager professed to speak no English, so our sleep was held hostage by the bad manners of this particular group. This marked the only night we wished we'd opted for a hotel.

spain

The Spanish hostel organization is REAJ, or *Red Española de Albergues Juveniles*. It runs about 120 year-round hostels and another twenty-five or so converted college dorms open only in the summer. The other six dozen hostels are open five to ten months or serve only groups. If you're traveling in the off-season, you may find few open hostels with family rooms. That's not a problem, though, as Spanish hotels are among the cheapest on the Continent.

The most interesting Spanish hostel we've stayed in was in Hondarribia, near San Sebástián, in a Basque cultural center. The downside was a registration form entirely (and mystifyingly) in Basque instead of Spanish. But the upside was that we were able to watch a group of boys playing traditional Basque wooden instruments.

As you can see from our experience, hostels aren't for everyone. We've had nights we adored hosteling and other times (as in Lüneburg) when we thought it was a big mistake—but the same can be said of hotels, campgrounds, restaurants, or life in general. Hostels are an important part of budget travel in Europe, so get a membership and check out the HI Web site before you go.

euro camping

Camping is a delightful way to see Europe, with many wonderful camp-grounds all over the Continent and Great Britain. Throughout Europe, in fact, some of the best lodgings are in campgrounds—like the one near France's Versailles Palace, or the one on an Italian cliff near Sorrento, with views of Mount Vesuvius and the Bay of Naples.

Are we recommending that you pitch a tent every night, wade through mud, and share your bed with insects? Not on your life. Camping Euro-style comes in four main varieties, none of which feature mud and bugs:

- Some families tent camp—also called car camping—enjoying Europe's rel-atively mosquito-free air to sleep outdoors on nice evenings, then seeking out hostels or hotels when it rains.

- Other families rent bungalows or deluxe tents (with separate bedrooms and a kitchen) available at many European campgrounds.

- A third option involves staying at vacation camps, a special breed of holi-day habitat popular with European families but practically unknown in the United States. Vacation camps are special resorts with family bunga-lows or deluxe tents for sleeping and with a wide variety of recreational activities organized during the day—something like summer camp for families.

- A final choice is to opt for a recreational vehicle (RV), or motor-home camping. Renting an RV is like renting a little apartment that goes every-where with you, eliminating the daily drag of searching for a hotel room and trudging all the bags up flights of stairs. You're protected in any weather, and the kids may enjoy tent camping when it's nice, giving the adults more room and privacy in the RV.

In this chapter we'll explain how each of these options works, why camp-ing is particularly suited to families, where you can rent a European RV, what to bring, and how to find the best campgrounds and holiday camps all over Europe.

to camp or not to camp

Should you camp your way through Europe, even if you've never been a camping family? There's no reason not to. Kids who don't like wilderness camping in the States—with its bugs, tents, and campfires—are often enthusiastic about camping in Europe.

Though camping may mean more work for the parents than hotels, it may actually set a more relaxing pace for your vacation.

Our family has gone camping for at least a month each summer of the six years I've been stationed here. The kids don't mind spending today in Lisbon if they know they can spend tomorrow at the camp swimming pool. Camping has given us flexibility, economy, and a lot of social contact. Our three kids meet German and French kids and play on the swings or play soccer. The younger they are, the less they need words!

—Dave Fittante, Würzburg, Germany

With an RV camper, the day ends as soon as everyone gets tired and you decide to pull off the road. You may not even need to find a campground: "Free-camping" in highway rest areas is common, legal, and safe in many European countries, making it cheap and easy to go with the flow of your family's energy span. (Check your guide, as free-camping is frowned upon in some areas.)

If you drive from one campground to another by car and rent bungalows, or stay at holiday camps, it's also likely that your vacation will be more low key. Your kids will enjoy the company of other children and will have more time to do the active kid things they like best, with less emphasis on stuffy museums and cathedrals.

meet the neighbors

Camping is an ideal way to meet other families. Whereas Americans usually camp to get away into the wilderness, Europeans approach camping with more of a social agenda. Many Europeans, in fact, will rent a campsite for the entire summer, setting up their gear in June, then come out each weekend to enjoy their summer neighborhood. (You'll note rates for annual or permanent site rental in many European campground guides.)

This difference suits the adventurous traveling family perfectly: Camping in Europe gives you a convenient location near everything and lots of opportunities to meet other people—not only from the local country but also from all over!

Dan and Wendy have fond memories of people they met in campgrounds. At one place in Greece, their children enjoyed playing with a two-year-old Dutch girl one afternoon. When the two families ran into each other again several campgrounds later, the parents got acquainted, too, spending eight hours in a Greek cafe eating squid, drinking retsina, and talking politics and art.

In another incident, the Hallinans stopped at a campground along the Mosel River near Trier in Germany, attracted by a small circus setting up in a nearby field. As their parents pitched camp, the kids made friends with seven-year-old Peggy, playing happily despite the lack of any common language. Everyone in the family was astonished that night to find that Peggy was the contortionist in the small family circus. She twisted her little body into relentless gymnastics, while three uncles provided the orchestra and an older brother meticulously tossed knives at Peggy's sister.

campgrounds

Free-camping is cheap and flexible. But if one of your goals is to meet other people, you're better off hanging out in campgrounds.

To give you an idea of what European campgrounds can be like, let's look at two examples. Here's what you'd find at Camping Tahiti (www.camping tahiti.com) on Italy's Adriatic coast 100 km south of Venice:

- Tent pitches and RV camper pitches
- Wooden bungalows and "caravans" (mobile homes)
- Miniature golf, gymnasium, archery field, tennis
- Two swimming pools; a beach 700 meters away
- Wellness garden with thermal baths and spa
- Supermarket, laundry, infirmary
- Cafeteria, pizza parlor, two discos

A family of four could stay overnight at Camping Tahiti in June on the smallest pitch for €52.30 or rent an air-conditioned two-bedroom caravan for €99. Even the cheapest pitch includes a satellite-TV connection!

At Camping Fichtelsee in Bavaria (www.camping-fichtelsee.de), in contrast, you can park your RV or tent camp surrounded by woods and mountains, but there's no spa or minigolf, and you'll share clean communal plumbing. On the other hand, you'll only pay €26 per night—and you still get cable TV.

facilities

Not all campgrounds are as well equipped as Camping Tahiti. At almost all campgrounds you can expect to find a restaurant or cafe (sometimes several) where you can enjoy reasonably priced—and often very good—meals. You will *not* need to cook burgers on a campfire every night when camping in Europe! Even if you do make your own dinner, you'll want to join the other adults in the cafe for coffee and conversation in the evening.

Most campgrounds have a playground (where all the kids gather day and night) and often a pool. Take note though: Even when a pool is available, it will not be filled until the summer months. This can be frustrating on a hot May day. The larger campgrounds have all kinds of activities for kids, usually organized by age group.

It's almost certain that there will be at least one camp store. The basic store will offer eggs, bread, milk, and canned goods, with occasional stores also offering fresh meat or local produce. Each camp store is different: You never know which one will offer a big tub of homemade yogurt, or where your kids will find their first jar of peanut butter after long deprivation. Camp stores are a big convenience but are often overpriced, so plan to stop at a supermarket for most food purchases.

Organization varies widely at European campgrounds. Sometimes the campground is divided into a finite number of sites, and you are assigned a numbered area. Other places are never full as long as you can squeeze in among the tents and trailers to establish your own little living area.

plumbing

Plumbing includes communal showers plus laundry and dishwashing sinks, with all the cold water you could want and hot water that is sometimes metered. (This varies, but the same small coin that buys a local telephone call usually buys you three to five minutes of hot water.)

Toilets will also be in a central block and vary widely in acceptability to the typical American. Many Europeans, for instance, prefer to squat over a seatless toilet bowl rather than use an "unsanitary" toilet seat—so often there just won't be any seat. In some countries, especially France, you may occasionally find Turkish toilets, even at some of the fanciest campgrounds. Most Americans are bewildered (at best) or repulsed (at worst) by these stand-up facilities that require both men and women to squat over a drain. Fortunately, they are rapidly becoming less common.

In fact, plumbing has improved vastly at most campgrounds in the past decade. Today some pitches even have their own private facilities. At Camping Tahiti, for instance, each top-end pitch includes a "lux-cabin" with sink, shower, toilet, two cooking burners, and refrigerator.

Stand-and-squat Turkish toilets are (happily) becoming rarer.

fees

What you pay in many campgrounds can be complicated. Sometimes there is a set fee per tent, per vehicle, or per person. More often your cost will be the total of several small charges for each adult, child, tent, camper, or hookup. As the examples above illustrated, a family of four will usually pay from €20 to €50 per night for a pitch, while chalets and bungalows range from €50 to €100 most places.

You'll be expected to pay when you check in. If you're not sure how long you'll be staying, pay for one night when you first register, then go back in the morning and pay again for subsequent days. Once you've handed over your money, many places will give you a tag to stick on your camper to prove you've paid.

safety

European campgrounds tend to be much safer than most other areas. In our experience neither theft nor personal safety should really concern you. (In fact, the only place in months of camping that Dan and Wendy were ever warned about theft was a Greek campground—where people advised them to watch out for all the Americans there!)

Why are campgrounds so theft free? Just as Willy Sutton robbed banks "because that's where the money is," thieves tend to avoid campgrounds because their efforts rarely pay off. No self-respecting thief wants a few pots and pans and a new gas stove when jewelry and car radios can be had on the city streets.

Most campgrounds have good security at the gates, leading Europeans to leave their sites set up and unattended for days at a time. If you have to choose between leaving some of your belongings in your tent or parking them all day on a city street, the tent's an odds-on favorite for safety every time.

typical campgrounds

There is a great range in quality among the campgrounds of Europe. Some bear a close resemblance to junkyards, whereas others are similar to high-class destination resorts, lacking only a hotel. Some campgrounds, especially those in recreation areas (lakes, beaches, ski slopes), are called "tourist villages." They have every possible amenity, including bungalows or trailers to rent. Many of the best campgrounds are found in Spain, Italy, and Greece. Why? Because the English and Germans are the most avid campers, and they bring their money to the sunny parts of the Continent.

One of our favorite places is the campground "the Residence" near Jesolo, Italy, opposite the lagoon from Venice. We would drive to the end of the jetty and take a boat (commuter) into Venice. It's beautiful and exciting both ways: traveling with the Italians going to work in the morning, or leaving at night, at sunset, and witnessing the lights of Venice and the Islands.

—Dave Fittante, Würzburg, Germany

country by country

Although each individual campground has its own personality, a few gross, utterly biased generalizations from our experience might help you plan your itinerary:

England: The British love to travel by "caravan" but often prefer to stay in holiday camps, highly organized resorts with activity directors. Regular campgrounds are simple but usually pleasant. London's Crystal Palace Caravan Harbour, in Bromley, is a great treat for visitors to the capital.

France: Many cities have their own municipal campgrounds, often with a bakery or a nice restaurant. Paris is well served by a huge campground at the Bois de Boulogne and another at Versailles. French campgrounds can be marginal in the north but improve as you move south, culminating in some very nice ones near the Riviera.

Germany and Switzerland: City campsites tend to be noisy and crowded. The best camping tends to be more on the U.S. model: a way to enjoy nature, out of municipal areas.

Spain: Some of the most luxurious campgrounds, with two or three restaurants and four or five stores. Many establishments on Spain's southern coast include clothing stores, movie theaters, record shops, hairdressers, and discotheques! And Barcelona's campground is spectacular. However, watch out for high costs at these deluxe campgrounds.

Italy: Almost on a par with Spain, often featuring pizza parlors, multiple restaurants, swimming pools, and real Laundromats. Even in Rome itself the campgrounds are great.

Greece: The majority of campgrounds offer great privacy, marking off 20-by-20-foot sites with a hedge up to 10 feet high. Most have great little tavernas with good, cheap food. In both Italy and Greece, look for a pool if your kids like to swim. Many areas of the Mediterranean are too polluted for bathing, with garbage, sewage, and tar washing up on the beaches.

Of course these are simplistic summaries. Let's look next at how to find the best campgrounds in any country.

finding a good campground

Look closely at the listings in your camp guide, taking special note of opening and closing dates. Most campgrounds are open May to September, so don't expect to do much camping in the off-season.

Nudist camps are usually denoted by the initials FKK, the name of a German naturalist group. These are not Club-Med-Gone-Naked: They're almost always family-oriented places without sexual overtones. If that's not your cup of tea, though, be aware that many European women bare their breasts much more casually than American women do—even at campgrounds and beaches not dedicated to nudity. (I have vivid memories of nuns in long habits strolling unconcernedly past bare-breasted women of all shapes and ages on the family-oriented beach near us in Brittany.)

There are many things that cannot be determined by reading lists of funny codes. After using your guide to locate likely looking prospects, it is important to inspect the property before committing yourselves. Start by driving in and checking out the general ambience. Then proceed directly to the all-important bathrooms for a thorough inspection. Are there sit-down toilets? Do they have seats? Is there hot water in the showers? Don't take anyone's word for it: Turn on the taps and make sure.

Almost any campground with good sanitary facilities will do, but you might want to take a few extra minutes now to check out any stores and restaurants or to visit the playground if you have young kids.

Once a camp passes inspection, find a good spot. The best one is relatively near the bathrooms, so you won't face a long, stumbling walk in the dark. At the same time, make sure you're not so near that any odors or the sound of people coming and going in the night will annoy you (100 yards away should be safe). Don't pick a spot near a restaurant or cafe, where young people are apt to be up drinking until all hours.

bring on the bungalows

While campgrounds in Europe often have bungalows for rent, finding them may be hit or miss. If you'd like to pursue this kind of beyond-pup-tents camping, look into an organization that specializes in this approach, like Eurocamp. This British organization, recommended by reader Lisa Towle, offers what I call "gourmet camping." Eurocamp leases land at campgrounds all over Europe. It sets up mobile homes and tents on these campsites, with beds (with real springs), linens, refrigerators, stoves, sinks, pots and pans, cutlery, tables, chairs—everything you need. You bring your kids and your clothes, and you're all set. Eurocamp even staffs the campgrounds with English-speaking workers who run activities for the kids every morning while you relax.

Basically, you get all the best of hotel life (even separate bedrooms!) with the interaction and low prices of a campground. The clientele at most sites is international, so chances are your kids will be playing with kids from all over

Europe about ten minutes after you pull into the campground. Check out Eurocamp's Web site at www.eurocamp.com.

holiday camps

Bungalows at places like Eurocamp usually coexist with tent campers and RVs. One step up are *holiday camps,* where the pup tents and RVs have been banished. As we said earlier, holiday camps can be thought of as sleepover camps for the whole family. You'll sleep in "caravans," "chalets," "supertents," or bungalows and enjoy all kinds of organized daily activities.

Keycamp (www.keycamp.com) is one good example, with 106 locations in nine European countries. It offers various accommodations including four-bedroom supertents and three-bedroom chalets, and many of its resorts have water parks and waterslides.

Another example is Center Parcs (www.centerparc.com), with sixteen villages in France, Belgium, Germany, and the Netherlands. Each Center Parc vacation camp has a marvelous year-round domed water park as its hub, with a slew of other activities, from trail rides to crafts, bike rentals to boating. Costs vary from about €60 per night in the off-season and €100 to €110 in August (French properties will cost about 40 percent more).

rv camping

Dan and Wendy chose the fourth option—RV camping—and recommend it highly. With their three kids, they lived out of a VW bus for five months, enjoying the fact that their "hotel" went with them everywhere they traveled.

Finding a camper for your trip can be surprisingly easy. Many of the car rental companies also rent campers and motor homes, so locating the vehicle you want can be as simple as renting a car. (We've included a list in chapter 22, Resources.)

The cost of renting an RV varies widely by country and by season. Germany seems to have the most competition and, therefore, the lowest prices. Through an agency like MC Rent, for instance, a four-berth motor home could cost as little as $102 per day rented in Germany in the off-season, or $165 at peak times. The least expensive comparable vehicle in France goes for $238 per day in the middle of summer!

Obviously, if you can plan your itinerary to start and end in Germany and you can travel in the off-season, you'll save a lot of money. One great way to compare your options is at www.ideamerge.com, a Web site that specializes in RV rentals for Europe.

On top of your rental fees, you'll need to factor in fuel. Most RVs require diesel fuel, which fortunately sells for about 20 percent less than gasoline. When you're comparing costs, ask about the estimated miles per gallon (or kilometers per liter) of any vehicle, as a fuel gulper will increase your costs immensely.

You can see from these costs that RV camping at $150 plus fuel plus campground fees may not save you tons of money, even if you free-camp as many families do. Any monetary savings come only from being able to cook your own meals. But the savings in sanity—from the flexibility of having a built-in hotel room—could be incalculable when traveling with kids.

what to bring

If you're booking a holiday camp, there's nothing special you need to bring, beyond what you'd need in a hotel. If you're staying at campgrounds (whether tent camping, RV camping, or renting bungalows), we recommend a good campground guide and a discount pass called a Camping Carnet. Plus, you may need some camping equipment.

a good guide

A good guide to European campgrounds is essential. Two of the best are published in Britain. The first, available at www.amazon.com, is from the AA (Britain's equivalent of our AAA); it's called *AA Caravan & Camping Europe*, and it lists 3,500 campgrounds all over Europe. The second is the *Alan Rogers Guide to Europe.* This guide includes 900 continental European campgrounds that have been inspected by the Rogers organization. Rogers also offers his guide online at www.alanrogers.com, useful for preplanning or if you have Internet access while you travel. Note that in both cases the Europe guide doesn't include Britain—British campsites are in a separate volume from AA or Alan Rogers.

Two good supplemental books that include campground listings as well as pages and pages of general information are *Europe by Van and Motorhome* by David Shore and Patty Campbell and *Traveler's Guide to European Camping* by Mike and Terri Church. General guidebooks such as *Let's Go* also list campgrounds.

Specific-country guides are helpful, too, if you're staying in one region. For example, the French Camping Federation, at www.campingfrance.com, puts out an inch-thick *Guide Officiel* for €12. Its cryptic listings are useful, but its full-color ads are even more helpful, showing various campgrounds and listing all the amenities, from soundproofed discos and supermarkets to water parks, private beaches, and rental bungalows. See chapter 22, Resources, for information on where to get all the books and guides listed here.

equipment

A rental camper should be fully equipped and outfitted with bedding and cooking gear. Check to make sure who provides the following recommended equipment:

_____ Tent, even if you're sleeping in a van or camper (A tent holds your place at the campground while you sightsee and gives you a place to stow your luggage.)

_____ Sleeping bags or sheets and blankets

_____ Towels

_____ Stove (Open fires are not permitted at most campgrounds, and grills are not provided.)

_____ Lights

_____ Cooking and eating utensils

_____ Folding chairs and tables (Optional, but fun and very European—picnic tables are not provided at campsites.)

Everything is readily available in Europe in all-purpose stores similar to our discount department stores. If you have good gear at home, though, bring it along, since everything costs much more on the Continent. Folding chairs and tables can be purchased in many outdoor markets, as can used pots and pans and kitchen tools.

One thing you *must* buy overseas is your cooking stove, as airlines *do not allow* gas stoves and fuel on board. This is no problem, because a great line of products, Camping Gaz, is available everywhere in Europe. Their large, refillable tanks are very economical and can be used to power stoves, lights, and heaters.

camping carnet

Another necessity is a Camping Carnet *(car-nay)*, an internationally recognized pass that is good for a discount of up to 20 percent at about two-thirds of the campgrounds in Europe. Why the discount? Because the carnet guarantees that your bill will be paid (by the club that issued your card) if you skip camp. And because it provides insurance coverage for bodily injury, a great comfort to the campground owner.

Without a carnet you'll be asked to surrender your passport when you register. It will be held hostage until your departure, a fact that can make people uneasy. Some campgrounds may even require a carnet for entry. They're open only to members—but with your carnet, you're a member, too.

There are two ways to get a carnet. One is to contact Family Campers and RVers, near Buffalo. They'll sell you a family membership in their organization (2007 dues were $25), then offer you an International Camping Carnet for another $20.

Carnets are also widely available in Europe from all sports and auto clubs (AAA equivalents) that are members of the International Federation of Camping and Caravaning. (Come prepared: You'll need two passport photos of an adult in your group.)

your aaa card

If you're not already a member, join AAA (American Automobile Association) before you go. Your AAA card gives you all sorts of reciprocal privileges in local automobile clubs in Austria, Belgium, Denmark, Finland, Germany, Great Britain, Greece, Italy, Luxembourg, the Netherlands, Norway, and Switzerland. Check with AAA for an updated list and for emergency road-aid numbers in the countries you'll be visiting, if you'll be RV camping.

Armed with the information in this chapter, you should be able to enjoy camping your way through Europe, meeting new friends, and having great adventures with your kids. Happy camping!

We spent almost six weeks car camping with three kids eighteen, eleven, and two and enjoyed every minute of it. We originally planned to camp one-third of our trip and stay in pensions and youth hostels the other two-thirds. The camping was so much easier that we camped the entire time! No worries about reservations, directions, language barriers, car safety, kids' excessive energy. We were always able to get a bungalow at the campground when it was raining. I actually miss sleeping in a tent with three kids. If we get a chance to return, I won't even consider bothering with B&Bs or hostels!

—Shannon Latson, Agoura, CA

road-trip survival

Even though our big trip was planned around long-term homestays, we still spent hundreds of hours on the road. The first few days were great. Traveling was still a novelty; every tree, every bicycle, every house, every road sign was different and exotic.

By the end of the first week, car travel was close to a nightmare. We were tired of being cooped up in a car together. We couldn't agree on where to stop—and when we did, we couldn't agree on when to go again. With relief we settled into our first "home" in Spain, trying not to think about our next stint on the road.

Eventually we learned a lot about road-trip survival. In this chapter I'll pass that experience on to you.

daily schedules

We learned through trial and error that certain schedules and travel patterns suited our family and others didn't. In sharing these scheduling tips, it's good to keep in mind that what worked for us won't necessarily work best for your family. But if I tell you *why* we did what we did, you can tailor our experience to fit your needs.

pacing

Pace yourselves. It may seem like a good idea to divide your road time into equal travel segments. We tried this approach first but gave it up. For us a more successful way was to travel as far as possible on travel days, then stay put for two or three days in the same place.

Why was this? Arriving in a new town or city is hard work. By the time you find the tourist office and get a map, find a hotel, and get the bags in, a good hour has probably passed. Then, cramped from sitting in the car, everyone wants to stretch out for *just* a minute before setting out to explore the town.

Suddenly it's dinnertime, then bedtime—and you've seen nothing of this place but your hotel room and the restaurant on the corner.

Compare that with the stay-put system. Instead of driving for four hours, you drive for six, or even eight. You arrive just in time for dinner, then collapse into sleep. Next day you're fresh and ready for sightseeing the whole day. One of our best "stay-puts" was in France's Dordogne Valley, where a three-day stay gave us not only time to tour the prehistoric caves that had brought us there but also time to explore old ruined castles and build dams of rocks and sticks in a bubbling stream.

For us car travel and staying put were definitely two different gears. We grew to enjoy both immensely. But changing gears from one to the other was never easy, so we learned to minimize the switching.

Also make sure to account for *real* distances. What looks like a few hundred kilometers on the map may take hours and hours on winding mountain roads.

Even though Europe is small in comparison to the United States, one shouldn't underestimate the time it actually takes to get places. It made me wish for "time travel" when it literally took us a day to get from Paris to Wengen [Switzerland] and another day back. All those trips had their enjoyable memories. But the person who is planning the trip, while planted in their living room, needs to recognize and allot the time needed for actual change of locations in their itinerary.

—Lillian Souers, Dallas

---

getting up

Getting up can become a family battleground on vacation. Who sleeps latest in your family? In some families it's the kids, who are used to sleeping in on any day that there's no school. In other families maybe the parents are night owls who just don't function before the first cup of coffee.

In our family the kids inevitably wanted to sleep much later than we did. Mornings started off badly, with a lot of up-and-at-'em urging on our part and a lot of grumbling from them. It was not, as they say, a pretty sight.

The solution turned out to be as simple as discussing our schedule the night before, then asking for their input. "Since we agreed on an early start tomorrow, what time do you think you could be ready?" we'd ask. We quickly realized that our morning battles had been over power as much as sleep: When the kids could decide their own destiny, they almost always picked a reasonable time. (Mind you, I don't mean dawn when I say reasonable. But the kids often volunteered to get up at 8:00 or 8:30, not 10:00 A.M.)

Did they wake up on their own? Never. But having come to a consensus the night before, we could say, "It's time to get up. Remember you asked me to wake you at seven so you'd be ready at eight?" This way, we weren't the brunt of nearly as many snarls.

Once the kids are awake, it's really helpful to leave them alone to get dressed at their own pace. Take a walk if you're in the country, or shop at a bakery for picnic supplies. Kids—like all of us—almost always get more done when no one is standing over them expectantly. And you'll be more relaxed if you don't feel like you're wasting a beautiful morning in Italy. Also this is a perfect quiet time to go over maps, read, and plot possibilities before the kids are up.

Occasionally (once or twice a week on a longer trip) let the kids simply sleep in. Go off on your own and do something adult: Chat over coffee in a small cafe, or visit an art museum. Take a vacation from the kids, and you'll all be better off. Don't worry; responsible school-age kids will be perfectly safe in a hotel room alone for a few hours.

Once in Bern we left the kids in our hotel, watching the Olympics, while we went out for a walk. We wouldn't do that here in the United States, but they're real trustworthy kids, and we stay in little family hotels that don't have that many rooms. We just make sure to tell the clerk or the concierge downstairs that we'll be back in a while—you'd want someone to know, in case of fire.

—Lisa Geibel and Doug Alexander, Austin, TX

Let the kids sleep in occasionally, while you spend time alone.

Are *you* the slug in your family? Make sure the rest of your family reads this, so your inner clock won't become a time bomb.

letting off steam

Build time into your schedule for physical activity. Younger kids, especially boys, need almost constant physical activity. Watch a group of ten-year-olds at recess: They're running and chasing each other, and even rolling in the grass like puppies.

When you're traveling *en famille,* though, your kids won't have other kids with whom to let off steam. Allow for this, and take up the slack yourselves. When Sam was ten we kept a soccer ball in the trunk of our car. At rest stops we'd kick the ball around for ten or fifteen minutes to get the itchies out of him. Other times Lew would suddenly tag Sam and yell, "Race you to the next corner," as we walked down a city street.

Pushing ourselves into activities like this did wonders for our circulation, too. More important, though, it resulted in more peaceful and relaxed mealtimes and museum visits. *Plan* some physical release for your kids, and it won't surprise you at inappropriate times.

lack of privacy

Privacy becomes a big issue on anything less than a deluxe tour. Budget travel means double rooms at best and often a single family room at a hotel or hostel. We had never discussed this reality before our trip started. I'll never forget the quiet dismay on Libby's face the first night she realized she would be sharing a room with her little brother. On an intellectual level she wasn't surprised. But suddenly the ramifications hit her: "I have to find someplace to get dressed. I have to go to sleep the same time he does. I have to get up when he does. I have to breathe the same air."

Don't get me wrong: These are two kids who like and respect each other and have always gotten along well. But both—especially Lib at thirteen—like privacy, too. And the reality of constant togetherness was very different from the theory.

It worked out fine. You can always change clothes in the bathroom or under the covers. Or you can stay in bed until your roommate gets up and leaves. The kids worked out their own patterns before too long.

Should you discuss this with your kids so they'll be prepared? I'd say yes. But my daughter disagrees. "Sharing a room is *not* fun," she recalls. "You don't get any time to yourself." Yet she insists, "Don't tell them the grisly details before you go. They'll hate you and they'll say they won't go."

Maybe she's right. Certainly don't lie if the subject comes up. But don't dwell on the issue and blow it all out of proportion. Somehow your kids will work it out, no matter what their initial reaction. And in working it out, they'll learn a lot about adaptability.

toilet survival

Toilets are an issue you may not even think about, but you should. Public toilets in the United States are all alike: They feature the same fixtures, just in different states of cleanliness. European toilets have much more variety. A few—especially in small villages and inexpensive cafes in France—are Turkish toilets that require you to squat over a drain while you stand on two foot-shaped platforms. There is no good way to use these toilets, especially in pants. Yet it's also in France that many street corners have high-tech coin-operated kiosk toilets that automatically self-disinfect after each use (a great French invention that I've noticed recently in other countries, too).

In between are fixtures more comparable to ours. Except in England, though, you'll rarely flush by pushing down a handle. Instead, you'll use an overhead pullchain, or pull up on a knob on the top of the tank, or press on a rectangular button recessed in the tank top. Use your imagination and you'll figure it out.

On the top end of the scale, two toilets stand out in the annals of sanitation. One, in a hotel in Grenoble, France, was christened "the nuclear toilet" by our kids. Not uncommon in Europe, this type of toilet uses compressed air to flush, so that only a little water is needed. Stand up first—or you may be startled by the incredibly loud whoosh of air when you press the button.

The second toilet is of a type starting to become more popular in France and Germany. Instead of a normal oval seat, this one has a seat shaped like a horseshoe, with the open ends disappearing into the body of the toilet. The horseshoe is encased in a paper sleeve. Before you sit down, you press a button on the toilet, and a mechanism advances the paper sleeve, providing you with a clean surface on which to sit. Quite a contrast to a Turkish toilet!

Speaking of toilet seats, you'll encounter many toilet bowls without them in Europe. Are you supposed to sit on the cold bare rim or squat over the bowl? I'll leave that up to you, but I've been told many Europeans opt for squatting, considering a toilet without a seat to be more sanitary.

Whichever type of toilet you encounter, bring along your own paper. Europe sells the finest paper tissues in the world; make sure everyone in the family carries his own little packet every day to be ready for a possible lack of toilet paper.

backseat basics

Your kids will be much happier in the car if you pack basic survival gear. A few good ideas include the following:

- **Water bottles.** Each person in the family should have his or her own individual water bottle. Buy bottled mineral water in screw-top plastic bottles on the first day. (*Note:* Germany's strict recycling laws limit plastic bottles, so buy over the border if possible.) Then let each person be responsible for refilling his own water supply each day from the tap.

- **Pillows.** Pick up some small throw pillows at a discount department store. They're great for car naps. Get different colors so everyone knows whose is whose.

- **Personal music player,** with extra headphones. Our kids got a lot of use from a player with two earphone jacks. Both of them could listen to rock music while we talked—or one of them could retreat to solitude, finding the illusion of privacy where there was often too little. Younger kids would enjoy a personal music player just as much, with some of their own kiddie music or stories.

Having a Walkman helped in the car. Our daughter could listen to French rock and roll on the radio and hear familiar tunes, but she'd be hearing lots of new songs and listening to the DJs in French at the same time.

—Louise Goldenberg, Eliot, ME

- **Books.** Reading is a great way to pass the time on long car trips. Even if you're the type who gets queasy reading in the car, a book is a good idea: It gives you something to do during sightseeing stops, when your interests don't match other people's.

- **Quiet toys.** Younger kids need small toys to occupy them. We thought Sam was too old, and we didn't bring toys from home. He filled the gap by buying Legos with most of his souvenir money. Stored in a fishing-tackle box we bought in Spain, the Legos were easy for Sam to manage neatly in the backseat.

- **Snacks.** Car snacks are tough. Salty things make everyone too thirsty. Bread and rolls generate crumbs. Fruit leaves sticky drips. Juice spills. You may prefer to pull over for an organized snacktime on the roadside. But, in any case, bring food. If you're stuck in traffic past lunchtime, suddenly realize the stores close Tuesday afternoon, or learn too late that restaurants don't serve dinner until 9:00 P.M., you'll be glad you brought snacks for the kids.

- **Day bags.** Where does all this stuff go? Each family member needs his or her own backpack or zippered tote for daytime paraphernalia. Leaving anything—even books and toys—lying around in your car at night is an open invitation to break-ins. With individual bags, it's easy for everyone to pack up and clean up as the night's destination approaches.

- **Litter bag.** When you live in your car for hours at a time, it gets dirty quickly. We also kept a small dustpan and brush under the seat, so we could gather up crumbs and sand easily.

reading aloud

One of the items listed above—books—is worth saying a bit more about. Why? Because reading aloud can be a real addition to your trip.

Almost by accident we started reading out loud in the car. It began when one of us, reading silently, would share short passages: "Oh, this is great. You've gotta hear this." The others, bored after many miles, would say, "Read a little more." And so we read for mile after mile.

The reading led to discussions that were some of the best of the trip. We read Anne Tyler's *Accidental Tourist* and thought about the importance of being open to new experiences. We read Bernard Cornwell's *Redcoat*, a Revolutionary War story told from the English point of view, then discussed American government, freedom, and how to look at life from the other side. When we were living in Brittany, we read *Assignment in Brittany,* a thriller about the French Resistance in World War II.

The list goes on and on. But I won't mention them all because I have no intention of suggesting you read what we read. I would like to urge you, though, to bring along some good books for car or train travel.

What's a good travel book? As you can see by what worked for us, it can be almost anything with a good plot and interesting characters. Try to find stories that relate to the areas you'll be visiting. Jean Auel's *Clan of the Cave Bear* series would be great for a trip through France's Dordogne; Edward Rutherfurd's *Sarum* would lend depth to a trip to England; a book of Greek myths would be almost mandatory for Greece.

One way to start is to check your library for ideas before you go. Ask your librarian to show you *Children's Books in Print,* then look up appropriate topics (France, cathedrals, World War II, etc.) in the subject guide.

Just about any book should be suitable. Don't worry that you can't get hold of books specifically written for children. We started reading adult books to Sam simply because we had no alternative, but it worked out beautifully. If we ran across some particularly adult topic, we'd either skip a few paragraphs or simply plow ahead.

Often this would lead to a discussion—about war, greed, poverty, or whatever—that somehow seemed easy to handle in the privacy of our car. In fact, Sam enjoyed some of the topics so much he'd continue on by himself. At an age when he'd rarely read even a child's book voluntarily, Sam read several chapters of Ken Follett's spy thriller *Triple* on his own.

If your family likes a good story, the reading probably won't stop when you get to your destination. Again, without the television, toys, and friends of home, your kids will be more interested in books than they've ever been.

driving in europe

Don't be apprehensive about driving in Europe. Overall, most drivers in Europe are more predictable than the typical American driver. At all times—

except in Italy and in the fast lane of the German autobahns—we felt much safer than we often do at home.

traffic conventions

All European countries use a common system of iconic road signs that don't depend on words. Most of these are so obvious—tunnel ahead, slippery road, falling rocks—that you wonder why we use words in the United States. Many guidebooks offer lists of common signs. We recommend you review common European road signs by clicking on "Road Signs and Signals" at www.idea merge.com/motoeuropa/guide.html.

One of the most obscure signs that you really *must* understand is a yellow diamond with white borders. This signifies that the road you are on has priority at intersections and merges. When this sign is crossed with a black bar, it means *end of priority.* Then you must yield to traffic on your right.

Your road has right-of-way

Road to your right has priority.

In fact, this is the default in Europe: The driver on the right has priority. This applies even when you're on a major road, with a little side road on your right. Unless you have the "Your road has right-of-way" sign, you'd better expect cars to pull out of that little side road right into your path. Europeans know this. Many intersections that would sport a stop sign or traffic signal here work very smoothly in Europe because *everyone* understands that traffic on the right always goes first unless signs indicate otherwise.

Be aware that the American system of turning right on red is *not* observed in Europe. A red light means a red light, and you must wait until the light changes, even if you're turning right. Most traffic lights turn to amber just before the red turns to green, though, so you can get a good jump start.

Another important convention in Europe is flashing one's headlights. When used by the driver behind you, this gesture has the same angry get-out-of-my-way-you-jerk meaning as it does in the States. It's heavily used in the fast lane of superhighways. At an intersection, though, flashing lights invariably mean that the other driver is politely telling you to go first.

Speaking of superhighways, it's worth noting that divided highways in Europe most often have just two lanes in each direction. The fast lane is *very fast.* A Mercedes or BMW will swoop down on you before you realize they're there. Always stay in the slow lane (which is often very slow) unless you're passing.

direction signs

How do you find your way? In America we're accustomed to route numbers on all our highways. When we give directions, we'll say something like, "Take 495 to 95 north. Get off at exit 3, and go east on 101."

This system doesn't hold sway in much of Europe. As a holdover from ancient times, major cities and towns are used for guidance instead of route numbers. Someone in Paris, for instance, might have given us directions to our house on the Breton coast by saying, "Leave Paris *direction le Mans,* then take *direction Rennes.* Then continue in *direction Dinan,* then take *direction Dinard."*

It's a tricky system that requires you to know the local geography. You must check your map and figure out the name of the next major town or city, then watch for that name on signs at each intersection. Then, when you approach your first target city, you have to know enough to switch to the next goalpost. If you keep following signs for le Mans, you'll drive right into downtown le Mans instead of turning toward Rennes.

My husband had the foresight to purchase a compass before our trip. It assured us we were headed in the right direction when we didn't know if a certain town was east or west. The most stressful part of the trip was driving: unknown roads, with unfamiliar signage, in an unfamiliar car. Another reason for staying put with younger kids!

—Jennifer and Tim Woods, Chicago

This is not to say that route numbers don't exist in Europe. Look closely on your map: They're there in tiny letters. They may even be posted at some intersections in equally tiny letters. But route numbers change almost randomly—there's nothing like our Route 66 across the nation—and they're almost impossible to see from a moving car, so you're better off using the *direction* system.

There are two exceptions to this. In northern Europe and in England, route numbers are used more consistently. And in all countries, major autoroutes (comparable to our biggest interstates) are usually clearly marked with numbers like "the A1" or "the M4."

on the left in england

Driving on the left in England sounds much harder than it actually is. Just be sure not to start your trip by heading straight for downtown London. Get the hang of things out in the country first! We had our children chant *Left, Left,*

Left for the first few miles (yes, miles—England isn't entirely metric yet), and we did fine.

Watch out when you back out of driveways. Somehow, long after you've gotten the hang of driving on the left going frontward, you'll still get confused when you're turned around. Think hard about which way to turn the wheel as you reach the main road.

Speaking of turning, don't worry about those notorious roundabouts—they're really quite civilized. Lanes are clearly marked, and drivers behave predictably. The rules are as follows:

- Yield as you enter the roundabout. This is a real yield—almost a full stop—if there's traffic. Don't just blurt into the roundabout.

- Roundabouts usually have two lanes. As you enter the roundabout, stay on the inside, close to the "hub" of the roundabout. Go around as many times as you want until you're sure of where you're going.

- Move into the outside lane one "spoke" before you're ready to exit the roundabout. It will be easy to move over because everyone in the outside lane will have just exited.

motoring guide

One of the best ways to prepare for your trip is to check out an online European motoring guide called *Moto-Europa*. Once published as a traditional book, this guide is now available free online at www.ideamerge.com/moto europa. Once you get there, click "Online Guide," then choose the topic or country of your choice.

Moto-Europa will tell you that Italian cops can collect traffic fines on the spot, that *Farligt sving* means dangerous curve in Danish, that some Spanish cities indicate resident-only parking with a blue line along the curb, and that the black letters *HR* on a yellow background in the United Kingdom indicate a "holiday route"—a more scenic but often longer option. In short, this wonderful Web site can answer all your questions and make you much more confident if you're at all insecure about driving overseas.

Don't let these few paragraphs on road rules make you apprehensive. In all our months of European travel—and in spite of often finding ourselves lost or confused—we've never once run afoul of any traffic regulations. Go. Drive. Enjoy.

renting and exchanging homes

Why get a house? Having a house instead of staying in hotels is essential to the success of an extended overseas trip for three main reasons:

- **Savings:** With a home exchange, your house is free—and a car may even be included. When you rent, you can pay as little as $250 per week, instead of paying almost that much per night in a hotel. Your savings are compounded by having a kitchen—you can avoid the huge expense of restaurant meals.

- **Sanity:** In a house there's enough room to ensure privacy for everyone, and most likely a yard for the kids to play in, too. Some houses include toys and bicycles.

- **Learning:** Living in a house makes it easier to compare "real" life in another country with the life to which your family is accustomed. One of the great pleasures of nontourist travel is doing ordinary things like grocery shopping—but doing them in extraordinary places.

All this is true in spades on a longer trip. But even on a shorter trip, hotels can be one of your largest expenses. Getting a house for even a week can save both money and sanity—making traveling with children a more positive experience.

home exchange

How would you like a vacation in Europe with no hotel costs, rental car costs, or restaurant costs? Home exchanging makes it possible to travel for little more than the cost of airfare. You move into another family's home in Italy, France, England, or wherever, while they watch over your home during your absence. You use their car and cook in their kitchen and pay about what you would for groceries and utilities at home.

While savings are an undeniable advantage of home swapping, another big plus is the chance to really connect with another community. Home exchangers often arrange with their neighbors to greet you on your arrival. This means you and your kids have built-in friends from day one. Your initial swap can sometimes lead to an ongoing friendship with subsequent exchanges in future years.

While home exchanging beats hotels any day, it offers several advantages (besides cost) over renting an overseas home:

- Cars are often included, eliminating the cost of a rental car.

- Houses are better equipped for daily life than vacation rentals. Exchange with a family, and toys and bicycles will be included.

- Your own house won't sit empty during your absence. Many home exchangers report that they feel more comfortable with a relative stranger in their house than they would with the house a sitting target for thieves.

- You can take side trips and stay in hotels without paying double for every night. Home renters find it galling to pay for their home base, then pay again for on-the-road lodging.

- You may even be able to leave your pets behind at home, cared for by your overseas counterparts.

A car exchange often goes along with a home exchange.

Dan and Wendy exchanged their California home for one in England a few summers ago. Their exchange partners stayed an extra day after the Hallinans' arrival and threw a welcoming party that night. For the next two weeks, Dan and Wendy's biggest "problem" was that their kids preferred hanging around with their new friends to sightseeing. "We didn't mind. We think meeting other people is more important than seeing another castle, anyway," reported Dan. Based on this success, the Hallinans made a swap in Provence two years later.

Inevitably you'll be anxious at first about turning your home over to perfect (or probably imperfect) strangers. What about your silverware and stereo, or family heirlooms? If you want you can box up your most precious possessions and leave them with a friend, but exchangers universally claim no loss of possessions. Remember, you're holding their house and possessions hostage. Most exchangers are more careful than they would be in their own home.

If you want to exchange your home, the first step is to join an exchange club. Your home will be listed in the club's directory and online database, and you'll get access to everyone else's listings. Depending on the agency, you'll pay between $90 and $100 for your listing plus online access to other members' listings. Scan the listings—the Internet makes this so easy!—and find a match: a location you want, with someone who wants to be in your area during your desired time frame. Then write off, while others overseas are writing to you. Your biggest problem will be having too many good options from which to choose! To try it out go to www.HomeExchange.com; at this service, nonmembers can access the entire database for free. We've listed additional home exchange clubs in chapter 22, Resources.

save big with local tourist office rentals

Let's say you decide to rent instead of exchanging homes. Especially if you'll be traveling for several weeks, you can save hundreds of dollars by renting through an overseas tourist office instead of through an agency.

European tourist offices are an awesome resource for travelers. Existing in every city and town and in many small villages, tourist offices are usually staffed by helpful, multilingual people. Before you leave the States, they can send you lists of rentals, sightseeing brochures, or information about kids' clubs and craft classes. When you arrive, they're your prime resource for maps and pamphlets and for finding a hotel in your price range. We'll talk about all these things in different chapters. For now let's consider them your prime resource for rentals, or self-catered cottages, as they're often called.

Once you've decided where you want to live, just contact several tourist offices in the area. These days it's easiest to find them on the Web. For instance, if I wanted to find rentals in York, England, I might type "tourist office York UK" in my search engine. That would lead me to the Web site, where a full list of rentals might be posted. At the least there would be an e-mail address for requesting the list. You can also find tourist office addresses in guidebooks, or get them from a country's national tourist office in New York (see chapter 22, Resources). In response, you'll receive a list of possible rentals, with brief descriptions of the properties and prices.

The savings, compared to agencies, are considerable. If you wanted to stay in the Dordogne, for instance, you could visit www.justfrance.com, a Pennsylvania agency, and rent a stone house with a pool twenty-five minutes from Sarlat for $2,000 to $6,000 per week. Or you could contact the tourist office in Sarlat, and select from ninety rentals that would sleep a family of four, starting as low as €120 to €150 per week from September to June and €400 per week in July and August.

Here's a typical listing from Sarlat, for a property that rented in 2007 for €150 a week in June and September and €500 to €600 a week in July and August:

> *Quiet one-story house, perfect for a couple and 2 or 3 young children. 2 bedrooms (one with double bed, one with twin beds), dishwasher, TV. 4 mountain bikes included in rental; tennis, horseback riding, hiking, fishing nearby. 12 km from Sarlat in Saint Genies, a tiny village with cafe, butcher, restaurant, market. Tastings of local gourmet products each Wednesday night.*

Granted, some of the ritzy rentals from the agencies have swimming pools or tennis courts. I'm not saying you can't decide to splurge if you want to. I'm just telling you that it's possible to rent something very normal and nice—and pay about as much per week as you'd pay at most hotels for a single night.

catch #1: language

You knew there'd be a catch. Renting through tourist offices, in most cases, means you'd better speak a little of the local language. (That listing above was sent to me in French.) Even though tourist office personnel speak English, you'll be expected to make the arrangements with your overseas landlord yourself, and many home owners don't speak any English.

If you don't speak the language of the country you'll be visiting, find an agent who speaks English, and request information about rentals. While it's wonderful to try out a new language, this is not the place to do so; misunderstandings could be too disastrous.

You can work with either American or European agents. U.S.-based agencies usually cost the most—but then, their employees all speak English fairly well, too. Check our list of recommendations at the back of the book for ideas, but do stick to an agency: Almost all of them, no matter where, have at least one person who can answer all your questions in English and manage arrangements with your potential landlord.

There's no reason to plan your location around your language skills. Once the arrangements are made, it's fun to figure out how to communicate in the shops and with your neighbors. With two hands and a dictionary, almost anything is possible! But be aware that you'll find more English-speaking agents in tourist-oriented areas and very few in rural areas.

catch #2: effort

Working with tourist offices is a lot more work. You have to write lots of letters (not too hard by e-mail), sift through (and maybe translate) the replies, then write back again for more details on the ones you like. It takes time, and time is money. For a short trip of one or two weeks, you might prefer working with an agency. You'll pay a little more, but you'll avoid the work of looking into several different properties on your own.

For longer stays a lower per-week cost may be worth a little extra bother. Or you may just enjoy the whole process and not see it as a bother at all. When we were hunting for French rentals, I would look forward to the mail with its daily harvest of friendly letters and photos. For me it seemed as if the trip had already begun when I had a chance to learn about new places and "meet" new people.

catch #3: location

Not every tourist office handles lists of rentals. We've had excellent results with this approach in Great Britain and France, quickly receiving large lists of private homes for rent at reasonable prices. Most German tourist offices match or exceed this standard, while a few are more like Italy, where tourist offices often respond with lists of pricey "holiday houses" or complexes of commercial bungalows and apartments. In Spain a few tourist offices now provide great resources (a new and very welcome change!), while others are totally clueless.

Given these three caveats, let's look at some other resources besides tourist offices that may help you.

agencies

I'm a tightwad who enjoys finding my own rentals. But if you have more money and prefer to spend your time in more normal pursuits, by all means take advantage of some of the excellent agencies that handle self-catered properties. The peace of mind you gain from having a knowledgeable agent working on your behalf may well be worth the extra cost.

One agency you might contact in the United States is Interhome. Interhome, based in Zurich, has more than 20,000 rental homes in Europe, from $250 per week and up. All their listings are examined, scored, and rated with one to six stars. A new "budget houses" search feature shows there are 1,000-plus choices at under $350 per week. The Florida office is connected to computers in Switzerland, so you can get instant, accurate information on availability and prices.

Overseas agencies, especially those in England, are another option—and not just for properties in Britain. Whether you're looking for rentals in Spain, Italy, Greece, or France, British agencies have a surprising supply of choices, often at a reasonable price. (Because of the airfare investment American families must make to travel to the Continent, American agencies often assume they're catering to a well-off crowd. British folks with more modest incomes

Tourist offices are often a gold mine of rental information.

often bop across the channel and want a modest cottage in Spain for a week or two.) Through Internet access, overseas agencies are now more easily accessible, so look into them! We've listed several agencies in chapter 22, Resources.

rural cottages

Some European countries specifically encourage tourists to stay in less-frequented rural areas. They'll set you up with simple furnished homes, usually in the countryside or in small villages, often requiring a car. These properties range from basic to more than comfortable but will almost never be deluxe.

France's program is most organized. The Maison des Gîtes de France publishes ninety-five regional guides with photos and descriptions of available properties. You buy the guide(s) you want, then book directly with the owner, through the regional *gîtes* (pronounced *jheet*) office, or online. *Gîtes* can be simple old farmhouses or modern vacation homes. A *gîte* my parents rented in Brittany, for example, was a new, four-bedroom home in the country complete with a small swimming pool and lovely views of grazing sheep. In 2007 a similar *gîte* cost €310 per week in May or September.

In Italy the program is called Agriturismo, and it offers Italian cottages and farmhouses for vacation rental. About half of Italy's *agriturismo* properties are self-catering cottages, while the other half are more like B&Bs, where you rent only rooms without kitchen facilities. Many regional tourist offices can also supply you with free lists of *agriturismo* properties, but then it's up to you to write (most likely in Italian) to find out cost and availability.

Spain's program goes under several names: *casas rurales, casas rusticas, casas de aldea,* and *casas de labrana;* the program is offered through most tourist offices around the country. The Spanish National Tourist Office has a long list of *casas rurales* links on its Web site at www.okspain.org (click on "Rural Lodgings" under "Accommodations").

All rural rentals are likely to require language skills. Even though you may book the property with someone at a central office who speaks English, you will often have to make final arrangements for payment and arrival with an owner who is unlikely to speak English.

Do check the U.S. papers—even our local paper sometimes has neat far-away vacation rentals. With a toddler, we knew we wanted an apartment in Paris. We called the agencies and found their rates extremely high (one was more than $2,000 per week!). Then we checked the New York Times *and found an apartment in a working-class neighborhood for only $400 per week. This is where we truly experienced "living in Paris."*

—Carolyn Barnabo, Darien, CT

---

online sources

When we first traveled to Europe, finding rentals in some countries was a huge challenge. Today the Internet makes it easy, giving you access to both individual listings (comparable to the newspaper listings discussed above) and agencies.

It's serious fun to shop for European rentals on the Web. All those juicy pictures, complete contact and price information—the Web cuts your search time to almost nothing. Three of our favorite pan-European home-rental sites are Internet Holiday Ads (www.iha.com), Interhome (www.interhome .com) and Homelidays (www.homelidays.com).

The first, IHA, lists more than 7,000 private rentals in Western Europe, including about 2,500 each in France and Italy, and another 700 in Spain. Because the home owners set their own prices individually (this is not an agency but is basically a big cooperative bulletin board), the weekly rents are quite reasonable: about 20 percent of these rent for €250 or less per week. For instance, wouldn't you love a six-bedroom mountain chalet in Bavaria for just €380 per *month* (yes—month, not week) in July, or a three-bedroom traditional stone house in Andalucia, Spain, for €133 per week, any month of the year? IHA's search engine lets you put in all sorts of variables for price, location, and amenities, and listings include photos and sometimes even videos of the property. You pick the property you like, then contact the owner from the details listed.

Homeliday is, like IHA, a French-based owner-advertisement site. It features about 30,000 European listings, about half of which are in France, with another 10,000 or so split between Italy and Spain. There are more listings here than on IHA, but we like IHA's interface and prices better.

Another dependable source is Interhome. As we mentioned a few pages ago, Interhome is an agency with a U.S. office. Their Web site has 20,000 rentals; you can search by many criteria such as region, number of bedrooms, and maximum price. Some are purpose-built vacation resorts with less charm than a "real house," but every listing has a photo so you can see for yourself if you're getting a chalet with window boxes or a high-rise apartment.

We've listed many more good rental Web sites under individual countries later in this chapter. If you're an Internet user, though, you know that available sites change daily. Type "rent house Italy" or whatever into your favorite search engine and find your own cool Web sites! There's no limit to what you might find.

personal connections

One last option is the personal touch. Personal connections are an obvious approach in any country but can be even more useful in places like Spain or Italy, compulsively sociable countries where personal contacts and family ties are everything. Has anyone in your family ever visited Italy and made friends with any local folks? Was there a Spanish exchange student at your town's high school four years ago? Is your neighbor's sister-in-law Danish? Talk up your trip, and ask everyone you know for connections.

If you have no other personal connections, try working through a college or university that maintains a foreign-study program in your target area. Our apartment in Salamanca, Spain, in fact, materialized through an appeal to Lew's alma mater, Dartmouth.

Would this work for you? It's worth a try when your only alternative may be a characterless condo surrounded by other tourists. Call a university near you, or the college you attended, or even the one from which your second cousin or your mail carrier graduated. Any college with an overseas program knows someone in that city who's familiar with local housing opportunities. Get that someone's name and address, and give it a try.

If you do obtain housing through informal connections, don't forget to show your appreciation. Politely ask about a fee, and if one isn't requested, offer your thanks in some other way when you arrive—money, discreetly tucked in an envelope, and a small gift of some typically American product would be appropriate.

timing is everything!

Getting a rental—especially a nice one at a reasonable price—depends on when you travel and when you book.

High season for rentals is July 15 through August 31, when the majority of Europeans vacation. June 15 through July 15 is sometimes referred to as "high-saver" season because it's slightly less in demand and slightly less expensive. Other months are vastly cheaper. That means if you can possibly travel in late May and early June or in September, you can save big bucks.

Book early. Agencies and tourist offices say the biggest mistake Americans make is to wait until a few months—or even a few weeks—before vacation to book a rental. Europeans plan their vacations months in advance. We've known people who started in January and ended up with the fifth or sixth choice on their list—for a July vacation. Get trip-cancellation insurance from a travel agent if you're worried about making plans so far ahead.

If you rent through an agency (like Interhome), you'll be able to pay by credit card for your rental. If you rent directly from the owner, you will most likely need to pay by bank wire transfer. This sounds daunting if you haven't done it before, but banks do this without batting an eye. Our bank, for instance, charges $20 for sending a wire transfer.

rental checklist

Whether you're renting through an agency, through tourist office listings, or through personal connections, you'll need to get some basic information about each potential property beyond what's included in the listing. Although the answers you need depend on your family's size and interests, your list might look like this one we use:

_____ How many bedrooms? What size are the beds?
_____ How many bathrooms? Describe them.
_____ Is there a clothes washer? Or a public Laundromat nearby?
_____ Is there parking close by? Where? Is it free?
_____ What other special features or amenities are there?
_____ General description: Is the house old, new? Stone, wood?
_____ Is it in a village or in the countryside?
_____ If in a village—in the center or on the outskirts?
_____ What's the population of the town?
_____ Are there other kids nearby? How far? What ages?
_____ How far to food stores and to the main road?
_____ What's the price per week? Any discount for multiple weeks?
_____ Does that price include all taxes and utilities?
_____ What about bed linens and towels?
_____ Is there a telephone? If so, how much extra does it cost? If not, where is the nearest pay telephone?
_____ What is the minimum rental period? Is there a specific changeover day when we must arrive and leave?
_____ If we're interested, how much deposit do you want? When? When will the balance be due? Will you accept dollars, or must I pay in local currency? Do I pay by credit card, check, or wire transfer?

Check out every detail on a rental house to avoid surprises.

Here's why we suggest you ask about bed size. Beds throughout Europe are small. You are not likely to find a queen- or a king-size bed anywhere in your travels, and many double beds are closer to the size we call "three-quarter" beds. In northern areas (especially Germany), it's common for a double room to have two twin beds pushed together—but you won't see this often in southern areas. Be prepared if anyone in your family is 6 foot 3 inches!

For any likely rental choices, ask for a floor-plan sketch: Sometimes the only access to one bedroom is through another, or the bathroom is far from the bedrooms. Insist on multiple photos, too, including one that shows a little of the surrounding neighborhood.

Now that we've outlined the overall attack plan, let's run down specific countries and detail how to find rentals. For each of several countries, we'll tell you what's available through local tourist offices and how to get addresses for the tourist offices. We'll tell you about any good materials available from national tourist offices (NTOs) in the United States and whether the country has a *gîtes*-type organization of rural rentals. We'll include a list of foreign terms that may be helpful to know in your housing search and finish off with a suggested strategy and information to calibrate your expectations. Chapter 22, Resources, has addresses for all national tourist offices and for other agencies and organizations mentioned here.

english rentals

England is the easiest place to find rentals. It's not only the lack of a language barrier but also the huge number of choices that make England a snap. Now the only barrier is the high cost!

British Tourist Authority (BTA): At its Web site, www.visitbritain.com, the BTA has a searchable database of apartments and cottages.

Local tourist offices: Excellent web and print resources. Cities usually offer full-color listings including hotels, B&Bs, and self-catering properties; smaller towns have text-only lists with basic information or hook into the BTA's Web site.

Rural rentals: No specific program. Agencies and tourist offices handle rentals in all parts of England, both urban and rural.

Strategy: It seems that every home owner in England must move to a tent in the summer and rent out his or her house as a "self-catering cottage." Nothing else could explain the thousands of fully furnished rental units available in that country.

One good place to start is at www.cottageguide.co.uk, a Web site that lists over 6,000 self-catering properties all over the United Kingdom. Browsing the site you'll find listings like "Crofter's End," a two-bedroom stone cottage in Cornwall starting at £160 per week in the off-season and up to £450 per week at the height of summer. Or "Millers Cottage," an old water mill in Lincolnshire, surrounded by a bird sanctuary, for £225 to £325 per week.

Rentals in Britain will be more expensive than anywhere else in Europe. A rental that might cost €250 per week elsewhere will be £250 here—almost 50 percent more, thanks to the premium the British pound holds over the American dollar.

The prices at www.cottages.co.uk are not as high as some others, but you may still save a lot by contacting towns directly. Tourist offices may send you listings whose terse style—"Mrs. Eunice Palfrey, 48 Vicar's Close. Sleeps 5"—sounds so pallid that you may be tempted to return to the agencies and pay a bit more for something with a complete description. But don't forget this is England, and you speak the language: You can pick up the phone and get any amount of detail on any of the simple town listings. Sure, you might spend $25 on phone calls. But since the unadorned listings sometimes start at less than half the price of the to-die-for cottages, phoning makes sense, especially for a long stay on a limited budget.

Expectations: Like so many British traditions, self-catering has clearly defined rules. Rentals are almost always from Saturday to Saturday. The property is clean when you arrive, and you are expected to leave it that way; there's no maid service except in very rare (and expensive) circumstances. Linens are not often included (though they may be available for an extra fee), and neither is gas or electricity. Usually the meters are read when you arrive and again when you leave—but sometimes electricity and heat are coin-metered, and you must feed in 50 pence coins, just as you would feed a parking meter.

The English consider a daily bath essential and a shower a shoddy substitute. As a result, your rental is apt to feature a tub with no shower and no curtain or surround. If this is a problem, you can buy a shower hose at many household goods and department stores. This Y-shaped rubber gadget has a shower nozzle on a short tube at one end and cups that get jammed over the hot and cold taps on the other ends. Don't expect stand-up showers, even with this solution: The hose is too short, and remember—there's no curtain. In England's typically deep tubs, a sit-down shower can actually be quite reasonable.

You may want to pick up two of these shower gadgets and use the extra on your kitchen sink. Almost all English sinks feature separate hot and cold taps, making it impossible to rinse a few dishes under running water. Your extra "shower" combines the two taps into one stream, giving you warm water as an option to scalding or freezing. As dishwashers are uncommon, this may come in especially handy.

British electrical outlets are not the same as those on the Continent. Even if you have appliances that will work on European 220V current, you'll need a different plug adapter while you're in England. Strangely, we found these hard to come by: Most stores sell adapters from British to European or American plugs (for Brits to take with them on vacation), but the ones to change continental and U.S. cords to fit British outlets are rare. Buy before you leave (see the Magellan catalog in Resources), or try a good hardware store after you arrive.

Like houses throughout Europe, your English house is not apt to include window screens. Mosquitoes are less common in Europe, but in some areas it's helpful to avoid sitting around with the windows open and the lights on at night.

french rentals

France is another easy country in which to find low-cost rentals.

French National Tourist Office: The French NTO's Web site at www.franceguide.com links to the Gites de France Web site (see below) but doesn't offer any additional resources. It doesn't *need* to, because the *gites* network is so comprehensive, and sites like IHA and Homelidays offer so many French listings.

Local tourist offices: Excellent resources. Local tourist offices offer you detailed listings, usually in French, of relatively inexpensive rentals. Then it's up to you to follow up on your own with individual owners. Many are now online, like the excellent Loire Valley listings at www.tourismeloiret.com. You can find a comprehensive list of local tourist offices at www.tourisme.fr/recherche/e_index.htm. Larger towns will have resources and other links listed; for smaller towns you'll be able to get an e-mail or snail mail address for direct contact.

All but the smallest villages have a tourist office; write and be assured that your inquiry will be delivered to someone whose job is to make it easy for you to visit that town.

Rural rentals: Extensive *gites* program with more than 50,000 properties exists through the Maison des Gîtes in Paris. Check their Web site at www.gites-de-france.fr, and use your credit card to order any of ninety-five regional guides describing listings, or simply browse online. Another great

Consider an off-season vacation if you're on a tight budget.

resource is www.gite.com, a private Canadian company that connects vacationers directly with French *gîte* owners. Information on each property is extensive and all in English.

Useful terms for French rentals:

LL	*Lave linge*	washing machine
LV	*Lave vaisselle*	dishwasher
BS	*Basse saison*	off-season (low season)
	Hors saison	off-season (out of season)
MS	*Moyenne saison*	shoulder season
HS	*Haute saison*	high season
1 lit 2 pl.	*1 lit 2 places*	double bed
	canapé convertible	sofa bed
cuis	*cuisine*	kitchen
ch	*chambre*	bedroom
s. de bain	*salle de bain*	bathroom
d	*douche*	shower
séj	*séjour*	living room
	meublé	furnished rental
	prix à la semaine	price per week
	prix à la quinzaine	price for two weeks
	prix au mois	monthly price

Note: Prices are almost always quoted by the week, unless otherwise noted.

Strategy: All in all you're better off staying outside popular areas like Provence, Normandy–Brittany, the Riviera, and the Dordogne, unless you come in the off-season.

Renting directly via tourist office listings is realistic only for those with intermediate-level French language skills. After all, it's easy to read a listing like "Mrs. G. Rae-Fraser. 3 BR, Kit, DR, LR, bath," then pick up the phone and call England. It's a challenge—for most of us—to decipher an entry like "Mme COLAS E. Cuis. Toilettes, S. de Bain, 3 ch. 3 lits, dist mer 15 km village très calme," and even more of a challenge to phone or e-mail and ask for more details in French. If you can surmount the language barrier, the procedure for renting directly is similar to that in England: Contact the tourist office for lists of possibilities, then follow up by phone or in writing with questions to find out more.What if you don't speak French? Language skills aren't really an issue these days, with so many Web sites offering online searches and booking in English. One tip: Be wary of sites that cater especially to British owners of French rentals, as their prices will be based on the oh-so-expensive British pound.

Expectations: French houses most often feature a small toilet room (*le w.c.,* pronounced "vay-say") separate from the bathroom. The bathroom is literally that—a room for bathing, containing a tub (often with flexible shower nozzle), sink, and bidet. For active families, the separation of washroom and toilet room eases bathroom traffic jams tremendously.

In the kitchen you're apt to find the same tiny refrigerator that's common throughout Europe, with virtually no freezer capacity (forgo ice cream and stick to French pastries). Fresh food is a priority in much of Europe: Many homes that could afford larger refrigerators have small ones simply because it's all that's needed to keep a day or two of food. If you're used to shopping weekly and buying four gallons of milk for the kids each trip, prepare to change your shopping habits.

Sheets and towels aren't provided with many French rentals. Beg your landlord to provide them for a small fee if possible. Bringing sheets isn't practical: They're heavy, bulky, and unlikely to fit French beds, which are different sizes from ours. Buying also isn't practical. If you usually buy double-bed sheets at a Sears white sale for around $10 each, you'll find French sheet prices of $25 to $35 hard to swallow when you have to buy two of them for each bed.

We rented a French gîte that didn't come with sheets. So I wrote in my pathetic French and asked if they could supply them. They never replied, so I brought a whole suitcase of sheets. When we arrived our landlady said, "Here's your sheets and towels. Your letter was wonderful—we thought you were a professor of French!" I thought they hadn't written because they were in stitches over my French.

—Louise Goldenberg, Eliot, ME

French pillows are different from American ones, too. Your beds may be equipped with *traversins,* hard cylindrical bolsters, or with *oreillers,* softer rectangular pillows, more like the ones we're used to—but often smaller and thinner.

german rentals

There are not as many readily available rentals in Germany, but when you only need to find one, it doesn't matter that the available sites may offer only 600 choices rather than 6,000.

German National Tourist Office: The NTO's Web site at www.germany-tourism.de includes a list of links to some pan-European rental sites. Choose "Info Center" then "Accommodation," then "Holiday Villages" (assuming they don't rearrange their Web site!), and you'll get a list of pan-European sites with listings in Germany.

Local tourist offices: There's a list of regional tourist offices on the German NTO site, above, but it's a bit hidden. To find it, click your way from "Info Center" to "Accommodation" to "Guesthouses" (even though you're not looking for guesthouses). Local tourist offices are generally known as *Fremdenverkehrsverband* (literally, "stranger-travel association"). Occasionally you'll see slight variations on the name, but this word will work most places. On sites like www.rlp-info.de, the Rheinland-Pfalz state tourist office site, you'll find extensive listings in German and in English.

Rural rentals: *Urlaub auf dem Bauernhof* (farmhouse vacation) is popular in Germany. Check out the central Web site at www.landtourismus.de for a good selection with descriptions in English and reasonable prices.

Useful terms for German rentals:

EZ	*Einzelzimmer*	single room
DZ	*Doppelzimmer*	double room
MBZ	*Mehrbettzimmer*	3–4 bedroom
D	*Dusche*	shower
B	*Bad*	bathtub
WC	*WC*	toilet
BK	*Balkon*	balcony
FeWo	*Ferienwohnung*	apartment
FH	*Ferienhaus*	cottage or bungalow
ÜF	*Übernachtung/Frühstück*	overnight with breakfast
KB	*Kinderbetten*	cots
NS	*Neben-Saison*	off-season
HS	*Haupt-Saison*	high season
NK	*Nebenkosten*	extra costs acc. to usage
einger.	*eingerichtet*	furnished/equipped
	Schlafzimmer/Schlafraum	bedroom
	jede weitere Pers.	each addl. person
	Waschmaschinenbenutz	use of clothes washer
	Fahrräder	bicycles
	Bettwäsche	bed linens
	Sandkasten	sandbox
	Gartenmöbeln	lawn furniture
	Kamin	fireplace

Strategy: By all means use tourist offices. While some are little help, others rank among the best in Europe. They'll offer you two choices of rentals: *Ferienwohnungen* (vacation apartments) and *Ferienhäuser* (vacation houses). Note that "apartments" are often a wing of a farmhouse rather than a downtown dwelling. Since apartments vastly outnumber houses, don't hold out for a freestanding home.

One small but good German rental source is www.vacation-apartments .com, with 600-plus listings. Browsing these listings in mid-2007, we noted a two-bedroom unit in the Black Forest for €20 per day and a restored 1835 farm in Lower Saxony where DSL access is included in the €10 per day cost. Here's one that sounds especially good for families:

> *Ecologically run cattle farm surrounded by the mountains of the Bavarian Forest National Park offers two new and very comfortable holiday flats with high-quality furnishings. The flats are approximately 75 m² in size, and provide rest and relaxation for 2 to 5 people. €26 per day.*

Listings almost universally quote costs by the day. Once in a while you'll see weekly rates, but monthly rates are virtually unheard of. A survey of 2005 rates shows plenty of listings for around €200 to €300 per week, with some nice properties for less.

Expectations: In both *Ferienwohnungen* and *Ferienhäuser, Zentral-heizung* (central heating) and *Bettwäsche* (bed linens) are usually included. *Endreinigung* (cleaning when you leave) and *Strom, Gas, Wasser* (electricity, gas, water) may be included or may be *zuzüglich* (extra). If you're looking for the comforts of home, ask about a *Waschmaschine* (clothes washer) or a *Spülmaschine* (dishwasher).

Apartments may be modern condolike dwellings in a holiday complex, or they may be an ell or wing of a private house or farmhouse. Houses can be recently built second homes but may just as easily be farmhouses. Either way bedrooms will usually feature very firm, thin mattresses with a bottom sheet (often of stretchy knit material), no top sheet, and a down comforter. Pillows are much like ours. "Double" beds are often two single beds pushed together.

In the bathroom, showers are widespread. Make sure to ask how the hot water heater works; here, as in much of Europe, hot water is often activated on demand (i.e., just before you take a shower) rather than being constantly heated throughout the day. You don't want to discover, when you're naked and dirty under a deluge of icy water, that you can't read the directions on the water heater!

italian rentals

Renting in Italy is totally haphazard. As with so much in this country, if you have absolutely no expectations, you may be pleasantly surprised.

Italian National Tourist Office: There are no resources for rentals on the NTO Web site at www.italiantourism.com.

Local tourist offices: Tourist offices are a confusing mishmash. Larger cities have either an EPT (Ente Provinciale per il Turismo) or an APT (Azienda di Promozione Turistica). Smaller towns have an AST (Azienda Autonoma di Soggiorno e Turismo) or a Pro Loco. These are not very good resources, so you're better off on the pan-European rental sites with lots of Italian listings.

Rural rentals: *Agriturismo* is officially promoted in Italy. More than 2,000 farms offer lodging, about half of which are apartments (the rest are B&Bs). One good online resource with English descriptions and prices is www.holiday farm.net. Another, for Tuscany alone, is www.agriturismo.regione.toscana.it.

Useful terms for Italian rentals:

Cam.	*camere*	rooms
Let.	*letti*	beds
IVA	*imposto sul valore aggiunta*	VAT tax
	doccia	shower
	bagno	bath
	matrimoniale	double bed
	camera doppa	twin-bedded room
	cauzione	deposit
	prezzo settimana	price per week
	riscaldamento centralizzato	central heating
	allogio con stufe	heated by stove

Strategy: It's tough to find sources for direct rentals. But that's fine, because sites like www.iha.com offer plenty of rentals at reasonable prices. If you ask for listings in the Siena area of Tuscany, for instance, you'll get a wide choice of properties for as little as €250 per week.

Expectations: Most rentals are described as "villas" rather than houses. The word is used a bit loosely, to say the least: Villas from even the best agencies are sometimes crumbling farmhouses in the countryside that have been divided into several eccentric apartments.

Rentals in Italy tend to be older farm properties that the younger generation, bound for the cities, has turned its back on. It's a curious mix: About half are converted outbuildings—yet as many as 35 percent of the available rentals include a swimming pool! As you might expect with old farm buildings, the state of repair in Italian rentals is variable. Make sure you ask lots of in-depth questions about the property and insist on pictures.

When you walk through the door of your Italian villa, you'll most likely find yourself in the kitchen or dining room. This is a lovely commentary on Italian social life: Why make the living room the first room guests encounter, when what you really want to do is feed them? The living room is most often in the back, away from "guest" areas.

Bathrooms, as in many other European countries, are more apt to include a tub than a shower, but plumbing is usually fine. Bedrooms generally will include linens, but make sure to ask.

spanish rentals

Spain has been a frustrating country in which to find rentals in the past. Recently, however, the situation has vastly improved.

Spanish National Tourist Office: On their Web site, www.okspain.org, you can find a list of agencies offering rentals in Spain. Choose "Accommodations," and then "Apts & Villas."

Local tourist offices: Known as the Oficina de Turismo, these tend to concentrate on rural rentals (see below).

Rural rentals: Several names are widely used for rural rentals, including *casas rurales, casas rústicas, casas de aldea* (village houses), and *casas de labranza* (farmhouses), or simply *agroturismo*. Again, the NTO Web site at www.ok spain.org has become the central clearinghouse. Choose "Accommodations," and then "Rural Lodgings," and you'll find an extensive list of links to explore online. One good site for owner-direct listings is ecoturismorural.com

Useful terms for Spanish rentals:

E	*estudio*	studio apartment
1D	*un dormitorio*	one bedroom
2D	*dos dormitorios*	two bedrooms
PY	*playa*	beach
AM	*alta montaña*	mountainous area
TA	*temporada alta*	high season
TM	*temporada media*	shoulder season
TB	*temporada baja*	low season
CX	*cama supletoria*	extra bed
CC	*casa completa*	whole house
Ta	*todo el año*	year-round
	quincena	two weeks

Strategy: Spain can be simplistically divided into three areas: the cities, the country, and the tourist strip along the Mediterranean coast.

Organized tourism in Spain focuses largely on the east coast, so rentals here are abundant. Spending a few weeks in a concrete high-rise tourist playground, however, may not be the best way to catch the flavor of Spain. If you do want to stay on the coast, agencies like www.iha.com and www.homelidays .com have listings anywhere from $350 to $3,500 per week.

Renting in the country is certainly a more authentically Spanish option, and finally there are starting to be plenty of available properties. Spain has undergone massive waves of migration to the cities in recent decades; you can drive through many abandoned villages in rural areas, where the entire population moved to the city during the 1950s and 1960s in search of work. The Italians recycled such old farmhouses into tourist moneymakers early on, but in Spain most old houses until recently sat forlornly by the roadside, still lacking electricity and plumbing.

Rural tourism has caught on big-time in the last decade. Properties are being made over and marketed both as B&Bs and as rentals. Today, in fact, rural rentals are much easier to find than those in town. Most Spaniards aren't interested in living anywhere but in the cities. This makes city housing tight. The villagers who left Spain's small towns a few decades ago have filled the drab high-rises that guard the outskirts of every Spanish city, leaving no room for travelers like us.

In contrast to America, where the poor live in the inner city and the rich live in outlying suburbs, in Spain the pattern is reversed: The poorer you are, for the most part, the farther from the center of town you live. For Spaniards an apartment in the city makes it easy to wander through the streets during the evening paseo (a ritual nightly stroll) and meet friends in the neighborhood bar. Living in the suburbs would mean two commutes a day for everyone in the family, since many businesses and schools still observe the split workday and close for three hours at lunchtime. Other cultural factors compound Spain's housing situation. Freestanding houses are uncommon in urban areas, and three-fourths of Spanish apartments are owner occupied and never offered as rentals.

At a time when Spanish rentals were harder to find, we called on personal ties to find an apartment in Salamanca. Lew's alma mater gave us the name of the woman who finds housing for their exchange students, and she hooked us up with a friend whose mother had just entered a nursing home. Mama's apartment was no palace. It needed routine repairs, but our rent was low, and we learned a lot about normal Spanish life by scurrying here and there for window glass, plywood, a dish rack, and a mailbox lock. Lew felt he'd taken his final exam in Spanish—and passed with flying colors—when he called a repairman to fix our water heater and was able to explain the problem. We were reimbursed for our expenses and, in the end, grew rather attached to our little apartment. The location was convenient to everything, and the building's central courtyard teemed with kids, providing Libby and Sam with many good friends.

Expectations: As in much of Europe, central heating is less widespread. Your Spanish rental may include a portable space heater or the traditional *brasero,* a heater that's built into the base of a table. Historically a charcoal heater, the *brasero* has fortunately evolved into a safer electrical heater. *Braseros* don't heat a room, let alone an entire dwelling: They're only useful if everyone in the family sits at the table, legs tucked under the long, thick tablecloth. If you're in Spain during a cold spell, you'll find the *brasero* strongly rewards family togetherness!

Bed pillows encourage closeness, too. Double beds throughout Spain may have a single, wide pillow that stretches the width of the bed. If you sleep with a pillow and your spouse doesn't, or if one of you regularly kneads the pillow into a ball, be prepared to work out a plan for peaceful coexistence.

Your home is unlikely to sport a dishwasher, so be prepared to wash your dishes by hand, then hang them on the wall—in the *escurridor* (dish rack)—to drip. You also may not find a washing machine and almost certainly not a dryer: Spanish women hang their laundry out to dry daily, as clotheslines on every floor of every apartment building attest. If this isn't your idea of a vacation and you decide to take your wash out, you'll find that coin laundries are much rarer in Spain than in most other European countries. Don't despair, though: There's a *lavanderia* on almost every corner that will wash, dry, and fold your clothes for not much more than you'd pay to sit all morning feeding coins into the machines yourself.

other countries

We've gone into great detail for the five countries most often visited by American tourists. It used to be challenging to find rentals in smaller countries. But today, thanks to the Internet, you can find a great house or apartment almost anywhere with relatively little effort. You can check Interhome, Homelidays or IHA for almost every country, so start there first. Or simply type "Austria rental house" or "Switzerland self-catering" or something similar into your favorite search engine. Following are some additional specifics for other European countries; see chapter 22 for more details.

Austria. Interhome, based in neighboring Switzerland, lists a large number of Austrian properties starting at about $325 per week. Local tourist offices may also be able to help with self-catered cottages or arrange farmstays of a week or more. Write to Verkehrsverein, followed by the name of any town. A great site for booking rural accommodations is www.farmholidays.com.

Belgium. The NTO's Web site at www.visitbelgium.com has limited listings of apartments and farm stays under "Where to Stay"; you can also check out www.gitesdewallonie.net. Beyond that, check out the pan-European rental Web sites mentioned in this chapter; we're not aware of any Web sites or agencies that specialize in Belgium.

Denmark. Two Web sites stand out for Denmark: www.cottage-rental.com and www.novasol.com. Reasonable listings start at under $300 per week in the off-season and about $450 per week in summer. Properties are mainly compact, modern bungalows built as vacation homes in the country.

Greece. This used to be a tough country in which to find rentals. Now things are better. Try the Web at www.greeklodging.com or www.greecetravel.com/villas for a good selection of properties.

Ireland. Start on the Web at www.irelandvacations.com (the Web site of the Irish National Tourist Board) or at Irish Cottage Holiday Homes (www.irishcottageholidays.com). Prices are about $160 to $800 per week, and rentals range from newly built vacation colonies to ancient thatched cottages.

Norway. Norway is well served by Novasol (www.novasol.com), which bought out the previously recommended Norwegian agency Fjordhytter and took its great catalog online. The site provides detailed listings and clear booking information, plus a great search engine, for more than 12,000 holiday properties. Homes are almost always private vacation homes, and prices start at about $180 per week in the off-season and $320 in high season. Read listings carefully, as some homes are rustic, with no hot water and electricity or with outside toilets.

Sweden. Destinations Stockholms Skårgård (www.dess.se) offers cottages in the Swedish archipelago starting at about $250 off-season and $350 midsummer. Book seven to eight months ahead for high season. Another great Web site, www.swedenhomerentals.se, covers rentals all over Sweden, starting at about $300 per week.

Switzerland. On the Web, www.holiday-home.ch and Interhome are the best places to start, with hundreds of rentals all over Switzerland. Schweizer Reisekasse (www.reka.ch), a nonprofit organization devoted to inexpensive family vacations, offers some 1,100 rentals, but the Web site is only in German, French, and Italian. The national tourist office has information on farm holidays *(Ferien auf dem Bauernhof)* as well as an online booking service at www.myswitzerland.com.

I was very impressed by Switzerland's Tourism Office. They provided us with two books on farming vacations that had a lot of detail, from how many languages were spoken at the farm, to how many children lived there, ages, if guests could help with farm work, what animals they had, housing facilities, distance to train or bus, meals included—incredible how organized they were.

—Patty Dodd, El Segundo, CA

---

f'rinstance

All the theoretical information in the world just doesn't substitute for real-world examples. I hope the following ones will help you picture yourself in your own overseas rental or exchange home.

Cheltenham, England. Cheltenham, an elegant small city in the Cotswolds, two hours west of London, is known throughout England as a genteel place for military widows to retire. Our house—half a 1960s duplex—was neither elegant nor regal. But it sported three bedrooms, bath, kitchen, dining room, and living room and included color television, washer and dryer, and clean linens each week. We found this monthlong rental through the local tourist office.

Uninspiring in itself, our Cheltenham rental shared the street with Victorian brick row houses and half-timbered thatched-roof cottages. A community cricket and soccer field, an elementary school, a convenience store, and a city bus stop were within blocks. *(Harrimans)*

Chard, England. Our house in this small market town, halfway between Exeter and Salisbury, was on the main street, near all the small shops. Seeing us day after day for two weeks, the shopkeepers overcame their British reserve and became quite chatty. Our kids loved the newsagents—the local variety/candy store—and the butcher and baker were fascinated by "their first Americans."

The house we rented was two-thirds of a greystone "maisonette" with three bedrooms, bath, sitting room, kitchen, and color television. Linens weren't provided; Dan and I brought sheets, and the kids used sleeping bags. We shared a lovely yard and swimming pool with the owners, who lived in the other third of the house, but sharing wasn't difficult: Only our hardy kids were tempted by the pool in England's mild climate. *(Hallinans)*

Upton-on-Severn, England. Near Tewksbury, in Gloucestershire, we rented a half-timbered cottage on the grounds of Puckrup Manor. It was classic English countryside—down a winding lane lined with hedgerows, surrounded by wandering cows, and complete with a pretty garden and a little teahouse. The kids enjoyed exploring the Iron Age hill-fort on the property, but we missed the daily contact with the townspeople that we had had in Chard.

To our initial disappointment, the cottage was much modernized inside, with only one original wall remaining. But when it came to living there for a week, we appreciated its modern plumbing, color television, and washer. *(Hallinans)*

London, England. The London flat we rented for four weeks—two weeks at the start of our trip, and two more at the end—was a real bargain compared with hotel rooms. With two small bedrooms, bathroom, and living/dining/kitchen, it was crowded for five people, but very "homely"—as the English say when they mean homey.

Our building, though new, had character, as it had been built in the middle of an old cemetery. The ancient graves had been removed, and the gravestones were incorporated into the walls of the obligatory garden. And the location was great: right near Marble Arch tube and bus stops, just a half block from Hyde Park.

The most important thing to consider in London is location, since it's a large city, and access to public transportation is essential. Almost any residential area close to a tube stop is good, but try to stay close to the city center; if you end up north of Hampstead Heath, you'll spend at least an hour each way on the tube to reach the center of London. *(Hallinans)*

Plouer-sur-Rance, France. Our only disappointment. This home, rented through a local tourist office listing, sounded great: three bedrooms, garden, near quiet village center on a tidal estuary in Brittany. But an honest description might have read, "One-half a former funeral parlor, surrounded by a cemetery and a huge old-folks home in a grimy, deserted village in Brittany, where half the buildings are for sale. 3 bedrooms, 1 bath, kitchen, living/dining room. Only redeeming points: lovely flower garden and a surprising palm tree."

We left after one night, concerned that the kids would meet no other children and we'd be miserable. We lost the $600 we had paid—Madame denied deceiving us and took offense at our aversion to the funeral parlor and to the motorcycle gangs that raced up and down the "quiet" street. But it seemed senseless, at that point, to waste a month's vacation. And my French, adequate for the basics, was not up to arguing with an angry Frenchwoman. How could we have avoided this disaster? We should have asked for a sketch of the neighborhood, or, on arrival, have expressed our misgivings before we foolishly paid up the rent in full. The third option might have been to simply stay put, meet the neighbors, and make the best of it. Who knows? Plouer might have turned out to be a wonderful, warm village, and we may have missed the cultural experience of our lives. *(Harrimans)*

St. Enogat (Dinard), France. An honest listing for the replacement house we found in Brittany might have read: "Freestanding granite cottage surrounded by grass and trees of a public park, within 200 feet of the English Channel. 2 bedrooms, kitchen, living/dining room, 1 bath (sink, bidet, tub), 1 w.c., extra sink on landing near bedrooms. Barbecue, lawn chairs, and beach umbrella included."

We escaped from the Plouer disaster to the lovely Edwardian coastal resort of Dinard. This time we dealt with an agency: We wanted a more professional approach and the chance to debate in English if problems arose. Our agent quickly found us the perfect house in the outlying district of St. Enogat. St. Enogat featured two wonderful bakeries and a clean, wide beach with rocky cliffs bordered by safe promenades. This wonderful area is inundated with Brits in the summer, so many people speak some English. Yet in the off-season (before June 15) the weather can be beautiful, prices are cheaper, and the atmosphere is very French. One disadvantage to the off-season was that most neighboring houses were unoccupied, and French children were still in school. We didn't meet many local families as a result, but we had lovely picnics, hiked for miles along the cliffs, and dug elaborate canal systems in the sand. *(Harrimans)*

Paris apartment and boat. A week in a Paris apartment can cost almost as much as a month in the country—but it's still cheaper than putting five people up in a hotel. Chez Vous, a U.S. agency, found us a charming small apartment with two bedrooms, bath, tiny kitchen, and even tinier living/ dining area.

A fifth-floor walk-up in a nondescript building near the Eiffel Tower, it was located just off a wonderful shopping street, full of the best France has to offer: patisserie (pastry shop), boulangerie (bakery), and charcuterie (rather like a deli), all within walking distance. It did not take us long to discover the wonders of French charcuterie—salmon puff pastries, little quiches, pâtés, and so many other wonderful things—that could be brought home and reheated in our own kitchen for dinner, without taking the kids out to an expensive restaurant every night.

Our children enjoyed Paris so much they wanted to return later. Chez Vous's French office rented us a *peniche*—a barge moored on the Seine alongside the Tuileries Gardens. It was one of the highlights of our trip. We had the entire boat to ourselves—two bedrooms, kitchen, bathroom, and an immense living room the kids could play in when it rained. Unfortunately this barge is no longer available, but Chez Vous rents apartments in a neighboring barge, which is much ritzier. The price is high, but the experience is unforgettable. *(Hallinans)*

Salamanca, Spain. We found our Salamanca apartment through personal connections. It consisted of two bedrooms, living room, kitchen, and bathroom in a large, older building arranged around a courtyard. We huddled around its *brasero* in an unexpected April cold spell and generated a little extra warmth by actively scrubbing down its neglected interior.

But although this rental was neither modern nor spotless, it was just what we wanted. The rent was low, and the neighbors were kind. Our landlady plied us with extra blankets, gifts, and love, and our kids joined in courtyard soccer games from the second day of our visit. It was an easy walk to Salamanca's beautiful Plaza Mayor or to the neighborhood bar for wine and tapas. On reflection, the apartment worked out great, and we're grateful to Mari-Tere for her help. *(Harrimans)*

Bagni di Lucca, Italy. Our Tuscan villa was a large rambling building in a medieval hill town where the houses grew organically into each other—it was impossible to tell where our house stopped and another began.

In our case, the word villa was appropriate. Not only did we have five bedrooms, two baths, a huge family room, kitchen, and dining room, but we also had two huge halls, a small courtyard for play and outdoor dining, and our own chapel. What's more, the deal (arranged through a friend of our travel agent) even included some modern amenities such as a black-and-white television and a washer/dryer.

The house turned out to be geographically isolated, a fact that was both an advantage and a disadvantage. What appeared on the map to be an easy twenty-minute drive from Lucca (between Pisa and Florence) was in fact a forty-five-minute trip to the base of the hill and another ten minutes of terrifying turns up to the village. We then had to park outside the town and walk to our house through narrow passages—a lovely stroll, but one that added to the trek.

On the other hand, Bagni di Lucca's isolation was also its strongest point. All of us, including the kids, enjoyed this place especially, as the foreignness of the town was totally unlike anything we had experienced. If this charming hill town had been easier to get to, it probably would have lost its medieval Italian flavor long ago! *(Hallinans)*

chapter 13

home cooking

If you've decided to spend some time in a rental home, you'll be cooking in instead of eating out and concerning yourselves with several issues involved in shopping and cooking in any foreign country.

what is food?

Europeans tend to have different attitudes toward food from most Americans. As Americans we aren't often reminded that our food once grew in the mud or ran around a farmyard on four legs. We demand unblemished produce, as if dry spells and bugs didn't exist. We eat only meat that's shaped like a serving and turn up our noses at anything that resembles a recognizable animal.

Europeans are more apt to believe in live food, fresh food. Even in supermarkets, you're apt to see whole skinned rabbits, fish with glassy eyes, calves' brains, and pigs' ears, all unmistakably tied to their sources by appearance. European cooks find a close-to-the-source product their best guarantee of freshness, a testimony to a historic lack of refrigeration. I once read an interview with a famous Italian cook who said she got discouraged and lost her appetite in American supermarkets because "all the food is dead and in coffins of plastic."

To people in areas where cooling hasn't always been prevalent, dead means unsafe, spoiled, low quality. To Americans, dead has come to mean guaranteed, sanitized. To us, food comes from supermarkets; it doesn't come from fields and barnyards. The Spanish housewife doesn't see it as a disadvantage that she has to look her fish in the eye at the market—she finds it reassuring.

Most of us won't have the same reaction. The realities of facing real food may take a bit of mental adjustment. But learning to appreciate real, local food can be a huge benefit of a European trip.

where to shop

Most European towns and cities offer three options for food shopping: the traditional open-air or covered market, the modern supermarket, and the small mom-and-pop store.

traditional markets

Traditional markets are what most of us imagine when we conjure up a vision of shopping for food in Europe. There we are, wandering into a narrow village street of covered stalls on market day and picking over the brilliant red tomatoes. Or ducking under the iron-and-glass dome of an immense art nouveau covered marketplace, where scores of pleasant peasants offer quaint baskets of fruit and cheese. After all, one of the reasons we take trips like this is to immerse ourselves in local tradition, to escape the plastic anonymity of American supermarkets.

The reality of the traditional market is very different. And it can be a bit disconcerting at first, especially to your kids. The smells and sights of such a market—strong cheeses, pickled vegetables, hanging meat carcasses—can turn the stomachs of the uninitiated. Even if you're not a hopeless Hamburger Helper cook, you more likely associate "fresh and unprocessed" with "in raw, moist slices" or "sold in a wooden bin," not with "feathers and eyes still intact" or "still moving vigorously."

You may prefer to enjoy the traditional market for its rich sights, smells, and sounds, then scuttle to the neighborhood supermarket to do your shopping.

supermarkets

Shopping at the supermarket in Europe has several advantages:

- Your neighbors are there, too, so it's not a complete cop-out. Europe is not really a continent where grandmotherly types in kerchiefs spend their whole day loading fresh vegetables into a handy string bag. Women here are just as busy as anywhere and love the convenience of supermarkets.

- You'll be able to pay your bill with VISA. Supermarkets in many countries readily accept credit cards at the checkout counter, cutting down on the amount of local cash you'll have to carry around.

- You won't need as much knowledge of the language to get by. For many this may be the biggest advantage. In the open market you'll need to know all the words for all the foods you want. You'll need to know how to think in kilos and grams, and how to express your thoughts in the right numbers. At a supermarket much of your shopping will consist of pulling things from shelves and sticking them in your cart, then thrusting a handful of bills or a credit card at the cashier. (Consider this from both sides: Many of you may enjoy the extra learning that comes from the challenge of face-to-face marketing.)

- You'll be able to find some American foods there to ease the transition for any finicky eaters in the family. Breakfast cereals, milk, tortellini, dry soup mixes—all these more familiar foods helped our kids eat well at one meal, while we tried new things at the next.

- You'll be able to find foreign junk food. Why on earth is this an advantage? Because junk foods are a wonderful way to encourage the unadventurous to try new foods. Amazingly, many countries far surpass the United States in their ability to concoct utterly useless packaged snack foods. Let your kids pick one each time you go shopping. Once they've successfully ventured beyond the known in junk food, they're more apt to experiment with more useful foods, too.

mom-and-pop stores

In addition to these two options, European countries all feature a large number of small neighborhood markets. Some of these are like our convenience stores and offer the same no-language-needed impersonality of supermarkets, as described earlier.

Others, though, reflect a long tradition of specialty stores: butchers, bakers, greengrocers, and so on. Almost always these stores offer very high quality and excellent service for a little more money than the open markets or the supermarkets. And shopping in these stores almost invariably requires some mastery of the local language.

If you do have the necessary language skills, getting to know these local purveyors is a rewarding part of living in a town or neighborhood. In Spain you might shop at your local *fruteria* (fruit shop) or the neighborhood *despacio de pan* (store where bread is sold but not baked). In France you'll probably get addicted to the nearest charcuterie, a delilike place that offers a wide variety of ready-to-warm-up main dishes.

when to shop

You're likely to shop more often in Europe than you do at home. European refrigerators are small—commonly 4 to 6 cubic feet, like the small "dorm" or office refrigerators sold in the States. American fridges, by contrast, are commonly 18 to 23 cubic feet, with a freezer compartment only slightly smaller than a typical European family refrigerator.

This difference is partially due to smaller houses and apartments and to higher energy costs. But that can't be the whole answer—larger fridges aren't even displayed in most appliance stores for those with larger houses and paychecks. The truth lies in the European preference for fresh food and in most people's different eating habits. If you're going to buy fresh meat, vegetables, and dairy products every day or two and if you don't buy fresh milk by the gallon, you just don't need that much storage space for your perishables.

The days and hours when stores are open become important when you must shop frequently. Don't count on the twenty-four-hour supermarket you've gotten used to at home! Find out about the local hours when you first arrive so you won't be caught by surprise. In Spain, for instance, stores are usually closed from two to five in the afternoon. And in France stores are often closed on Monday—though each town usually makes sure one bakery and one small grocery remain open. In all countries Sunday hours may be limited.

what's for dinner?

Once you get your food home and packed into your tiny refrigerator, it's time to start cooking. Your rental home will come with pans and dishes, but the rest is up to you.

You have two obvious choices: You can cook your family's favorite dishes from back home or cook local specialties. Either way, you'll face a few small hurdles. If you opt for old favorites, you may find certain ingredients are unobtainable locally. (I couldn't locate cornstarch for Chinese sweet-and-sour pork in Spain, though a helpful reader in Spain has since told me what to look for.)

You may also find that you don't know as many recipes by heart as you thought you did. It's a good idea to bring a basic American paperback cookbook for reference, unless you will have online access to recipes.

Even better, bring one that features the specialties of the region you're visiting. Unless you're utterly fluent in the language, you'll be lost with a local cookbook—a traveler's normal vocabulary doesn't extend to phrases like "fold in egg whites" or "whip until frothy with stiff peaks." Remember, though, that if you use an American cookbook, you'll need to bring a small measuring cup and a set of measuring spoons. The only measuring devices that come with your rental will be metric ones.

If you've decided to wing it without a cookbook, even cooking supermarket packaged foods can be an experience. In Spain, for instance, there are no instructions on a box of rice; using the same amount of water and cooking time as Uncle Ben's Converted Rice requires at home will produce nothing but a gluey mess. And yet as recently as the 1990s, a box of Rice Krispies came with full instructions: "Pour into bowl. Pour on just enough milk to cover cereal. Eat with a teaspoon or soup spoon." Every housewife in Spain knows how to cook rice, but breakfast cereals are newer and less familiar to some.

grocery shopping, country by country

Exploring grocery stores can be one of traveling's greatest everyday pleasures. In our travels we've devoted as much as three to five hours each week to "sightseeing" at the markets. If you're spending less time overseas, however, you might want to get up to speed as quickly as possible. Let's look at some generalities about European supermarkets, then delve into some local peculiarities in England, France, Italy, and Spain.

European supermarkets

These common tips on food and procedures apply to most supermarkets throughout Europe.

- Carts are usually neatly chained to each other in designated areas—a system getting off the ground in parts of the United States. To get a cart you slide a small coin into the slot of a little box attached to the cart's handle. As the coin drops the chain hooking your cart to the next one in line disconnects, freeing the cart. When you're done shopping, simply reattach the chain, and your coin is returned to you.

- You will usually be expected to bag your own groceries. In some places you will also be charged a small fee for each bag, so you may want to bring your own string bags like the locals. Credit cards are accepted almost everywhere (and were long before U.S. grocers accepted them).

- As you browse prices, remember to convert currency and weight. European food is sold by the kilo, which is 2.2 pounds, making everything look twice as expensive even before you factor in the euro (or pound or Swiss franc).

- Fruits and vegetables must usually be weighed in the produce department. You will be scolded at the checkout if you arrive with unlabeled produce! Either there will be a produce clerk to do this or an automatic icon-driven scale. Place your peaches on the scale, push the button with a picture of a peach, and the machine spits out an adhesive label for your bag. Your kids may eat more fruits and vegetables in Europe because they like to push those buttons so much.

- Milk is most commonly sterilized and found on unrefrigerated shelves in paper cartons (larger versions of the juice brick packs common in the States). Sterilized milk tastes best served up hot for breakfast with Nestlé's Quik (the most common chocolate powder in many countries) mixed in. When fresh milk can be found, it's often in small quantities (never gallons) and rarely low-fat or fat-free.

- Cheeses are abundant and delightful. Try something new every time! Store personnel may not be willing to slice it for you. In Europe cheese is more often eaten as a dessert course than sliced on sandwiches, and some countries' health laws prohibit deli department meat slicers from cutting cheese. Sliced cheese can usually be found in the dairy case.

- Produce is generally of higher quality. It's almost as if the vegetables were bred for taste instead of their ability to stand up to automated harvesting equipment (novel idea)! The combination of excellent vegetables and nonexistent freezer compartments will encourage you to cook more fresh vegetables than you might at home.

- Breakfast cereals are increasingly common. General Mills cereals (like Cheerios) are sold under the Nestlé name.

- Even if you avoid soft drinks, as we do, it's fun to try a few that are unavailable at home. In Europe it's common to mix flavored syrups into tap water or fizzy water. Two common flavors not found in the States are black currant (*cassis* in French) and almond (*orgeata* in Italian).

- While Europeans in general eat a healthier diet than Americans, junk food comes in an impressive variety of options. Potato chips come in bizarre flavors like ham and shrimp; they compete for snackers' attention with every manner of flavored, fried, and extruded cheese puff imaginable.

- Watch out if you try to bake. Both sugar and flour are processed differently and may react differently in your favorite recipes. Baking powder sometimes comes with vanilla already added.

- Ah . . . chocolate. Notice we didn't put it with the junk food. Good dark chocolate—the kind most often found in Europe—actually has surprising health benefits. Most supermarkets have delightfully complete selections at a variety of price points, and with various nuts and dried fruit mixed in.

english supermarkets

English supermarkets often include many extras that make them pleasant places to shop: in-house coffee shop and pharmacy, miniature shopping carts for Mommy's little helpers, and ample diaper-changing areas in the clean bathrooms. The stores are large, modern, and well stocked. Some major observations about price and products:

- Milk is widely available and similar in taste to American milk, since milk drinking is more common in England than on the Continent.

- Produce is not up to French or Italian standards but is better than American and extremely varied. Exotics like star fruit are common. The English use different French-derived names for several vegetables. A few you're apt to encounter include aubergine (eggplant), courgette (zucchini), and mange-tout (snow peas).

- Beverage aisles include shelf after shelf of ales, including thick Scottish ales that taste as if they're made with oatmeal, and shandy, a drink made of half beer and half lemonade. Squash is a common soft drink, usually a sort of watery orange soda. Ginger beer is a stronger (and sometimes slightly alcoholic) version of ginger ale. Apple juice is often carbonated— look for the word *sparkling* on the bottle or can.

- Snack foods run largely to biscuits (cookies), crisps (potato chips), and sweets (candy). All of these can be found in exhaustive variety in English supermarkets. Your kids, like ours, will probably try to convince you that it's their cultural duty to explore as many varieties as possible.

- Bake mixes are very common, including all manner of cakes and puddings. One look at the baking-mix aisle serves to remind visitors that pastry shops, so widespread in France and Spain, are not as ubiquitous here.

- Meats are of lesser quality than in France or Spain and more expensive (as is everything in England). Ham roasts are very salty and don't come pre-cooked as they do in the states. Dan and Wendy's request for spareribs was met with incredulity: "You mean you want us to cut off most of the meat and just give you the bones???" And their order for beef patties sent the butcher into gales of laughter. In England "patties" refers only to cow pats left on the floor of the barn.

french supermarkets

French supermarkets are much like ours—a mix of smaller in-town establishments and mall superstores. But the superstores are even larger than ours, often combining an enormous grocery with a discount store that sells everything from underwear to lawn chairs. There's also a chain of 600 frozen-food stores called Picard, which sells an amazing range of gourmet frozen foods—freezer after freezer of tuna tartare, fois gras, snails, stuffed duck, and artichoke mousse.

A few observations:

- Meats are very good. Routine cuts of beef and pork sell for a bit more than at home. But the meats that are most expensive in the States—veal, lamb, and special beef cuts—are cheaper in France. French people on a tight budget buy *abats*—brains, kidneys, heart, tongue, and so on—for one or two dollars per pound. Most supermarket meat is precut and plastic sealed.

- Cheeses are wonderful in France, as you might expect. We like to buy a quarter kilo each of two cheeses we know we like and an equal amount of two unknown cheeses whose appearance or name appeals to us (a few of our favorites include Carré Breton, Port Salut, and St. Paulin). In many stores your cheese will be custom cut, laid on a piece of paper, then heat sealed into its own special envelope.

- Snack foods don't include many crackers but are otherwise extremely varied. Flavored peanuts, often with a crunchy, fried coating, are very common, as are many flavored, fried, and extruded junk bits. Our kids love Nutella chocolate spread, which can be eaten on bread or simply on fingers. Cookies are easily found, though in not nearly as many varieties as in America. The best source for sweets is the pastry shop!

- Bake mixes exist, though there's nothing like the row after row of cake, cookie, and biscuit mixes in a Stateside supermarket. If you want to bake, you can also choose from several brands of puff-pastry mix in the freezer compartment.

italian supermarkets

Italian supermarkets are among the best in the world—just as you might expect in a country where good food is almost revered. Some generalizations about Italian grocery-store food:

- Meats are of comparable quality to those in France, with rabbit surprisingly common. Most supermarkets have a working butcher, who will slice or grind any cut of meat to order (if you speak enough Italian to ask!). There's usually some ready-packaged meat available if you prefer to silently grab and run.

- Deli departments feature sliced meats and an incredible variety of cheeses. Try the cheeses you think you know—like mozzarella, provolone, and Gorgonzola: The authentic version is probably very different from what you're used to. (This may not always work out well. Dan and Wendy's kids turned their noses up at real Parmesan cheese, accustomed as they were to Kraft's grated Parmesan.)

- Vegetables are of very high quality, often presented very artistically. Picture mounds of red, orange, and yellow peppers next to four colors of broccoli in purple, blue, green, and white.

- Beverages for kids include lots of brick-pack juices and at least two dozen flavors of syrups. Make sure to try *tamarindo* (from the tropical tamarind fruit) and *orgeat,* an almond flavor similar to Spain's almond *horchata* drink.

- Vacuum-packed pasta products, like tortellini and gnocchi, are of very high quality. In every supermarket there is at least one aisle of dry packaged pasta, in every size and shape, from big, floppy elephant-ear rounds to tiny spiraled noodles. Stay long enough to try them all!

spanish supermarkets

Since most Spaniards live clustered in urban areas, Spanish supermarkets are small and tucked into the urban fabric. At most supermarkets everything is self-serve except produce and meat, for which you must place your order and be served by store personnel. Some major observations about price and products:

- Meats are of good variety and excellent quality. Spanish pork loin *(lomo)* is especially good—tender and lean. Our kids love it. The butcher will cut what you want to order. You're not likely to see hamburger, but you can ask the butcher to grind any of his meats for you at no extra charge. Meats are priced about the same as in the United States.

- Cheeses are found both in the meat case and packaged in the dairy case. There's wonderful variety, which is good, since you're likely to prefer chewing calcium to drinking it in Spain. Our kids especially like *manchega,* a cheddarlike cheese.

- You'll find favorite cereals like Corn Flakes and Rice Krispies, along with supersweetened local variants like Miel Pops (corn pops made with honey) and Estrellitas (heavily honeyed stars). Our kids experimented with several of these, then switched to a typical Spanish bread-and-jam breakfast when they decided they didn't care for the cereal or the milk.

- Produce is of mixed quality. Fruits—especially citrus—are excellent. Vegetables are less impressive, partly because you can't pick the ones you want in most markets: Order a half kilo of peppers, for instance, and you take the peppers the produce lady decides you will have (unless you're willing to discuss the matter in rapid Spanish).

- Snack foods are big in Spain. *Marias* are small round cookies (called "digestive biscuits" in England) that taste something like an animal cracker. They're sold in boxes as big as those that hold paper diapers in an American supermarket, and Spanish kids eat a lot of them.

- On the other hand, you won't find many crackers (just a few varieties, in very small boxes) and, aside from *Marias,* almost no cookies. The Spanish are more apt to stop at a pastry shop when they want a sweet.

- Beverages sold include a wide variety of fruit juices (in large brick packs at reasonable prices), a good variety of wines and beer, and plenty of soft drinks. Try *gaseosa,* a sweetened, fizzy water. Our kids like it plain, and we enjoy it mixed with red wine to make a wine cooler–like drink the Spaniards call *tinto con gaz.*

- Bake mixes are virtually nonexistent. The Spanish housewife who thinks nothing of hacking up a whole fish and deep-frying it from scratch will almost always duck into her neighborhood pastry shop and buy a prepared dessert. Join her, and your family will appreciate it!

In Spain you'll rarely choose your own produce at the market.

communicating

I believe in a simplistic solution to world peace: If everyone in the world just got to know everyone else, war would be much less likely. I picture the globe, with threads connecting every pair of acquaintances, until eventually the whole world is bound tightly and securely together. I like collecting new threads wherever I go, and our trips to Europe have been no exception.

Yet meeting people in our European travels has proved more of a challenge than we expected. In this chapter I'll explain why, then I'll outline some ideas that may help *you* do better. Finally I'll talk about language—how you can talk to the people you *do* manage to meet.

why it's hard to meet people

We're typical outgoing Americans. We thought we'd meet people at the grocery store and on the street and make new friends all over Europe. But it hasn't happened. With very few exceptions the only connections we've made are ones we planned before we left.

Stop and think about it. How do you make friends at home? Almost exclusively through people you already know: through coworkers, through members of clubs you belong to, through relatives and neighbors. Chance meetings just aren't that common. When was the last time you made a new friend in the checkout line at Wal-Mart? Have you picked anybody up at the beach since you turned nineteen?

Even when you do make these infrequent chance encounters at home, they often occur when you're alone. Family togetherness on your trip will make it all the less likely that you'll hook up with other people. The family unit eliminates a lot of the need to reach out and makes reaching in seem more daunting to others.

And that's assuming that they *want* to reach in. *You've* set out to meet the world, but those around you are just trying to go about their daily business. *You're* away from work, and they're trying to rush home in time to catch the plumber. Meeting you and your family is not first on the agenda of every inhabitant of Europe.

Cultural factors intrude, too. People in other countries make social contacts differently from most Americans. Coworkers may work cordially for years side by side without feeling compelled to attend each others' weddings, exchange birthday presents, or even find out where the other lives. (For an interesting discussion of the differences between French and American socialization, read *Cultural Misunderstandings: The French-American Experience* by Raymonde Carroll.)

Many Europeans find amusing our American tendency to disclose every detail of our personal lives at the drop of a hat. Some are offended, some are charmed, and others simply dismiss us as a bit childlike. Try to take some cues from those around you before you launch into your life story, and by all means realize the people are not personally snubbing you when your overtures aren't returned in kind.

Many families worry that anti-American feelings will mar their overseas trip, in light of Europe's differences with our government over the Iraq war. We have not encountered any problems with this in our travels since the war started. Most Europeans understand that Americans may have their own differences with the U.S. government and do not display any awkwardness in their interactions with us.

how to meet people

Despite all these obstacles, making contacts overseas is still very rewarding. But it requires you to plan ahead and take advantage of every possible connection before you leave home. A few ideas:

- **Service clubs.** If you're a member of Rotary or some other worldwide organization, you're in luck. You have a built-in network of contacts wherever you go. Write ahead, and make plans to meet someone in the group as soon as you arrive at your "home base." If you're not a Rotarian, perhaps a friend who *is* can make some contacts.

- **Sister city programs.** More than 1,200 American towns and cities are partners with more than 1,900 sister cities and towns in 121 different countries. Go to your own city or town hall—or contact Sister Cities International—and find out if any official connection exists between your hometown and someplace in Europe. Then find out how to arrange a visit.

- **Churches.** If you attend church at home, make sure to seek out the local congregation or parish overseas. Again, make contact before you leave if at all possible. Otherwise you may just get things going when it's time to leave.

- **Professional interests.** If you're a doctor, write to the local medical society or hospital, and ask to meet with other doctors. If you're a teacher, arrange to visit a school. As a computer consultant, I made contacts with Apple dealers in Spain and England that were very interesting. But in both cases it took almost three weeks of a four-week stay to get something off the ground; I should have arranged things ahead of time. Write to the local tourist office for advice long before you depart.

- **Volunteer work.** If you can speak the local language, your services as a volunteer might be helpful. Ask at city hall if there's a volunteer bureau in town or any specific charities. Even if you just stuff envelopes two afternoons a week, it's a way to learn a lot and meet other people.

- **Personal connections.** Earlier on, we suggested "Pushpin Planning" to collect ideas for places to visit. Don't limit yourself to *places,* though: Collect people, too. Does your plumber know someone in Portugal? Isn't this year's high-school exchange student from Greece? Didn't your neighbor's sister marry someone from Spain?

We met a Polish family through an international Catholic organization we belong to. The wife was studying to be an English teacher and the husband also spoke good English. They invited us to their home outside Krakow for dinner. This was certainly a highlight of the trip—spending several hours talking with a family with whom we had so much in common. "I love Polish food!" our six-year-old exclaimed to our hosts.

—Jennifer and Tim Woods, Chicago

Before our first trip, Lew wrote to a half-dozen men he had met briefly on a business trip three years before. Two, in England and in the Netherlands, made plans to meet him for a business lunch. Another, in Germany, blocked out a day when he and his wife could give all four of us a tour of their city, complete with lunch at a restaurant and afternoon strudel at their home.

The fourth, Pedro Ramos, invited us to his house in Spain for a long weekend. This shocked us: After all, Lew had met Señor Ramos only once. But Pedro and his wife, Juana, had children the same ages as ours and were eager to exchange ideas. Sam learned that Spanish ten-year-olds liked computer games as much as he did; Gema Ramos was surprised to learn that Libby, her same age, got *paid* by the neighbors for babysitting. Without a word of common language, Juana taught me how to slice up a whole fish and peel potatoes *fast,* while Lew and Pedro chattered away about the industrial dehumidification business in Spanish.

The point here, of course, is that what seems like an unlikely and tenuous connection could bring you the best cultural exchange of your trip, as it did for us. (Gema and Libby, in fact, corresponded for years after their brief meeting.) So don't dismiss any possible contact. Work to hunt up potential new friends, drop them a note with your plans, and see what happens.

pen pals and exchange students

Pen pals offer a quick way to make contacts in another country. They're also a cheap way to introduce your kids to other cultures before you're ready to invest in a trip.

Several U.S. and overseas organizations can find you pen pals in the country of your choice. World Pen Pals, in New York, is typical. Contact them and for $3 they'll match your child with another from a foreign country (your choice of gender and continent guaranteed; they'll do their best to meet country-specific requests).

Pen-pal options exist on the Internet, too. At www.kidscom.com, for instance, pick "Make Friends," then "Find a Key Pal." Then you can fill in information about your interests and some variable about what you want in a pen pal (country, age, gender, etc.), and you'll be matched up electronically for an e-mail pen-pal relationship.

You might also consider hosting an exchange student in your home now so you'll have some overseas contacts when you travel. This may not be true in all communities, but in our town of Portsmouth, New Hampshire, we see frequent announcements in the local paper asking for families to host visiting students.

In Strasbourg we visited the family of our exchange student who had lived with us for two weeks in the States. That was an amazing experience! They invited us to their home, took us around Strasbourg and the Black Forest and took us out for flambé in a traditional Alsatian restaurant. That type of insider tour guide and perspective is so invaluable. Mathieu was with us two years ago, and it was so fun to see him and his home.

Kaira Sturdivant Rouda, Columbus, OH

Make friends now, before it's time to leave home. By the time your family is ready to travel, your child will already have a "best friend" in the country you're planning to visit.

meet-a-family programs

If despite all your efforts you can't find a personal contact in some location, look to official organizations, either locally or globally.

Many countries or individual towns will help you hook up with local families. Once you decide where you'll be traveling, contact all tourist offices on your itinerary, tell them your travel dates, and say you'd like to meet a local family with similar-age children. Some have formal "Meet the People" programs; others will find you a contact even if they have no specific program.

You can also turn to worldwide friendship programs. An excellent program of this type is SERVAS, dedicated to promoting peace and understanding through home hospitality in more than 130 countries. You join either as a "host" or a "visitor" (or both), a process that involves a personal interview. (The interview weeds out those merely interested in free lodgings from those who relish the rewarding but exhausting process of trading ideas.) Once your membership is approved, you can contact other SERVAS members from the directory provided to arrange homestays (usually two days) or "day hosting" without lodging. After you return home, you can also look forward to visits from SERVAS members.

Less structured programs exist, too. One of the largest is CouchSurfing (www.couchsurfing.com), with 200,000 members in more than 200 countries. Eighty-four percent of CouchSurfing members speak English, and a large number of them are in Europe, so this organization offers copious opportunities for connecting with other families. While the name refers to the possibility of sleeping on someone else's couch, overnight stays are usually difficult for more than two people. But that's okay, because Couch-Surfers can also specify that they're just looking for coffee and connections.

Sign up online, then search members' profiles in the places you'll be visiting. There's no overt category for families, but if you put "family, kids, children" in the keyword field, you'll quickly find listings like this one in Belgium:

Not everyone welcomes kids, and not everyone has room for an entire family to stay overnight. But all of the members are gregarious people sincerely interested in international friendship. Stay in a hostel, and share dessert or a playground visit with a family. Write to a CouchSurfing member for advice on meeting local families. Clubs like this are a great resource for any family with imagination.

what to do with your contacts

So now you've managed to gather some good potential contacts. What should you do next?

You should *not* try to get yourself invited to stay. Unless a program like SERVAS encourages home hospitality, you should never assume or suggest this.

Instead write a friendly letter explaining who you are and what your itinerary is and ask if you can take them to lunch when you are in their town. Carol Andrus, in *Transitions Abroad* magazine, writes about her experience using this approach for a visit to India.

> [I said] that I was planning my first trip to India that summer and that I was interested in absolutely everything—music, art, history, people, customs, food, handicrafts, wildlife, etc.—and that I would appreciate any consideration or hospitality they could extend me. I said I would call them when I got there. Might I invite them (and spouse) to dinner to tell me about their city? Would they be my guest at a concert or museum? This clearly signaled that I was not just trying to line up a date or a free meal.

Andrus's contacts were even vaguer than our contact with the Ramoses: They included a gift-shop owner in Kashmir where her dentist had once bought a souvenir, a student from Calcutta who once sold a Bible to her aunt, and the mother of a New York cabbie. Yet each of these turned into rewarding meetings where she learned a lot about local culture and history. There's no reason this approach couldn't work for you, too. It's worth the effort.

meeting other kids

Children needn't plan ahead as much as adults: They're much more likely to make chance encounters. Your part in helping this happen lies in choosing a home base that's conducive to kids getting together. Make sure to ask about nearby parks and schools, and find out whether many other children live nearby.

We were very fortunate in Spain because of the large central courtyard (*patio*) in our apartment building. That architectural serendipity, together with the fact that Spanish schools have limited hours, made it easy for Lib and Sam to make plenty of friends in Spain.

France was different. Our second house lay between a park and a beach, yet we met no French kids our entire stay. After the first week I asked the friendly clerk at the bakery where all the children were. Eyeing my kids a bit suspiciously, she answered, "In France, Madame, the children are in school in May." "But after school," I persisted. "After school," she said patiently, "they are doing their homework."

In England we left nothing to chance. Though Libby is perfectly content on her own, Sam depends on packs of active friends for happiness. Therefore, as soon as we arrived at our English home base, we signed him up for day camp from an ad in the local paper. It was a simple affair at a local school and not too expensive as camps go. Sam thrived, making friends quickly and coming home each day with a thick (and entirely unconscious) British accent. "Camp was smashing today, Mum. I did shooting and fencing with Angus and Jenkins, but cricket was *ever* so boring."

Look into organized activities like this for your kids before you leave. The local tourist office can send you a schedule of summer crafts and sports classes. If your child's in Scouts, you might also try to hook up with the local Scout troop while you're in town.

language and communication skills

How much language is enough? Is there any point in making contact with people who might not speak English? Should I take an intensive language course before I leave?

Language skills are an important issue. Certainly it's helpful if at least one member of your family speaks the language of your home base. You can save money, for instance, dealing directly with landlords instead of using an agency. And you'll have a wider universe of potential contacts if they needn't speak English.

Yet these language skills are *not* essential to a successful trip to Europe. And in fact, some language ability in your family can cause surprising tensions between family members. In some ways it may be better if you're all stumbling along equally.

We left for our first European trip with two strong languages in the family (Lew had learned Spanish in a year spent in Spain at age thirteen; I had majored in French in college; and Libby was just finishing second-year Spanish). We came back with some surprising convictions about the place of language skills. Our experience taught us that:

- Attitude is more essential to communication than language.

- Language skills aren't easy to pick up on a family trip. There's no "total immersion" when you're with your family.

- Language skills—who has them and who doesn't—can play a big part in family dynamics.

Our experience in Spain clearly illustrates these three points. Before we left I plunged myself into an unsuccessful crusade to learn Spanish and to teach it to Sam. We repeated mindless dialogs from a children's tape-and-book set called *Teach Your Child Spanish*. We had a few vocabulary sessions with Lew and learned how difficult it is to translate a family relationship into a student/teacher one. We bought a children's picture-dictionary book called *The First Thousand Words of Spanish* and devised games that helped both of us learn a few words. I even took a half-dozen hourlong lessons with a Colombian woman who advertised "Native Spanish speaker will help you learn or brush up on your Spanish."

Through these ploys I arrived knowing enough Spanish to pick out a few words on a menu. But I was paralyzed by the knowledge of how little I knew. I stayed inside, studying my books. Sam, meanwhile, had no such inhibitions. On our second day in Salamanca, without any hesitation he joined the swarm of Spanish kids eternally kicking a soccer ball around the courtyard of our apartment building. After he came in from his first encounter, we asked him who his new friends were.

"I don't really know their names. I think maybe one of them is called Oscar."

"Are they about your age?" Lew persisted.

"I don't *know,* Dad. We were just playing soccer."

He'd been out there for three hours and had done fine without Spanish—because he spoke soccer.

Libby illustrated the same essential communication skills in France. Without knowing a word of French, she'd often run up to the grocery or the bakery on her own to get sweets. "After all," she reasoned, "all you have to do is put something down on the counter, and hand them the money."

"But what if they say something to you?" I asked.

"Easy," she replied. "I just say something complicated in English, and they leave me alone."

Amused at this effective survival strategy, I asked Libby how she had arrived at this approach. "I figured it out in Spain," she reported. "One day when you were out, a guy came to the door. I think he was trying to get me to donate organs for transplant or something. I told him I didn't speak Spanish, but he didn't believe me—I guess, because I was saying it in pretty decent Spanish. I repeated it over and over, but he kept making his pitch. Finally I just said to him real fast in English, 'Hey. I can't speak Spanish, already. I'm really not going to donate any organs today, so excuse me while I shut the door'—and he backed off." She looked up at us with a triumphant grin. Pretty good system, huh?

Both my kids had learned what I had not: Make do with what you already know, and get out there and use it! A sincere wish to communicate will eventually overcome any language barrier.

seven basic words and phrases

Still, a few small efforts will help you hurdle the language barrier more smoothly. If you don't speak the language of the country you're in, take the time to memorize seven key words and phrases in the host language:

Hello	*Please*	*Do you speak English?*
Thank you	*You're welcome*	*Where are the toilets?*
Excuse me		

Trust me: These key phrases will go a long way. If you walk into a store or restaurant and simply start speaking English, you're rudely assuming the employees speak your language; you're making it clear you don't even care to try. The difference in effect is magical when you do nothing more than preface your English with *Hello, do you speak English, please?* in their language.

We carry phrase books with us for the major countries we plan to visit. But for small countries we visit briefly, like Holland and Denmark, we make it a practice to start our visit at a local tourist office. There we ask the inevitably bilingual clerks to teach us the seven key words and phrases. We write them down phonetically, so we can remember the approximate pronunciation, then we're ready to go forth.

a little notepad

Also essential to better communication is a small notepad for drawing and writing what you'd like to communicate. Pictures and written words can often succeed where spoken words are misunderstood completely. If someone is giving you directions, for instance, it's much easier to whip out your pad and ask them to draw a map. Shopkeepers will be glad to write down the price of an item so you can see the numerals instead of having to listen to the words. Keep your pad someplace where you can always take it out quickly and easily.

be silly

Above all, don't forget that most of the height of the language barrier is made up of dignity. If you can let go of your pride, you'll communicate much more easily.

A waitress in Germany illustrated this beautifully. We were in Lüneberg at a neighborhood tavern where none of the three employees spoke English—and we, at the time, spoke no German. One waitress, on seeing us painstakingly decipher every menu entry with our dictionary, rushed over, grabbed the menu, pointed to the first item and snuffled deep in the back of her throat—a rather startling and unappetizing sound. In seconds Sam realized we were taking part in a game of international charades. "She's a pig!" he shouted. We caught on immediately: The first menu item was some kind of pork.

On it went, down the whole menu. A loud "Mooooo" for beef and a smaller, quieter one for veal. Chickens clucking. Only one dish stumped this wonderfully uninhibited actress—what kind of noise *does* a cream sauce make? —forcing her to snatch my phrase book and point out the meaning of *sahne.*

We ended up with four delicious dinners and about ten minutes of uproarious entertainment, thanks to a waitress who didn't stand on ceremony.

three language levels

This isn't to say that a good repertoire of grunts, a lack of self-consciousness, and a phrase book are enough to get everyone through every situation. Our experience makes me think there are three levels of fluency in a foreign language, levels that I'll call *survival, literacy,* and *complete fluency.*

survival

Survival describes the German waitress who communicated in English without knowing a word of it. Survival-level skills have allowed us to order meals, fill the tank, find a room, and follow road signs in countries like Denmark, Belgium, and Germany, even when we didn't speak a word of Danish, Flemish, or German. Road signs usually use icons and internationally accepted symbols. Menus often include French or English translations. Memorizing a few simple lines from a pocket phrase book takes care of gas stations and hotels. Survival gets you around any country just fine when everything's going well.

Why don't we just speak English? We could. Today English is recognized increasingly as the lingua franca of a United Europe and of the world, a badge of international community rather than American dominance. But we are reluctant to speak English if it is at all avoidable, as we do not want to be seen as Ugly Americans, unwilling to make the effort to communicate in another language.

literacy

Literacy, the second level of language proficiency, kicks in when you get beyond survival skills, when you can carry on simple conversations and understand a newspaper or book. Lew and I are literate in Spanish and French, respectively: We can enjoy reading almost anything in our second languages, and people regularly tell us how well we speak them. Literacy got us through a weekend with Spanish friends and gave us the skills we needed to tell a French auto mechanic where the squeak was in the back of our car. Literacy would have probably carried us through any medical or police problems, too—though we didn't have to test it that far.

Literacy is a dangerous stage. If you're literate with a good accent, people don't believe your claim that you speak only a little of their language. They respond to your simple conversational volleys with an explosion of volatile words. You're left standing there, shell shocked, with the shrapnel of assorted adjectives and verbs embedded in your ears but with no idea of what really hit you. I resolved while in Europe to believe people who assured me their English was not so good—despite the evidence—and to converse with them slowly and in simple phrases, as I would have them do unto me. It is easy to get carried away and assume fluency where only literacy exists.

fluency

Complete fluency is literacy with much more speed and with a much larger vocabulary, including slang and cultural allusions. As good as my French got toward the end of a month in France, I still got lost in movies, when informal dialogue flashed by so quickly. Fluency's just not there if you find yourself, as Lew and I both do, holding back in conversations, simplifying the ideas in our heads to match what our mouths could put forth.

I am always reminded of what a large part culture and slang play in fluency when I visit England. Here I am often unable to understand the *meaning* of an advertising slogan or headline at first glance—despite the fact that I can obviously understand the words. The best illustration of this came when a youth-hostel warden offered to "knock me up" in the morning—and meant nothing more nefarious than knocking on my door to awaken us.

So how much language is enough? Our long trip, in the end, required both less foreign language expertise than I expected and more. I had vastly overestimated the Spanish I needed to be a tourist. I might even have been better off without any knowledge of Spanish: Knowing enough to be convinced I could "do it right" with just a little more work kept me holed up studying when I should have been out on the Spanish streets learning by doing.

On the other hand, I just as largely underestimated the knowledge of any language that's necessary to meet new people and exchange *ideas* instead of just small talk. Our inability, even in Spanish and French, to speak as quickly as we could fashion our thoughts became a real obstacle to any but the most elementary encounters. Our expectations of making new friends and learning *all* about their lives and aspirations were unrealistic and will have to wait for another trip, when we've achieved better fluency.

picking up language skills

What if you arrive in Europe without language skills? Won't you pick up quite a bit just from being there, especially if you're able to stay for a few months?

The answer to that depends on your own learning style. Even those who aren't linguistically inclined can pick up a few words when they're plunked down in a foreign country.

The problem is, you're not really "plunked." Traveling with your family, loneliness won't impel you to learn the language. Supermarkets allow you to grab your choices off the shelf without asking anyone for anything; hunger won't force you to increase your vocabulary. And few places in Europe are way off the beaten path; when you try to practice, someone's bound to jump in in English and "make it easier" for you.

All these factors make it almost impossible to start from ground zero and learn more than a few words of a language when you travel abroad. So, if learning a language is important to you, get a good foundation before you leave.

That may not be as tough as it sounds. Language experts Cal and Marya Urponen report that in most languages, 300 to 500 words comprise 50 percent of all communication. If you can pick up a set of 1,000 flash cards and learn them before your trip, you have the foundation you need to build on when you arrive. (See chapter 22, Resources, for sources for flash cards, tapes, and books.)

This still doesn't mean you'll be fluent when you return. Starting with a few hundred words guarantees you a good survival-level mastery of your language by the time you leave. But even reaching the level of literacy will still take months or years.

don't force the kids

My efforts to teach Sam some French and Spanish were a dismal failure. Despite the fact that he's a natural mimic, he was not interested in vocabulary or verb tenses. Yet he did end up learning a lot *about* language. He picked up the accent and inflections of each language and could spout gibberish syllables, complete with body language, that could almost have made a native stop to listen carefully. He was fascinated (as most of us are) to see little toddlers speaking a foreign language and was mightily impressed by kids his age who had mastered a second—or even a third—language. All of these things served him well when he studied his first foreign language in junior high. But in the meantime he learned exactly what he needed in both languages: enough words to play games with the guys.

All you can really do is set an example, and if the kids are ready, they'll want to join in with you. Libby, at thirteen, refused to work with me on French, saying, "It's annoying to have your parents teach you stuff." Later, at fifteen, she elbowed in on me often, quizzing me and asking *How do you say…?* as I worked to pick up the basics of Italian for a business trip.

language and power

Language is power, and those without it have none. You may be surprised, as I was, at how much language issues can affect your state of mind. In Spain, for instance, even while I leaned gratefully on Lew's translation skills, I resented the powerlessness of my dependence. It had never occurred to me how the equality of our relationship would be affected. I felt out of control and uncomfortable. I began to wonder if blind people profoundly resent their guide dogs, even though they love them dearly.

Lew felt the same way in France. Although he spoke some French, Lew still peppered me with questions. *Could you tell me what kind of sauce the menu says is on the beef? How much did he say they want for that book? Did that sign I just drove past really say* ROAD CLOSED AHEAD?

For Lew in France and for me in Spain, these trivial transactions went on hour after hour. Although we both got better at providing unprompted translations of the most mundane matters for the rest of the family, these efforts were outnumbered by at least as many translations that went undone and unasked, as we declined to bother each other one more time. The strain on our relationship was always there.

Your kids will experience similar feelings of powerlessness. Libby complained from the first day we entered France: "To be in France without French is dull. You can't read any signs, you can't listen to other people's conversations, you don't know what the waiter's saying. Even when someone translates for you, you have the feeling something's being left out." This can, of course, be especially frustrating for teenagers, whose growing independence is essential to their self-esteem.

If you're the one "in charge of" language in a particular country, remember how disenfranchised everyone else in the family must feel. Translate as much as you can, without waiting to be asked. If you're not sure what some-

Communication is the goal. Go ahead, be silly if it works.

thing says, take a stab at it rather than clam up; your family won't know if your translation isn't perfect, but they'll surely resent your leaving them in the dark if you say nothing.

Don't take the role of teacher, though, unless invited. As I mentioned, kids are apt to resist anything that smacks of vocabulary lessons. And any effort on your part to correct grammar or pronunciation will only bring on resentment and the total extinction of any effort to learn.

Besides, if you get too caught up in the mechanics, you'll forget to relax and simply communicate. In his excellent book *Europe Through the Back Door,* Rick Steves recounts a conversation he had with an old man in Italy. Eager to communicate with an interesting-looking cobbler on the streets of Sicily, but knowing no real Italian, he made do with what he had. He recalls:

> "Spaghetti," I said with a very saucy Italian accent.
> "Ronald Reagan," was the man's reply.
> "Mama mia!" I said, tossing my hands and head into the air.
> "Yes, no, one, two, tree," he returned slowly and proudly.
> Then I whispered secretly, "Molto buono, ravioli."
> He spit, "Be sexy, drink Pepsi!"
> And I waved goodbye saying, "Arrivederci."
> "Ciao," he smiled.

Steves and the cobbler never managed to exchange their views on nuclear disarmament or women's rights, but each left the interchange feeling happy and connected. Another thread was stretched, tying the world together more securely.

homestay survival

What makes up a typical day at home for your family? Inevitably there's school and work, shopping, friends, cooking, laundry, and myriad other activities.

But what if you stay in Italy for a few weeks or a month? What will you do all day? Surely you're not planning to go sightseeing all day, every day. The laundry only needs to be taken care of once a week. There's no school or work. It's too exhausting to run around sightseeing every minute. Exactly *what* are you planning to do all day? This chapter will share with you some concrete ideas about what to do all day on a trip that includes a "stay-put" segment.

It will also touch upon some sensitive problems in interpersonal dynamics that can arise when the whole family is together for weeks at a time. Even if your family has always communicated well, you may be surprised at the level of tension that can arise with your spouse or with your kids when your daily lifestyle is completely altered.

what to do

As you read the first few lines of this chapter, you may have answered my question in your mind. What will you do all day?

Nothing, some of you responded with relish. *It's my vacation, and I can't wait for the pleasure of simply...doing...nothing.* Others had a different reaction: *We'll do whatever the French do. We're just going to live like the natives, experience typical everyday life in another culture.*

Both of these approaches are actually a little trickier than they sound. And the best approach lies somewhere in the middle.

doing nothing

Prepare to plan ahead if your goal is to do nothing. Don't laugh. Stop a minute and think what "nothing" means to you. If it conjures up lazy Sunday mornings with music on the stereo and the Sunday paper on your lap, you'd better bring a portable radio and plenty of English-language reading material. If "nothing" is long hikes in the country, pack your walking shorts, poncho, and hiking boots.

The point here, obviously, is that when you do nothing at home, what you're doing probably calls on equipment or resources you take for granted. If a certain flavor of "nothing" is important to you, pack the ingredients in your suitcase.

living like the natives

Going local was the group I signed up for, mentally, before our long trip. *I'll shop where my neighbors shop, cook what they cook—I'll just blend right in,* I remember thinking. For me living locally was going to be a full-time job.

In reality, three problems stood in my way. The first was my family. Already savoring another culture outside, they wanted our rented homes to be more of a refuge from new experiences. *Please make us sweet-and-sour pork,* they begged, requesting a Chinese favorite over Spanish *paella. Can't we ever have hamburgers?* Even though they were, for the most part, adventurous eaters in restaurants, home was *different.* Eventually I came to agree: Building a little home-away-from-home was important to all of us in avoiding sensory overload.

The second difficulty in living like the natives was our lack of language skills. Unless you are completely fluent, it's impossible to live exactly as your neighbors do in a foreign country. If you can't read the cookbooks and food packages, if you can't sit down with the local newspaper or understand what is on television, you have to revert to doing the things you know how to do.

The third obstacle was life itself. In another country your neighbors are going to work, and their kids are attending school. They're serving on juries, shopping for a new car, getting braces for their kids' teeth, and visiting their sick mothers. Even if you speak the language flawlessly, your daily life will still be that of a visitor passing through.

the middle ground

Perhaps the best approach incorporates a little bit of "nothing" and a little bit of native living. Start by upgrading an empty "nothing" to some deliberate leisure activity. What have you been meaning to do for months or years? This may be sketching, watercolors, bird-watching, swimming, photography, or any number of activities. Consider your trip a sabbatical, one you'd like to return from with a new skill. Or use it to get back in shape from a life without time for exercise.

This idea has several benefits. Most obviously, it keeps you from getting bored on the days you're not sightseeing. More subtly, it gives you a "job" not unlike the real jobs your foreign neighbors hold. Your chosen activity gives you a focus for your days and a real reason to interact with other people. If you're seen sketching every day in your village, you may be more apt to meet other people. And you'll force yourself to learn a whole new vocabulary buying paints in an art-supply store or figuring out how to get a pass for the city pool.

At the same time, look for opportunities to pursue some everyday activities "like the natives." I was extremely let down in Spain when I realized I couldn't create a little Spanish home in our apartment. But things perked up when I realized what we *could* do.

We spent a whole day, for example, getting supplies to fix a broken window. We learned that window glass isn't sold at hardware stores but at *cristalerias,* or glass shops. We learned to read the yellow pages of the phone book to locate a *cristaleria* and explored a new part of the city to find the shop. Finally, Lew picked up several new vocabulary words (and some practice in metric measurements) in buying the glass and putty. We could have left the window securely patched with cardboard. But it was more interesting to take advantage of a real-life experience, humble as it was. Living like a native doesn't have to be all or nothing.

teenage tensions

No matter what you find to do with your time, you'll end up with more family togetherness than ever before. All in all, that's a positive thing—isn't it one of the main reasons you wanted to take this trip? But intense family togetherness can contribute its own unexpected tensions, especially when it comes to teenagers.

Why is this a special problem? At home, "together" means in the same house, each of you with his own room and each room with its own door. During an extended trip, "together" frequently means sitting in a car for six hours, followed by sharing four bunk beds in a single hostel room. Or being in a small apartment with no friends and no television.

Libby's reaction to all this, at age thirteen, was probably quite typical. At home she had begun to spend more and more time in her room with the door shut. Now in Europe, with no physical doors to close, Lib resorted to shutting mental doors. It took us all a long time to understand this. We interpreted the unanimated expression she often wore as proof of boredom at best and misery at worst. We didn't realize that her emotional "shades" were simply pulled down temporarily.

Compounding the problem, the trip forced our daughter into increased dependence at a time when growing independence would have made more sense. When only Lew and I spoke the right language, knew the right way to turn, or had the right currency on hand, Libby felt dependent in ways she couldn't begin to imagine at home, where she operated competently in her own sphere. This made her feel uncomfortable—and caused us to slip back into old habits of treating her more like a child than we had in months.

Put yourself in your teenager's shoes and try to minimize the inevitable inequities as much as possible. A few ideas may help:

- Hand out some foreign currency to your child in every country. The ability to buy snacks and souvenirs without asking permission is important.

- Leave your teenager alone regularly. Don't insist that the whole family do everything together. Figure out what *you* want to do, then go do it, leaving your son or daughter behind. What seems like a wasted day to you may be essential to the ongoing sanity of an adolescent.

- Other times, *you* be the ones to stay home while your teenager goes out. Older kids will want to go to the movies or to discos, or just hang around in public places, either by themselves or with local kids they've met. I wouldn't advocate this in a city you're just passing through, but you should quickly feel comfortable with this kind of freedom someplace where you've settled in for a few weeks.

Ironically, although the trip put added strains on our family's adjustment to adolescence, it also helped us get through the tough times more quickly. We had our clashes with Libby, as any teenager and her parents will. But we had nowhere to hide. Lew and I couldn't cut an argument short to rush off to work. Libby couldn't slam her bedroom door and sulk when she didn't have a bedroom. By the end of four months we had evolved pretty good patterns of talking out our differences—patterns that stood us in good stead throughout her teen years. I'm convinced that the pressure cooker of growing up on the road helped us bypass several years of more intense fury.

I don't mean to leave you with the impression that life on the road with a teenager is impossible. It can be difficult, but the same maturing forces that cause problems also show up as increased thoughtfulness, vivacity, and wit. One day, for instance, I asked Libby if she'd like to go to Oxford the next day. Without even blinking she replied, "Sure. I'd love to. But do you think they'd accept me on such short notice?" And just when we were convinced she would prefer to be an orphan, she'd overwhelm us with love—like the time in France when she planned a lovely picnic for our anniversary and purchased all the ingredients at the corner grocery without a word of French to call on.

marriage tensions

Those of us well out of adolescence can produce our share of tensions, too. Lew and I were surprised at the strain an overseas trip put on our marriage.

Why does this happen? If your marriage has lasted this long, you and your spouse have almost certainly arrived at a complex series of trade-offs and compromises for everyday situations. Some of these are the product of edgy negotiations, while others have evolved totally unconsciously.

Lew and I are probably typical. I've turned off the lights he leaves on for about as long as he's closed the bureau drawers I leave open. But I seem to recall that we sulked at each other for about six years before we agreed he would trade bathroom cleaning for my laundry skills. After two decades together, though, we've sorted out life pretty fairly between us.

Over the years a good marriage becomes soft and well worn, shaped to fit so closely that it rarely rubs the wrong way. Completely changing routines can be in many ways like starting over with a new marriage. You'll have to break in your relationship all over again and put up with the blisters it causes in the meantime.

Where are you likely to encounter these sore spots? Here are a few areas to watch out for:

- **Household chores.** If you and your spouse split housework along traditional lines—she does the cooking and cleaning, he does repairs and yard work—renegotiate the chores for homestays. The reason's obvious: Cooking and cleaning are much more work than usual, while there may be little or no "men's work" to do. Even if your usual split is more even, beware of differences abroad. Lew had to take our laundry to the *lavanderia* when only he spoke Spanish, and I reluctantly agreed to scrub the toilet in return.

- **Shopping.** Avoid any arguments about shopping by treating it like a special kind of sightseeing. As a rule our whole family goes to the grocery store when we're overseas. This helps everyone agree on the menu and lets each person in the family choose new and different foods.

- **Driving and navigating.** Driving in a strange country is a two-person job: one to actually steer the car and the other to watch maps, guidebooks, and road signs. Don't automatically split the time in the driver's seat with your partner. It took weeks for us to discover that Lew really *liked* to drive while I handled the maps, but that both of us felt uncomfortable the other way around. Usually it's best for the person with the better language skills to be the navigator, not the driver.

- **Planning.** Share the planning for sightseeing trips whenever possible (see "Family Decision Making" in chapter 6). If one person takes on this whole responsibility, he or she will soon be resented by the others if the entertainment isn't up to par. Take turns being in charge, so everyone—even the kids—can take an active rather than passive part.

- **Finances.** If you're watching your budget, make sure that everyone agrees on this goal. Don't let one person end up being the heavy, always reminding everyone to keep it cheap.

Lew and I found ourselves squabbling about the most unexpected and inconsequential things—how to translate a menu, whether to navigate by street names or by landmarks, when to stop for gas. It took us a few weeks to realize the problem: We had begun to assume, after two decades of marriage, that we both saw everything the same way.

A long trip made us realize this wasn't so. Once we were alert to such differences, we usually managed to find them before they caused a crisis. We discovered that Lew picks up a new language orally, while I must see it written down. I need to see a map of any new city, while Lew prefers to find a central landmark and explore, mentally recording patterns. Aware now of such basics, we could profit from them: I'd take over translating if we had a phrase book, and he'd navigate when we couldn't find a good map.

Discovering (or rediscovering) each other's strengths leads not only to a more peaceful and productive trip but also to an increased closeness that can last long after your trip has ended. Facing scores of daily differences just when you have time to discuss them at length can result in the emergence of Great Truths that help you understand each other so much better.

Lew and I might have made the same discoveries in a summer at home, or we might have taken another twenty years to find out how different we really are. But these revelations were bound to happen on an intensive trip. With so many new experiences and emotions happening in such a compressed time span, we could hardly fail to see some patterns emerge. Our trip stretched the fabric of our relationship in ways that introduced unexpected strains but that eventually enlarged our marriage and left it in one piece.

visits from relatives

Other family members can upset your mental equilibrium, too. Many of those nearest and dearest to you will see your trip as a great opportunity to do a little traveling themselves. "You're going to be in France in June? You're renting a house? That's great—we'll come over and join you for a week!" They think it's a great idea, and you agree. After all, you'll all be homesick by then, and these are people you dearly love.

But how can I say this so my mother won't be upset when she reads it? Be very careful about inviting your parents or any other relatives to meet up with you in Europe. Dan and Wendy sum it up this way: "Tell people *not* to invite family. You get things working as a unit, and you don't want to upset the pattern. We wanted our family to be with us so much—but then we felt uncomfortable until they left. I think if they'd been with us the whole time, though, it would have been fine."

Our experience was identical: a confounding awkwardness, despite our joy at seeing family. I'm still glad we did it. All four of the kids' grandparents managed to meet up with us during our travels, and all had a great time. But I wish someone had warned *me*—as I'm warning you—that it's very difficult to change emotional gears in the middle of an extended overseas trip.

Oh, go ahead and do it anyway. You know you want to, and how on earth can you say no? Just listen to one piece of advice: Logic says you should get together with relatives later in your trip, when you've been gone long enough to really miss them. Contrary to this, our collective experience suggests that joining up with relatives early in your trip may work out best. The longer you've been functioning as a self-contained unit, the more your loved ones may seem like outsiders to you.

expectations

In addition to acting like a magnifying glass on the normal pressures of marriage and family, a trip can introduce its own pressures. The worst of these often stem from expectations.

Your expectations may be a lot like ours. We were betting our all on our big trip. We'd spent almost two years planning it and even longer saving up. We'd left our house and all our possessions with strangers and had abandoned our business clients, no matter the consequences. We knew we were unlikely to take such a trip again soon, if ever. Though we planned to pack light, mentally each of us carried an extra suitcase loaded with expectations.

I was the worst offender. My expectations, in fact, would have filled a steamer trunk. I was sure I could learn fluent Spanish in a month if I tried really hard. I was convinced the kids could make friends wherever we went if I just engineered it carefully.

I knew we could pick the right routes and see the best sights if I just studied enough guidebooks. And I knew it could all be done within budget if I watched every expense. I was the one who would claim the glory if our adventure was a success—but I was the one to blame if the trip was anything short of brilliant.

Family tensions run high when expectations aren't met.

Expectations are like chemicals in a laboratory beaker. On their own they can range from harmless to highly volatile. Mixed with the rest of the family's expectations, explosions are almost inevitable—it's just a matter of when. Your daughter may equate vacation with sleeping late every day and doing exactly what she wants. Your son may think vacation means ice cream twice a day. Your husband may want to see every museum on the Continent. All these expectations can't coexist for long.

They certainly didn't in our family. Less than a week into the trip, on a miserable rainy day, I was ready to give up. Why did we ever decide to do this? What were the kids actually going to learn? The whole adventure seemed so futile, so stupid. We'd already gone over budget, even though we'd stayed in rooms with sagging beds and peeling paint. We were cold and uncomfortable and regularly snapping at one another. I was tired of feeling cut off from everything around me by the language barrier. Sure, we'd had a few pleasant experiences, but nothing to overcome the brutal feeling that the whole thing was a huge mistake.

What goes up must come down. My expectations were just too high to begin with, so my tumble into depression was inevitable—especially the first week, when we were still adjusting to constant togetherness. (All of us took a few such tumbles in the course of our travels—but luckily, one at a time, when the rest of the family was usually calm enough to put up with a little ranting and raving.)

How can you avoid the same problem? Just knowing the problem exists will help. Talking about each person's expectations will help even more. Just before you leave, ask family members to write down ten things they're most looking forward to on the trip. Exchange lists, and talk through several of the choices. *What is it about Paris that you're looking forward to? How much Italian do you think you'll learn? Will you be really disappointed if we don't get as far as Legoland?* Each point you discuss helps lessen the explosive potential of the family chemistry.

Is there any way to avoid family arguments entirely? Certainly not. And if you think there is, you *definitely* have unrealistic expectations!

chapter 16

can we afford this?

You know you want to take the kids to Europe. But how can you afford it? That depends on what "it" is. "It" can be a one-month house swap. You lend your house and car to a family from overseas, and they let you borrow theirs. You have no hotel costs, no car rental costs, and you avoid restaurant costs by cooking at home, using only the money you would have spent on groceries if you'd stayed in the United States. That leaves you with no expenses except airfare—and a lower total cost than a typical vacation at home. Think about what the average family spends for a week in Florida at Disney World!

On the other end of the scale, you could eat out almost every night, stay in lots of hotels, rent expensive villas, and put yourself in hock for a decade.

Your trip will likely mix a little of each: lots of cost cutting, with a few fun splurges thrown in. In this chapter I'll give you a rough idea of what each component of a family trip can cost, so you can assemble the package that best suits your family and your finances.

Throughout I'll stress the low end of the budget scale, emphasizing the *least possible you can comfortably pay*. That way if you're scraping by and taking this trip only at great sacrifice, you'll feel comfortable. If you're better off, I'm sure you can figure out how to pay more without any help from me!

currency rates

Your costs will depend heavily on currency exchange rates, which can fluctuate wildly. As this book goes to press, the U.S. dollar is somewhat weak compared to European currencies, which means most prices are higher than two years ago when we did our previous update. However, what will happen by the time you read this is anyone's guess.

Costs in this edition are based on prices in mid-2007 and on major currencies rounded off to the following exchange rates:

Euro*	€0.74 (euros) = $1	€1.00 = $1.36
England	£0.50 (British pounds) = $1	£1.00 = $2.00
Switzerland	1.21 CHF (Swiss francs) = $1	1.00 CHF = $0.83
Denmark	5.48 DK (Danish kroner) = $1	1.00 DK = $0.18

*The euro is the standard currency of thirteen countries:

Austria	Greece	Portugal
Belgium	Ireland	Slovenia
Finland	Italy	Spain
France	Luxembourg	
Germany	the Netherlands	

Check currency rates when you're ready to travel, and adjust our numbers up or down to allow for changes in exchange rates.

four best ways to cut back

You can stay in clean, conveniently located hotels, eat nutritious and delicious meals, and visit all the important sites in Europe without spending an outrageous amount of money. I know—because our family has done it, and so have many of our readers.

How can you do this, too? What factors can blow your budget the fastest? Don't spend time debating whether to take the rental house for $1,100 or the not-so-nice one for $950. Spend your time instead on the four major categories that will make or break your budget:

1. **Airfares.** Airfare from the East Coast of the United States to Europe is likely to cost you anywhere from $375 to $1,100, depending on special fares in effect when you go. June 1 through October 15 will be most expensive, and West Coast fares are usually $200 more. You can easily save $300 to $500 per ticket by shopping carefully, with total savings in the thousands for the typical family of four.

2. **Car rental.** Rentals vary wildly from one company to another—and from one country to the next. Leasing and purchasing plans sometimes make more sense than renting. It pays to invest several hours of your time in calling around. Details are explained in chapter 2, Planes, Trains, Boats, and Cars.

3. **Hotels.** Guidebooks call a $130 double "moderate" or "inexpensive." Yet if you booked two of these every night on a six-week trip, you'd waste more than

$7,000 compared to staying at youth hostels for $18 per person. How do all the options stack up for a family of four? Camping will cost perhaps $50 per night (tent) to $120 (bungalows); youth hostels about $72; and budget hotels—cheaper than "moderate"—from $100 to $180 for two doubles (cost depends heavily on country). See chapter 8, Budget Hotels, and chapter 9, Youth Hostels, for in-depth information.

4. Restaurants. Meals will almost certainly be the biggest category in your budget. If you eat out—even at modest restaurants—it's not difficult to spend $10 per person for breakfast, $15 for lunch, and $35 for dinner. Instead, follow the plan we advised in chapter 7, Restaurants. Buy breakfast at a neighborhood bakery, raid a grocery store for a picnic lunch, then eat where the local folks eat for dinner. You can do it all for under $40 per person per day—less with preteen appetites—a savings of more than $1,600 on a three-week trip. And the savings may actually add to the fun of your trip!

We all enjoyed the street food market on the rue de Buci in Paris, with vendors selling chickens and rabbits roasting on spits, fruit vendors, stores of cheese, sausages, fruits, and hot and cold prepared foods. Our best meal of the trip was a picnic in our hotel room.

—Diana Raimi, Ann Arbor, MI

Picture two families, the Smiths and the Joneses. The Smiths follow the advice in *Take Your Kids to Europe* (TYKE). They shop around for plane fares and car rentals, stay at youth hostels and family hotels, and enjoy bakery breakfasts and picnic lunches. The Joneses take the first plane and car prices they find. They overnight at moderate two-star hotels and eat three meals a day at inexpensive restaurants. At the end of a six-week vacation, one family has spent $11,000 more—even though both families visited all the same places and watched expenses carefully.

	Jones Family Conventional budgeting	Smith Family The TYKE way
Plane	$4,400	$2,900
Car rental	$2,722	$1,759
Lodging	$10,920	$5,712
Meals	$10,080	$6,720
Total	$28,122	$17,091

stay put

The other way to cut expenses to the bone is to stay put as much as possible. Let's look at two more families. The Whites spend a month of their vacation in a rented house, cooking meals at home, and the other two weeks on the road. The Greens spend the entire six weeks in a home swap with car included. If both families eat in while they're home based, here's what they might spend:

	White Family *Rental and hotels*	**Green Family** *Home exchange*
Plane	$2,900	$2,900
Car rental	$1,759	$0
House rental	$1,600	$0
Hotels/hostels	$1,904	$0
Meals	$3,200	$1,440
Total	$11,363	$4,340

As you can see from these four families, the basic decisions you make on airfares, car rental, lodging, and meals can make an enormous difference in the total cost of your vacation. The differences are, of course, less spectacular for the "normal" two-week vacation, but they're still striking.

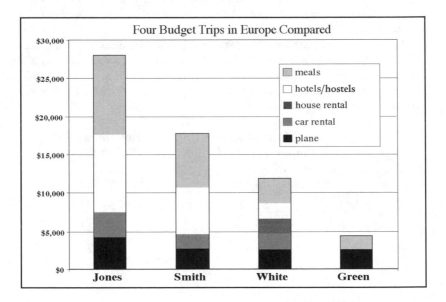

expense categories

Yet these four categories are not the only expenses you'll have. Let's look at all the other typical expenses on a family trip to Europe and analyze each just a bit. Then I'll show you how you can estimate your own trip costs.

gasoline

Gasoline is much more expensive in Europe than in the States, running the equivalent of $6 to $7 a gallon in mid-2007. Expect to pay $100 to $125 every time you fill up your tank, thanks to very high taxes on gasoline. Aside from staying put, there's no real way to minimize this expense. (Fortunately, most European cars get very good mileage; rent a diesel car for best economy.)

groceries

Grocery prices overall are roughly comparable to U.S. prices, although many individual items differ widely. When we stayed in rental homes, we could easily have spent about the same per week for groceries as we normally do at home—if we hadn't been lured by all the unusual snack foods and convenience foods we just *had* to try. (We budget about $50 per person per week at home and $60 in Europe.)

laundry

When you pack light, you'll need to do laundry every week. Northern countries have plenty of Laundromats. Southern ones like Spain and Greece have far fewer—but they have many family laundries where you can drop your clothes off and pick them up later washed, dried, and even folded. This can be an excellent deal; often you'll pay about the same as you'd spend sitting in a muggy Laundromat feeding coins in all day. (And you'll avoid confusion. Did you realize Laundromats in some European countries have an extra step between washing and drying? It's a giant squisher, sort of like a trash compactor, that forces excess water from your clothes to cut down drying time and energy use.)

How much can you expect to pay for laundry? Allow about $5 per person per week, unless you have a rental home with a washer. Dry cleaning is extra.

house rentals

Greece and Portugal are probably the least expensive Western European countries in which to rent houses. Spain offers an eclectic mix of good countryside bargains—and overpriced concrete condos. France offers the best combination of value and plentiful choice, while everything tends to cost more in Italy, Germany, Switzerland, and the Scandinavian countries.

If you're traveling in the off-season and you speak the local language, you may well be able to find a rental for as little as $150 a week. Prices go up as you add middlemen (agencies) to help hurdle the language barrier and as you approach high season. In major cities in midsummer, you could easily pay $500 to $700 per week for the least expensive rental—but you'd still beat hotel prices. And you'll often get a discount if you're staying several weeks. It's all explained in chapter 12, Renting and Exchanging Homes.

Holiday-rentals.com absolutely saved our budget. We stayed in a rental in Ferney Voltaire in France, just over the border from Geneva. We saved a ton and were able to cook some meals there.

—Barbara Knight, Sterling, VA

---

sightseeing

Even though we don't recommend that you make your trip a steady blur of castles and museums, you'll still want to do a good bit of sightseeing. Prices vary widely, from free parks and beaches to midpriced museums to very expensive amusement parks.

A small budget can go a long way when it's propelled by a big imagination. Check local newspapers and tourist offices for country fairs and other inexpensive treats. For instance, we spent hours at an elementary-school fund-raiser in Brittany. There we learned a lot about children's games and songs in France, and Sam won a small prize for his archery skills. Disneyland Paris might have a higher wow factor, but our little school fair had a lot more local flavor—for a lot less money.

When you do visit the usual sites, figure on an overall average cost of about $10 per site per adult and about $7 for each child—more if your taste runs to extravagant amusement parks.

snacks

You budget for groceries, and you budget for restaurant meals, but cold drinks and ice creams still inevitably pop up midafternoon. Obviously you can keep this to a minimum if necessary. But we've found a comfortable budget to be about $5 per person per day.

special events

Make sure to leave enough slack in your budget to allow for special opportunities. Have you always yearned to ski on a glacier? Would you like to learn a native craft? Or maybe your child would like to go to day camp with the local children? Keep a little reserve for that special opportunity.

transportation

Aside from car rental, you'll need to pay tolls. Though some countries (notably Germany) have none, other countries such as Spain, France, and Italy charge tolls on their major autoroutes. Then in big cities you'll need to pay for parking, buses, and subways. (Allow about $6 per person per day for public transportation in cities and about $35 per day to park your car on big-city days.) You may also need to pay for ferries, depending on your itinerary.

miscellaneous

Even with all these major categories, there will still be plenty of expenses that try to slip through the cracks. What about film and videotape? Batteries? Pens and paper, envelopes and stamps? Souvenirs? On top of that, you may have expenses for clothing when things wear out or unusual weather strikes.

Our biggest weakness was reading books and guidebooks. We hadn't allowed for this expense at all in our planning and were rather surprised to find, when we made our final tallies, that we'd spent almost $25 a week just on books, magazines, and newspapers.

budget estimator

Our worksheet is designed to give you a rough, *ballpark* idea of how much your family vacation in Europe might cost. Fill in the blanks, and see what you come up with!

Take the final figure with a grain of salt. Of *course* our budget estimator can't predict your costs to the last penny: Costs depend on exchange rates, the season, the countries you visit, and your own preferences. Some families would picnic three meals a day before they'd share a bathroom with strangers. Others insist on fancy restaurant meals but don't care where they flop at night. With that caveat, take your budget for a test drive.

the rough estimate

If you're just looking for a very rough order of magnitude, plug your family size and length of trip into the various blanks on the form, grab your calculator, and figure it all out. The figures for meals, hotels, and so on are continentwide low-end averages and assume you'll be traveling the TYKE way, with picnic breakfasts and lunches and overnights at campgrounds, hostels, or small family hotels.

fine-tuning your estimate

Some costs, as we've discussed in earlier chapters, vary widely from country to country. If you're traveling largely in one or two countries, you may want to make your estimate more country specific. To do this:

BUDGET ESTIMATOR FORM

Airfares	Actual quoted fares						=	_____
Car rental or purchase/repurchase		_____ days	x	$50	per day		=	_____
Home Rental	July or August	_____ wks	x	$600	per week		=	_____
	Other months	_____ wks	x	$400	per week		=	_____
Special events	Special event #1	_____						_____
	Special event #2	_____						_____
	Special event #3	_____						_____
	TOTAL costs knowable up front					**A**		_____

"At home" days										
Groceries	_____ # of people	x	_____ wks	x	$6	p.p./per week	=	_____
Snacks/rest.	_____ # of people	x	_____ wks	x	$22	p.p./per week	=	_____
"On the road" days								
Hotels (big city)	_____ # of people	x	_____ nights	x	$50	p.p./per night	=	_____
Hotels (elsewhere)	_____ # of people	x	_____ nights	x	$30	p.p./per night	=	_____
Hostels	_____ # of people	x	_____ nights	x	$18	p.p./per night	=	_____
Camping	_____ # of people	x	_____ nights	x	$9	p.p./per night	=	_____
Breakfast	_____ # of people	x	_____ days	x	$7	p.p./per day	=	_____
Lunch	_____ # of people	x	_____ days	x	$9	p.p./per day	=	_____
Dinner	_____ # of people	x	_____ days	x	$24	p.p./per day	=	_____
Snacks	_____ # of people	x	_____ days	x	$5	p.p./per day	=	_____
Gasoline	_____ trip length, in kilometers			x	$0.14	per km	=	_____
Sightseeing	_____ # of adults	x	_____ sites	x	$10	per site	=	_____
	_____ # of kids	x	_____ sites	x	$7	per site	=	_____
Laundry	_____ # of people	x	_____ weeks	x	$5	p.p./per week	=	_____
Fudge factor	_____ # of people	x	_____ weeks	x	$50	p.p./per week	=	_____
	SUBTOTAL variable daily costs							_____
	Multiply x country factor (see next page)					**X**		_____
	TOTAL variable daily costs					**B**		_____
	GRAND TOTAL Estimated Cost				**(Add A + B)**			_____

Nail down the costs that are knowable up front:

1. Check specific airfares on a Web site like Expedia or Orbitz (www.expedia.com or www.orbitz.com).

2. Check specific car rental costs on a Web site like Auto Europe (www.autoeurope.com).

3. Check specific home rentals on Interhome or IHA (www.interhome.com or www.iha.com).

4. Add in any known "big splurges" you're planning, like a ferry trip or Chunnel crossing, those polo lessons, or the hot-air balloon ride.

Then multiply your variable costs by a country factor:

Britain	χ	1.5
France	χ	1.00
Germany	χ	1.15
Italy	χ	1.20
Spain	χ	0.90

Of course, even with these country-specific figures we can't predict your budget to the penny. But now you'll at least have some idea of the damage you might be inflicting on your savings account.

please stay awhile

I hope the preceding chapters of this book have convinced you that you simply must take your kids to Europe—and that this chapter has convinced you that you can afford it.

Now I'm going to twist your arm one more time to please stay as long as you can. It takes a while to change gears and get attuned to different cultures, and a week or two just isn't long enough. Rationalize it to yourself this way: The weekly cost of your trip goes down the longer you stay, so why not stay several weeks?

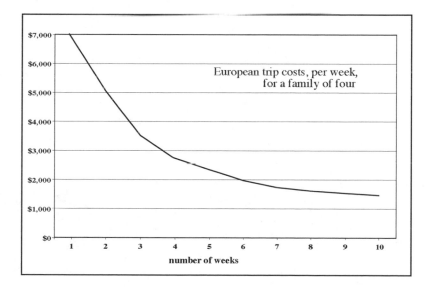

European trip costs, per week, for a family of four

number of weeks

The preceding chart illustrates the situation pretty well. The family that travels for two weeks has the same airfare expenses as one that stays ten weeks, plus much higher short-term car rental fees. On top of that, our short-term family stays in hotels and hostels the whole time. They have so little time and they want to see everything, so they don't rent a home and stay put.

On the other end of the scale, families that stay four weeks or longer are apt to spend about three-fourths of their time in rentals instead of hotels, eating from the grocery store instead of from restaurants. And they have the benefit of long-term car leases or purchase/repurchase deals.

Please stay as long as your circumstances can possibly allow. You only go through life once, and your kids are growing up fast. Can you *really* think of anything more important to do?

the totally biased guide to what to see and do

Don't you just hate guidebooks that say, "You're sure to love the town of Santa Maria. The grocery store there is run by a little old lady in black who will remind you of your Italian grandma."

Excuse me? How do you *know* I'll love it? And didn't I tell you my grandmother was Lithuanian?

I don't know you or your family, so I couldn't begin to say what will surely appeal to your kids. But you wanted my advice, or you wouldn't have bought *Take Your Kids to Europe*. So without further ado, we give you "The Totally Biased Guide to What to See and Do."

how it's organized

We've divided the Continent geographically into five chapters: Great Britain; France; Benelux and Denmark; Germany, Austria, and Switzerland; and Italy, Spain, Greece, and Morocco. All in all we've included information on more than 200 places you and your kids can visit. We haven't attempted to cover every place in Europe, but rather we show you the *types* of places that appeal to kids. Our choices concentrate most heavily on England and France, where our readers say they're most likely to go. But we include ideas for more than a dozen countries in Europe, and we hope you can make your own additional choices anywhere in the world based on the examples we've included.

For each site we've given a short description plus all the facts—telephone and Web site, hours and days open, location or directions, and approximate costs in local currency when known. Prices can stay the same for years or double without notice, though, so use these figures merely as an indicator of whether the site is likely to be a budget buster. (Even though everything was double-checked at press time, hours and days can change, too. Forgive us if this causes you any inconvenience.)

but really—will my kids like it?

Will your kids like this stuff? Would my kids like the same places another day or another year? It's hard to say. Some places we visited when we were tired or cold or hungry might have left us feeling differently if we had visited on a sunny day. Some days we were happy just to be alive, and we looked at everything through rose-colored glasses. Some places were suggested by our readers, who may have different interests altogether. We've even included a few great possibilities we've read about and plan to visit next time we save up enough pennies to cross the pond.

All I can say is, use this section as a source of ideas for how some kids react to specific types of sites. *And then be prepared for your kids to be their own totally individual selves.*

even more great ideas!

The sites included in this chapter are not meant to be comprehensive. We could have included scores more ideas, but after a while the choices get redundant. Please hunt down your own good ideas. Here are some additional places to look into in some of the categories kids like best. Readers' recommendations are marked with their names and double asterisks; Web sites are listed when available.

miniature worlds

Madurodam, The Hague, Netherlands; www.madurodam.nl

Miniatura Park, Goonhavern (Cornwall), England; www.miniaturapark.co.uk

Miniature Italy, Rimini, Italy; www.italiainminiatura.com

Miniature Walcheren, Middelburg, Netherlands; www.miniatuurwalcheren.nl

Minimundus, Klagenfurt, Austria; www.minimundus.at

Portugal dos Pequenitos, Coimbra, Portugal

Swiss Vapeur Parc, Le Bouveret, Switzerland; www.swissvapeur.ch

underground

Mines

Beddgelert, Wales (copper); www.syguncoppermine.co.uk

Blenau Ffestiniog, Wales (slate); www.llechwedd-slate-caverns.co.uk

Ponterwyd, Wales (silver, lead); www.silverminetours.co.uk

Natural caves

Cheddar, England; www.cheddarcaves.co.uk

Dachstein and Werfen, Austria; www.eisriesenwelt.at

Dinant, Belgium; www.dinantourism.com

Mira de Aire, Portugal; www.grutasmiradaire.com

Porto Cristo, Spain; www.cuevasdeldrac.com

Pozzuoli (near Naples), Italy

Savonnières, France; www.grottes-savonnieres.com

St. Beatus, Switzerland; www.beatushoehlen.ch

Salt mines

Berchtesgaden, Germany; www.salzwelt.de

Bex, Switzerland; www.mines.ch

Hallein and Altausee, Austria; www.salzwelten.at

storybooks, myths, and legends

Heidi: Statue and ninety-minute mountain hike, Maienfeld, Switzerland; www.heidi swiss.ch

King Arthur: Tintagel Castle ruins, Cornwall, England; www.english-heritage.org.uk/tintagel

The Little Mermaid: Statue in Copenhagen

Little Red Riding Hood: Statue in Alsfeld, Germany

Peter Rabbit: Beatrix Potter's cottage, near Sawrey, England; www.visitcumbria.com/bpotter.htm

The Pied Piper: Statue, skit on summer Sundays, Hameln, Germany; www.hameln.com

Rapunzel's circular tower: Neustadt (near Marburg), Germany

Robin Hood: Edwinstowe and Nottingham, England; www.robinhood.co.uk

Sound of Music Tour: Salzburg **(Marti Huisman, Debra Jangraw); www.panoramatours.at

animals, fish, and birds

Aquarium du Val de Loire, Amboise, France ** (Steven Roth); www.aquariumduvaldeloire.com

Bear Pits, Bern, Switzerland ** (Lisa Geibel); www.berninfo.com

Frankfurt Zoo, Frankfurt, Germany ** (Sandy Perez); www.zoo-frankfurt.de

Natural History Museum, London ** (Sandy Perez); www.nhm.ac.uk

how things are made

Cheese: Emmentaler Schaukäserei, Affoltern, near Bern, Switzerland (www.showdairy.com); Appenzeller Schaukäserei, Appenzell, Switzerland (www.appenzeller.ch); Cheese Market, Alkmaar, Holland ** (Saundra Middleton) (www.kaasmuseum.nl); Société des Caves, Roquefort, France (www.roquefort-societe.com)

Chocolate: Schoggiland, near St. Gallen, Switzerland; www.schoggi-land.ch

Glass: Waterford Crystal factory, Waterford, Ireland; www.waterfordvisitorcentre.com

Paper: Basel Paper Mill/Museum of Paper, Basel, Switzerland; www.papiermuseum.ch

Pottery: Delft, Netherlands (www.delftsepauw.com); Denby, England (www.denby.co.uk)

open-air museums

Bunratty Folk Park, near Shannon, Ireland; www.shannonheritage.com/Folk_Park.htm

Freileichtmuseum Ballenberg, Meiringen, Switzerland; www.ballenberg.ch

Lyngby (www.natmus.dk), Århus (www.dengamleby.dk), and Hjerl Hede, Denmark (www.hjerlhede.dk)

Museumsdorf Düppel, Düppel (near Berlin), Germany; www.dueppel.de

Nederlands Openluchtmuseum, Arnhem, Netherlands; www.openluchtmuseum.nl

Österreichisches Freilichtmuseum, Stübing, Austria; www.freilichtmuseum.at

Zuiderzeemuseum, Enkhuizen, Netherlands; www.zuiderzeemuseum.nl

history, art, and music

Armor museum, Leeds, England ** (Melanie Nelson-Smith); www.royalarmouries.org

Castle Howard **(Connie Knowles); www.castlehoward.co.uk

Corrie Ten Boom's Hiding Place, Haarlem, Netherlands **(Nancy Fletcher); www.corrietenboom.com

Monet's artworks, Giverny, France ** (Debra Jangrow, Diana Raimi); www.giverny.org

Musical Instrument Museum, Brussels; www.mim.fgov.be

Rijksmuseum, Amsterdam ** (Nancy Fletcher); www.rijksmuseum.nl

Tower of London, England ** (Mimi Ansbro); www.tower-of-london.com

offbeat ideas

Ballooning Museum, Balleroy, Normandy, France; www.chateau-balleroy.com

Bread Museum, Ulm, Germany; www.brotmuseum-ulm.de

Canal boat for homeless cats! Poezenboot, Amsterdam ** (Saundra Middleton); www.poezenboot.nl

Dog Collar Museum, Leeds, England; www.leeds-castle.com

Kermis-en Circusmuseum, Steenwijk, Holland (with minicircus); www.kermisencirqsmuseum.nl

Lawnmower Museum, Southport, Lancashire, England; www.lawnmowerworld.co.uk

Pencil Museum, Keswick, England; www.pencils.co.uk

Umbrella Museum, Gignese, Italy; www.gignese.it/museo

the totally biased guide to great britain

More American families travel to England than to any other country, perhaps due to the lack of a language barrier or the strong English roots of the American colonies. Despite new free-admission policies at many state-owned museums, however, England is astonishingly expensive and, in our opinion, a poor value. *Let's Go England* warns that you'll pay an average of £95 (about $190) for a double with a down-the-hall bath. We paid £54 (about $108) for a lunch of pizza, salad, and beverages for five people in early 2007. In general, price tags on most goods and services carry numbers similar to those in the States—but the prices are in pounds, not dollars, so you're really paying twice as much.

Budget carefully; choose free state museums over pricey private ones—then cut your visit short and head for France, where prices are much lower! If your wallet allows, this chapter describes some of the sites your family might want to visit in five regions: London; South England; the Cotswolds and Wiltshire; Wales and the Midlands; and Yorkshire and Scotland.

london

London is bustling, exciting, overwhelming, like most other major cities. Take time to enjoy the cityscape. Ride the Underground, double-decker buses, and the city's traditional oversize black taxis, since all three are oh-so-British (and oh-so-much-less nerve-racking than driving on the left in a big city!). Take a walking tour and attend the theater. The Queen will approve.

london walks

London Walks are a series of themed guided tours of the city, led by very entertaining actors and actresses. The walks are aimed at adults, but many are popular with kids, including "Historic Greenwich" (which starts with a great boat ride) and Saturday night's "Ghosts of the Old City," given by "delightfully spooky" black-garbed guides—who are parents and relate well to kids.

england, scotland, and wales

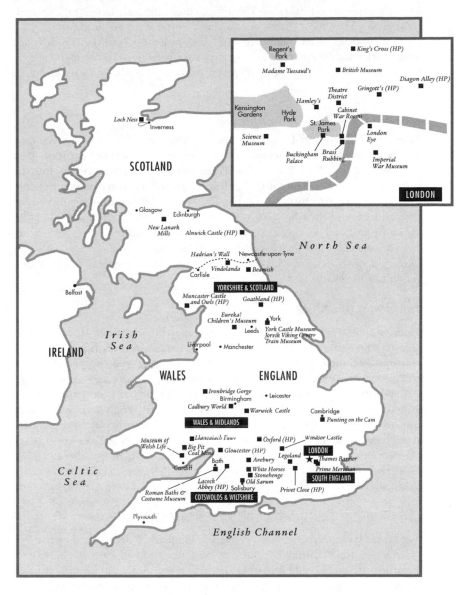

LONDON (inset)

Regent's Park · King's Cross (HP) · Madame Tussaud's · British Museum · Diagon Alley (HP) · Theatre District · Gringott's (HP) · Hamley's · Cabinet War Rooms · Kensington Gardens · Hyde Park · St. James Park · London Eye · Science Museum · Buckingham Palace · Brass Rubbing · Imperial War Museum

North Sea

Loch Ness · Inverness

SCOTLAND

· Glasgow · Edinburgh
New Lanark Mills · Alnwick Castle (HP)

Hadrian's Wall · Newcastle-upon-Tyne
Vindolanda · Beamish
Carlisle

YORKSHIRE & SCOTLAND

Belfast

Muncaster Castle and Owls (HP) · Goathland (HP)

Eureka! Children's Museum · York
Leeds · York Castle Museum / Jorvik Viking Centre / Train Museum

Irish Sea

IRELAND

Liverpool · Manchester

WALES · **ENGLAND**

Ironbridge Gorge · Leicester
Birmingham
Cadbury World · Warwick Castle · Cambridge
WALES & MIDLANDS · Punting on the Cam

Museum of Welsh Life · Llancaiach Fawr · Oxford (HP) · Windsor Castle
Big Pit Coal Mine · Gloucester (HP) · Legoland · **LONDON**
Cardiff · Bath · Avebury · ★ Thames Barrier
White Horses · Prime Meridian
Lacock · Stonehenge · **SOUTH ENGLAND**
Abbey (HP) · Old Sarum
Roman Baths & Costume Museum · Salisbury · Privet Close (HP)
COTSWOLDS & WILTSHIRE

Celtic Sea

Plymouth

English Channel

The "Thames Pub Walk" is a surprise winner for families, too. It includes a boat ride, views of replicas of Shakespeare's Globe Theatre and Sir Francis Drake's sixteenth-century ship *The Golden Hinde,* and a shriveled (fake) corpse in an iron gibbet. Now there's even a Harry Potter walk on Sunday.

The Original London Walks (020–7624–3978; www.walks.com). Most walks last around two hours. No need to reserve. Get a schedule (online or at London tourist offices) and simply show up at the designated meeting place and time. Adults £6, under age fifteen free.

the london eye

London's Millennium Dome was an embarrassing flop. But the London Eye—a huge "observation wheel" also celebrating the new millennium—gets rave reviews. Think of it as a slow Ferris wheel, 450 feet high (the fourth-highest structure in London). Climb into one of its thirty-two completely enclosed high-tech capsules, and you'll take a full thirty minutes to revolve just once around the wheel. It's not scary for even the smallest kids—but the views are amazing, as long as there's none of that London fog!

The London Eye (0870–990–8883; www.londoneye.com) is located near the Waterloo tube station. Open daily 10:00 A.M. to 8:00 P.M. (later June through September). Adults £14.50, children £7.25.

hamley's toy store

Hamley's bills itself as the world's biggest toy store, with seven floors of playthings. A few years ago the store underwent a massive refurbishment and now features a haunted staircase, a huge model railroad, moving displays, and talking books. After visiting Hamley's years ago, Sam wrote in his journal, "They have a Lego building table there with all kinds of Legos, and they let you sit there and make things. And they have some really rich stuff like a motorboat with a real gas engine, only kid size." The displays and specific toys change, but the attraction for all kids remains as strong as ever.

Hamley's (0870–333–2455; www.hamleys.com) is at 188 Regent Street, London. Tube: Oxford Circus. Open Monday through Friday 10:00 A.M. to 8:00 P.M., Saturday 9:30 A.M. to 8:00 P.M., Sunday noon to 6:00 P.M.

changing of the guard and royal mews

Your kids have seen pictures of the Buckingham Palace guards on every "Come to Britain" tourist brochure in existence and will want to come here. Families, though, should know this event is a peculiarly British mix of utter boredom and pomp. Warn your kids that the whole procedure takes a *long* time—more than an hour, in fact. At the beginning and end, a red-uniformed band marches in and out, and partway through, the cavalry approaches with glittering gold breastplates. In between the show is tedious, consisting largely of one guard at a time marching forward and saluting another guard.

The crowds for the daily 11:30 A.M. show are terrible, so if you must go, get there early—or better yet, go very late. Because of the slow pace, many tourists wander off after twenty or thirty minutes, leaving a clear view to those remaining. If you're early and trying to figure out where to stand, the band comes in around the traffic circle in front of the palace, and the cavalry approaches from the direction of Constitution Hill on the road to the right of the palace. Try to climb Victoria Memorial in the middle of the circle, or line up along the far side of the fence. Smaller kids may have to go on your shoulders to see much of anything at all.

A better alternative, especially for kids who like horses, may be the Royal Mews in the back corner of Buckingham Palace. These stables offer pageantry at your own speed, in a small, doable dose. Star of the show is the Queen's golden coach, used for coronations.

Changing of the Guard (www.changing-the-guard.com) takes place at Buckingham Palace, at the edge of St. James Park and Green Park. About equidistant from three Tube stations: Hyde Park, Victoria Station, and St. James Park. The pageantry, such as it is, takes place between the palace and the Victoria Memorial at 11:30 A.M. daily April through October; alternate days off-season. No admission fee, as you are simply standing on public streets.

The Royal Mews (020–7839–1377; www.royal.gov.uk) is at the corner of Buckingham Palace Road and Hobart Place, just southwest of the palace. Open daily except Friday March through October 11:00 A.M. to 4:00 P.M.; 10:00 A.M. to 5:00 P.M. in August and September. Adults £7.00, kids £4.50, families £18.50.

brass rubbing

All over England cathedrals and churches are full of *brasses,* engraved plates decorating tombs and sanctuary walls. For many years tourists enjoyed placing paper over these brasses and rubbing with crayons to create a striking copy of the angels, knights, and ladies that graced these ornate plaques.

As the craze spread, Brass Rubbing Centres opened all over the country to save wear and tear on the original brasses, cut down on tourist traffic jams at the best brasses, and turn the practice into a moneymaker. We visited the center in York, then went on to enjoy the process again at Salisbury Cathedral and Westminster Abbey. All three observed the same procedure: You look through the available designs, then pay to rent the imitation brass you like (fees are usually a few pounds). You're issued paper and your choice of colored wax sticks, and you're off and rubbing. Once Libby had rubbed her namesake, Queen Elizabeth, Sam just *had* to do one, too!

Check at any church or cathedral, or ask at any tourist office for the nearest Brass Rubbing Centre. Salisbury no longer offers brass rubbing.

london theater

School-age kids are definitely old enough to enjoy a night out at the theater. Since we had watched every one of the Jeremy Brett Sherlock Holmes stories at home on public television, we bought tickets as soon as we arrived in England to see Brett play this role on the London stage. We looked forward to it for weeks, only to arrive at the theater fifteen minutes before curtain to find that Brett was ill and the performance was canceled.

What to do? Make a dash for that old standby, Agatha Christie's *Mousetrap*. This play's been running at the St. Martin's Theatre since 1974—after twenty-two additional years at the Ambassador's Theatre. The cast has changed, but the play goes on—a simple mystery that's perfect for kids. Libby and Sam, who hadn't seen anything more professional than the local high school play, were entranced and rated it one of their favorite outings of the entire trip.

Definitely go to the theater at least once while you're in London. London's *Time Out* weekly entertainment guide has reliable reviews of shows that will aid you in deciding which shows to consider. Check it out online before you go at www.timeout.com or buy a copy at any London newsstand. The Leicester Square Ticket Booth sells half-price tickets on the day of any show, but the line here is so unbearably long you may decide to simply see a "lesser" play at full price. If there's something you really want to see, reserve ahead of time. British theater tickets are usually cheaper than American ones, and theaters are small enough that the cheapest tickets are usually good seats.

the british museum and library

Let's Go once described the British Museum as "the closest thing this planet has to a complete record of the rise and fall of Western civilization." That's why it's important to buy a guidebook first and get your kids' opinions on what they'd most like to see. Ask for the "short guide."

In fact, there are specialized guidebooks for separate sections of the museum. Take a look at the Egyptian one first: The mummies (including the curse-of-the-mummy's-tomb one) are such a hit with most kids that you may spend the most time here. Sam was fascinated by the cat and bird mummies.

Your kids' interests may surprise you. Dan and Wendy found their kids weren't old enough to appreciate the Elgin marbles (pieces of the Parthenon) and the Rosetta Stone but were completely intrigued by the signature room in the British Library. They pored over copies of the Beatles' original manuscripts, as well as handwritten copies of *Alice in Wonderland* and *Winnie the Pooh*. Even four-year-old Morghan felt a strong link with history when she recognized nursery rhymes from the sixteenth century as old favorites.

While many of the collections—such as the manuscripts and various Viking and Iron Age archaeological artifacts—are "home grown," the scope of the collection reflects the British Empire's conquests around the world. Does Britain have the right to keep and display treasures garnered (some countries say "stolen") from around the world? It's a topic worthy of a family discussion.

The British Museum (020–7323–8000; www.thebritishmuseum.ac.uk), Great Russell Street, London. Tube: Tottenham Court Road or Holborn. Open daily 10:00 A.M. to 5:30 P.M.; extended hours to 8:30 P.M. on Thursday and Friday. Free. The British Library (020–7412–7332; www.bl.uk), formerly at the British Museum, has moved to 96 Euston Road, near St. Pancras railway station. It's open 9:30 A.M. to 6:00 P.M. Monday through Friday and 11:00 A.M. to 5:00 P.M. on Saturday and Sunday. Free.

Most kids love the Egyptian mummies at the British Museum.

london science museum

Any family could spend a week at the London Science Museum, a sprawling building chock-full of hands-on activities and cutaway displays.

Favorite of most kids is the sixty-exhibit Launch Pad, a noisy, chaotic space where children can explore fiber optics by plugging in a spaghetti of plastic tubes, try to sneak past the "Tip-Toe Tester" vibration detector, or use a giant Sound Disk to whisper to a friend across a crowded room. Each exhibit sports a three-ring binder full of background information, or you can ask a green-shirted "Explainer" for details.

The Science Museum's lobby acts as a giant index to the whole museum, helping you choose your priorities. Or you can purchase one of the Children's Trail guides to help you link related exhibits into a meaningful visit. Sam loved the cutaway Plexiglas model of a 1959 Morris Mini-Minor car and the train collections, where push buttons and cranks let you examine locomotive power. Small pedestals are strategically placed near most exhibits, so even small children can see and take part.

The Science Museum (0870–870–4868; www.sciencemuseum.org.uk) is on Exhibition Road, Kensington. Tube: South Kensington. Open daily 10:00 A.M. to 6:00 P.M. Free.

imperial war museum and cabinet war rooms

Whether because they're relatively recent or because mankind keeps coming up with new ways to kill, contemplating the twentieth century's two World Wars can be upsetting to children. Two excellent sites in London are worth a visit but are only recommended for older kids.

The Imperial War Museum, despite its name, does not glorify war. Instead, it presents an arrestingly interactive representation of the sounds, sights, and smells of war. Your family can get down in the trenches or live through the Blitz, complete with shaking floor, booming explosions, and the smell of burning. In an age where TV and video games make war seem trivial, the experience can be a sobering one for older children ready to handle this much reality.

On to the Cabinet War Rooms. As the London Blitz was reducing much of England's capital to ashes, Winston Churchill ran the war from twenty-one reinforced rooms 17 feet underground. When the war ended, these rooms were closed up—pencils and coffee cups still on the desks, pillows and blankets on the cots—and forgotten for almost two decades.

Nineteen of these Cabinet War Rooms are now open to the public, of which the most interesting include the Cabinet Room, where Churchill met with his advisers; the Transatlantic Telephone Room, whence the prime minister phoned Franklin D. Roosevelt; and the Map Room, where pins still mark the progress of each supply convoy across the Atlantic.

Audioguides (in both adult and kid versions) provide a wonderful mix of explanation, period music, and speeches: As you look at the Cabinet Room, for instance, you'll hear Churchill and his chiefs of staff discussing matters of state. Older kids with an understanding of history will enjoy this most, but the Family Trail treasure hunt (complete it and you get a wartime security pass) and kids' audioguide make this museum surprisingly accessible to all ages.

The Imperial War Museum (020–7416–5000; www.iwm.org.uk) is located south of the Thames on Lambeth Road, London. Tube: Lambeth North or Elephant and Castle. Open daily 10:00 A.M. to 6:00 P.M. Free.

The Cabinet War Rooms and Churchill Museum (020–7766–0120; www.iwm .org.uk) are entered at the Clive Steps on King Charles Street across from St. James Park, London. Tube: Westminster. Open daily 9:30 A.M. to 6:00 P.M. Adults £11, under age sixteen free.

madame tussaud's wax museum

Alas, Madame Tussaud's, once a classy museum that my kids adored on their first trip to Europe, is now way overpriced and largely disappointing. Visitors are herded along a though-shalt-not-deviate route past wax statues that are often not very lifelike. Museum shops and roving photographers try hard to make you spend even more—if you have any money left after paying a fortune in admission fees for a family of four. The "Spirit of London" time-taxi tour of London's history is good. But overall we can no longer recommend this museum and include it only to warn you off.

Madame Tussaud's (020–7935–6861; www.madame-tussauds.com) is on Maryle-bone Road, London. Tube: Baker Street, then head east on Marylebone about 2 blocks. Open 9:30 A.M. to 5:30 P.M. weekdays, until 6:00 P.M. weekends. Buy online and save with a family ticket for £54. In person you'll pay £23 for adults and £19 for kids, or £84 for a family of four.

south england

Within roughly an hour of London lie several other sites interesting to kids, whether they're interested in science, history, or those enduringly endearing little blocks, Legos.

windsor: legoland and windsor castle

About forty-five minutes west of London in the town of Windsor, families can mix history and fun by visting both the Queen's castle and Legoland park.

Windsor Castle is a one-stop royal treat where you can see goose-stepping guards in tall black hats, a huge breathtaking dollhouse, King Henry VIII's rotund armor, an ivory throne, and sumptuous furnished rooms. Make sure to ask for one of the age-specific treasure hunts for kids before you enter.

At Legoland kids can build Lego creations from a limitless supply of blocks and test them on the Earthquake Table, race through the treetops on a series of walkways and chutes, drive cars at the popular Traffic School—or boats at the Boating School. Younger kids enjoy special attractions in DuploLand. Highly recommended as a special treat. (See also Legoland Germany and Denmark—just as much fun and a lot less expensive, due to differences in exchange rates.)

To reach Windsor take the M4 to Junction 6, then follow the B3022 Bracknell/Ascot Road 2 miles from Windsor. Or take the train from London (Paddington Station to Windsor Central via Slough, or Waterloo Station to Windsor and Eton Riverside station), then walk to the castle or enjoy shuttle bus service to the park. Windsor Castle (020–7766–7304; www.windsor.gov.uk) is open 9:45 A.M. to 3:00 P.M. November through February and until 4:00 P.M. March through October. Adults £14.50, children £8.00, families £36.50.

Legoland (www.legoland.co.uk) is open daily April through August plus some days in September and October, 10:00 A.M. to 5:00 P.M.; later in July and August. Park closes when capacity is reached, so reserve ahead online. Adults £31, children £24 at the gate; small discount for booking online.

Windsor Castle was awesome. It was huge and the dollhouse was really, really cool. I liked seeing how the Queen lives and seeing Henry VIII's armor.

—Hannah Rausch, Rowley, MA (age ten)

---

hedge mazes

While hedgework mazes are popular worldwide, they're an absolute mania in England, which boasts about one hundred throughout the country. These bushy labyrinths are often located at important historic sites, making it easy to mix a dose of culture with a bit of intriguing adventure. (If you want to skip the culture, there are also three mazes at Legoland.)

Longleat Maze was great. We got lost for a long time, but it was fun. Finally we met up with some teenagers whose friends had made it to the tower in the center. They called instructions to their friends, we followed them, and we all made it out.

—Marilyn Lewis, Boise, ID

Don't worry too much about getting lost. The most complex mazes have spotting towers to help you out if you get totally frustrated. Just to make sure the experience is fun, though, make sure to visit the toilets before you go in! Some of the best mazes include three in the London area, along with two farther afield.

Hampton Court. Britain's oldest maze is the small but challenging maze at Hampton Court, the palace where Henry VIII dallied with Anne Boleyn.

Kids will also enjoy touring the kitchens and the chapel of the palace, located 10 miles southwest of London in East Molesey.

Hever Castle. A half hour away is Hever Castle (3 miles southeast of Edenbridge; take the Sevenoaks exit from the M25 and A21); its narrow, tall hedge maze is in gardens studded with odd-shaped topiaries.

Leeds Castle. Also near London, Leeds Castle is located off the A20, west of Hever Castle, 4 miles from Maidstone. This maze is made up of 3,000 yew trees and has a secret underground room decorated with seashells in its center.

Longleat. The world's largest maze is midway between Bath and Salisbury on the A32 at the sixteenth-century Longleat House. Visit the sumptuous mansion and fourteen other attractions on the estate, including a children's adventure park and a safari park. Highly recommended by several readers.

Jubilee. Farther north, off the A40 near Gloucester, is the Jubilee Maze in Symonds Yat, complete with a Maze Museum that explains how mazes evolved from mystical pagan rituals to symbolize Christian pilgrimages.

All mazes are open Easter through October; Longleat is also open weekends in March. All charge admission fees.

punting on the cam

No picture of British university life is complete without an image of young men in white flannel trousers and straw hats lazily poling boats along the river. In Cambridge, England, the river is the Cam and the boats are called punts—but you needn't be a student (or a young man) to join in. Anyone can rent a boat and head out on the water.

Once you've paid your rental fee, you'll get a low, flat-bottomed boat that easily fits four to six, plus a long, heavy pole. The proprietor will explain how to push the pole into the shallow river bottom, then "climb" hand-over-hand up the pole to move upriver. It's not as easy as it looks, but it's a lot of fun for an active family. (Don't raise your kids' expectations: Only older teens and adults will be able to handle the heavy pole.)

The most popular route takes you along the Backs, an aptly named area made up of the backyards of several of Cambridge's famous colleges. The most popular stretch offers about 800 meters of good punting and great architecture between Silver Street and Magdalene Bridge, but intrepid souls can go as far as they want. Chauffered punts are offered for the less intrepid. Life jackets are available free at most locations. Rental options include:

Scudamore's (01223–359–750; www.scudamores.com), four locations including Mill Lane and Magdalene Bridge. Open daily year-round, 10:00 A.M. to dusk (9:00 A.M. to dusk in summer). Punts £16/hour weekdays, £18/hour weekends + £60 refundable deposit. May offer hostel card discount.

Granta Boat and Punt (01223–301–845; www.puntingincambridge.com) at Granta Inn, Mill Pond, Newnham Road. Open daily April through October 9:30 A.M. to dusk. Punts, £10/hour weekdays, £12/hour weekends + £60 refundable deposit.

thames barrier

Closer in again to London, a scientific marvel awaits in Woolwich. Imagine building a wall across the Thames River. That's what the British did in 1982 when they installed a series of rotating gates across the river—gates that can be raised whenever floods threaten the Greater London area. In fact, the gates were raised eighteen times in the first twelve years of the barrier's existence.

Your visit to the Thames Barrier Visitor Centre starts with a ten-minute video and a series of showcases explaining the barrier's eight-year construction. Your kids can even press a button on a model of the barrier and see how the gates lie flat on the river bottom until they're rotated up into position. An eighteen-minute multimedia presentation finishes the trip. If your itinerary is flexible, call ahead and see when the barrier's monthly test gate closing is scheduled.

Thames Barrier Visitor Centre (020–8854–1373; www.greenwichengland.com /tourism/barrier.htm), Unity Way, Woolwich. Open daily 10:30 A.M. to 4:00 P.M., April to September and 11:00 A.M. to 3:30 P.M. off-season. Adults £2, kids £1.

greenwich meridian and maritime museum

Not far from the Thames Barrier, in Greenwich, is the Prime Meridian and the Royal Observatory, which one of our younger readers highly recommends to you:

The Meridian itself is lit up rather well, with a long lighted line stretching across the observatory courtyard. We had a good time standing with one leg in the Eastern Hemisphere and one in the Western. For about 50 pence, a machine next to the line will make a neat-looking card that has the exact Greenwich Mean Time that you were at the Meridian, down to a tenth of a second. These cards make a great souvenir.

—Forrester Cole, Manchester, MA (age fourteen)

Nearby is the National Maritime Museum, which traces the spread of the British Empire. It's been revamped to include the point of view of the conquered as well as the conquerors, which can make for great family discussions. Kids can run around reconstructed ship cabins and decks or even attend Saturday "Shipmates Sessions" interactive workshops.

The Royal Observatory and National Maritime Museum (020–8312–6565; www .nmm.ac.uk) are open daily 10:00 A.M. to 5:00 P.M. Free.

harry potter in southern england

It's almost inevitable that your kids will think of Harry Potter as you travel in England. Alas, no one castle was used for Hogwarts, but movie locations are scattered throughout Britain. You can pay homage no matter where your itinerary leads. The British Tourist Authority puts out a map called "Harry Potter—Discovering the Magic of Britain" that pinpoints movie locations and non-Potter mystical sites related to dragons, ghosts, and wizards. In southern England, consider these possibilities:

gloucester and lacock abbey

The beautiful eleventh-century cloisters of Gloucester Cathedral, with their vaulted ceilings, became Hogwarts hallways in many scenes. Several classroom shots were filmed at Lacock Abbey. See if the sacristy and the warming room look familiar!

Lacock Abbey (01249–730–459; www.nationaltrust.org.uk) is near Chippenham, about 14 miles east of Bath. Open daily 11:00 A.M. to 5:30 P.M. March to October. Adults £8.30, children £4.10, families £21.20.

Gloucester Cathedral (01452–528–095; www.gloucestercathedral.uk.com), about two hours west of London, is open daily (hours vary). Admission is free, but a donation of £3 is appreciated.

oxford

Many scenes were shot in Christ Church College. Check out the Great Hall, the stairway leading to it, and the cloisters for familiar sights. Oxford's main research center, the Bodleian Library, starred as the Hogwarts School library in all those scenes where Harry and his friends were trying to discover the identity of Nicholas Flamel (who, by the way, was an actual fourteenth-century French alchemist).

Bodleian Library's Old Reading Rooms, Broad Street, Oxford (www.bodley.ox.ac .uk), are open 9:00 A.M. to 10:00 P.M. weekdays and 9:00 A.M. to 5:00 P.M. Saturday. Free. Christ Church College, St. Aldate's Street, Oxford (01865–276–150; www.chch.ox.ac.uk), 9:00 A.M. to 5:00 P.M. Monday through Saturday, 1:00 to 5:00 P.M. Sunday. Adults £4.70, children £3.70, families £9.40.

bracknell

Number 4 Privet Drive is actually 12 Picket Post Close in Martins Heron, Bracknell, Berkshire, about 8 miles southwest of Windsor. You can't go in, but you can view the exterior.

london

King's Cross Station, where Harry boarded the Hogwarts Express, has no barrier between platform nine and platform ten, so "Platform 9¾" was actually shot between platforms four and five. If you visit the London Zoo, you'll recognize the Reptile House where Harry first discovered he was a Parselmouth.

Gringott's Bank scenes were shot in Australia House (the Australian embassy), and Diagon Alley was patterned after Leadenhall Market, a covered market with cobbled streets.

King's Cross Station is located on Euston Road in north London. You can reach it on the Metropolitan, Circle, Northern, Piccadilly, and Victoria lines.

The London Zoo is in Regents Park (020–7722–3333; www.londonzoo.org). Tube: Camden Town (Northern Line) and then a twelve-minute walk. Open 10:00 A.M. to 4:00 P.M. daily, until 5:30 P.M. March through September. Adults £14.00, kids £10.75, families £45.00.

Australia House is on the Strand (Tube: Aldwych). Leadenhall Market (www.leadenhallmarket.co.uk) is located to the south of Leadenhall Street between Gracechurch and Lime Streets. Tube: Monument or Bank. Open 8:00 A.M. to 3:00 P.M. Monday through Friday; restaurants open later.

cotswolds and wiltshire

An hour west of London lies an area called the Cotswolds, once the center of a thriving wool trade and now best known for its charming scenery of golden-gray stone houses in villages with names like Lower Slaughter, Wotton-under-Edge, Chipping Norton, and Little Badminton. One of our kids' favorite villages is Bourton-on-the-Water, where the shallow River Windrush flows under a series of tiny stone bridges and over several stone fords.

Driving anywhere in the Cotswolds is a scenic treat but offers few specific family attractions. Just to the west and south, however, lie some interesting and well-known destinations—including Stonehenge.

stonehenge

Stonehenge is a better place to see formations of tourist buses than rings of stones. The stones are huge, and their genesis is intriguing. But there's very little mysticism in marching around a roped-off blacktop path while being jostled by hordes of tourists.

British tourism advocates, well aware that a visit to Stonehenge leaves something to be desired, have long debated ways to enhance the experience. In December 2002 the British government announced it would support boring a tunnel to make adjacent highway A344 invisible. But the project is mired in protests from Druids and environmental groups. Until the tunnel is built, our recommendation is to drive by on the A344 in early morning or at sunset and enjoy the view of the deserted stones from the road. Or simply focus on other prehistoric relics, as Stonehenge is far from the only stone henge in England.

While we were in Britain, we bought a fascinating book telling how archaeologists are discovering more and more buried henges and other ancient ruins from growth patterns of crops planted above them. In times of drought, we learned, crops planted over stone ruins languish; aerial photos clearly show henges, walls, and foundations as circular or rectangular shadows in the fields.

Stonehenge (0870–333–1181; www.english-heritage.org.uk/stonehenge) is located in rural fields on the A344 near Amesbury, about 10 miles north of Salisbury. Open

9:30 A.M. to 4:00 P.M. daily; until 7:00 P.M. in summer. Adults £6.30, children £3.20, families £15.80. Includes audio guide.

avebury

While many of England's prehistoric structures are buried under the sod, some are not. One of the best is Avebury, just to the north of Stonehenge. Avebury is the largest of the open-air temples, consisting of a 1,400-foot-diameter ring of about 100 stones and a deep ditch surrounding much of the village of Avebury.

Why come here instead of Stonehenge? The stones are smaller and ruder, and only some have survived. But here the kids can run around, or the whole family can picnic without getting trampled by armies of tourists. Your family is more likely to ponder the significance of a henge in this less frantic setting. And while Stonehenge's main building is a very crowded and commercial gift shop, Avebury offers a small but recently expanded museum usually staffed by archaeologists, who are more than happy to answer any questions you might have.

The village of Avebury is on the A4361 about 10 miles south of Swindon and 8 miles south of the M4 throughway. Check details at www.english-heritage.org.uk. No admission fee or hours for Avebury henge. Alexander Keillor Museum (01672–539–555), open 10:00 A.M. to 4:00 P.M. daily; adults £4.20, children £2.10, families £10.50.

At Avebury the stone henges are smaller but more approachable.

west kennett long barrow

On your way out of Avebury, stop by the West Kennett Long Barrow. Long barrows, which are actually ancient Iron Age burial mounds, are scattered throughout England. Visiting this particular ancient burial chamber requires a hike of some three-fourths of a mile from the road. But the farmland trek makes you feel like you're the first ones to discover the barrow: It becomes part of the experience. There's no admission fee—just walk in and explore the stone-lined chambers by the light that filters through a panel of glass bricks in the roof.

After you've visited one barrow, the kids will spot them everywhere as you drive through the countryside, adding to your appreciation of the landscape. (On a trip through the Cotswolds, we picked up a great tourist map that marked many of that area's best-known barrows and used it to treasure hunt for the ages-old mounds.)

To find West Kennett Long Barrow, continue on the A4361 south from Avebury to the roundabout. Then head toward Marlborough on the A4. Less than 1 mile later, you will see signs on your right for the West Kennett Long Barrow. No admission fee; www.stonepages.com/england.

wiltshire white horses

In the area roughly between Stonehenge and the M4 motorway, your kids will enjoy looking for the famous white horses—eight equine forms looking rather like giant cave paintings that grace hillsides in the area. Are they ancient? Not for the most part. The one at Uffington (just north of the M4) is an original, dating back more than 1,000 years. But the others were carved into the chalk hillsides by schoolboys, clerks, and local landowners in the past two centuries. They're fun to watch for if you're touring the area and can lead to great discussions about what differentiates a work of art from its "wannabe" imitators.

White Horses are found at Uffington, Pewsey, Alton Barnes, Westbury/Bratton, Cherhill, Hackpen, and Marlborough. Local tourist offices have a pamphlet and map called A Tour of the White Horses, *or visit www.wiltshirewhitehorses.org.uk.*

salisbury

We had read Edward Rutherfurd's book *Sarum* for mile after mile from Paris to Scotland. Rutherfurd writes like James Michener, inventing characters from every era, prehistoric to Celt to Roman to early Christian and on up, to illustrate the great phases of English history. Once we finished the book, a pilgrimage to Salisbury, nucleus of the book, was essential.

Your visit starts above the modern city of Salisbury at Old Sarum, originally an early Iron Age hill fort. In Roman times it was the town of Serviodunum, an important crossroads between Winchester and Exeter. Saxon and

Norman settlements replaced the Roman town, culminating in the erection of a cathedral before A.D. 100. Only a few short centuries later, peace and commerce favored the development of the new city of Salisbury nearer to the river, and the defensible hilltop was abandoned.

Today you can drive across the outer moat of the old fort-city, park your car, and walk across the inner moat to explore the excavated foundations of Old Sarum. Buy the guidebook at the ticket booth and take a self-guided tour of the castle and cathedral areas, or learn from the new illustrated information panels.

If you haven't had a chance to read *Sarum,* plan a picnic here and simply enjoy the moats and the view from Old Sarum's heights. Walk on the paths that lead down from Sarum toward the main road: They're made of chalk, glistening white, and your children can pick up big lumpy pieces of chalk for souvenirs.

Below on the plain, the "new" Salisbury is a small, pleasant city with a lovely cathedral. *Sarum* readers will be compelled to visit the cathedral to see the pillars that almost collapsed and the carvings in the chapter house, and to muse on where the little statue might be hidden. Adults may want to see one of four original copies of the Magna Carta.

In any event, look up as you approach the far end of the nave, in the area known as the New Sanctuary. Here the ceiling has been "polychromed"—painted in many colors—in the fashion original to most European cathedrals. Your kids may be surprised to know that cathedrals were the Disneylands of their day, often covered in bright colors, in contrast to the cold, gray appearance so many of them evince today.

Old Sarum (01722–335–398; www.english-heritage.org.uk/oldsarum) is a few miles north of the city of Salisbury on the A345. Open 10:00 A.M. to 4:00 P.M. daily in winter; longer hours April through October. Adults £2.80, children £1.40. Guidebook highly recommended. Salisbury Cathedral (01722–555–120; www.salisburycathedral .org.uk) is in the center of the city of Salisbury. Follow High Street through the city center and into the Cathedral Close, or just look up and follow the cathedral's spire! Open daily 7:00 A.M. to 6:15 P.M., until 8:15 P.M. in summer. Suggested donation adults £5, children £3, families £12.

bath

The city of Bath in southwest England was a Celtic spa even before the Romans arrived, but they made it into a major resort. In the eighteenth and nineteenth centuries, Bath was a cultural center and spa where fashionable Brits went to see and be seen.

the roman baths

The Roman baths here are beautifully preserved. You can see the main pool, a large rectangle of stone surrounded by the bases of sturdy columns and filled with mysterious-looking, green-tinged water. Around the pool, stone steps, platforms, and niches make it easy to imagine the Romans soaking and socializing in the warm waters. (Unfortunately the baths themselves closed in the second half of the twentieth century, when a visiting eleven-year-old died of cerebral meningitis contracted there.) The accompanying museum includes several carved monuments, archaeological remnants, and scores of coins thrown into the baths over the centuries.

The usual way to see the baths is to wander slowly through a self-guided tour of the many remains, eventually to come out at the actual main baths. With kids it's probably a better idea to circle the top level, looking down on the baths, then head straight down to the baths, bypassing the museum in what's called the Temple Precinct. If your meanderings bring you to the actual pools on the hour, consider the free thirty-minute guided tour. It will help everyone in the family understand the system of hot and cold pools involved in a proper Roman bath.

The Roman baths (01225–477–000; www.romanbaths.co.uk) are in the center of town, next to Bath Abbey. The main pool of the baths can be seen from the Pump Room above, for free. Open daily, at least 9:30 A.M. to 5:00 P.M., with longer hours in warmer months. Adults £11.25, children £6.50, families £29.00.

costume museum

For many girls, costume displays are one of the biggest magnets that exist. Take advantage of that attraction for a great mother-daughter outing to the Bath Costume Museum. (Few males, young or old, are terribly fascinated by old clothes.)

This museum has one of the largest and most comprehensive collections of men's, women's, and children's fashions from the sixteenth century onward. How could women do anything useful wearing those bustles and hoopskirts? Did the rich dress differently from the poor? Did kids have their own "look," or were they treated like miniature adults? Costumes have a wonderful way of emphasizing the different roles played by every member of a society.

If you have time while in Bath, enjoy lunch at the Pump Room, the oh-so-elegant Regency-style room where the rich and famous used to enjoy the spa waters in the early 1800s. The paneled Pump Room, with its linen napery and soothing harpists or violin trios, fits every upper-crust British stereotype and makes for a lovely treat. You can sample the spa waters, but remember to hold your little finger in the air while you drink your tea (just kidding).

Museum of Costume (01225–477–173; www.museumofcostume.co.uk), in the Assembly Rooms, Bennett Street. Open daily 11:00 A.M. to 4:30 P.M.; adults £6.75, kids £4.75 (joint family ticket with Roman baths, £38.00). The Pump Room is in the Abbey Courtyard next to the Roman baths; it serves morning coffee 9:30 A.M. to noon, lunch noon to 2:30 P.M., and afternoon tea 2:30 to 4:30 P.M.

wales and the midlands

The Midlands are England's industrial heartland, and there are some who would say that visiting here is like vacationing in Detroit or in Gary, Indiana. Yet the very industrialization of the area points up its place in history: It was here that the Industrial Revolution began. Over the border, in Wales, coal mines turned green valleys into scarred, black wastelands to feed the appetite of England's factories.

Our visit to this area covers some early factories, a coal mine, and a look at the life of both the "winners" and the "losers" in the Industrial Revolution. It also includes a visit to a modern-day chocolate factory and a quick look at the English Civil War.

the museum of welsh life

A great introduction to Welsh life over the centuries exists at the Museum of Welsh Life, outside Cardiff, Wales, where more than thirty traditional Welsh homes, chapels, shops, and mills have been moved to the grounds of a small Elizabethan castle. It's a great place, but it's spread out over one hundred acres, so be prepared for lots of walking.

There's an old schoolhouse, a gristmill, a tannery—even a cockfighting pit. There are also several homes, including a row of identical miners' houses furnished in several different periods. Our kids especially liked the animals here. As Lib said, "Not just a token horse or a few chickens, but lambs, and pheasants, and everything."

There's an excellent museum here, too, with everything from furniture to musical instruments to courting spoons. Sam liked some of the old farm machinery, while Libby was attracted to the costumes. We all got a kick out of the dog tongs, designed to separate dogs fighting in church.

The Museum of Welsh Life, Amgueddfa Werin Cymru (029–2057–3500; www .nmgw.ac.uk/mwl), is at St. Fagans, west of Cardiff. Take the M4 past Cardiff, then take exit 33. Go south on the A4232 about 3 miles, following signs to the Museum of Welsh Life. Open daily 10:00 A.M. to 5:00 P.M. Free.

big pit coal mine

Britain's industrial revolution was fueled in large part by coal mines that erased much of the green, rural countryside of Wales and replaced it with grimy black piles of tailings. At the Big Pit Mining Museum in Blaenafon, Wales, you'll go down under the earth to see how the coal was brought up and to understand the conditions coal miners faced.

Big Pit coal mine was a working mine until 1980. Before you descend into the mine, you'll be outfitted in a hard hat, complete with miner's lamp, a hefty battery pack, and an emergency oxygen canister hooked to your belt. Then you'll be led for more than a mile underground, while a former miner explains the workings of the mine from the early nineteenth century until the time of its closing.

It's cold, dark, and wet—but fascinating. You'll learn about the pit ponies that lived their whole lives underground, about the little children who sat in the pitch dark and worked the ventilation doors, and about the men who lay on the wet rocks in tunnels sometimes only 2 feet high, chipping out the coal.

The Big Pit (01495–790–311; www.nmgw.ac.uk/bigpit) is in Blaenafon, South Wales, about 24 miles from Cardiff or 16 miles from Newport. From the M4, turn off at junction 26 (Newport), then take the A402 to Pontypool, then the A4043 to Blaenafon. Watch for signs for Big Pit about a mile out of Blaenafon on the B4248. Open daily March through November, with the first tour at 10:00 A.M. and the last starting at 3:30 P.M. Free. Children must be at least five years old or 1 meter tall to go underground. Visitors should wear warm clothing and sturdy walking shoes.

llancaiach fawr manor

Wales has always been at best ambivalent about the British monarchy. Who, then, would the country support when the Civil War raged from 1642 to 1648?

England's Civil War broke out when major landowners got fed up with King Charles I, who had dissolved Parliament in 1629. By the time Parliament was reconvened eleven years later, England's gentry had compiled a long list of grievances against a king who exacted huge taxes and spent much of the resulting revenue on his own lavish lifestyle. For six years the King's soldiers fought the army of Parliament, until finally Charles was beheaded in 1649.

During this period Britain's upper class agonized over its loyalties. Llancaiach Fawr, near Cardiff, Wales, depicts the dilemma of allegiance in a semi-fortified Tudor manor house filled with costumed period actors. It's 1645, and Col. Edward Prichard's manor is preparing for a visit from King Charles. Kids can join in with servants crushing herbs in the kitchen; they can try on the colonel's seventy-pound armor or explore the privy tower and reflect on the advantages of modern toilets.

A highlight of our trip: My twelve-year-old son loved trying on the armor and trying to understand the guides as they spoke in the style of the seventeenth century. When they asked us, "From whence do ye hale?" I answered, "The United States." They said, "I'm not familiar with that place!" My husband then said, "The colonies." This they understood and launched into a discussion about the difficulties of the New World. It was all great fun.

—Marilyn Lewis, Boise, ID

Llancaiach Fawr (01443–412–248) is located thirty minutes north of Cardiff, just off the A470 on the B4254 at Nelson in Wales' Rhymney Valley. Follow MANOR *signs. Open daily 10:00 A.M. to 5:00 P.M.; closed Monday November through February. Adults £5.00, children £4.00, families £16.50.*

ironbridge: birthplace of a revolution

In Coalbrookdale, England, in 1709, Abraham Darby invented a way to produce cheap cast iron, and the Industrial Revolution was born. Today, in the Ironbridge Gorge northwest of Birmingham, a rich complex of six major museums memorializes this great leap of history.

Start with a quick visit to the Museum of the Gorge for a 40-foot model of the gorge in the eighteenth century and an audiovisual program that explains the history of the area. Then continue along to the Blists Hill Victorian Town, a re-creation of an entire industrial town of the 1890s. Here, on forty acres, you'll find a candlemaker, blacksmith, cobbler, and carpenter, as well as High Street shops, including a bank, bakery, sweetshop, butcher, and a chemist (and his leeches always seem to be a big hit). Furnished homes are open to the public, and you can see iron products made at the foundry—the only working wrought-ironworks in the Western world.

Ironbridge Gorge is a must. It's part working village, with ironworks where you can see a blast furnace in operation and you can see glass and pottery being made. Don't miss the bridge itself. It was the first iron bridge in the world and was built to show the world that iron could be a usable architectural material.

—Paul Snook, Strongsville, OH

If your kids haven't had enough, seek out one of the Gorge's specialized museums: The Jackfield Tile Museum, the Coalport China Works, and the Museum of Iron all detail different manufacturing specialties, while the Tar Tunnel shows how natural bitumen was mined. Added in 2002 is Enginuity, a hands-on science museum where kids can experiment with gadgets as "apprentice engineers."

Ironbridge Gorge (01952–884–391; www.ironbridge.org.uk) is located just south of Telford, off the M54 midway between Birmingham and Shrewsbury. It has been designated a World Heritage Site—a distinction given by UNESCO to fewer than 250 sites worldwide, including the Pyramids and the Taj Mahal. Gorge museums are open mid-March through October (some open year-round) from 10:00 A.M. to 5:00 P.M. Each museum has its own entry fees, but you can buy a passport for all the museums for £14.00 for adults, £9.50 for children, or £46.00 for a family. The passport is valid indefinitely until you've visited all sites.

warwick castle

Who benefited from the Industrial Revolution? Certainly the Welsh miners don't appear to have. Life for the poor was not easy, as you might learn if you read aloud from Charles Dickens's *Hard Times* on your way to Warwick Castle.

Warwick Castle was built in medieval days, but today it's furnished as it was in the 1890s, with wax figures of the Prince of Wales and a young Winston Churchill, among others, enjoying an upper-class weekend. The fine clothes, the light airy chambers, and the ubiquitous servants make a powerful commentary on the divisions in England at the height of the British Empire if you visit—as we did—just after a trek down the Big Pit.

In the private apartments Warwick Castle features the late nineteenth century, but on the outside it's medieval all the way. You'll see knights jousting, and twice a day you can watch the world's largest trebuchet (catapult) in action. "Dream of Battle," a special-effects simulation of the dreams of a twelve-year-old-squire about to go to war, is too scary for younger kids but a good history lesson for older ones.

Warwick Castle (01926–406–600; www.warwick-castle.co.uk) is in Warwick just off the M40 in the triangle formed by Coventry, Birmingham, and Stratford-on-Avon. Open daily 10:00 A.M. to 5:00 P.M. (until 6:00 P.M. in summer). Prices vary and are higher at peak periods. Adults £15.95 to £17.95, children £9.95 to £10.95, families £45.00 to £48.00. Bring a picnic, and eat among the peacocks in the garden.

cadbury world

Cadbury World is a bit hokey and definitely commercial. But who can resist the Willy Wonka charm of visiting a chocolate factory? Your tour takes about ninety minutes and starts with the history of chocolate, from the Aztecs onward. Much of the story is told in the multisensory cinema, opened in 2001.

Most popular with kids is the Demonstration Room, where workers mold chocolates and invite visitors to dip their own centers in a bath of molten chocolate. If the plant is operating, your tour will also include part of the packaging plant, where up to 118 million chocolate bars are wrapped each year.

An extensive playground with ample picnicking areas makes this a very family-centered place to visit. Allow three hours.

Cadbury World (0845–450–3599; www.cadburyworld.co.uk) is located on Linden Road, Bournville, just south of Birmingham. Take the M5 to exit 2 or 4 and follow signs. Hours vary widely; check the online calendar for specifics. In general, open daily mid-February through October at least 10:00 A.M. to 3:00 P.M.; often longer. Call ahead to reserve or book online, as limited capacity means walk-ins may be denied admission. The packaging plant is closed four or five times a year for maintenance. Adults £13.50, children £9.95, families £40.00 to £48.50.

yorkshire and scotland

Too often travelers focus on London and the south when visiting England. But the northern counties offer natural beauty, from rolling hills to misty moors, and many excellent museums. This area is also a great jumping-off place for a visit to Scotland.

york

York is one of our family's favorite cities in England, with a lovely small scale, lots of pedestrian streets, and plenty of interesting things to do, both within the city bounds and nearby.

york castle museum

Folk museums are always a good bet when traveling with kids. Because they display everyday clothes, tools, toys, and even buildings, they invite comparisons to your children's own daily life. For family travel I'd pick a folk museum over an art museum any day of the week.

The York Castle Museum is not another empty castle—it's a wonderful folk museum with artifacts from nineteenth-century local life. Here you can trace the development of household items, from vacuum cleaners to bathtubs, and marvel at old kitchen gadgets or elaborate clocks and watches. Everything's in realistic settings rather than flat museum cases. Victorian and Edwardian toys, lamps, jewelry, and clothes, for instance, are displayed in shop windows as part of two reconstructed streetscapes. There's even a working gristmill on the grounds. This was my favorite museum of our travels.

York Castle Museum (01904–687–687; www.yorkcastlemuseum.org.uk) off Tower Street, York. Open daily 9:30 A.M. to 5:00 P.M. Adults £6.50, children £4.00, families £19.00.

trains!

National Railway Museum and York Model Railway are both located near the York train station in northern England. The museum features more than 200 full-size carriages and engines with related displays. Sam, at ten, enjoyed this but liked the smaller Model Railway with its model trains the most. He recalls, "It was a whole room full of a huge complex of trains, and you could do things like start other trains and turn on lights by pressing buttons that said PUSH. I would recommend it for kids that like either models or mechanical things."

National Railway Museum (0870–421–4001; www.nrm.org.uk) is on Leeman Road, York; continue under the tracks from the railway station. Open daily 10:00 A.M. to 6:00 P.M. Free. York Model Railway (01904–630–169) is on Station Road, York, right next to the railway station. Open daily 9:30 A.M. to 6:00 P.M.; 10:30 A.M. to 5:00 P.M. November through February. Adults £3.40, children £2.00.

jorvik viking centre and DIG

In the ninth and tenth centuries, the British Isles were terrorized by Viking raids. In northern England a city founded by the Romans as Eboracum and called Eoforwic by the Anglo-Saxons was rechristened Jorvik by its Viking invaders.

Today the city is York, and the Viking raid has been immortalized in the Jorvik Viking Centre, hugely renovated in early 2001. A state-of-the-art exhibit includes a high-tech time machine to transport visitors back through 1,000 years of the city's history; time capsules that fly visitors through the re-created Viking city; a new artifacts gallery; and realistic sights, sounds, and smells that make the experience memorable. It's a great mix of archaeology and amusement park.

If this visit awakens an interest in archaeology in your kids, go on to DIG, where kids can practice sorting through their own pile of historic residue, write their name in runes, or try sewing a Roman shoe. DIG lets visitors explore not only Viking times but the Roman, medieval and Victorian eras, too, bringing out the archaeological detective in virtually anyone. We highly recommend a combined visit to DIG and Jorvik.

Jorvik Viking Centre (01904–543–400; www.jorvik-viking-centre.co.uk) is located at Coppergate Walk, York. Open daily 10:00 A.M. to 5:00 P.M. Adults £7.95, children five to fifteen £5.50, families £21.95. DIG 01904–543403) is in St. Saviour's church, St. Saviourgate, York. Open Monday through Friday 10:00 A.M. to 5:00 P.M. Adults £5.50, children £5.00. Discounts are available for joint tickets to Jorvik and DIG. Book ahead by phone.

eureka! children's museum

One of Europe's best children's museums opened in 1992 to the west of York in Halifax. Designed as a hands-on experience for five- to twelve-year-olds, Eureka! (as it's called) offers fascinating options. Even the building itself is an exhibit, with its structure, heating, and ventilation explained.

Younger kids gravitate to the "Living and Working Together" exhibit, a minitown with houses, shops, and factories. Here they can make toys, drive a simulated car, or flush a transparent toilet. School-age kids enjoy climbing inside an oversized human body to see how the brain, organs, and senses work in the "You and Your Body" display—or play "Digestion Pinball" to learn how their bodies process food.

"Soundspace," an interactive exhibit on sound and music; "Desert Discovery"; and "Our Global Garden," with an environmental theme, are the museum's newest galleries.

Eureka! (01422–330–069; www.eureka.org.uk) is located on Discovery Road in Halifax, Yorkshire. Take the M1 from London to Leeds, then go west on the M62 to exit 24. Follow signs to the center of Halifax, then follow signs for Eureka! Open daily 10:00 A.M. to 5:00 P.M. Adults and children £7.25, toddlers £2.25, families £31.00.

beamish open-air museum

Visiting an open-air museum is a fun and effective way of opening your kids' eyes to another culture. Not far from York is the Beamish Open-Air Museum in Stanley, south of Newcastle near Chester Le Street.

Beamish combines town and country for a complete look at turn-of-the-twentieth-century, small-town life in Britain. Kids will enjoy riding an electric tramcar to Old Town, where they'll see a pub, stables, a grocery, and other shops, all reconstructed buildings from the region. After Old Town, you can tour Colliery Village, with its coal mine and miners' housing, and Home Farm, with live animals and a farmer's wife demonstrating traditional cooking and crafts skills. Costumed staff in all parts of the 300-acre museum add to the mood but don't volunteer much information.

Note that some parts of the museum are closed in winter, and fees are reduced accordingly.

To reach the Beamish Open-Air Museum (0191–370–4000; www.beamish.org.uk) in Stanley, south of Newcastle near Chester Le Street, take the M1 from Durham or Newcastle, then head east on the A693 toward Stanley and follow the signs. Open daily 10:00 A.M. to 5:00 P.M. April through October, 10:00 A.M. to 4:00 P.M. November through March. Adults £16, kids £10 (summer); everyone £6 (winter).

harry potter in northern england

Earlier we listed a few Harry Potter movie locations in southern England. The northern part of the country—where literary Hogwarts is nebulously located—offers three more opportunities to feel the magic of J. K. Rowling's tales.

alnwick castle

All the Quidditch matches were filmed here, as well as that memorable scene where Harry first learned to ride a broomstick. Harry Potter aside, it's the second-largest inhabited castle in England (only Windsor tops it!); it's been home to various Dukes of Northumberland since 1309. The castle even rents out cottages on the extensive grounds if you'd like to stay and explore the Scottish borderlands.

Alnwick Castle (01665–510–777; www.alnwickcastle.com) is located on England's east coast about halfway between Newcastle-upon-Tyne and the Scottish border, just a mile off the A1. Open April through October, 10:00 A.M. to 6:00 P.M. Adults £9, children £4.

goathland

Hogsmeade station is in actuality the 1865-era railway station in the tiny moorland town of Goathland. See it from a ride on the steam trains of the North Yorkshire Moors Railway, which pass through on their 18-mile trip from Pickering to Grosmont.

Goathland Trains (01751–472–508; www.nymr.co.uk) start at Pickering, about 35 km northwest of York via the A64 and A169. Round-trip day-rover tickets let you get on and off as you please to explore the stations or hike in the moors. Adults £14, children £7, family discounts. Five to eight trains per day depending on season; schedule varies.

Not a movie location, but a haunted thirteenth-century castle that serves as headquarters of the World Owl Trust. More than 180 birds of fifty species take part in "Meet the Birds" flying demonstrations.

Muncaster Castle (01229–717–614; www.muncaster.co.uk) is on the west coast, in the Lake District National Park. Take the M6 to Carlisle, then the A595 toward Barrow; follow signs. Muncaster is open mid-February through October. The castle is open noon to 5:00 P.M. daily (closed Saturday). The Owl Centre is open seven days a week 10:30 A.M. to 6:00 P.M; "Meet the Birds" demonstrations are at 2:30 P.M. Owl Centre: Adults £7.00, children £5.00, families £22.00; castle add-on: adults £2.50, kids £1.50, families £5.00.

hadrian's wall and vindolanda

The Romans occupied much of England from the first to the fifth centuries. Between A.D. 117 and 138, they built Hadrian's Wall across the narrowest stretch of Britain to mark the northern extent of their conquered territory. Today remnants of the wall remain, along with forts, milecastles, temples, and towers built for 18,000 soldiers and their camp followers. It's all mapped out in *A Guide to Hadrian's Wall,* a brochure widely available at local shops and tourist offices.

We walked along a small piece of wall at Walltown Crags. The kids were disappointed to find the wall only a few feet wide and less than 6 feet high. "I could've climbed right over this if *I* was invading!" scoffed Sam, who had been expecting the Great Wall of China.

Sam was right. Although you can easily see Hadrian's Wall snaking off across the desolate hills, it is a sorry shadow of the original wall. Sheep and cows graze on either side of the old stones, while tourists clamber along the top of the wall. The idea that a simple stone wall—even in its original uneroded form—was expected to be a major defense system was incredulous to our Star Wars–era kids.

At nearby Vindolanda we were able to see what the wall really looked like in its heyday. Here, at the site of a Roman fort, pieces of both the original turf wall and its stone successor have been rebuilt. You'll realize that the Roman wall was up to 10 feet wide and more than 15 feet high. Sam no longer scoffed as he climbed the towers of the reconstructed wall.

Vindolanda, like so many European sites, lets visitors wander freely. You can explore the foundations of a complex of Roman buildings—an inn, a few homes, a bathhouse, and a fort. Without any ropes or DO NOT TOUCH signs, we were able to spend time studying the *hypocausts,* or heating ducts, under the floors and the sensible draining system in the baths. Did the introduction of modern plumbing and heating benefit the conquered Celts?

Once you've had enough of the ruins, visit the museum, housed in a small cottage at the edge of the excavations. Vindolanda's unique soil has preserved items usually lost to history—a Roman housewife's invitation to her birthday party, old socks, pieces of tents—as well as the more usual durable items of pottery and metal. This museum is small and special, with just the right number of displays for a kid's attention span.

Hadrian's Wall (www.hadrians-wall.org) runs roughly parallel to route A69(T), from Newcastle-upon-Tyne to Carlisle in northern England. The best extant section runs for 7 miles between Once Brewed and Carvoran. The wall runs freely through open country, with no hours and no admission charges.

Vindolanda (01434-344-277; www.vindolanda.com) is in Chesterholm, between routes A69 and B6318, 1.5 miles north of Bardon Mill, about equidistant from both Newcastle and Carlisle. Open 10:00 A.M. to 5:00 P.M. daily (later in summer). Eratic hours November through mid-February. Adults £4.95, children £3.00, families £14.00. Joint ticket for Vindolanda and museum is adults £7.50, kids £4.70, families £22.00.

new lanark mills

Ever wondered what it was like to be a ten-year-old mill worker in the year 1820? Annie McLeod is waiting in New Lanark, Scotland, to fill you in. Although countless mills and factories in Britain are open to visitors, this one best penetrates kids' consciousness by telling its story from a child's point of view.

"Annie McLeod's Story" vividly reproduces the sights, sounds, and even smells of life in the early days of the Industrial Revolution, when the mills of New Lanark were built. You'll ride in "time-taxis" while holograms, projectors, and digital sound tell the story. Then you'll visit actual millworkers' houses, a village store, and even a school (where kids can dress up in period costumes). This great mix of restored reality and technical whizbang led to New Lanark's selection as Britain's Best New Tourist Attraction in 1991.

Finish off your visit with an active hike to the nearby Falls of Clyde, an enjoyable romp and a great way to understand how mills were dependent on ample hydropower. *Bonus:* One of Scotland's nicest youth hostels, with plenty of family rooms, has been built in one of the old mill buildings in the center of New Lanark.

New Lanark and Annie McLeod's Story (01555-661-345; www.newlanark.org) are located between Glasgow and Edinburgh. Take the M74/A74 north from the English border, or drive an hour southwest of Edinburgh on the A70. Open daily year-round 11:00 A.M. to 5:00 P.M. A family ticket is £17.95 (two kids) or £21.95 (three or four kids). The hostel charges £14.00 for adults and £9.75 to £10.75 for kids.

loch ness

Another name-brand mystery that appeals to any kid is the Loch Ness Monster. If you travel to Scotland, start pondering Nessie at the Loch Ness Exhibition Centre, halfway around the north shore of the loch. This high-tech multimedia show was totally refurbished in 1999 and serves as a good prelude to Nessie-watching on the edges of the loch (the real attraction).

We chose Urquhart Castle as our lookout point because several sightings noted in the museum had taken place near there. The castle's a wonderful ruin over which kids are allowed to romp freely. A small guidebook describes the original structure in relation to today's ruins; it's fun to walk around looking for the chapel, the kitchen, and the Great Hall. Watch for Nessie from the walls of the castle or from the loch's edge, where there's a good cove with lots of flat skipping stones. Looking out over the loch for monsters is addictive. You stare and stare at the water, and every minute you're convinced you see a curved black hump just beginning to rise above the waves.

Loch Ness was an important destination for our kids, and I'm glad we detoured to include it. At best you might spot the elusive monster or get caught up in a discussion of evolution; at worst a spring or summer drive around the loch can be beautiful, with grazing sheep and brilliant purple rhododendron everywhere.

To hunt Nessie, start at Inverness, on the east end of Loch Ness. Take A82 16 miles to Urquhart Castle (www.castles.org/Chatelaine/urquhart.htm). Castle open daily 9:30 A.M. to 4:30 P.M., later in summer. Adults £6.50, children £3.25. The Loch Ness Exhibition Centre (01456–450–573; www.loch-ness-scotland.com) is 2 miles away at Drumnadrochit. Adults £5.95, kids £3.50.

chapter 18

the totally biased guide to france

France has an adults-only image that's hard to shake. Maybe it's the idea of romance in Paris and all that wine. Maybe it's the phrase "dirty French post-cards" and an image of cancan dancers. Maybe it's the reputation France has for luxury and expense—surely this can't be the best place to take a budget vacation with children?

Surprisingly, though, it is. We think France—outside of Paris—provides a better value for less money than almost any other country in Western Europe, along with a wonderful atmosphere for kids.

The country also offers marvels from many periods of history which, collectively, can reset your family's sense of historic scale. If you've been soaking in Renaissance palaces and medieval cathedrals elsewhere in Europe, France will show you how trivially modern your idea of history has been up to now. Just look at this time line of French history:

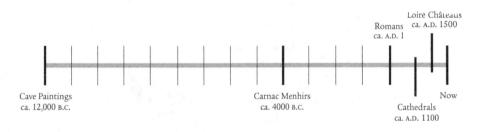

Loire Châteaus
ca. A.D. 1500

Romans
ca. A.D. 1

Cave Paintings
ca. 12,000 B.C.

Carnac Menhirs
ca. 4000 B.C.

Now

Cathedrals
ca. A.D. 1100

In this chapter we'll give you ideas for visits in six different regions of France, including Europe's highest sand dune, some great Roman ruins, the Paris sewers—and of course, the Eiffel Tower.

france

UNITED KINGDOM

Plymouth

English Channel

Pointe du Hoc   Le Havre

Bayeux Tapestry   Caen   ★ **Paris**

Battle Museum

Brest   Strasbourg   Karlsruhe

Oceanopolis   *Monkeys & Eagles*

Port-Musée   **BRITTANY/NORMANDY**   *Storks, Cormorants, Otters*

Quimper Pottery   **LOIRE VALLEY**   Orleans   *Ecomusée d'Alsace*   **ALSACE**

Carnac Menhirs   *Clos Lucé*   Blois   Mulhouse

Ussé   Tours   *Chambord*   *Auto Museum*

Nantes   *Cheverny*   Guédelon   *Fire Engine*

Chenonceau   *Museum*

Bern   Zurich

★

FRANCE   SWITZERLAND

Clermont-Ferrand   Geneva

Bay   *Prehisto Parc*   Lyon

of   *Font de Gaume*   *Palais Idéal*   Torino

Biscay   *Commarque Castle*   (Turin)

DORDOGNE VALLEY   Les Eyzies   Valence

Bordeaux   Sarlat   *Gouffre de*

Padirac   ITALY

Canoes   Rocamadour   *Ardèche*

Gorge & Caves

Dune du Pilat   *Roman Amphitheater*

Orange

Bayonne   *Roman Aqueduct*   **RHÔNE VALLEY**   **Monaco**

Temple, Arena   Nîmes

Toulouse

Marseille

Bilbao

ANDORRA   *Mediterranean*

SPAIN   *Sea*

PARIS inset

■ Parc Astérix

● Charles de Gaulle Airport

Flea Markets   *Science Museum*
Marché aux Puces   *Cité des Sciences*

Paris-Story   *Musée des*
Arts et Métiers

Paris   *Doll Museum*
Sewers

Eiffel   *Louvre*
Tower   *Notre Dame*

Musée   *Musée*   *Cluny*
Rodin   *d'Orsay*   *Museum*

Disneyland Paris ■

To Chartres

● Orly Airport

PARIS

paris

As so many places in the world become homogenized into a bland international stew, France somehow remains very French. People really do ride around on bicycles with long *baguettes* under their arms. The countryside really is covered with vineyards, and the roads are lined with tall, skinny Lombardy poplar trees. Still, many of the things that most say "France!" are found right in Paris.

paris street life

Paris, like any other big city, can be overwhelming with its noise and smog. Yet it was one of the true meccas for our kids throughout the trip: Whenever we mentioned the word *Paris,* Libby and Sam broke into a singsong chant of "We're go-ing to Pa-ris! We're go-ing to Pa-ris!" Their enthusiasm was still intact when we left, so I'll share some helpful logistics that worked for us. (Also be sure to see the "Special Pointers for Cities" section of chapter 6, Sightseeing Survival, for general city tips.)

Paris is full of museums. There's a bread museum, a moviemaking museum, a holography museum, and dozens more. But the real Paris is in the streets, not in glass cases. Ride the Métro, and see puppet shows and singers perform between stops—in your subway car. Sit in a cafe and watch the crowds mill by. Eyeball the gorgeous array of foods in the many street markets, or walk along the *quais* of the Seine. Do all these things, but don't take your kids to many museums.

Paris is a shopping capital, so consider ogling the richer side of Paris on a window-shopping expedition. Libby and I started near the Louvre and followed rue de Rivoli as far as rue de Castiglione, poking into all the *très chic* shops on the way. Then we spilled into the Place Vendome and past the Ritz Hotel, where we watched the rich and famous get out of a long row of waiting limousines. Of course we couldn't afford to buy anything, but the fun was in browsing along the windows of Cartier, Gucci, and so on, choosing one "purchase" from each display until we reached rue du Faubourg St. Honoré.

Kids will want to see how Paris kids spend the day. If your child's a skateboard lover, visit the Palais de Chaillot (see Eiffel Tower, below) or the Fountain of the Innocents (near Forum des Halles). In both places local skateboarders can usually be found in abundance. In summer take younger kids (under age nine) to the Jardin des Tuileries, where a mini–amusement park is located along rue de Rivoli right by the Tuileries Métro station. The Ferris wheel offers a great view of Paris. In many city parks you can find a tiny traditional merry-go-round, too, where kids try to snatch brass rings on a stick.

Street markets are free and delightful. A dozen permanent daily food markets and almost sixty roving ones exist in Paris, offering a great opportunity for your kids to see the reverence in which the French hold food. The flower and bird market is a fixture on Ile de la Cité, near Notre Dame, with birds on Sunday and flowers the other six days of the week (Métro: Cité). The flea markets on the northern edge of the city—the Marché aux Puces de Saint-Ouen—are another Paris favorite with older kids. This market, open Saturday, Sunday, and Monday, covers acre upon acre of narrow alleys full of stalls selling food and drink, antiques and junk, old and new clothes. The old stuff is especially fun: military medals and badges, china dolls, flags, and bins of coins from all over the world for just a few euros each. Though many antiques are pricey, there's something within the budget of the smallest allowance and unlimited fun in the looking. At thirteen Libby could have spent all of our Paris days here.

Marché aux Puces (Flea Market) (www.vernaison.net). Take the Métro to Porte de Clignancourt station on the line of the same name. You'll see signs for the Marché aux Puces directing you north from the station right into what appears to be the market—clusters of street peddlers line the sidewalk, making it almost impossible to pass. This is not the flea market. Keep walking roughly north, through a highway underpass, then turn left into the market area. No admission fee; open 9:30 A.M. to 6:00 P.M.

paris-story

One good place to start a visit to Paris is at Paris-Story, an award-winning multimedia presentation. This forty-five-minute show uses twenty-five projectors, period music, and headphones with your choice of eleven languages as it charts the history of the city. Parents and older kids will get a great overview of the development of major cities in general and Paris in particular, while younger kids will spend their time happily fiddling with the headphones and enjoying a symphony of rich sounds and images.

Paris-Story, 11 bis rue Scribe, 75009 Paris (01–42–66–62–06; www.paris-story .com). Métro: Opéra. Show on the hour, every hour from 9:00 A.M. to 7:00 P.M. Adults €10, children €6, families €26.

art museums—rodin, d'orsay, louvre, cluny

Art museums will never be the first choice of most kids, yet where better to see art than in Paris? We recommend four different museums for four different reasons.

The Musée Rodin is a good bet on a nice day, especially with younger kids. The trick is to pay only for admission to the garden, where Rodin's best-known pieces (including *The Thinker*) are displayed. Kids will enjoy trying to imitate the pose of each statue, and the sandbox is a bonus.

The Musée d'Orsay gets high marks from many of our readers. Housed in an ornate and cavernous restored railway station, it's the home of most of France's Impressionist paintings. Some of the best paintings are on the fifth level, along with a simple cafe and an outdoor terrace with great river views. But don't miss the scale model of part of Paris on the ground floor.

The Musée d'Orsay is more accessible and kid-friendly than other museums. It is less crowded than the Louvre and still has world-class art. The second-story restaurant has a good buffet, reasonably priced (for Paris!), and walls and ceiling encrusted with rococo murals and gold leaf. My eight-year-old daughter loved it!

—Diana Raimi, Ann Arbor, MI

The Louvre, like any other museum, is best visited with a specific plan of attack (see "What You'll Want the Kids to See" in chapter 1 for recommended museum tactics). Even if you decide to do nothing more than pay homage to the *Mona Lisa* and leave, spend a few euros for an English-language guide called *Guide for the Visitor in a Hurry*. It features good maps and a few paragraphs on the major works you'll want to see. You'll wander aimlessly without it, as signs in the museum—although recently redesigned—can be confusing. Pace your visit with cafe stops. The shopping mall under the Louvre has several.

My nieces surprised me by enjoying the Cluny Museum on our recent trip to Paris. The Cluny is one of my favorites, with room after room of polychromed statues and gold reliquaries from medieval and Renaissance times. Plus it's all housed in the original Roman baths, the ruins of which are visible. Emma, age thirteen, explained her attraction first. "The Roman ruins were amazing to see. Even though I know better, I kept thinking people back then were living in caves and running around with sticks. But of course they weren't." Hannah, ten, chimed in, "I liked the giant tapestry of the Lady and the Unicorn and all the carved sculptures. When things are on a piece of paper, like a painting, it's not as real as a sculpture." Roman ruins and the increased tangibility of 3-D art made these two kids museum fans.

Older kids may in fact appreciate museums, though you may not be able to tell right off the bat. We mistakenly attributed Libby's detached reaction at the Louvre to boredom and found out later we were seriously off the mark. Months afterward she told us, "I really *loved* the Louvre. If everyone hadn't continually stressed the boredom factor, I would have enjoyed it a lot more." In fact, Libby insisted on a return visit the next year, when her grandmother unexpectedly took her along on a trip to Europe. "I think I bored Grammy by staring at each painting for five minutes," she reported. "I like to find at least two weird details in each that aren't visible right off. It's kind of fun to point them out to someone, too."

Try one good museum, then have a frank talk with your kids about whether they want to visit more of them. You may be surprised.

Musée Rodin (01–44–18–61–10; www.musee-rodin.fr), 77 rue de Varenne, 75007 Paris. Métro: Varenne. Open daily except Monday, 9:30 A.M. to 5:00 P.M. Adults €1 (garden only) or €7 (museum and garden), under eighteen free.

Musée d'Orsay (01–40–49–48–14; www.musee-orsay.fr), 62 rue de Lille, 75007 Paris (Left Bank, across from the Tuileries Gardens). Métro: Solferino. Open daily except Monday, 9:30 A.M. to 6:00 P.M. Adults €7.50, under eighteen free.

The Louvre (01–40–20–50–50; www.louvre.fr) is in the center of Paris on the Right Bank of the Seine. Métro: Palais-Royal stop, not Louvre. Open daily except Tuesday, 9:00 A.M. to 6:00 P.M., until 10:00 P.M. Wednesday and Friday. Adults €8.50, under eighteen free. Enter through the downstairs shopping center (Carrousel du Louvre) to avoid lines, then save time by buying at the automatic ticket machines in the lobby. Free (and crowded!) the first Sunday of the month.

Musée Cluny (01–53–73–78–16; www.musee-moyenage.fr) is also known as the Musée National du Moyen Age; 6 place Paul Painlevé, 75005 Paris. Métro: Cluny-La Sorbonne. Open daily except Tuesday, 9:15 A.M. to 5:45 P.M. Adults €7.50, under eighteen free.

Note: It's important to visit d'Orsay and the Louvre as soon as they open to avoid the lines that form later.

musée de la poupée (doll museum)

Tucked into a small dead-end street near the Centre Pompidou is the charming, tiny, doll museum, or Musée de la Poupée. The museum showcases the private doll collection of a father-son team, Guido and Samy Odin. The 300 dolls are wonderful, all sizes, boy dolls and girl dolls, all dressed in beautiful original costumes.

Two things made this museum stand out in our eyes. First, the dolls are all posed in thirty-six tableaux that tell a story, complete with furniture, tiny toys, and other props. Second, it's a wonderful place for your kids to see scads of French kids their own ages, chattering and oohing and aahing. Perhaps because of the small scale of the place or because tourists have not yet stumbled upon it, this museum seems like a secret discovery.

Musée de la Poupée (01–42–72–73–11; www.museedelapoupeeparis.com), Impasse Berthaud, near 22 rue Beaubourg, 75003 Paris. Métro: Rambuteau. Open daily except Monday, 10:00 A.M. to 6:00 P.M. Adults €6, children €4.

cité des sciences (science museum)

The French take pride in being on the leading edge of technology. (If you listen carefully, you'll hear the English word *gadget* used frequently in French conversation.) From automated credit-card toll booths and push-button vegetable scales to portable car washes, you'll often see innovative technological devices here years before they arrive in the States.

Not long ago France decided its future depended on awakening in its children a strong interest in technology. As part of the effort to reach this goal, the country built a new science museum—the Cité des Sciences et de l'Industrie—in 1986. It's located on the northern edge of Paris at La Villette and features three huge floors of hands-on science exhibits.

The museum is divided into two main areas, Explora (for adults and older kids) and Cité des Enfants (for younger kids). Explora has eighteen topical sections, such as Health, Math, Space, Ocean, and Computers. Gadgets, buttons, and videos (some in English) abound, drawing kids in. Most exhibits are so hands-on and visual that lack of French will be no barrier—but if it is, just move on to the next exhibit. You can wander at will, with no time limit in Explora.

Cité des Enfants has two sections, one for three- to five-year-olds and the other for five- to twelve-year-olds; your admission buys you a ninety-minute session at a set time. Here little kids delight in working with gears and pumps, shoveling dirt at a miniature construction site, or ogling an ant farm. Cité des Enfant's exhibits and time limits match shorter attention spans well, but if your kids are older, you'll probably prefer Explora for its more flexible schedule.

Cité des Sciences (01–40–05–70–00; www.citesciences.fr), 30 avenue Corentin-Cariou, 75019 Paris. Métro: Porte de la Villette, then follow signs. Open daily except Monday, 10:00 A.M. to 6:00 P.M. (7:00 P.M. on Sunday). Explora adults €7.50, children €5.50; under seven free. Cité des Enfants €5.00 (adults and kids).

les égouts (paris sewers)

Paris was at the forefront of technology long before La Villette was built. Its sewers, known as Les Egouts de Paris, have been hailed as a model of urban engineering—and Paris is proud to have you and your family visit them.

This is your chance to follow in the underground footsteps of Jean Valjean, hero of *Les Misérables*. In the nineteenth century, in fact, whole families lived in the sewers—but you'll be glad you don't. (The stench is not as bad as you might expect, but you won't forget you're in the sewers.) Your tour starts with an interesting video presentation in English, French, German, or Spanish that explains Parisian efforts to manage water through history. After that, a sewer worker will lead you through a small fraction of the city's 2,100 km of sewers. Be prepared for surprises: In 1984 a small crocodile showed up in the *égouts!*

Paris Sewers (01–53–68–27–81; fax 01–53–68–27–89) entry at the Pont d'Alma, two bridges upstream from the Eiffel Tower. Métro: Alma-Marceau. Paris sewer tours are given Saturday through Wednesday, 11:00 A.M. to 5:00 P.M.; 11:00 A.M. to 4:00 P.M. in winter; closed last three weeks in January. Adults €4, children €3.

musée des arts et métiers (arts and trades)

One goal of the French Revolution was to replace privilege and religion with a meritocracy born of science and reason. In 1794 an ancient abbey was taken over by the Revolutionaries to form a repository for scientific models and instruments. The collection grew quickly; the French upper class left their toys behind as they fled the country or met their end on the guillotine.

For two centuries leading inventors contributed barometers, bridge models, printing presses, early airplanes, and vacuum tubes, which piled up in dusty rooms filled with glass cases. Then, in the late 1990s, the museum closed and was rebuilt from the ground up. When it reopened in 2000, the

motley collection had been transformed into a fascinating chronology of discovery and invention over the ages, well signed in both French and English.

While the Cité des Sciences teaches the present and future of technology, Arts et Métiers documents the past admirably. It's not for younger kids, but may be just the thing for curious teens.

Musée des Arts et Métiers (01–53–01–82–00; www.arts-et-metiers.net), 60 rue Réaumur, 75003 Paris. Métro: Arts-et-Métiers. Open daily except Monday, 10:00 A.M. to 6:00 P.M. (9:30 P.M. Thursday). Adults €6.50, under eighteen free.

eiffel tower

A trip to the Eiffel Tower is inevitable: It draws kids like a 975-foot magnet. But reaching it by Métro requires a hike from the nearest stations. *Don't* get off at Bir Hakeim station as most guidebooks recommend. Take the RER to Champ de Mars station instead. Or use the Pont de Sevres/9 line to Trocadéro station. The walk is about as long but much more interesting, passing among street artists and skateboarders through the fountains of the Palais de Chaillot. Keep your eyes on the fountains: They periodically erupt with huge jets of water in a magnificent display.

Once you're at the tower, you'll find long lines at the ticket booths. Put part of the family in line just in case, then send a scout up to the ticket windows: Often the lines on the back side of the tower (toward the field called the Champ de Mars) are much shorter. Study the ticket prices while you're in line. What you pay for admission depends on how high up you go and whether you walk or take the elevator (you can only walk as far as the second level).

The Eiffel Tower has a small post office. Postcards mailed from there will have an Eiffel Tower postmark. Make sure to bring your addresses and a pencil.

—Marti Huisman, Raleigh, NC

There are three levels to the Eiffel Tower. The first level is uninspiring; the second is spacious, with a snack bar, a fancy restaurant, and lots of fresh-air observation areas; the top is tiny, cramped, and enclosed. Our kids decided afterward that the view from the second level was best—but, as most kids inevitably will, they insisted on going all the way up.

The Eiffel Tower (01–44–11–23–23; www.tour-eiffel.fr) is open daily 9:30 A.M. to 11:00 P.M. Métro: Trocadéro. Admission depends on how high you go and whether you walk or take the elevator. Elevator: €4.10 to first level; €7.50 to second level; €10.70 to third level (children three to eleven €2.30–€4.10–€5.90, under age three free). On foot: €3.80 to first or second level. Tickets also sold at the vending machine in the east corner.

rooftops of paris

The Eiffel Tower has competition in the "Let's go up and see the view" department from the Arc de Triomphe and Notre-Dame's roof. Many people are unaware that these two Paris icons let you climb up on their roofs and look out over the surrounding cityscape. But be aware that scaling either of these monuments requires climbing a seemingly endless narrow, spiral, stone staircase—an activity we don't recommend to the unfit or claustrophobic. For anyone else, the aerobic but exhilarating jaunt is worth the effort.

The Arc de Triomphe is for traditionalists with sturdy legs. Your climb is rewarded with an intimate view of Paris rooftops in the center of the city. You're only six or seven stories up, but the experience is both exhilarating and charming.

The stairs at the Arc de Triomphe end in a small (boring) museum, topped by the upper level of the arch. You can look down the Champs Elysées or eyeball the entire city from the Eiffel Tower to Sacré-Coeur. The roof here is flat and open, so you will not feel too crowded or rushed.

At Notre-Dame the views are equally lovely. But you might not notice—as you'll be too busy looking at the wonderful gargoyles, now at eye-level, and at the enormous thirteen-ton bell in the south tower. The walkway around the edge of the roof is fenced and entirely safe for kids of any age.

Arc de Triomphe (01–55–37–73–77; www.monum.fr), Place du Général de Gaulle, 75008 Paris. Métro: Charles de Gaulle Etoile. Open daily 10:00 A.M. to 10:30 P.M. Adults €8.00, under eighteen free.

Notre-Dame Cathedral is located on the Ile de la Cité. Métro: Cité. The tower is open daily 10:00 A.M. to 5:30 P.M. Adults €7.50, under eighteen free.

Our absolutely magical favorite in Paris was climbing to the top of Notre-Dame Cathedral. Instead of waiting for hours and paying too much to go up the Eiffel Tower, we waited just half an hour here. The spiral stone steps were worn smooth by nearly 1,000 years of use. Halfway up we came out on the balustrade to an incredible view . . . the rooftops of Paris and all the fantastical gargoyles, so close you can reach out and touch them. While we were in the famed belltower of Quasimodo, the more than twenty bells began to ring. It was breathtakingly beautiful.

—Ellen Manuel, Belleview, NE

---

parc astérix

Not only children but also adults by the millions in France read comic books (*bandes dessinées*) regularly. Join them in the fun! In doing so you'll inevitably make the acquaintance of Astérix, a friendly Gaul who stars in comic books that are wildly popular with European children. In fact, surveys show that Astérix and his friend Obélix are better known by youngsters on the Continent than Disney's characters.

Sam had "met" Astérix briefly in the States, where he's less widely known, and was delighted to find Astérix comics in every country, in every language, on our trip. All of us took great joy in reading about the little fellow's adventures in outwitting the Roman conquerors of long-ago Brittany; they're filled with very sophisticated humor that both kids and adults can appreciate.

Thirty-eight kilometers outside Paris lies a theme park dedicated to Astérix and his band. Parc Astérix is in six parts: the Ancient Road (shops); the Roman City (water rides, gladiators, and the Roman camp); the Big Lake (dolphin shows and an enormous roller coaster); Astérix Village (theater plus life-size costumed characters); Gergovie Place (chariots and magic potions); and the Streets of Paris (an atmosphere of medieval Paris).

Kids will like the roller-coaster rides and the Three Musketeers–style live sword fights on the ramparts best; on hot days they'll enjoy soaking themselves in the "rain" at the edge of Panoramix's cave. Bring a picnic to avoid overpriced "boar" hot dogs.

To reach Parc Astérix (03–44–62–34–34; www.parcasterix.com) take the autoroute du Nord (A1) from Paris, past Charles de Gaulle Airport, then take the exit marked PARC ASTÉRIX. *Or by train or Métro from Paris, take the RER line B3 to Roissy, then catch the Astérix shuttle bus (adults €6, kids €4). Open daily 10:00 A.M. to 6:00 P.M. April through August. Adults €35, three to eleven years €25, under age three free.*

disneyland paris

Disneyland Paris stumbled a bit in its first few years. While it was being built, French farmers protested; once it was open, local citizens were incredulous to find its restaurants didn't serve wine. Tourists stayed in Paris instead of at the overpriced hotels on the site, and EuroDisney, as it was then called, hemorrhaged cash.

Today, though, Disney's park has settled in. Cafe menus have been adjusted to the French palate, farmers have returned to protesting the potential loss of farm subsidies, and Disneyland Paris has become Europe's most popular tourist attraction.

Visit if your kids insist and you've got money to burn. The park is pricey, but hey, it's Disney. It's small compared with Orlando, but the special effects at some of the rides are *formidable*. It's frighteningly crowded in summer, so take advantage of evening discounts when the mob thins. We still recommend small local fairs and circuses over international spectaculars like Disneyland Paris, but if you do go, these pointers may help:

• Language is not a problem. Although everyone from staff to robots officially speaks French, most employees sport lapel pins that indicate the languages they speak—someone who speaks English is usually just a few feet away if you have a question.

- Plan on brown bagging? Disneyland's picnic area is outside the gates, and you must leave all food in "Guest Storage" before you enter: The *New York Times* reports that security guards search all totes and backpacks and will confiscate children's peanut-butter-and-jelly sandwiches as quickly as a terrorist's bomb. Luckily, food inside has gotten cheaper, with burgers starting at about €1.50.

- If you've already visited Disney World in Orlando, concentrate on the differences at Disneyland Paris. One attraction not found in Florida is Alice's Labyrinth, a maze at the heart of Fantasyland. Kids especially enjoy the labyrinth at night, when the maze of hedges is lit up by tiny blue lights.

Thunder Mountain and Windmill not worth the wait. Star Tours was fantastic!!! Caves were fun. Pirates of the Caribbean a little bigger and better than regular Disney. Captain Nemo not good at all—long wait for a very poor walk-through museum.

—Sandy Perez, Paris (one-year stay)

Disneyland Paris (01–64–74–30–00; www.disneylandparis.com) is located in Marne-La-Vallée, 32 km east of Paris on the A4 autoroute (exit 14). Or you can take the A4 RER train from Châtelet-Les-Halles (takes about forty-five minutes). One-day park entry: Adults €46, children €38 (ages three to eleven). Avoid long ticket lines by buying admission tickets ahead online. Hours vary from 10:00 A.M. to 6:00 P.M. on winter weekdays to 9:00 A.M. to 11:00 P.M. on summer weekends. Check the Web site for updates.

chartres cathedral

If your children seem allergic to cathedrals, take them to Chartres, about an hour southwest of Paris. There they'll meet tour guide Malcolm Miller, who makes historic Christianity come alive to kids of any (or no) religious background. Our kids battled this unwelcome delay on the way to Paris. But Miller's tour left them actually begging us to stay long enough to take the tour again.

On the day we visited, Miller suddenly perceived that our group didn't properly appreciate the cathedral's architecture. "I need six volunteers!" he barked, immediately grabbing six men. He stood the recruits in two rows, facing each other and instructed them to link their raised arms in such a way as to imitate the vaulting of the cathedral roof. "Here's how the columns and vaults work together to support the weight of the roof," he explained, ducking under the outstretched arms and chinning himself on the tangle of hands. Predictably, the men groaned and bent forward from the strain.

"Flying buttresses!" Miller exclaimed. "As you can see, we need flying buttresses." Six women were selected to stand behind the "columns" and push their own arms against the men's backs. Again the "roof" weighed down, and this time the "building" stood strong. None of us would ever forget how cathedrals were built—especially Lew, who had played the part of a column.

Miller depicts cathedrals as giant libraries with each frieze or stained-glass window a book to be read. He "read aloud" some of the windows, and our kids listened with amazingly rapt attention. Later, as we passed the cathedral on the way back from dinner, our pagan kids lagged behind, and we could overhear them pointing to different parts of a carved door frame, retelling Bible stories to each other. I can't say these kids ever came to *adore* cathedrals, but now at least they could welcome short visits with some interest. If your itinerary passes anywhere near Chartres early in your trip, stop here before you visit any other cathedral.

Chartres Cathedral is in the town of Chartres, one hour southwest of Paris via the A10 and A11. Malcolm Miller tours twice daily at noon and 2:45 P.M., Monday through Saturday. Miller charges €10 (adults) and €5 (children) for his marvelous tours, including free headsets. (Note that tours may be canceled for marriages, funerals, or other religious priorities.) For information call 02–37–28–15–58 or e-mail miller-chartres@aol.com.

brittany and normandy

France's western seacoast offers wonderful beaches and tidal pools, along with a wealth of history from its Stonehenge-like menhirs to more recent memories of the D-Day assault in World War II.

bayeux tapestry

The area of Normandy around Bayeux is a great place to learn about two of the most famous invasions of all time: William the Conqueror's invasion of England in 1066, and the Allied invasion of Normandy nine centuries later in World War II. Both proved enormously interesting to our children.

After the Battle of Hastings, William the Conqueror commissioned the Bayeux Tapestry to tell the story of his conquest, from *his* point of view. The Tapestry Museum in downtown Bayeux gives a more balanced account through an excellent audiovisual show screened alternately in English and French. It tells the entire story of the invasion, narrating scenes from the tapestry in a way that makes them come alive to adults and children. By the end of the film, one of our kids said, "I get it. It's a giant medieval comic strip!" And so it was: 225 feet long and less than 2 feet tall, covered with colorful characters. (If you can't tell who's who, the English have the mustaches and the Normans are clean shaven.)

In the gift shop we bought an embroidery kit to re-create one small section of the famous tapestry. Both kids contributed a few stitches to the finished product that now hangs in our dining room.

Centre Guillaume le Conquérant (William the Conqueror Center; 02–31–51–25–50; www.bayeux-tourism.com), rue de Nesmond, Bayeux. Open daily 9:00 A.M. to

7:00 P.M. year-round, but closed 12:30 to 2:00 P.M. November through March. Adults €7.50, children €3.00.

normandy invasion

On the edge of Bayeux another museum, La Musée de la Bataille—the Battle Museum—tells the story of the Allied invasion of 1944. Invasion museums abound in Normandy, but this one is the most comprehensive. Its opening exhibits feature the usual clean uniforms and shiny weapons that come too close to glorifying war. But it also portrays the words and thoughts of those involved, with an excellent collection of leaflets, old newspapers, and newsreel footage. Kids who delight in climbing on a real tank outside may sober up considerably as you read Nazi propaganda leaflets together and scan a letter from a soldier to his mother back home. Lots of life-size dioramas make for a very three-dimensional display.

The realities of the invasion are made even more immediate by a visit to the Normandy beaches, and especially Pointe du Hoc. Pointe du Hoc, where American soldiers scaled a sheer, rocky cliff while German machine guns fired from above, has been preserved as it was after the battle. The area has been swept for mines, and grass has grown over the wounded earth, but deep shell craters and shattered concrete gun emplacements evoke the invasion.

On a blustery early-June day, it's not hard to envision how much colder those wet and frightened soldiers would have been. Sam reported our visit quite vividly (and with imaginative spelling) in his journal: "There was a tunnel with all sorts of shell marcks on the walls. We could imagen the American soldier walk in saying 'Why didn't I listen to my mother and just be a medic' then spraying machine gun fire all around to hit the hiding Nazies." For weeks afterward, our son asked questions about World War II, suddenly determined to try to understand how such terrible events happen.

Musée de la Bataille (02–31–51–46–90; www.normandiememoire.com) is on Boulevard Fabian Ware, Bayeux. Open daily 9:30 A.M. to 6:30 P.M. year-round; closed 12:30 to 2:00 P.M. mid-September through May 1. Adults €5.50, children €2.60, under age ten free. Pointe du Hoc, Route N814, 15 km outside of Bayeux. Head north on D6 from Bayeux to the sea, then west. On the way you'll pass Omaha Beach, where the Americans landed once Pointe du Hoc was secured, and the U.S. Cemetery. Pointe du Hoc is open daily 9:00 A.M. to 5:00 P.M.; no admission charge.

On our visit to Brittany in September 2004, we stayed in Cancale, a cheaper and less touristic town where we stayed in a chambre d'hôte (B&B) for €40, including a big breakfast. My son loved watching the fishing boats and the tractors hauling oysters on the local oyster farm.

—Barbara Dallao, Philadelphia

---

oceanopolis

Reaching out into the Atlantic as France's westernmost port in its western-most province, Brest is a great place to enjoy underwater creatures at Ocean-opolis, Europe's largest open-air aquarium.

You'll start your tour of the crab-shaped building with an exploration of navigation and safety at sea, and you can even try your hand at maneuvering model ships from a mock ship's bridge.

From here you'll continue past the seal's pool to visit seabirds, whales, and dolphins, all in a natural coast-of-Brittany setting. Finally you'll study the food chain; get a chance to handle sea urchins, starfish, and sponges in the "Touch Me" tidal pool; and learn about modern aquaculture.

Because of the fresh seawater and natural light available to the Ocean-opolis aquariums, you'll feel like you're truly walking on the ocean floor instead of merely visiting a museum.

Oceanopolis (02–98–34–40–40; www.oceanopolis.com) is located at Brest's marina. Follow signs for Port de Commerce, Port de Plaisance once in Brest. Open 9:00 A.M. to 6:00 P.M. daily April through September; 10:00 A.M. to 5:00 P.M. Tuesday through Sunday October through May. Adults €15.80, children €11.00.

port-musée (seaport museum)

Kids love boats, and France offers a museum—Brittany's new Port-Musée—that mixes active romping with a good overview of maritime history.

Like Mystic Seaport in Connecticut, the Port-Musée is a full-size outdoor celebration of the nautical life, with more than thirty original and replica boats. In the fishing harbor you'll see tuna and shrimp boats; in the coasting harbor, a steam-powered tugboat, a one-hundred-year-old topsail schooner, and a Thames barge; and in the yacht harbor, a flotilla of gems including *Viviane,* the oldest-known pleasure boat (1859).

Many of the ships offer exhibitions and guided tours that augment the displays, slide shows, and videos in the Musée du Bateau (Boat Museum) associated with the Port-Musée. But since most kids like active scenes, you may want to skip the museum and visit the workshops, where you'll see ships' carpenters, sailmakers, and even blacksmiths at work. Then end your stay by renting a small boat and taking to the waters yourselves.

Douarnenez is located about 35 km south of Brest, on the west coast of Brittany in France. The Port-Musée and Musée du Bateau (02–98–92–65–20; www.port-musee .org), on the banks of the Port-Rhu River, are open daily 10:00 A.M. to 7:00 P.M. mid-June through September; 10:00 A.M. to 12:30 P.M. and 2:00 to 6:00 P.M. (closed Mon-day) off-season. Adults €6.50, children €4.00, families €17.10. Both museums closed January; Musée du Bateau (floating boats) closed off-season.

quimper pottery

Overall, France is a good place to visit factories. Many French factories let visitors wander quite freely, seeing interesting processes at close range. (See chapter 22, Resources, for a recommended guide to factory tours.)

Quimper (*kam pair*), located about 60 km southeast of Brest along the N165, offers a chance to see traditional faience pottery being made. Les Faïenceries de Quimper H. B. Henriot have been producing their distinctive wares for three centuries on the banks of the River Odet.

It's all quite interesting, from the initial turning and molding of the clay to the final application of bright folk-art pictures. Most fascinating are the people who handpaint the dishes. Somehow, they manage to be oblivious to gawkers standing behind them as they deftly add colorful designs to the plates and cups.

Organized tours are normally given in French but are offered in English "on demand" (yes, a single family constitutes enough demand!). Watch younger kids carefully: Racks of pottery just out of the kiln are dangerously hot. At the tour's end you can buy factory seconds at much reduced prices.

Les Faïenceries de Quimper H. B. Henriot (02–98–90–09–36; www.hb-henriot .com) are on the south side of the River Odet, on rue Haute near the beginning of Route de Bénodet at Place Berardier. Open Monday through Friday 9:30 A.M. to 6:00 P.M. Adults €4, kids €2. You must call ahead to arrange tours.

carnac menhirs

As you travel through Brittany, remind your kids that the local population has more in common with the Gaelic tribes of Wales, Scotland, and Ireland than with the inhabitants of the rest of France. Look at a map, and talk about how bagpipers extend into Brittany then continue on to Galicia in northwest Spain.

Once these connections have been made, it won't seem strange to learn that the same nomadic tribes that built Stonehenge erected massive rows of stone megaliths near Carnac on Brittany's southern coast. Three groups of *alignements,* as they are called, stand today. Menec has 1,169 stones in eleven rows; Kermario, 1,029 stones in ten rows; and Kerlescan, a mere 555 stones in thirteen rows. These stones, or *menhirs,* range from about 1 meter tall to as much as 22 meters tall and stretch over an area of about 4 kilometers. Some authorities call this the most important prehistoric site in Europe.

For centuries visitors were allowed to wander freely among the stones of Carnac, a peaceful, mysterious experience in stark contrast to the managed tourist hordes at Stonehenge. In the early 1990s, however, the French government decided the menhirs were falling over due to trampling of the earth and vegetation around the stones. Vast areas of menhirs were cordoned off to allow the vegetation to regenerate.

At the same time, plans were made to build visitor centers, toilets, parking lots, and ticket booths to manage future visits. Protesters staged sit-ins, and a public-interest group was formed to fight the commercialization of the site; this group offered its own plan for conservation while still allowing free wandering. As of press time, most of Carnac's menhirs were still "behind bars," though a compromise plan allowed free wandering for limited hours in the winter.

Still, the stones are impressive. They march in disciplined rows, as far as the eye can see, in the midst of a peaceful rural countryside. It's startling to imagine how many there must have been originally, if this is what remains after 6,000 years. Certainly worth a visit if you're in the area.

To reach the Carnac menhirs (http://carnac.monument-nationaux.fr) from Quimper, take the N265 to L'Orient, then the N165 to Auray. Head southwest on the D768 and look for signs saying Route des Alignements. Open daily 10:00 A.M. to 5:00 P.M. (longer in summer). Adults €4, teens €3, under twelve free.

loire valley

If you visit both the Loire Valley and the Dordogne (see below), invite your kids to ponder the differences between Renaissance pleasure palaces and medieval fortress castles. They're both called *châteaux* in French, but fortresses have gray, thick walls, crenelated towers, and small window slits, whereas the palaces sport airy spaces, white and gold flourishes, and gleaming inlaid wood. What changes in the economy and public safety might be reflected in these architectural changes?

But don't expect architectural observations to hold children's interest for long. In fact, the Loire chateaus can be a disappointment for kids who expect thrones, crowns, and golden dishes but find instead an overdose of architecture.

loire châteaus

We started our Loire Valley tour at Chambord, largely because guidebooks describe it as the "largest and most extravagant of the Loire châteaux," with more than 300 rooms. Libby and Sam raced through the whole building in under an hour, enchanted by the double-spiral staircase but severely disappointed by the sparsely furnished rooms. "I don't think a king would want to hang around here," sniffed Lib. Their reaction to Chenonceau, stretching magnificently across the River Cher, was similar.

We scoured our guidebook for a furnished château and found Cheverny, where the *Mona Lisa* was hidden during World War II. Cheverny, though tiny in comparison to Chambord, suited all of us, with rich drapes, huge curtained beds, and a tiny suit of armor designed for a prince. For Sam a hunting lodge with both walls and ceiling covered in antlers was the finishing touch. The owners have begun offering visitors rides in the world's largest tethered hot-air balloon—a safe and unusual (if expensive) thrill 150 meters above the château.

A few readers have reported equally satisfying experiences at the Château d'Ussé because of its association with fairy tales and at Clos Lucé, Leonardo da Vinci's modest home near Amboise, where the attraction is the scale models of Leonardo's inventions.

My nine-year-old daughter really enjoyed the Château d'Ussé. The required tour was short, and when we were there they had wax tableaux telling the story of Sleeping Beauty. They weren't everywhere—but every so often there was a little glass window, and we'd peek in and see the King and Queen by the cradle, or we'd see the witch.

—Louise Goldenberg, Eliot, ME

Plan a trip to the Loire carefully, taking into consideration your own kids. At most sites the interest is mostly architectural—a low priority with your average child—and tours are either in French or are self-conducted with an English-language brochure. Either way, it's not a very captivating experience for kids.

When I originally wrote this section, I advised skipping the châteaus altogether. Libby says a better recommendation might be: "Take them to Cheverny. It's neat. And go see a few others. They are pretty. Just don't plan to spend very long there because your kids will get bored quickly once they've looked around."

Most Loire châteaus are open daily year-round for at least the hours listed below, but with later closings in summer. French route numbers are not marked prominently, so count on a good local map and direction signs for each château.

Chambord (02–54–50–40–00; www.chambord.org) is about 12 km west of Blois; open daily 9:00 A.M. to 6.15 P.M. Adults €9.50, children under seventeen free.

Chenonceau (02–47–23–90–07; www.chenonceau.com) is on route D140 about 35 km south of Blois; open daily 9:00 A.M. to 7:00 P.M. mid-March through mid-September; closes earlier off-season. Adults €9.50, children €7.50.

Cheverny (02–54–79–96–29; www.chateau-cheverny.com) is 18 km southeast of Blois. Open daily 9:15 A.M. to 6:15 P.M. (closes earlier in winter). Adults €6.80, children €3.40.

Ussé (02–47–95–54–05; www.chateaudusse.fr) is near the D7, 10 km north of Chinon, open daily 9:30 A.M. to 6:30 P.M. February through mid-November. Adults €12, kids €4.

Clos Lucé (02–47–57–00–73; www.vinci-closluce.com) is 2 km north of Amboise; open daily 9:00 A.M. to 6:00 P.M., later in summer. Adults €12, children €7, families €34.

guédelon medieval worksite

If the fancy palaces of the Loire fail to interest your kids, take them to see a medieval fortress castle being built farther upriver. Near the town of Saint-Fargeau, a group of enthusiasts is creating a castle from the ground up. It's a twenty-five-year project, using entirely local materials. A discovery trail with a dozen stops shows visitors the stone-hewer's hut, the stables, the rope maker, the woodcutter, the forge—every craft needed to build a castle. The location's a bit out of the way, but the Guédelon project is like nothing else in Europe. Visit their outstanding Web site to learn more and get hooked.

Guédelon (03–86–45–66–66; www.guedelon.org) is in Saint-Fargeau. From Paris take the A6, then the A77 to exit 21 and follow signs. Open daily except Wednesday, 10:00 A.M. to 6:00 P.M., mid-March through October. Adults €9, kids €7.

dordogne valley

More than 15,000 years ago Cro-Magnon man settled into a valley with narrow sides for easy hunting, shallow rivers full of fish, and hundreds of tiny caves. This Paleolithic paradise is known today as the Périgord region, or the Dordogne Valley, and it's located in the southwest of France about 130 km east of Bordeaux.

les eyzies prehistoric caves

The Dordogne was a priority for Lew, who had enjoyed reading Jean Auel's *Clan of the Cave Bear* series, which is evocative of the area. We stayed for three days in the small village of Les Eyzies, where some of the houses are actually built in the side of the great pockmarked cliffs.

Les Eyzies is the center of a cave region that offers nearly a dozen caverns open to the public. Go to the tourist office first and find out all your options, then decide which you want to visit. In general the caves are divided into two groups: those with prehistoric paintings and those whose appeal hinges on stalactites and stalagmites. In any event avoid the prehistory museum built into a wall above the town: It's *exceedingly* dull for children—and even for most adults.

The most famous caves in the area are the Lascaux caves in Montignac, 20 km northeast of Les Eyzies on N704 (toward Brive). The original Lascaux caves are closed to visitors; what's open here is a complete reproduction of the Lascaux caves, down to the last painting.

We opted for fading originals over bright imitations and visited the Grotte de Font-de-Gaume. Here small groups of visitors are shepherded through the caves in near-total darkness. The curators do this to protect the original cave paintings from light and moisture—the villains that eventually led to the closing of Lascaux. This protective measure, rather than diminishing the experience, actually enhances it, making the paintings come alive historically and artistically. In the brief flashes of dim light, we saw the paintings almost as if we were wandering, torch-bearing Cro-Magnons ourselves.

Grotte de Font-de-Gaume (05–53–06–86–00; www.monum.fr) is on Route D47, 2 km east of Les Eyzies. Open daily except Saturday, 9:30 A.M. to 5:00 P.M.; closed for lunch 12:30 to 2:00 P.M. September through May. Adults €8.50, children €5.50. Reservations are required at least two weeks in advance, as only twelve people may enter on each forty-five-minute guided tour. It is possible that Font-de-Gaume may be closed to the public soon.

prehisto parc

Perhaps because our forty-five-minute cave tour was in French, it didn't interest the kids quite as much as our trip to Prehisto Parc the next day. Prehisto Parc is a collection of about twenty life-size dioramas of people and animals, living and hunting at the time the caves were painted. Despite their initial disappointment in learning that the "cavemen" never actually lived in the caves—anthropologists now believe the caves were for worship and small lean-tos against the rocks were used for shelter—Libby and Sam liked Prehisto Parc because we could wander through at our own pace, English guidebook in hand, under the trees in the open air. Since our visit, Prehisto Parc has added workshops in spear throwing and fire making. Try your hand!

Prehisto Parc (05–53–50–73–19; www.prehistoparc.fr) is located on Route N706, in Tursac, 6 km east of Les Eyzies. Open daily March through mid-November 10:00 A.M. to 6:00 P.M. (later in summer). Adults €6, children €3.

rocamadour

A town that is the second-most-visited place in France must have something to recommend it. On the other hand, it must also be expensive and overrun with tourists. All these facts are true of Rocamadour, located about 65 km east of Les Eyzies.

Rocamadour is a charming, ancient village clinging to a rocky cliff high above the Alzou River. In the early Middle Ages, it was a favorite destination of pilgrims because of its association with the hermit St. Amadour and its famous statue of the Black Virgin. Many pilgrims have ascended the 216 steps to the sanctuary on their knees, but today you can opt for an elevator or ride the little train that circles the village and its parking lots.

Enjoy the architecture, then head to the edges of town for three great treats: the Monkey Forest (la Forêt des Singes), where 500 Barbary macaques roam freely; Eagle Rocks (le Rocher des Aigles), where rare birds of prey are raised and demonstrate their skills; and Euro Miniland (Féerie de Rail), an enormous model train layout of more than 300,000 buildings, trains, and cars. Rocamadour is a delightful destination in the off-season. Visit outside of July and August if at all possible!

Rocamadour elevators run year-round and cost €4.00 (lower, round-trip) and €1.85 (upper, round-trip). The train runs every fifteen minutes. Adults €3.50, children €2.00 (round-trip). Go to www.rocamadour.com for information.

Forêt des Singes (05–65–33–62–72; www.la-foret-des-singes.com) is open daily April through September, 10:00 A.M. to 6:00 P.M. (closed noon to 1:00 P.M. for lunch except July and August). Adults €7.50, children €4.50.

Rocher des Aigles (05–65–33–65–45; www.rocherdesaigles.com) is open 1:00 to 6:00 P.M. in July and August, 1:00 to 5:00 P.M. April through June and September, 2:00 to 4:00 P.M. October and November. Adults €8.00, children €4.50.

Féerie de Rail (05–65–33–71–06; www.la-feerie.com) is open April through mid-

November, with forty-five-minute demonstrations two to nine times per day (depending on season). Adults €6.50, children €4.50.

gouffre de padirac

Don't leave the Dordogne without seeing at least one stalactites-and-stalagmites cave. We especially like the Gouffre de Padirac, about an hour east of Les Eyzies, just beyond Rocamadour.

The tour of Padirac starts with a descent of 250 feet by stairs or by elevator down a deep, moss-lined sinkhole dripping and seeping with water. After a short trek underground, small groups of visitors are loaded into aluminum boats, then poled along a mysterious underground river by friendly French gondoliers (this is the most popular part with many kids). When the river becomes impassable, the tour continues on a rockbound path through fantastic natural formations and pools, stalactites, and stalagmites.

The ninety-minute tour is usually in French (some English tours during peak periods), but with plenty of movement and physical activity, the guide's words hardly matter. (If you're curious, he's mostly telling you the size, in meters, of the most impressive stalactites and stalagmites.)

The Gouffre de Padirac (05–65–33–64–56; www.gouffre-de-padirac.com) is on Route D673, 17 km east of Rocamadour. Open 9:00 A.M. to noon and 2:00 to 6:00 P.M. April through mid-October (9:00 A.M. to 6:00 P.M. July and August). Adults €8.30, children €5.20.

commarque castle

If the crowds at Rocamadour or at the more celebrated caves become depressing, hit the backroads in search of the Dordogne's many deserted corners. The region is littered with castles—not the lush châteaus of the Loire, but small fortresses built by barons and minor counts protecting their small territory from roving bandits. *Bastides,* or fortified hilltop towns, crown the landscape, and scores of brooks and streams provide a pleasant way to pass a few hours with the kids building waterworks and dams.

One good way to explore any area is to buy a picture book and browse for interesting castles and towns. We picked up *Wonderful Périgord,* available in several languages in almost every area gift shop. Each of us then "adopted" an interesting site, and we set off by car.

Our best pick was Commarque Castle, described in the book as "a phantom castle—a vast ruin overrun—once a perfect example of a Périgord medieval fortress." Built in the twelfth century, the castle today is still in the hands of the Commarque family. Whereas in the United States such a site would be fenced off for insurance reasons, here we were able to climb and poke in the most interesting set of deserted ruins we could imagine. Below the castle are prehistoric caves (complete with a significant wall carving of a horse) and fortress caves from the ninth and tenth centuries, where local residents hid from the periodic incursions of Viking raiders.

Recently the castle has been "discovered"—given a Web site, signage, and entry fees. We hope it retains its special magic.

To find Commarque Castle (www.commarque.com), follow Route D47, about 6 km from Les Eyzies, past Font-de-Gaume (toward Sarlat). Look for signs for the village of Bénivés. The castle is 5 km east of Bénivés. Open daily 10:00 A.M. to 6:00 P.M.; later in summer. Adults €5.50, children €2.50.

canoes on the dordogne

If your family enjoys boating, another way to appreciate the serenely beautiful Dordogne Valley is to hop into a canoe. Your voyage starts at Carsac, about 7 km from Sarlat. There you can rent two-person canoes by the hour or arrange a half- or full-day excursion. (We recommend a half-day at most, unless your kids are experienced at sitting still in canoes for hours on end.) No matter which option you select, you'll be traveling on calm stretches of the Dordogne River, past castles and villages best seen from the water.

When the kids get antsy, you can pull up on one of the many beaches and islands to snack or let off steam. At the end of your trip, a bus returns you to your car—there's no tedious paddling upstream!

The river is quite gentle, scenic, and historic. Especially interesting are the medieval castles and cave dwellings on the river's golden cliffs. You can bring a picnic lunch or stop en route to visit one of the many restaurants bordering the river. It was especially exciting for the kids to imagine English soldiers sailing up this same river in the Hundred Years War!

—Steve Roth, Pacific Palisades, CA

Rental of a two-person canoe is €4 per person per hour; half-day trips with bus return are €12 per person, and full-day trips with bus are €19 per person. Be forewarned that the river may be placid in the off-season but can be wall-to-wall boats in midsummer. Contact the Randonée Dordogne (05–53–28–22–01; www.canoerandodordogne.com) for more information. This organization also arranges longer trips, with overnight camping, with or without guides, and rents tents, air mattresses, and so forth.

dune du pilat

You may have already known that France is home to Europe's tallest mountain (Mount Blanc). But did you know the country also boasts the Continent's biggest sand dune?

One of France's unsung attractions, the Grand Dune du Pilat, stretches for more than a mile along the coast near Bordeaux, rising higher than a thirty-two-story skyscraper. A steep flight of weathered wooden stairs (fortunately just a few stories high!) scales the back of the dune to help visiting crowds reach the rim. We climbed them and found ourselves high on a clean white drift, looking down on the blue waters of the Bay of Biscay.

The sun came out just as we arrived, and we spent several hours jumping and sliding on the sand mountain. Hang gliders sailed off the edge of the dune, while school groups picnicked (like us) on its summit. College students outdid one another cartwheeling and somersaulting down the slope of warm, clean sand. As we left we even passed a skier hauling boots, poles, and snow skis up the back of the dune to prepare for an off-season schuss.

The Dune du Pilat is a wonderful place for physical and mental meanders. Your kids can let off steam as they run and cavort. And all of you can imagine almost anything from the heights. A few storm-battered World War II bunkers tilt at crazy angles on the edge of the dune, jump-starting an active imagination. From there, picture pirates sailing into the Bay of Biscay or giant sea creatures emerging from the depths. There's something about this site that opens the mind to any possibility.

It's fun to slip and slide down the biggest sand dune in Europe.

The Grand Dune du Pilat (www.dune-pyla.com) is located at Pyla, 10 km south of Arcachon, west of Bordeaux. Open daily. No admission charge. Wonderful, clean bathrooms near the souvenir shops for a small charge.

rhône valley

It's not surprising that Astérix is the most popular cartoon character in France. Astérix and his band of Gauls uphold French independence, after all, as they resist the soldiers of the conquering Roman Empire with both wiles and strength.

Astérix notwithstanding, the Romans *did* conquer France. And the proof of that conquest lies throughout the Rhône Valley.

nîmes: roman ruins

The city of Nîmes, along the A9 autoroute about 50 km north of the Rhône delta, makes a great base for exploring Roman ruins in southern France.

Known to the Romans as Nemausus, Nîmes abounds with Roman buildings, most of them within walking distance of one another. Its Maison Carrée is the best-preserved Roman temple in all of Europe, perhaps because it's been in constant use since it was built around A.D. 4. Nîmes's Roman arena is more complete than the Colosseum and comprises thirty-four tiers of seats for up to 23,000 spectators. Fitted with a removable roof in winter, the arena serves as the municipal stadium of Nîmes even today, hosting bullfights, plays, and concerts. Twenty km north of town, the Pont du Gard, a spectacular three-tiered Roman aqueduct, remains solid as ever, even though it was built (like the amphitheater) without any mortar.

The visitor center at the Pont du Gard has two great museums. The Ludo is a children's museum, where kids can make a Roman mosaic floor, play with an Archimedes screw, and open and close gates in a water system. For parents and older kids, a second museum traces the history of Roman settlement in the area and tells how the aqueduct was built. You can walk across the Pont du Gard—or drive to nearby Collias and canoe 8 km downriver, drifting under the aqueduct.

Nîmes is the center of bullfighting in France. If you're curious about the sport, you may want to ask about *courses camarguaises,* a variation in which the bullfighters snatch decorations from the bull's head rather than kill him. Oh—and before you leave, don't forget to tell your kids that Nîmes is the birthplace of denim. The heavy, blue cloth was originally known as "toile de Nîmes," or "cloth from Nîmes," leading to our word *denim.*

Nîmes (www.nimes-romaine.com/en) is in southern France, near Arles and Avignon. Maison Carrée and Arena are open 10:00 A.M. to 5:00 P.M. (9:00 A.M. to 7:00 P.M. summer). Maison Carrée free; Arena €7.70 adults, €5.80 kids. Pont du Gard center (www.pontdugard.fr) is open daily 10:00 A.M. to 5:30 P.M. Parking €5.00; Ludo €4.50; museum €6.00. Canoe trips (www.canoefrance.com/gardon) take about three hours and cost €19.00 for adults and €9.50 for kids.

orange: roman ruins

The ruins in Orange, about 50 km north of Nîmes, illustrate the difference between a Roman theater and an arena: Arenas are round or elliptical; theaters have a flat stage wall on one end.

The Théâtre Antique, or Ancient Theater, in Orange is smaller in scale than the arena at Nîmes, with seating for "only" 9,000 spectators. These stone seats step up the hillside in endless semicircular rows, all facing a stone screen wall that towers 120 feet. From the middle of the screen wall, flanked by solid columns, a 12-foot statue of Caesar Augustus—one of the tallest Roman statues in existence—has presided over the scene since before the birth of Christ.

By chance the Roman Amphitheater at Orange in southern France was our first encounter with Roman ruins. We didn't plan it; we were simply beguiled by a freeway sign precisely when we were ready to stop for lunch. The success of this stop, however, taught us how important first impressions can be.

Sam's immediate reaction was one of awe. "How can all this be here?" he asked, in a much-quieter-than-usual voice. "This should all be *dust* by now." The quiet awe didn't last for long. Within minutes he and Libby were racing off together. Later they took us on a tour of all they'd discovered—secret passages, hidden staircases, and rooms where they were *sure* lions had been kept before they were let loose to battle the Christians. The best thing about the Orange Amphitheater is that, like many other sites in Europe, it's not roped off and managed. Kids (and adults) can wander and run anywhere, without offending anyone.

This site really whetted the kids' interest in things Roman. Months after, Libby explained it to me. "Standing in that amphitheater was like looking at an unfinished sentence. You know, like 'The cat . . .'—you just feel like you *have* to find out the rest. I wanted to be able to picture the people who had filled that whole amphitheater."

Orange is 445 miles south of Paris, not far from Avignon. Follow signs in town for the Théâtre Antique (04–90–51–17–60; www.theatre-antique.com). Open daily 9:00 A.M. to 6:00 P.M. (later in summer). Adults €7.50, children €5.50. Free audioguide and multimedia show. Your ticket also includes admission to a mediocre museum that won't interest most kids.

ardèche river gorge

When you've had your fill of history, continue northwest on the A7 about 15 km, then turn west along the Ardèche River Gorge. The area from Pont St.-Esprit to Vallon Pont d'Arc is filled with beautiful scenery and well-maintained freshwater beaches. Stop and wade, swim, or enjoy a picnic when your backseaters get bored.

The kids might also enjoy a side trip to the Grotte de la Cocalière. Here you'll walk for about a kilometer along a subterranean river, then retrace your steps aboveground in a little train. The cave tour is spectacular, with surprises like a spelunker's campsite—and special events such as underground biking are occasionally featured. Children who are afraid of the dark will do well to stay at the front of the group, and everyone should dress warmly.

The Grotte de la Cocalière (04–66–24–34–74; www.grotte-cocaliere.com) is at St.-Ambroix, 18 km from Vallon Pont d'Arc on the D104 and D904; open daily April through October 10:00 A.M. to noon and 2:00 to 5:00 P.M.; 10:00 A.M. to 6:00 P.M. in summer. Adults €7.50, children €5.50. Other recommended caves in the area include the Grotte de la Madeleine and the Aven Grotte de Marzal, both at Saint-Remèze; the Aven Grotte d'Orgnac at Orgnac l'Aven; and the Aven Grotte de la Forestière at Vallon Pont d'Arc.

the mailman's ideal palace

If you're on the road from the south of France to Lyon, detour to the little town of Hauterives for an oddity sure to delight everyone in the family: le Palais Idéal de Facteur Cheval (the Ideal Palace of Mailman Cheval).

Built stone by stone over thirty-three years by mailman and self-taught mason Joseph Ferdinand Cheval, the "palace" is a folk-art delight. Look closely at the facade and you'll see parts of a Hindu temple, a medieval castle, and a Swiss chalet; you'll also spot ostriches, geese, and flamingos in the mosaics and glass chips. This is one of those weird places that will never make most guidebooks, but it is odd enough to totally charm most kids.

Is it worth the side trip? If you're heading for Lyon, Grenoble, Annecy, or Switzerland anyway, we vote yes. This place epitomizes the quirky, artsy individualism that is so typical of the French!

To find le Palais Idéal de Facteur Cheval (04–75–68–81–19; www.facteurcheval .com), a remote but endearing attraction, take the A7 north to Valence, then head northeast on the N532 to Romans. From there the D538 takes you to Hauterives (about 50 km total from Valence). Open daily year-round 9:30 A.M. to 12:30 P.M. and 1:30 to 6:30 P.M. Adults €5.20, children six to sixteen €3.70.

alsace

The two northeast provinces of Alsace and Lorraine have been a political football between France and Germany over the ages. Most recently the area was snatched away by Germany in the Franco–Prussian War of 1870–1871, then returned to France in the Treaty of Versailles—only to be invaded again by the Germans in the Second World War. The result of all this back-and-forth battle is an interesting hybrid culture, reflected in the language, architecture, and cuisine. It's like visiting two countries for the price of one, and the area abounds with some great attractions.

alsace ecomusée

This cultural mix is clearly displayed at France's largest and best open-air museum, the Ecomusée d'Alsace. It's located just outside Mulhouse, in a location convenient to travelers from all over Europe. Kids like open-air museums, and this one is no exception.

The museum started in 1980 when a charitable organization, appalled at the number of historic houses being demolished for new development, bought up several and moved them, stone by stone, to Ungersheim. Today more than fifty houses trace Alsatian history. Most of them are furnished and "inhabited" by costumed guides. Others are still being reconstructed and serve as architectural displays. Still others house shops where you can watch bakers, wheelwrights, blacksmiths, and clog makers ply their trades. Stable, sawmill, train station—a complete village has been reconstructed.

Though we don't usually mention hotels, it's worth noting that the Ecomusée rents apartments and reproduction half-timbered cottages on the grounds of the museum for about €90 to €105 per night. Go to the Web site at www.ecomusee-alsace.com and choose "hotellerie" to learn more or reserve.

The Ecomusée (03–89–74–44–74; www.ecomusee-alsace.com) is 12 km north of Mulhouse toward Guebwiller in Ungersheim on the CD 430. Open daily 9:30 A.M. to 7:00 P.M. in July and August and 10:00 A.M. to 5:00 P.M. September through June. Adults €15.50, kids six to sixteen €9.50.

wildlife!

If your kids like wildlife, several outstanding options exist in Alsace. These include the Montagne des Singes (Monkey Mountain) and the Volerie des Aigles (Eagles' Lair), both located at Kintzheim, and the Centre de Réintroduction des Cigognes (Center for the Reintroduction of Storks) and the Spectacle d'Animaux Pêcheurs (the Fishing Animals Show) in Hunawihr.

monkey mountain and eagles' lair

At Montagne des Singes (Monkey Mountain), more than 150 Barbary macaques roam freely in a forest. Baby monkeys cling to their mothers' stomachs, and small apes store wads of popcorn in their large cheek pouches. Curiously, these North African natives have adapted well to northern Europe; in winter they dash contentedly in the snow.

Nearby lie the ruins of the Château de Kintzheim, the perfect backdrop for the Volerie des Aigles (Eagles' Lair). Time your visit to arrive in the afternoon, when a wide range of birds of prey give demonstrations. You'll see eagles swoop down to grab live fish from a pool, falcons zeroing in on their trainers hidden in the crowd—and if you sit in the front row, tame vultures may tickle your legs. Far from exploiting these endangered species, the *volerie* is also a research center where forty-five falcons have been born, and where two pairs of royal eagles have given birth to three babies, now living happily at the bird sanctuary.

Montagne des Singes (03–88–92–11–09; www.montagnedessinges.com) and the Volerie des Aigles (03–88–92–84–33; www.voleriedesaigles.com) are located in Kintzheim, halfway between Mulhouse and Strasbourg and about 20 km north of Colmar. Montagne des Singes is open daily April through October 10:00 A.M. to noon and 1:00 to 5:00 P.M. (6:00 P.M. in summer). Adults €8, children €5. The volerie at Château de Kinzheim is open daily April through October from 2:00 P.M., two to four shows per day; check times on Web site. Adults €9, children €6. (See Rocamadour in the previous Dordogne Valley section for similar attractions.)

stork center and fishing animals show

The stork is the symbol of Alsace, but the local stork population dwindled from 145 pairs in 1960 to only two in 1982. At that point the Centre de Réintroduction des Cigognes (Center for the Reintroduction of Storks) worked to reintroduce the bird—decimated by high-tension wires and pollution—to the area. To rebuild the population it was necessary to extinguish the birds' natural migratory instinct by offering rich food and warm quarters for the winter (and by clipping the birds' wings and enclosing them in an enormous net). Now more than one hundred storks live and reproduce in the park and are gradually being reintroduced to the surrounding countryside. The birds are an awesome sight, with wingspans of up to 2 meters!

At the same site at Hunawihr, you and your family can also enjoy the unusual spectacle of otters and cormorants diving for fish at the Spectacle d'Animaux Pêcheurs (Fishing Animals Show). Seated in rows of seats rising above an enormous aquarium, you'll watch as a handful of fish are dumped into the water. Suddenly cormorants dive out of the sky, plunging as deep as 7 meters or even 20 meters to capture their prey. Soon after, before your fascinated eyes, a playful otter plops into the water to catch the remaining fish.

Centre de Réintroduction des Cigognes (03–89–73–72–62; www.cigogne-loutre .com) is in Hunawihr. To reach Hunawihr from Kintzheim, take the D35 through Ribeauville—then look for the stork's nest on the tower, telling you that you've arrived. Open daily April through November 11, 10:00 A.M. to noon and 2:00 to 5:30 P.M. (6:00 or 7:00 P.M. in summer). Adults €8, children €5. Shows at 3:00, 4:00, and 5:00 P.M.

mulhouse: museum city

Mulhouse (pronounced *mul-OOZE*) has many other attractions, including a train museum, a car museum, and a fire engine museum. The nearby Ecomusée (above) is best of all, but these are all good options if your outdoor plans get rained out.

The train musem (Musée Français du Chemin de Fer) and the Fire Engine Museum (Musée du Sapeur Pompier) share a site with an OMNIMAX-type theater. The train museum features scores of real engines and cars on real tracks and is quite the treat for train lovers. The fire engines follow suit: lots of trucks from all eras, displayed in a large hall.

The National Car Museum (Musée National de l'Automobile) is even better, featuring almost 500 vehicles from around the world. Completely renewed in 2000, the museum now includes a way-cool hands-on area called "Espace Animé," where your kids can sit behind the wheel of some cars, start the engine, and even learn about wind-tunnel experiments.

The Wallpaper and Printed Cloth Museums in Mulhouse are also world-famous but probably of decidedly less interest to kids. Nearby is the Musée Electropolis, a science museum celebrating electricity over the last three centuries.

The Musée Français du Chemin de Fer (03–89–42–83–33; www.citedutrain.com) is at 2 rue Alfred de Glehn in Mulhouse. Open daily 10:00 A.M. to 5:00 P.M. (10:00 A.M. to 6:00 P.M. April through October). Adults €10.00, children €7.50. Family discount.

The Musée National de l'Automobile (03–89–33–34–34; www.collection-schlumpf .com) is at 192 avenue de Colmar, Mulhouse. Open daily 10:00 A.M. to 6:00 P.M. Adults €10.50, children €8.00. Family discount. Joint ticket to both museums: Adults €17.50, children €12.50.

the totally biased guide to benelux and denmark

Benelux is the name often given to Belgium, the Netherlands, and Luxembourg—a quick shorthand for three small countries. We've lumped them together here with another small country, Denmark. Even though these four countries cover only a small corner of Europe, their selection of things to see and do is large.

Solid burghers are what you'll find in Benelux and Denmark. Housewives in Holland scrub their windows daily. Everyone in Belgium works to learn at least three languages. France's *joie de vivre* and Spain's *mañana* are not to be found in this corner of the continent.

But that doesn't mean people here don't have fun once their work is done. And some of that fun can be a little strange, too: In Ieper, Belgium, they throw stuffed cats from a tower, and in Billund, Denmark, you'll find the original amusement park made of Lego building blocks.

belgium

Belgium is an often-overlooked country with lots going for it. It's a country of transitions, a place that's long been smack in the middle of great happenings. Two thousand years ago the outer edge of the Roman Empire bumped up against German tribes here; even today you'll note a surprisingly obvious line where houses turn from stucco to brick, language changes from Romance to Germanic, bread turns from long sticks to "normal" loaves, and beds are made with coverlets instead of blankets.

Six hundred years ago Belgium was one of the greatest and richest trading centers of the world, when names such as Flanders and Brabant identified the area. Today Brussels is the capital of the European community and once again in the center of modern Europe. Our tour of this tiny country will start at the coast, with a look at Belgium's glorious past.

benelux and denmark

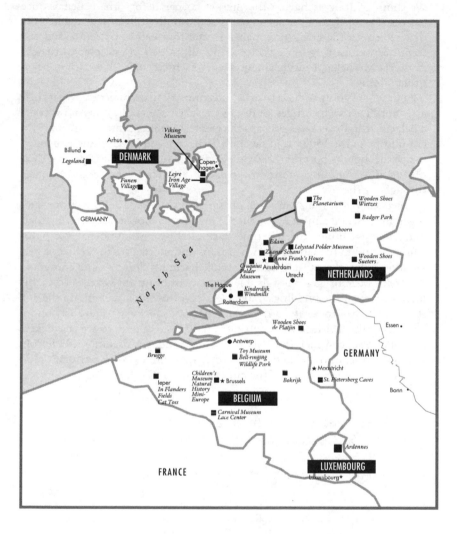

DENMARK

Billund •
Legoland ■

Arhus •

Viking Museum

Copen-
hagen •

Lejre
Iron Age
Village ■

Funen
Village ■

GERMANY

North Sea

The
Planetarium ■

Wooden Shoes
Wietzes ■

■ Badger Park

■ Giethoorn

■ Edam
Zaanse Schans ■ ■ Lelystad Polder Museum
Cruquius ★ ■ Anne Frank's House
Polder Amsterdam
Museum ■

Utrecht ●

Wooden Shoes
Sueters ■

NETHERLANDS

The Hague ●

Kinderdijk
Windmills ■

Rotterdam ●

Essen •

Wooden Shoes
de Platjin ■

GERMANY

Antwerp ●

Toy Museum ■
Bell-ringing ■
Wildlife Park

★ Maastricht

Brugge ■

Children's
Museum
Natural ■ ★ Brussels
History
Mini-
Europe

Bokrijk ■

■ St. Pietersberg Caves

Bonn •

Ieper
In Flanders
Fields
Cat Toss ■

BELGIUM

Carnival Museum ■
Lace Center

Ardennes ■

FRANCE

LUXEMBOURG

Luxembourg ★

brugge (bruges)

We think of Italy as having the market cornered for ornate Renaissance palaces. Then Belgium sneaks up on us with wonderfully ornate architecture that attests to the area's dominance in the fourteenth, fifteenth, and sixteenth centuries. Belgium's glories aren't all hidden in one place: Brussels, Antwerp, Mechelen, Leuven, Ghent, Liège—each city offers a wealth of beautiful buildings.

But you're going to have to offer kids more than architecture to get their attention. That's why Bruges (or Brugge, as its citizens call it) gets our vote for a Belgian visit. Bruges was perhaps the greatest trading center of all of northern Europe in the 1300s, trading cloth, fish, wine, and everything else imaginable through its port on the Zwin estuary. Its rich merchants poured their profits into building mansions, palaces, churches, and grand squares throughout the city.

A century later the Zwin silted up; sandbars blocked the ships from trading in Bruges, and almost overnight the merchants moved away, leaving their grand homes behind, frozen in time. Backwater Bruges slumbered, except for a brief period in the late 1500s, when nuns and monks fleeing religious persecution hid in the city and added several charming churches and convents.

Today little Bruges is a walkable minicity of beautiful swan-filled canals lined with exquisite buildings. Most likely to please kids: a climb up the 366 steps of the bell tower (*belfort*) with its intricate clockwork and forty-seven-bell carillon or a visit to the Kantcentrum, or Lace Center, to see lacemakers at work. Also consider the Folklore (Volkskunde) Museum, with its old schoolroom, cooperage, and candy store. In summer, kids can play traditional games in the garden of the museum's Black Cat Inn.

Bruges is spectacularly picturesque, and the climb up the Bell Tower was taxing. But listening to those bells ring at noon was worth every one of the 366 steps! (My ten-year-old was patient and encouraging when I needed a "breath" break.) It's also a marvelous-size town to walk all over.

—Lillian Souers, Dallas

Another good option is to rent bikes and ride down Langestraat out of town, with a stop to visit the St. Janshuis and Koelewei windmills on the edge of the ring canal. Then continue on to Damme. Damme, just 4 km away, served as Bruges's port until it too silted up. It's smaller but almost as well preserved and is famous for its restaurants. Bike here for lunch, then get back to Bruges as the tourist buses leave for the day and a quiet sunset settles on the "Venice of the North."

Visit Brugge's Web site at www.brugge.be for other ideas. The Kantcentrum (050–33–00–72; www.kantcentrum.com), Peperstraat 3A, is open Monday through Saturday 10:00 A.M. to noon and 2:00 to 5:00 P.M. Adults €2.50, children €1.50. Belfort is open daily except Monday year-round 9:30 A.M. to 5:00 P.M. Adults €5, under thirteen free. Museum voor Volkskunde (050–33–00–44), 40 Rolweg, is open same hours as Belfort. Adults €3, under thirteen free.

Windmills are open May through September, daily except Monday, 9:30 A.M. to 12:30 P.M. and 1:30 to 5:00 P.M. Adults €2, under thirteen free. Bike rentals are available at the train station and a half-dozen other locations in town for about €9 per day; bike tours cost about €19 to €22 and include bikes. Complete list of bike rental locations and tours at www.brugge.be/toerisme/en/fietse.htm.

ieper (ypres)

Belgium has too often been the place where warring armies meet. Napoleon met defeat at Waterloo, and Ieper (also known as Ypres) was the site of some of the worst slaughter of World War I. It was here that poison gas was used for the first time, and many of the battle sites—some with trenches still visible—are open to the public. Older children with some knowledge of World War I may be interested in a visit to the new interactive peace museum called In Flanders Fields. Here computers, video projectors, animatronic models, and CD-ROMs present 300 eyewitness accounts from ten different countries—including soldiers, nurses, refugees, and children. Hardy souls can even cross "No Man's Land" in the dark to feel a small iota of the tension experienced by the participants. The museum is excellent but presents the realities of war too graphically for younger children.

The trenches of World War I covered the countryside around Ieper. Just a few years ago, in fact, a woman was washing her windows when the ground under her gave way and she disappeared into an old trench. Outside Ieper, near the village of Passchendaele, the Sanctuary Woods museum has preserved an original network of trenches open to visitors. Today when trees and grass have returned to the area, it's impossible to truly visualize the appalling conditions suffered by soldiers in these trenches. But still, the site is very moving. Wear boots, as conditions can be muddy.

Every three years on the second Sunday in May, Ieper puts this sad chapter aside to toss stuffed cats from the church belfry. The tradition goes back at least as far as A.D. 962, when live cats were thrown from St. Martin's church to symbolize the casting out of evil spirits. Today plush toys are given the heave-ho in a much more humane ritual that includes the Cat Parade, with dancers, floats, musicians, and giant puppets representing the history of the cat. The next parades are scheduled for 2009 and 2012.

Ieper is in southwest Belgium, about halfway between Lille, France, and the coast. In Flanders Fields Museum (057–23–92–20; www.inflandersfields.be) is in the historic Cloth Hall in the main square (Grote Markt). Open daily 10:00 A.M. to 6:00 P.M. April through September; until 5:00 P.M. and closed Monday October through March; closed most of January. Adults €7.50, children €3.50.

Sanctuary Woods Hill 62 Museum (057–46–63–73) is on Canadalaan 26 in Zille-beke. Take the Menim Road about 3 km out of Ieper and follow signs. Open daily 10:00 A.M. to 5:00 P.M.

binche carnival museum

New Orleans is famous for Mardi Gras and Rio de Janeiro for its riotous Carnival. Unbeknownst to most Americans, many European communities also enjoy lavish costumes, parades, and masks on the day before Lent begins.

Unfortunately for most traveling families, Carnival season usually comes in February when kids are in school and the weather's not conducive to travel. But you can find out about the fun you missed at Binche's Musée International du Carnival et du Masque. Here ten rooms transport visitors country by country through European carnival traditions. At the end Belgium—and specifically Binche—is featured, with a great collection of masks and costumes. A large-screen AV show helps you feel the chaotic delight of Carnival. A worldwide collection of masks, from Balinese treasures to works crafted by North American Indians, rounds out the museum.

Binche is a wonderful place to visit. It's the only remaining walled city in Belgium—surrounded by its original fourteenth-century walls—and offers a lace-making center (where you can see lace made) and a nearby Gallo-Roman museum. It's a nice "This is Belgium" capsule.

Binche (www.binche.com) is about 40 km south of Brussels, near the French border between Mons and Charleroi. Musée du Masque (064–33–57–41; www.musee dumasque.be), 10 rue St.-Moustier. Open daily 9:30 A.M. to 12:30 P.M. and 1:30 to 6:00 P.M.; closed Friday and on Saturday morning. Adults €6.00, kids €3.50. Lace Center (Centre de la Dentelle; www.dentelledebinche.be), Grand'Place 25/1. Open Monday through Saturday 9:00 A.M. to 12:30 P.M. and 1:30 to 6:00 P.M. Musée Gallo-Romain (064–33–95–50; www.viaromana.org) is in the nearby village of Waudrez. Open Monday through Thursday 9:00 A.M. to 4:00 P.M. and Sunday 2:00 to 6:00 P.M. Adults €2, kids €1.

mechelen toy museum and wildlife park

Bells are everywhere in Mechelen, Belgium—four carillons with 197 bells and an internationally famous carillon school that has trained most of the world's leading bell ringers.

If you visit Mechelen today, your eyes can take in the superb architecture (a legacy from the city's heyday around 1500, when it was the capital of the Netherlands) while your ears enjoy the bell-ringing concerts that emanate from the Cathedral of St. Rombout, Busleyden House, and Our Lady over the Dilje, on Saturday, Sunday, and Monday.

Also head for the Toy Museum, where 5,000 square meters of old and new toys await you, spread over thirty different departments. You'll enjoy looking at some of the elaborate old mechanical toys as well as the opportunity to play with lots of hands-on materials.

The Wildlife Park at nearby Planckendael makes a good final destination. A breeding ground for the Antwerp Zoo, Planckendael offers Belgium's safest playground for younger kids and the challenging Route of Adventures for older children. And of course there are the animals, from wolves to leopards to pygmy chimpanzees. It's minutes from Mechelen by car, or you can take a canal boat.

Mechelen is located on the E19, halfway between Brussels and Antwerp. The Toy Museum (015–55–70–75; www.speelgoedmuseum.be), Nekkerspoel 21, is open 10:00 A.M. to 5:00 P.M. daily except Monday. Adults €7, children €5. The Wildlife Park (015–41–49–21; www.planckendael.be) is open daily year-round 10:00 A.M. to 6:45 P.M., later in summer. Adults €16.90, kids €11.90.

brussels museums

Before you head indoors to sample the many museums of Brussels, delight the kids with a trip to the famous Mannekin Pis fountain depicting a boy who's . . . well . . . let's just say the "Pis" transcends any language barrier. Some

Some of the world's best bell ringers were trained at Mechelen.

say this 1619 statue, on rue de l'Etuve behind the town hall, honors a boy who put out a fire with the only water hose available to him. Others admit the statue is simply Belgium's way of thumbing its national nose at pretentiousness in art.

musée des enfants (children's museum)

The Brussels Children's Museum is a treat for four- to twelve-years-olds. Here kids can drive a tram or a raft, sit in a dentist's chair, be a fireman or a farmer, produce a TV program, knead dough, or become a fairy-tale hero. Most activities are so tangible and hands-on that kids won't feel any language barrier. Note the limited hours!

The Children's Museum (02–640–01–07; www.museedesenfants.be) is at 15 rue du Bourgmestre. Open 2:30 to 5:00 P.M. on Wednesday, Saturday, and Sunday and during school vacations. Admission €7.

natural history museum

You get some idea of the scale of the Natural History Museum when you realize it holds thirty iguanodon (dinosaur) skeletons found in a Belgian coal mine, several animated life-size dinosaurs, eighteen whale skeletons, and separate rooms for insects, spiders, shells, the Artic/Antarctic, mammals, minerals, and Belgian fauna. The museum is constantly updating its exhibits. Well worth the visit.

The Natural History Museum, or Institut Royal des Sciences Naturelles de Belgique (02–627–42–11; www.naturalsciences.be), is entered from Chausée de Wavre 260. Metro: Line 1 to Maelbeek (a ten-minute walk from the museum). Open Tuesday through Friday 10:00 A.M. to 4:45 P.M. and weekends 10:00 A.M. to 6:00 P.M.; closed Monday. Adults €4, children €3, families €11.

mini-europe and spirit of europe

Brussels, as capital of the European Union, celebrates old Europe and new together at Mini-Europe, on the outskirts of the city.

Your visit starts outdoors, where more than 300 models of famous European monuments, including the Acropolis and Arc de Triomphe, are built on a one-quarter scale and arranged on easily walkable paths. Why do kids like a scale-model village or town so much? Maybe because it makes them feel so big! When your life is spent looking at grown-ups' knees and stomachs and being unable to see over tall counters, it's pleasant to tower over Big Ben and Mount Vesuvius (especially when the volcano erupts, as it does at Mini-Europe).

In 2004 Mini-Europe opened a new attraction called the Spirit of Europe, designed to convey the promise and challenge of uniting a diverse group of countries into a single political entity. If you're scratching your head and wondering how this concept can be made into a theme park that gets kids (and adults) thinking, come see for yourself. In the "European Symphony" exhibit, for instance, visitors put their hands on a big map of Europe and hear the European Anthem played by a different instrument for each country. More hands placed on more countries create a fuller and more complex orchestration of the anthem. Special technology puts visitors' own likenesses into some of the animated games that explore the languages, former currencies, and flags of the European countries.

Mini-Europe (02–474–13–13; www.minieurope.com) is located off the Brussels Ring Road West (exit 8 by car) north of Brussels. By metro, take line 1A to Heizel (about fifteen minutes). Open daily 9:30 A.M. to 6:00 P.M.; until 8:00 P.M. in summer. Adults €12.20, children €9.20.

bokrijk

The usual dilemma: You want the kids to get culture and they want to have fun. The Open-Air Museum at Bokrijk admirably accomplishes both. The cultural part is the collection of more than 120 historic buildings from all over Belgium, reassembled here to give visitors an overview of Belgian history. Wander around and you'll see everything from a grand Renaissance Flemish town square to farmhouses, mills, and craft shops. Park staff demonstrate traditional activities like lace making.

The open-air approach to culture is one kids usually take to without bribes or inducements—but you've got those here in spades, too. There are fishing ponds, a deer park, horse-cart rides, and best of all, one of Belgium's biggest playgrounds, with some truly spectacular equipment.

The playground next to the Open-Air Museum at Bokrijk is huge: three-story-high tube slides, all kinds of swings, deer enclosure, and a small children's area with child-size construction equipment. And the price is just the cost of parking!

—Lee Loewenstein, Plano, TX (in Belgium for a few years)

Bokrijk (011–26–53–00; www.bokrijk.be) is located outside the town of Genk, not far from Hasselt in southeast Belgium. Open April through September, 10:00 A.M. to 6:00 P.M. daily. Adults €10, children €5.

luxembourg

Kids collect countries; they love to add a new one to the list of places they've been. The tiny duchy of Luxembourg offers medieval castles and beautiful scenery and a chance for older children to learn about the sad history of the Ardennes.

the ardennes

All too often warring armies have treated the lowlands like a superhighway, devastating the flat territory as they marched through to do battle elsewhere. In Belgium Napoleon met his Waterloo, and Ieper (Ypres) saw some of the worst carnage of World War I. More recent generations remember Luxembourg as the site of the Battle of the Bulge, on Christmas of 1944.

It was here that Hitler launched his last desperate offensive of World War II. The area was only thinly protected, since no one thought a weakened Germany would attack over rough and hilly terrain in the dead of winter. Allied soldiers were caught unaware as they dreamed of Christmas and home; local citizens died alongside them as Hitler's forces slaughtered entire villages. Kids who think World War II was easy sailing after the Normandy Invasion will be sobered to learn of the civilian massacres and shell-shocked exhaustion that marked the six-week Battle of the Bulge.

Reminders of the battle can be seen throughout the countryside, both here and in neighboring Belgium, in pockmarked walls and bombed-out castles. But a good place to get an overview is the National Museum of Military History in Diekirch. This museum largely ignores military strategy to focus instead on the personal stories of the war, with authentic paraphernalia including propaganda leaflets dropped from the skies at Christmas to demoralize the troops. Ten life-size dioramas add to the interest for children.

The museum (80–89–08; www.nat-military-museum.lu) is in Diekirch, about 30 km north of Luxembourg City, on Bamertal 10. Open November through March 2:00 to 6:00 P.M.; April through October 10:00 A.M. to 6:00 P.M. Adults €5, children €3, under ten free.

netherlands

The Netherlands is small and flat—perfect for biking and hiking. Make your stay in Holland a country one with picnics by the true-to-stereotype windmills and dikes. The biggest dikes, like the one along the inland sea (the IJsselmeer), have a paved pathway along the top. Walk along this pathway and see how obviously the water on one side looms above the land on the other.

edam: bikes, dikes, and cheese

Every so often when you're traveling with kids, the big attraction someplace may just be that there is no big attraction! Edam is simply a tiny, beautifully preserved slice of Dutch history: no hustle and bustle, no neon and sex shops, no endless traffic jams. Its small but ornate houses tilt and teeter over cobbled streets, and its quiet canals are spanned by delicate iron drawbridges.

Begin your visit in Edam with a stop at the town museum, built as a merchant's home in about 1550 and lived in until 1895. Now it's restored to reflect a typical Renaissance dwelling. Kids love the cupboard beds, but the real attraction here is the floating basement. This room is like a department-store box, with its lid firmly attached to the joists of the house—and its bottom floating on the water table that lies so close to the surface in all of the Netherlands. At high tide visitors must crouch on its rolling floor, while at low tide they can stand up straight.

After the museum we took a long self-guided tour of the town, using an excellent booklet from the tourist office (VVV). Next day we rented bikes—a big hit with the kids—and rode along the dikes. One possible destination is Volendam, just a few miles away. Although Edam cheese is no longer made in Edam, Gouda and other cheeses are made at the Alida Hoeve farm on the southwest edge of Volendam, and you can see it all happen during a free tour. Back in Edam, visit the cheese market, held on Wednesday in July and August.

Big cities have an international flavor and a fast pace that makes them less suited to catching the personality of a country. Whether you're traveling with kids or on your own, small cities and towns are a better bet. Another great place with Dutch flavor is Hoorn, an old whaling town just north of Edam, and Marken, a "costume village" on an island off Volendam.

The town of Edam (0299–315125; www.vvv-edam.nl) is located about 22 km north of Amsterdam on highway N247. For information, write to VVV Edam, P.O. Box 91, 1135 ZJ Edam, the Netherlands. They can supply you with the booklet A Stroll through Edam *for €2.*

The Edam Museum (0299–372644), on Damplein 8 near the Dam, is open Tuesday through Sunday, April through October 10:00 A.M. to 4:30 P.M. Adults €3; kids €1. Bike rentals from Ronald Schot (0299–372155; fax 0299–371533) Grote Kerkstraat 7/9 or Ton Tweewielers (0299–371922) Schepenmakersdijk 6. The Cheese Market (kaasmarkt) (0299–365830; fax 0299–361713) is open 10:30 A.M. to 12:30 P.M. on Wednesday in July and August only. Alida Hoeve (0299–365830; www.henri willig.com), Zeddeweg 1, Volendam. Open daily 9:00 A.M. to 6:00 P.M.; free.

bike-barge tours

If the idea of biking for more than just a few hours appeals to your family, consider a vacation with Cycletours Holland. You'll cycle all day along quiet canals and bike paths, then meet up each night with your hotel-barge, where a gourmet four-course dinner is served. Nights are spent rocking gently in your berth. The next morning, after a hearty breakfast, you'll assemble your own picnic lunch from the buffet while the barge cruises to a new takeoff point, then set out for another day of biking on Holland's blissfully flat terrain.

Although the organization has no minimum age, Cycletours are not geared to young children. But we'd recommend them for families with active, civilized teenagers. The itinerary we chose—Amsterdam to Brugge—was an invigorating challenge, with days averaging 50 km and a bit too much open-country biking for me. The in-country loops, like the Golden Circle and the Southern Tour, provide more interesting village scenes.

Cycletours Holland (20-521-84-90; www.cycletours.com). Prices vary according to itinerary and your choice of cabins. Check Web site for current prices, which include all meals, lodging, and bike rentals.

polder museums

Even the youngest elementary-school child can quickly grasp the fact that most of Holland would be underwater without its dikes. Just stand by the side of the IJsselmeer and it's easy to picture the drowned fields that would exist if the dikes were removed. A visit to either of two Polder Museums in Holland explains how the country drained its swampy land to create islands of arable land called polders.

The first, at Cruquius near Haarlem, is housed in an early steam pump-mill—the first in Holland to replace the old wind-driven mills. Here a huge relief map of the Netherlands is alternately flooded and drained every ten minutes to show how rivers and tides would inundate the country without its elaborate sea defenses. Models of windmills and steam engines are an added bonus for most kids at this eccentric little old museum.

The second museum—the Nieuw Land Heritage Center—is in Lelystad, an area that was in the middle of the Zuyder Zee until draining of the area started in 1932. This museum tells the polder story with high-tech models and a ten-minute multimedia presentation. Kids will especially enjoy "Playing with Water," a 30-foot-long basin where they can build bridges and dams, take ships through locks, and even reclaim land with dikes. Ask for an English version of the kids' treasure hunt.

The Cruquius Polder Museum (023–528–5704; www.cruquiusmuseum.nl) is on Cruquiusdijk 27 in Cruquius, a town about 5 km southeast of Haarlem. It's open daily March 1 through October 31, 10:00 A.M. to 5:00 P.M. weekdays and 11:00 A.M. to 5:00 P.M. weekends. Adults €4, children half price. The Nieuw Land Heritage Center (0320–260–799; www.nieuwlanderfgoedcentrum.nl) is at Oostvaardersdijk 01–13, Lelystad. Open weekdays 10:00 A.M. to 5:00 P.M.; weekends and holidays 11:30 A.M. to 5:00 P.M. Adults €7.00, children €3.50.

anne frank's house

We prefer smaller cities and towns to bustling capitals like Amsterdam, as we've said repeatedly. But we stopped in Amsterdam to visit Anne Frank's house, since Libby had recently read *The Diary of Anne Frank*.

The tour here first takes you through Otto Frank's offices and the secret attic where Anne and her family hid from the Nazis. You'll see everything just as it was the day the Franks were discovered. It may not seem like much to children who haven't read the book, so try to do so before your visit. Then seeing Peter's room or the bookcase door will mean much more.

After the attic tour your path leads through a photo exhibit of family pictures. To my mind the photos are the best part, detailing the Franks' happy, normal life before Hitler. The commentary along with the photos does an excellent job of putting everything in historic context. You'll need to read the commentary to younger kids, who may be overwhelmed by the amount of text and tempted to skip by. It's worth the effort if you want your children to begin to understand the tragedy of the Holocaust.

Anne Frank's house is another of those sites that *must* be visited as early as possible. The inevitable crowds detract from the quiet desperation of the annex and make it difficult to read the displays in the exhibit or discuss their import with your kids. Go early, take it all in, then sit in a cafe and reflect.

Anne Frank Huis (020–556–7100; www.AnneFrank.org), Prinsengracht 267, Amsterdam. Open daily 9:00 A.M. to 5:00 P.M., to 9:00 P.M. April through August. Adults €7.50, children €3.50, under ten free.

zaanse schans folk museum

The late seventeenth and early eighteenth centuries are often referred to as the Golden Age in Holland, a time when the tiny nation was powerful beyond its size in trade and exploration. Zaanse Schans, an open-air museum near Amsterdam, re-creates the rich social and industrial life of that time.

Kids will enjoy learning that windmills weren't just for pumping water. Here they'll see working mills engaged in making mustard, paper, linseed oil, and snuff and in sawing wood. There's also cheese making at the *kaasmakerij* and wooden shoe carving at the *klompenmakerij*. Typical shops, warehouses, a watch museum, and furnished homes are all original buildings moved here from across the country. (Look for the authentic toilet in the ditch by the bakery!)

As with all open-air museums, Zaanse Schans allows kids plenty of chances for running, being noisy, and otherwise being kiddish while immersing themselves in history. The stranger who recommended Zaanse Schans to us over pancakes in an Amsterdam restaurant steered us right!

Zaanse Schans (075–616–8218; www.zaanseschans.nl) is located in Zaandijk, about fifteen minutes north of Amsterdam. Take the Alkmaar train from Amsterdam to the Koog-Zaandijk station, then follow signs (eight-minute walk). Open daily 9:00 A.M. to 5:00 P.M.; some mills and museums in the complex are open on weekends only in winter. Entry to the site is free, but about a third of the buildings have individual entry fees.

We all really had a great time in Holland. Zaanse Schans was wonderful, and strolling around Haarlem during market on Saturday buying cheese and stroopwafels is high on the list. But the best time our kids had there (and we had to return!) was going to the beach and collecting mussel shells.

—Katy Wessel, U.S. Air Force, anywhere and everywhere

---

windmills and wooden shoes

You can't leave Holland without a good dose of windmills and wooden shoes.

You'll see windmills dotted throughout the landscape, but the largest concentration is at Kinderdijk, about 8 km east of Rotterdam. Nineteen windmills dating from before 1750 line the Kinderdijk canals. Each Saturday afternoon in July and August the mills are rigged, the brakes are released, and all seventy-six sails start to spin in the wind. From April through September you can tour the area by canal boat or visit one of the mills. Here your kids can see a mill family's traditional Dutch cupboard beds and get a closer look at how the mills work.

Kinderdijk is the only area in Holland where they have deliberately preserved a large number of working windmills, all spaced maybe a couple of hundred yards apart. They're each about four stories tall, and kids can go in them, all the way to the top. The wooden interior gears are very interesting from a mechanical standpoint.

—Paul Snook, Strongsville, OH

Wooden shoe museums and factories abound in Holland. Most offer three elements: a chance to see wooden shoes being made, a museum showing the surprising variety of traditional clogs, and a shop where you can (of course) buy them. We've listed three of the best known below, though you'll find others wherever your itinerary takes you.

Kinderdijk (www.kinderdijk.nl) is 30 km east of Rotterdam; take exit 22 off the A16. Canal boats: Adults €2.50, children four through nine €2.00. Interior mill visit: Adults €3.00, children under sixteen €1.80. Exterior viewing free.

Klompenmuseum De Platijn (0499–371–247; www.klompenmuseumdeplatijn.nl) is in Best, between Den Bosch and Eindhoven just off the E25. Open daily noon to 6:00 P.M. July and August; 1:00 to 5:00 P.M. daily except Monday off-season. Adults €4.50, children €3.00.

Sueters Woodenshoes (0575–463–030; www.sueters.nl) is in Keyenborg, near Hengelo, west of Arnhem in Gelderland.

Klompenmuseum Wietzes (050–309–1181; www.klompenmuseum.nl) is in Eelde, just south of Groningen. Open daily except Monday 2:00 to 5:00 P.M. April through September.

maastricht: fossils and caves

Maastricht, in the eastern corner of the Netherlands, was established in the fourth century as the Roman fort of Mosae Trajectum. The Romans built their town by excavating blocks of limestone, locally called "mergel," from the chalky ground. This excavation continued for centuries, creating a labyrinth of tunnels that extends for more than 200 kilometers. Look for the entrances all over the landscape.

Most of the tunnels, or "galleries" as they are called, are blocked off now, to prevent people getting lost in them. But you can visit the Grotton St. Pietersberg and enjoy looking for fossils embedded in the limestone walls of the caves. Your tour guide will point out lizard bones, shark's teeth, and even a giant turtle, visible in the stone.

You'll also learn about the "Blokbrekers," the men who sawed the big blocks of stone. They left behind tally marks counting the number of stones they cut and graffiti scribbled during breaks in the monotonous work. Over the years the galleries were cut deeper and deeper. The early Roman inscriptions, now 40 feet off the ground, are barely visible, but more recent doodling—such as that carved by Napoleon when he visited—is more evident.

St. Pietersberg caves (043–325–21–21; www.vvvmaastricht.nl, click on "trips") are located south of Maastricht, beyond the N278 ring road. Open daily April through October and Wednesday, Friday, Saturday, and Sunday in the off-season. Hours vary; English tours are given once a day. Adults €4.25, children €3.25. The tour takes about an hour and is recommended only to good walkers. The caves are chilly, so bring a heavy sweater.

giethoorn

The eastern Netherlands province of Overijssel is largely overlooked by visitors, but it's an area with many attractions. Chief among these is Giethoorn, a traditional village with canals instead of streets.

Everything travels by boat in Giethoorn, Netherlands.

In Giethoorn almost every brick-and-thatch house sits on its own island, and most travel is by flat-bottom boat—kids going to school, postmen delivering the mail, even cows heading for pasture. Those who don't travel by boat go on foot across rickety plank bridges that look temporary but have been there for centuries. Antiques stores, a Dutch tile museum, and a small farm-life museum round out this charming town.

Many towns between Giethoorn and Zwolle, the provincial capital, are known as "costume villages" because their inhabitants still sport traditional Dutch dress. Meppel, Rouveen, and Staphorst are among the most traditional towns; in Staphorst the conservative Calvinists (as is true of the American Amish) would prefer that you not take photos and that you not visit on Sunday. One way to enjoy the colorful folk costumes without intruding is to visit the weekly markets held in Meppel on Thursday and in Zwolle on Friday.

Contact the VVV (tourist office) (0521–361593; www.zwaantje.nl) at Beulahkerweg 114a, 8355 AL, Giethoorn, for more information on this beautiful region of Holland.

't Olde Maat Uus farm-life museum (0521–362244; www.oldemaatuus.nl) is open daily 11:00 A.M. to 5:00 P.M., noon to 5:00 P.M. on Sunday. Adults €3, kids €1.

verkeerspark (traffic park)

We've included this entry to remind parents that they can't always predict what will be a hit with kids. Here's a "Traffic Park" (reader Sage Cole calls it Badger Park because of their mascot) that's not in any of the guidebooks, and their Web site's only in Dutch. Yet a gloomy, rainy-day visit became one child's fondest memory of a three-week trip through Europe.

Badger Park is an amusement park in Holland. We think the best things there were these pedal cars. There are a whole lot of them, so you don't have to wait in line or get tickets as in Legoland. There are so many roads you can really pick out a route and your parents can walk on sidewalks right next to you. There are stoplights and a gas station. You can park on the side of the road and climb up these gigantic inflated balls covered with netting, then get back in your car and drive some more.

—Sage Cole, age eleven, Manchester, MA

Verkeerspark (0592–350005; www.verkeersparkassen.nl) is in Assen on the N-33, and can be reached from the A-28 between Zwolle and Groningen. Open 9:30 A.M. to 5:00 P.M. May through August, weekends in April, September, and October. €14.75 all ages. Sage recommends you find your own little surprises such as "Badger Park" wherever you go.

franeker planetarium

Late in the eighteenth century a Dutch clergyman predicted that the end of the world would soon arrive, due to a disastrous collision of the planets. His prediction was proved false, but the scare inspired one man to learn as much as he could about the actions of the planets.

A little tiny house—our kids loved the very oldness of it. They were amazed that he could do that so long ago. The guide gave his talk in Dutch, English, German, and French, and that fascinated the kids.

—Nancy Fletcher, Portland, OR

Eise Eisinga decided to build a replica of the solar system in his house, complete with orbiting globes hanging from tracks in the ceiling and intricate clockworks hidden in closets and attics. As you study Eisinga's moving astronomical masterpiece, challenge your children to figure out how his view of the planets differs from what's commonly taught in elementary schools today.

The planetarium (0517–393–070; www.planetarium-friesland.nl) is located in Franeker (at Eise Eisingastraat 3) on Holland's north coast not far from the east end of the dike that crosses the IJsselmeer. Open Tuesday through Saturday 10:00 A.M. to 5:00 P.M. year-round, plus Sunday and Monday 1:00 to 5:00 P.M. April through October. Adults €3.50, children under fourteen €2.75.

denmark

You may not have time to venture all the way to Norway and Sweden, but Denmark is the more accessible part of Scandinavia. For our kids Denmark was mandatory, since it was home, at that time, to the only Legoland park. Denmark is also the land of Vikings and is, overall, a very child-friendly country.

lejre: visit the iron age

For one of the most unusual stops on your vacation, travel back to the Iron Age at Denmark's Lejre Experimental Centre, west of Copenhagen near Roskilde. This re-creation of a 2,000-year-old village was opened in 1964 on the theory that progress, despite its many advantages, has resulted in the loss of innovative and environmentally sound solutions our ancestors may have used. Over the years new areas have been developed, adding a Stone Age settlement (ca. 4000 B.C.), a Viking Marketplace (ca. A.D. 800), and the 1850 Farm Cottages to the original Iron Age Village.

At any time a number of families and individuals are in residence, having made a volunteer commitment to dress, eat, and live like their distant forebears for days, weeks, or months, and rediscover lost knowledge. Your family can join them for a single day, visiting the sacrificial bog, viewing primitive plowing with oxen, scrambling through the dance labyrinth, and watching potters, weavers, and blacksmiths at work.

Your tour ends up at Fire Valley, where visitors—with the help of staff members—can try their hand at chopping logs, lighting fires, grinding grain, making bread, and even paddling dugout canoes in the lagoon. These hands-on activities start with a slide show (unfortunately only in Danish), but the show-and-tell format seems to transcend the language barrier for most visitors.

Lejre (045–4648–0878; www.english.lejrecenter.dk) is not in the middle of civilization. From Copenhagen take Motorway 21/23 west. When you're south of Roskilde, turn toward Ringsted, then immediately turn right toward Holbaek. Next turn left to Ledreborg and follow signs to FORSØGSCENTER. *Open 10:00* A.M. *to 5:00* P.M., *from May 1 until mid-September. Adults 80 DKr, children three to fourteen 50 DKr (100 DKr and 80 DKr July and August).*

roskilde: vikings!

For decades in the ninth and tenth centuries, the Vikings were dreaded throughout Europe. They conquered all of central England, took over Normandy, and left the citizens cowering in the caves of France's Dordogne Valley. Now that you're in Denmark, it's hard to imagine that the ancestors of these pleasant, calm citizens were once universally feared!

A good side trip while you're in the area is the Viking Ship Museum at Roskilde. Here are displayed five Viking ships unearthed from the Roskilde fjord, where they sank around the year A.D. 1000. Films on the excavation are shown throughout the day, including an English version. The new Museum Island offers hands-on exhibits, where you can watch a replica Viking boat being built and (at certain times) try your hand at woodworking and rope work. Besides the boats in the museum, other Nordic ships and replicas can be seen in Museum Harbor. Roskilde Youth Hostel is adjacent and charges about 480 DKr (about $86) for a family room.

The Viking Museum (046–30–02–00; www.vikingeskibsmuseet.dk) is at Vindebodr 12 in Roskilde. Open daily 10:00 A.M. *to 5:00* P.M. *Adults 80 DKr, children free.*

funen village folk museum

In Denmark, on the island of Funen, the Funen Village features about twenty-five rural buildings from the past two centuries—farms, a windmill, a water-mill, a school, and a smith, just to name a few.

Open-air museums let kids be active and noisy while they approach history on their own terms. Yet often these museums are spread out on so many acres that short legs—and short attention spans—get tired. Here at the Funen Village, buildings are clustered closely together, so there's always something interesting just around the corner. Your children will probably want to watch the baby goats, geese, and horses; see the farmers planting or harvesting grain; or try their hand at one of the many craft workshops.

We've recommended many open-air museums throughout the Continent. Don't visit them all, as there's enough overlap to create tedium if you do. But by all means include one or two on your trip.

The Funen Village (066–13–1373; www.odmus.dk) is at Sejerskovveg 20 on the southern edge of Odense just north of exit 51 from the E-20. Open daily 10:00 A.M. to 7:00 P.M. July and August, 10:00 A.M. to 5:00 P.M. spring and fall (closed Monday). Adults 60 DKr, children free.

billund: legoland

The original Legoland is a small, tidy amusement park in the tiny Danish town of Billund. (See chapters 17 and 20 for other European sites.) The main attraction is the Lego displays—whole villages, scale-model cathedrals, Alpine scenes, Mount Rushmore, the Taj Mahal, the U.S. Capitol Building, and many more—made entirely of regular, off-the-shelf Legos. Sam, who has an extensive collection of Lego building blocks, had anticipated our stop at Legoland for months. Now that he had arrived in the promised land, he spent hours just getting ideas for future creations.

A big favorite with most kids is Traffic School. Here twenty-five young-sters, ages seven to thirteen, drive little electric cars (like dodgems, but made of oversize Legos) through a cityscape of streets, traffic circles, intersections, and grade crossings. Children have flags on their dashboards that indicate their language, and a single, multilingual teenage traffic cop helps them all remember the rules of the road. "Number Eight," he'll yell. "Don't pass in a no-passing zone!" Then he'll swing around and shout, "Numéro Trois—il faut garder la gauche là!" German, French, Spanish, Danish, Dutch, Swedish, Norwegian, and more, this fellow keeps track of them all—an impressive example to American kids.

When we first visited, most of Legoland's rides were pretty tame (a plus for younger families). Now a few wilder rides have been added for jaded teens, including the X-treme Racers and 2003's addition, the Power Builder. You pro-gram the Power Builder yourself (like programmable Legos!) to choose the thrill level you want. Alas, prices have gone up to pay for the new rides.

Legoland (075–33–13–33; www.legoland.dk) is in Billund in West Jutland, Den-mark. Take the E-45 north from the German border, and turn off at Vejle. Follow signs for Billund, about 30 km west of Vejle. The Tourist Office, located at Legoland, can find you accommodations and change money, too. (Ask about B&Bs or campground bun-galows if the high hotel prices are beyond your budget.) Legoland is open daily May through August 10:00 A.M. to 6:00 P.M. (8:00 or 9:00 P.M. in peak season) and most days in April, September, and October. Adults 229 DKr, kids three to twelve 199 DKr. Traf-fic School is 50 DKr extra. Make sure to reserve for Traffic School as soon as you arrive—and remember, ages seven to thirteen only for this activity!

the totally biased guide to germany, austria, and switzerland

When people dream of European cities, they think of London, Paris, and Rome. When they dream of the countryside, though, it's more than likely they'll envision an Alpine meadow filled with wildflowers and peopled with Heidi, Maria von Trapp, and Hansel and Gretel.

Germany, Austria, and Switzerland will in fact fulfill your stereotypes. But there's lots more to do in these three countries than just yodeling and herding cows. You can learn about glaciers, visit a chocolate factory, or slide down into a salt mine, for instance.

English is widely spoken, but if you bring a little knowledge of German and a large wad of money, you'll have a great time in these three countries.

switzerland

Switzerland is a neat, clean, orderly country, where people are incredibly friendly—as long as you are neat, clean, and orderly. Dan and Wendy recall the warmth they felt when passersby exchanged friendly hellos, and even a pair of teenagers absorbed in the repair of their motorcycle stopped to call out a greeting to the visiting strangers. Yet when Nat momentarily put his foot on the opposite train seat, a proper Swiss man swatted it with a rolled-up newspaper and admonished, "Maybe in your country, but not here."

Kids are attracted to the stereotypes of Switzerland, and they won't be disappointed. The chocolate and cheese really are delicious. The Alps really are covered with glaciers. And the shop windows display plenty of watches.

Plan a visit to Switzerland carefully, though, because it's one of the most expensive countries on the Continent. Don't plan to stay long if your budget's important to you.

germany, austria, and switzerland

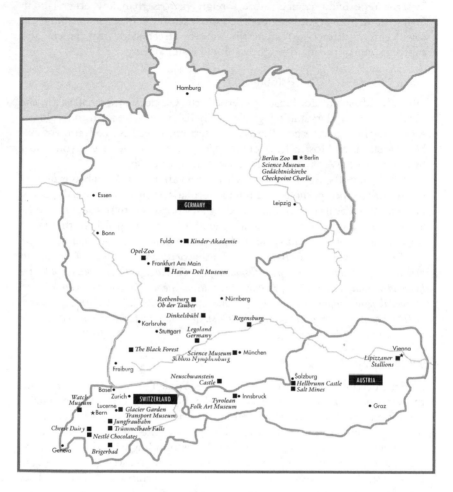

Hamburg

Berlin Zoo ■ ★ Berlin
Science Museum
Gedächtniskirche
Checkpoint Charlie

Essen

GERMANY

Leipzig

Bonn

Fulda ● ■ Kinder-Akademie

Opel-Zoo
● Frankfurt Am Main
■ Hanau Doll Museum

Rothenburg ■
Ob der Tauber
● Nürnberg

Dinkelsbühl ■
● Karlsruhe
● Stuttgart
Legoland
Germany
Regensburg
■

■ The Black Forest
Science Museum ■ ● München
Schloss Nymphenburg
Vienna
Lipizzaner
Stallions

Freiburg

Neuschwanstein
Castle ■
Salzburg ●
Hellbrunn Castle
■ Salt Mines
AUSTRIA

Watch
Museum ■
Basel
Zurich ●
SWITZERLAND
Lucerne ●
Tyrolean ● Innsbruck
Folk Art Museum
Graz ●

★ Bern ■ Glacier Garden
Transport Museum
■ Jungfraubahn
Cheese Dairy ■
■ Trümmelbach Falls
■ Nestlé Chocolates

Geneva ●
Brigerbad

lucerne

Lucerne reportedly attracts more foreign visitors than any other city in Switzerland. Even at the height of the tourist season, though, its medieval old town center is attractive. Wander through the streets with your camera, and capture some of the many brightly colored wall paintings.

gletschergarten (glacier garden)

One of the best sites for kids in Lucerne is the Glacier Garden. Officially, the focus here is understanding glaciers. There are relief maps and exhibits explaining how glaciers grind away at the terrain, as well as a collection of prehistoric skulls and fossils left from the last pass of the ice wave. If you're just heading into the Alps, this can be a useful introduction.

What your offspring are most likely to recall afterward, though, is exploring the strange-shaped potholes and unique formations created by actual glaciers' passage. And they'll enjoy the surrounding kitsch: caves with statues of gnomes, a tiny Swiss-chalet playhouse, and a maze of mirrors (Spiegellabyrinth) from a turn-of-the-twentieth-century carnival that's like walking inside a kaleidoscope.

The Gletschergarten (041–410–43–40; www.gletschergarten.ch), or Glacier Garden, is in downtown Lucerne on Denkmalstraße 4. Follow signs throughout town for the Löwendenkmal, Lucerne's trademark Lion Monument. The Glacier Garden and Spiegellabyrinth adjoin the famous lion. Joint ticket to both, adults CHF 12, children CHF 7. Open April through October 9:00 A.M. to 6:00 P.M.; 10:00 A.M. to 5:00 P.M. in the off-season.

verkehrshaus (transport museum)

Also in Lucerne is the Transport Museum, or Verkehrshaus. Sam recommends the very mountainous, very Swiss model railroad, especially the interactive exhibit on track switches. This exhibit is a series of tracks on a tilting, pneumatic turntable. You have to switch the right switches or a ball rolling along the tracks will make the wrong turn! In this astoundingly hands-on museum, kids can use simulators to fly planes and drive trains, see what it's like to be in a car crash, do outer-space experiments, or defend a ship against pirates. They can also take a virtual-reality tour of Switzerland by ship, rail, and postbus. You could spend your whole vacation in this one museum and never run out of things to see and do.

The Verkehrshaus der Schweiz (Swiss Transport Museum) (041–375–75–75; www.verkehrshaus.org), on Lidostraße 5 in Lucerne, is open daily 10:00 A.M. to 6:00 P.M. (10:00 A.M. to 5:00 P.M. in winter). Adults CHF 24, children six to sixteen CHF 12, families CHF 50 (IMAX theater extra).

alpine ups and downs everywhere!

Any ride up any Swiss mountain is popular with children. And there are certainly plenty of them: More than 400 aerial cableways, cog railways, and funicular railways welcome visitors year-round, while another thousand lifts operate during the ski season. Look at any map and you'll see the zipperlike ╂╂╂╂╂╂╂╂╂╂╂╂╂╂╂╂ lines of the lifts snaking up from most villages.

One good choice is to ride up and hike down. Hiking trails are well marked and well maintained, with yellow signs that give the time estimated for hiking to the next village. "Std." means *Stunden,* or hours; add a little to the times, as the Swiss are in better shape than most Americans. Free hiking maps are available from even the smallest tourist offices.

Boat rides on any of Switzerland's beautiful lakes are also a good bet. Again, shop by price and time available from among the 140 passenger boats on the country's lakes and rivers. Keep in mind that longer boat rides offer nothing but a lot more of the same; shorter trips are often best.

If you plan to take many train or boat rides, look into the Swiss Card, available at railway stations throughout Switzerland. It costs around $187 (first class) or $134 (second class) and allows foreign visitors unlimited half-price travel for one month on trains, boats, buses, and most mountain railways. And when you buy the pass, you also get a free "Swiss Family Card" that lets your children under sixteen travel free when they accompany you. A family of four could easily come out ahead if they planned to take more than a few boat rides and mountain railway excursions—and especially if they planned to travel regularly by train.

If you're staying in Switzerland longer than a month, ask instead for the Half-Fare Card, which offers the same half-price benefits of the Swiss Card for around the same price, but it is valid for a full year. It's a bit more of a hassle (you'll need a passport photo, and there's a ten-day wait for the card, during which you'll have use of a temporary card), but it's definitely worth the extra bother if you're staying longer.

Ask your travel agent or call Rail Europe at (888) 382–7245 in the United States for information about the Swiss Card and other discount passes.

berner oberland and valais

The area south of Bern, including that around Interlaken, is known as the Berner Oberland. It's an area of glaciers and Alpine villages that, although heavily touristed in the summer, is so expansive that the onslaught seems to be swallowed up by the mountain valleys.

Don't stay in Interlaken. Go into the country, head up a mountain road, and look for a ZIMMER FREI sign advertising a roadside B&B. Even better, head for someplace where cars aren't even allowed. Wengen, about 10 km south of Interlaken as the crow flies, can only be reached by cog railway, perched as it is on the side of the Alps.

Hikes in any direction present satisfying views, but one special outing takes you to the Trümmelbach Falls, not far from Wengen, near Lauterbrünnen. Take the underground funicular up to the seventh falls, hike up the last three, then follow these ten chutes of water as they make their way through caves and over glacier-carved gutters inside the rock. Be prepared for cold winds and a deafening roar—as well as a chance to explore great tunnels and little bridges.

Another great (but pricey) outing in this area is the Jungfraubahn train up the Jungfrau to Jungfraujoch, the highest train station in Europe at over 11,000 feet. The ride up is spectacular, and the views from the Sphinx terrace observation post (another 364 feet up, traveling by elevator) are breathtaking. You can take ski lessons on the 17-mile-long Altesch glacier, enjoy a dogsled ride, or dine in the restaurant. The Tripps' favorite part was the Ice Palace, a sequence of vaulted ice caves carved in the glacier and featuring ice sculptures of birds, animals, penguins, and even an igloo. A bonus: The Ice Palace is free to Jungfraubahn passengers.

Several valleys south of Lauterbrünnen in the Valais region, a very kid-friendly experience awaits you at the Brigerbad thermal spa. "Spa" brings up images of wealthy women getting seaweed wraps, but Brigerbad is essentially a giant water park, with the longest waterslide in Europe snaking down the mountainside. All this and educational value, too, because the water is natural and thermal. Every day the slides and wave pools are emptied and almost immediately clean, warm water—ranging from about 80°F to 100°F—gushes in to refill them. Explain to your kids how water percolates deep into the earth, is heated by proximity to the planet's molten core, then shoots back up through faults in the rock. Then relax and enjoy the fun as the Tripps, who lived five months in nearby Brig, recommend.

To reach Wengen (www.wengen.com), take a small Alpine train from Lauterbrünnen, south of Interlaken. Trümmelbach Falls is reached by postal bus from Lauterbrünnen (CHF 3) or by a half-hour hike. Falls are open April through November, 9:00 A.M. to 5:00 P.M. Adults CHF 11, children CHF 4. For information call 033–855–32–32, or go to www.truemmelbach.ch.

The Jungfraubahn leaves from Interlaken Ost station; check schedule or book at www.jungfraubahn.ch. CHF 152.60 round-trip per person—but this is where the Swiss

Card pays for itself. Buy the Swiss Card and your whole family can take the Jungfrau-bahn for the cost equivalent of two adult half-fare tickets.

Brigerbad (www.brig-belalp.ch—in German) is 3 km west of Brig and can be reached by postal bus from the Brig-Gamson-Brigerbad train station. Pools are open mid-May to mid-September, 10:00 A.M. to 7:00 P.M. (slides 1:30 to 6:00 P.M.). Adults CHF 13, kids CHF 6.

cheese and chocolate

What's more Swiss than cheese and chocolate? Your family can see how both are made with a visit to the Gruyères area.

Start at the cheese dairy where (what else?) Gruyère cheese is made. You'll see a short audiovisual presentation on the cheese-making process and then watch as milk is heated and stirred in huge vats to make the seventy-seven-pound wheels of cheese. While the tour is not terribly interactive, it won't strain a child's attention span, and the cheese samples at the end are excellent. There's also a cheese restaurant on-site where you can dine on fondue, *rösti* (a sort of potato pancake with cheese), or even macaroni and cheese. For months after his return, Sam wanted us to buy Gruyère cheese at the store—and he insisted that only the real Swiss variety tasted right.

What's more Swiss than chocolate and cheese?

> We spent a day visiting the Gruyère cheese factory (the restaurant there was wonderful) and the Nestlé factory. My seventeen-year-old son said it was one of the best days of his whole life.
>
> —Barbara Knight, Sterling, VA

Just north of Gruyères in Broc is the Nestlé factory, where the company's Cailler brand chocolates are made. Here you'll watch each step of the chocolate-making process through glass windows alongside the assembly line. First the whole cocoa beans are crushed and made into cakes of cocoa powder. This powder is mixed with milk, formed into bars, and packaged, all before your eyes. The best part comes at the end, when platters of chocolates are laid out before you in the samples room, and you can nibble to your heart's content for ten to fifteen minutes.

The Model Dairy (026–921–84–00; www.lamaisondugruyere.ch) is at the entrance to the town of Gruyères, near the railway station. Open daily 9:00 A.M. to 6:00 P.M.; cheese is usually made from 9:00 to 11:00 A.M. and 12:30 to 2:30 P.M. Adults CHF 5, children CHF 4, families CHF 10. The Nestlé factory (026–921–51–51; www.cailler.ch) is located on rue Jules Bellet 7 in Broc. Open April through October Monday to Friday, 9:30 A.M. to 4:00 P.M. Free entry.

swiss watches

In the not-so-charming industrial city of La Chaux-de-Fonds is a museum that salutes Switzerland's most famous industry: watchmaking. It's the Musée International d'Horlogerie (International Clockwork Museum). Through the display of more than 3,000 sundials, ancient water clocks, and intricate mechanical and musical clocks, the museum traces man's attempts to mark time over the ages. You can also see how clocks are made by watching actual craftsmen at work. Once you've seen all the little clocks and watches, finish your visit by taking in the fifteen-ton animated clock in the bell tower of the adjoining park. It's got something for everyone: music, bells, projectors—even a light show at night.

La Chaux-de-Fonds is in the Jura area of Switzerland, just north of the city of Neuchâtel, between Lake Neuchâtel and the French border. The Clockwork Museum (032–967–68–61; www.mih.ch) is at 29 rue des Musées. Open Tuesday through Sunday 10:00 A.M. to 5:00 P.M. Adults CHF 15, teens CHF 10, children under twelve free, families CHF 32.

germany

From Beethoven to BMWs to beer, Germany offers the world gifts worth sharing. By chance we've concentrated on sites that happen to be in the more heavily traveled western part of Germany. If you have time, visit the former East Germany, too: The comparison in this era of transition could fuel some interesting family talks.

If you are fortunate enough to travel in both halves of the country, compare road conditions, architecture, store signs, farm equipment, evidence of pollution—the list is endless. The differences are being rapidly obliterated, so visit now and witness a chapter of history.

Germany is a very large country, so we've organized our suggestions into five main areas: Southern Bavaria and Munich; Northern Bavaria; Frankfurt; the Black Forest; and Berlin.

neuschwanstein castle

Neuschwanstein Castle (pronounced *noy-shvahn-stine*) is like Stonehenge or the Eiffel Tower, a site so overhyped that you have to ask yourself, "Could it possibly be that good?" If you don't know the name, you know the castle: It stares at you from every German travel poster, with Disneyesque spires jutting into the mist against a background of snowcapped peaks.

If you visit you'll learn that the castle is little more than one hundred years old and was built by "Mad Ludwig" of Bavaria, who drowned mysteriously only months after the castle was finished. Unfortunately, the only way you'll learn all this is by hiking up the road to the castle and taking the obligatory tour in strongly accented English. Still, as long as your fairy-tale visions are tempered with these realistic expectations, it is a lovely castle. Bring a picnic in your backpacks, and hike up to the Marienbrücke over the gorge behind the castle for lunch.

At Neuschwanstein you can buy your tickets the day before at the tourist office near the parking lot. Then just go at the appointed time. You don't have to walk up to the castle. You can take a horse and wagon, but it costs extra. Another great spot to picnic is by the lake, near Hohen-schwangau.

—Maya D'Anjou, Morgan Hill, CA

Neuschwanstein (08362–939–88–0; www.neuschwanstein.de) is located in Fussen, about 75 kilometers southwest of Munich near the Austrian border. It's open daily 9:00 A.M. to 6:00 P.M. (10:00 A.M. to 4:00 P.M. off-season). Adults €9, children €8. Buy tickets for a set time, then picnic or explore while you wait your turn. Walking to the castle takes about forty minutes; by bus: €1.80 plus a ten-minute steep downhill walk; by horse carriage: €5.00 plus a five-minute walk.

legoland germany

Since we've already covered Legoland in Denmark and England, I'm going to turn this listing over to reader Ellen Manuel, who spent two months in Germany with her military husband and three kids.

What a clean, bright, wonderful park. The kids got German "drivers' licenses" with their photo, and after a driving instruction movie (in German), got to drive little Lego cars around, which they loved. They rode on Lego planes, Lego boats, Lego knights' horses, and a Lego roller-coaster car. Miniland was incredible, with Lego Venice (with singing gondoliers on moving boats), Berlin, Hamburg, Frankfurt, Washington, D.C., and the Munich airport with tiny Legomen loading luggage. All the cities and villages had cathedrals with ringing bells, fountains that worked, people that moved, etc. They also had Lego car-building centers, where we could build and race our own cars. We all had a super time. It was soooo much fun to watch the kids, as they felt that they'd arrived in heaven.

—Ellen Manuel, Belleview, NE

Legoland Germany (08221–700–700; www.legoland.de) is in Günzburg, halfway between Stuttgart and Munich. Open daily from June through most of September (Thursday through Sunday in April, May, and mid-September), 10:00 A.M. to 6:00 P.M., with extended hours to 8:00 or 9:00 P.M. in midsummer. Adults €26.50, kids three to eleven €22.50.

munich

Heavy bombing during World War II means that most German cities consist of an efficient, modern, characterless core, and an Old Town, or *Altstadt*, that's been carefully pieced back together or even rebuilt from scratch. (Many buildings that "date from 1215" may actually have been completed less than a decade ago.) Munich (München in German) typifies this fact, with a charming old town of mixed authenticity and a surrounding sprawl of rather soulless modernity. None of this will matter, though, to travelers with kids, who will find plenty to do.

outdoor treats

Start at Marienplatz, in the heart of the old town, where you'll find the *glockenspiel* (German for carillon). Stand in front of it at 11:00 A.M. daily to see the little doors on the clock open as jousting knights, working artisans, and costumed dancers, all made of enameled copper, perform for you. Or if you're here at 9:00 P.M., you'll see a mechanical watchman put Munich to bed.

Then head for the Englischer Garten, Munich's outdoor living room. Three miles long and more than a mile wide, this is Germany's largest city park. It holds four beer gardens, a Chinese pagoda, playgrounds, and even a surfing area! Mixing with normal German kids can be far more educational than visiting another church or *Rathaus,* so unwind here for a whole day. Rent bikes at the park's southern entrance, or take a rowboat out on the Kleinhesseloher See. Listen to the oompah bands that play on Sunday and on some summer afternoons. Munch on pretzels and enjoy! (A note to parents: Nude sunbathing is common in sections of the Englischer Garten marked on maps and signs by FKK. We tell you this so you can be alert. But the park is so vast you should be able to avoid surprises with a little care.)

Our kids really enjoyed Munich. We spent hours in the science museum exploring all the hands-on exhibits. Language was not a problem there at all. We even visited the Hofbrauhaus, where everyone was singing and dancing on the tables. Our kids loved that—I think they really liked seeing adults act crazy.

—Doug Alexander and Lisa Geibel, Austin, TX

deutsches museum (science museum)

If it's rainy, visit the Deutsches Museum, the world's largest science museum, with more than 17,000 items displayed in 12 miles of corridors. With this many choices, we recommend you start by buying the *Guide through the Collections* and thumbing through its pictures with your kids to set some goals. Also get the free English map and demonstration schedule. Kids love the hundreds of hands-on displays with buttons, levers, and switches they can activate. The simulated coal, salt, and iron mines in the basement are also popular, as is the high-voltage display that actually produces thunder and lightning. Kids from three to ten will especially enjoy the new Kinderreich (Kids' Kingdom), with its enormous guitar, a waterfall you can stand behind, pulleys and ropes to explore, a fire engine you can sit in, and a whole room of wooden blocks and giant Legos.

The Deutsches Museum (089–217–91; www.deutsches-museum.de) is located on an island in the Isar River, in the middle of Munich. It's open daily 9:00 A.M. to 5:00 P.M.; closed major holidays. S-Bahn: Isartor station. Adults €8.50; kids €3.00, families €17.00.

schloss nymphenburg

Ever wanted to see Cinderella's coach? It's waiting at Schloss Nymphenburg, about 5 km northwest of the Munich city center. The palace itself is impressive, an over-the-top rococo masterpiece. But architecture isn't usually kids' first choice. What makes this a nice side trip is the coach exhibit and acres of grounds dotted with interesting fountains and outbuildings.

The Marstallmuseum, in the former stables of the palace, houses three rooms of ornate coaches and sleighs. The Cinderella Coach was commissioned by King Ludwig I for his marriage to a duchess named Sophie; after the engagement broke off, Ludwig used the coach for joyrides around Bavaria. There's also a glass coronation coach and plenty of other high-class transport.

Schloss Nymphenburg (089–179–080; www.schloesser.bayern.de) is just to the northwest of Munich by the 41 bus or the 12 tram. Open daily 9:00 A.M. to 6:00 P.M. April to October (10:00 A.M. to 4:00 P.M. off-season). Adults €10, under eighteen free. Make sure to get the combined ticket not the castle ticket, so that you can visit the coach museum.

northern bavaria

Northern Bavaria is centered on Nürnberg (Nuremberg), once known as the toy-making center of Germany, but now, unfortunately, more closely associated with the Nazi War Crimes trials. It's a bustling industrial city, a jobs powerhouse of the region—and a place you'll want to pass by in favor of three charming nearby cities and towns.

regensburg

Regensburg makes a great base for exploring Northern Bavaria. It was the largest medieval city in Germany completely untouched by Allied bombing in World War II. Regensburg was first a Roman fort, then later the first capital of Bavaria and the site of the first German parliament. Now it's a charming university town, with a good mix of Bohemian dives and imperial mansions.

There's no one sight or museum to draw you to Regensburg—just the entire gestalt of the city. There is the charming Alte Kapelle with its ornate gilded rococo decor, gold and jewels in the cathedral treasury, the deep gorge of the Danube (Donau, in German) running through town, great public swimming pools and water parks. And then there are those beer parks. . . .

Our two weeks in Regensburg were great. It was easy to excite the kids by the history present all around them. An overwhelming urban blast from the past! Great inexpensive food, beer gardens with playgrounds. We spent many hours drinking beer and Apfelschorle (half apple cider, half fizzy water) and eating big soft pretzels (Brezen) while the kids played.

—Paul Heald, Athens, GA

Regensburg (0941–507–4410; www.regensburg.de) is 80 km southeast of Nürnberg via the E56. It's our choice of these three cities because it's not nearly as tourist-ridden as towns that lie on the Romantic Road.

rothenburg ob der tauber

We're talking seriously quaint here, folks. Rothenburg's reputation as one of the best-preserved medieval towns in Europe is well founded, as you'll see when you enter the city's thirteenth-century walls and wander around its narrow, jumbled streets.

Take your kids up on the ramparts of the old walls first for an active romp. Then head down to the *Rathaus* (town hall in German) and look across the marketplace for the old clock on the side of the drinking hall. The clock commemorates the heroism of Burgermeister Nusch, who saved the town from invaders by winning a bet that he could down a three-and-a-half-quart tankard of beer in just one slug! Hourly from 11:00 A.M. to 3:00 P.M., then again at 9:00 and 10:00 P.M., the clock demonstrates this feat as it chimes.

Rothenburg's architecture is just fabulous. Our kids (ten and thirteen) thought the Museum of Crime and Torture was most impressive. It's not all gory—for instance, we learned that liars had to wear a metal helmet with bells on it, to alert everyone to their fault. And women who squabbled were chained together until they learned to get along. We reminded our kids of these good ideas later in the trip when they misbehaved! When in Europe . . .

—Paul Snook, Strongsville, OH

When the kids get tired of soaking in the ambience, you might want to visit a museum. The Puppen und Spielzeugmuseum (Doll and Toy Museum) has a great collection of more than 800 dolls and dollhouses along with stuffed animals, toy soldiers, and trains. Older kids will opt for the ghoulish Mittelalterisches Kriminalmuseum, or Medieval Crime Museum. Some punishments—like the cage for bakers of underweight loaves and the "shame flute" for bad musicians—will fascinate, while others will gross out even the most hardened teenager.

Rothenburg is on the Romantic Road (Romantische Straße), about 45 km south of Würzburg. It's utterly overrun with tourists, so visit during the off-season if possible, or come as early in the morning as you can. Doll and Toy Museum (09861–73–30; www.spielzeugmuseum.rothenburg.de) is at Hofbronnengaße 13 and is open daily 9:30 A.M. to 6:00 P.M. Adults €4.00, kids €1.50. The Crime Museum (09861–53–59; www.kriminalmuseum.rothenburg.de) is at Burggasse 3 and is open daily 9:30 A.M. to 6:00 P.M., with shorter hours November through March. Adults €3.80, kids €2.30, families €9.80.

dinkelsbühl

Rivaling Rothenburg for the Quaint Award is Dinkelsbühl, 40 km to the south of Rothenburg. Dinkelsbühl residents sniff at their northern neighbor, noting that their half-timbered homes are authentic, while many of Rothenburg's are rebuilt.

You be the judge. Both are wonderfully attractive and horribly overrun with tourists at the height of the season. Both have old walls and towers you can climb to get a great view of the town.

But where Rothenburg sports its Toy Museum and Crime Museum, Dinkelsbühl celebrates kids. Legend has it that Swedish invaders, in the Thirty Years War (1618–1648), were turned back at the edge of town because they were moved by the tears of the village children (*Kinderzeche*). The town holds a yearly Kinderzeche festival to celebrate the event, in which kids dress up in old-fashioned costumes and reenact the event.

The Kinderzeche's great but crowded. Come another time, and enjoy Sunday concerts in the park from May through September, or climb the tower of St. George's Minster and enjoy a bird's-eye view of this beautiful town. Then, for something offbeat, visit the 3-D Museum, an oddball attraction that showcases all the ways people have tried to represent three-dimensional reality in two-dimensional media for the past 1,000 years.

Dinkelsbühl (www.dinkelsbuehl.de) is 40 km southeast of Rothenburg on Route 25, the road to Augsburg. The Kinderzeche (www.kinderzeche.de) is held in mid-July. St. George's Tower is open 1:00 to 6:00 P.M. on weekends from May through September; free admission. The 3-D Museum (09851–63–36; www.3d-museum.de) is housed in the Nördlinger Tor of the town wall. Open daily 10:00 A.M. to 6:00 P.M.; 11:00 A.M. to 4:00 P.M. weekends only November through March. Adults €8, kids €5.

frankfurt area

In an effort to bring more tourists to northern Germany, the German tourist bureau in 1985 decided that "the Frankfurt area" was not a very attractive name. So they dreamed up a promotion they call the Märchenstraße, or Fairy Tale Road. The route strings together various sites associated with the Brothers Grimm—from Rapunzel's tower to Sleeping Beauty's castle. The Grimm Guys really did hang out in Kassel, a city north of Frankfurt. And they really were inspired by their surrounding environment. But many of the sites are hokey and leave kids disappointed.

Why mention the Fairy Tale Road at all, then? Because you may hear about it and say, "This would be perfect for the kids!" It isn't, in our opinion (and that of some of our readers). But the neat thing is that this same area does have some other sites worth visiting with kids. In case you're traveling in the Frankfurt area, we'll recommend a few.

opel-zoo

Just west of Frankfurt in Kronberg is the Opel-Zoo, a wonderful zoo where more than 1,000 animals of 200 species loll about in their native habitats. Germans love zoos, and this is a good one, including as it does not only live animals but also a great nature museum with life-size models of animals and how they interact with their environments. For little kids there's also a petting-zoo area, where they can get up close to donkeys, sheep, goats, and the like.

A wonderful playground adjoins, with a 30-meter giant slide, a trampoline center, cable ride, and a little train. There are even pony and camel rides to finish off the day.

Kronberg has a vibrant history as an artists' colony and health spa (*Luftkurort*, or fresh-air-cure-place in German). Wander its late–Middle Ages streets of half-timbered houses, and don't miss the marvelous painted walls and ceilings of the ancient Johanniskirche (St. John's Church).

Opel-Zoo bei Kronberg (06173–79749; www.opel-zoo.de), Königsteiner Straße 35, Kronberg. From Frankfurt take the A66 toward Wiesbaden, then take the Königstein exit and follow the B8 and the B455 to Kronberg. Open daily 9:00 A.M. to 7:00 P.M. in summer; 9:00 A.M. to 5:00 P.M. off-season. Adults €9, kids three to fourteen €6.

hanau puppenmuseum (doll museum)

Hanau was where the Brothers Grimm were born, but your kids will be more interested in the Puppenmuseum (doll museum) here, which displays dolls from all over the world, both historic and modern.

Boys shouldn't turn up their noses at the idea of a doll museum because there's plenty here to interest any kid—from teddy bears and rocking horses to scale-model shops and schoolrooms. If you can read any German, you may also be able to help your kids learn a little about the lives of the kids who once played with these toys long ago. A hands-on area with dress-up clothes is fun, too.

Puppenmuseum (06181–86212; www.hessisches-puppenmuseum.de) is at Parkpromenade 4 in Hanau-Wilhelmsbad. From Frankfurt take the A66 toward Hanau or the B8/40 toward Hanau-Wilhelmsbad. Open Tuesday through Sunday 10.00 A.M. to noon and 2:00 to 5:00 P.M. Adults €2.50, kids under fourteen €.50, families €5.00.

kinder-akademie (children's museum)

In 1991 Helen Bonzel decided to transplant to Germany a concept she'd seen in the United States. The concept was the children's museum, or discovery center—a relatively unknown idea in Germany. Frau Bonzel succeeded at creating a great place where kids can play and experiment with crafts, science, and nature to their hearts' content. Now children's museums are catching on all over.

Exhibits include a giant human heart that kids can walk through, as well as exhibits about wheels ("Das Rad") and one on rabbits and Easter bunnies. Kids can take part in craft projects from papier-mâché to finger puppets. A good time was had by all.

Kids may enjoy the decidedly hands-on Deutsches Feuerwehr-Museum (Fire Engine Museum). Where else can they try out a fire extinguisher or set off a fire alarm with impunity? The town of Fulda even boasts a skateboard park, to top off a perfect day.

Kinder-Akademie (0661–90–27–30; www.kaf.de), Mehlerstraße 4, Fulda. From Frankfurt take the A66 in the direction of Hanau/Schlüctern, then continue on the B40 to Fulda. Open Monday through Friday 10:00 A.M. to 5:30 P.M. and weekends 1:00 to

5:30 P.M.; *closed Saturdays in summer. €3 for adults and kids over five; €6 for museum and "Walk-through Heart" exhibit. The Feuerwehr-Museum (0661–750–17; www.dfv.org/feuerwehrmuseum) is at St.-Laurentius-Straße 3. Open daily except Monday, 10:00 A.M. to 5:00 P.M. Adults €3, children €2, families €10. A Museum Pass (adults €9.50, children €7.50), available at the tourist office at Schloßstraße 1, gives you entry to both these plus four more museums. Visit www.tourismus-fulda.de to download an English brochure detailing everything there is to do in this great town.*

black forest

Whereas the Romantic Road and the Fairy Tale Road are pure inventions of the German Tourist Board, the Black Forest, or *Schwarzwald*, is real. Sure, the forest has suffered a bit from encroaching population and acid rain, but the area bounded roughly by Freiburg to the west, Stuttgart to the east, and Switzerland to the south is still rather lovely. This is the land of fairy tales, of dark forests and cuckoo clocks, of traditional thatched-roof homes. It's a great area to wander around freely or to hike, but here's a suggested itinerary of places to stop along the way.

Start just outside Freiburg, near the French border, by taking a cable car up Schauinsland, a 1,284-meter peak. The marvelous views will give you a preview of coming attractions. After you come back down to earth, start driving through the beautiful countryside, heading north to St. Märgen. This tiny village makes a great hiking base for a day. Pack a picnic and stop at the tourist office for hiking maps that detail a variety of one-hour to daylong treks. Hit the trails, or enjoy a boat ride at one of the many small area lakes. The tourist office can also find you inexpensive lodgings for the night.

Next day continue north on Route 500 through Furtwangen and Triberg. Furtwangen was the birthplace of the cuckoo clock, invented by Franz Ketterer in the early 1700s. His original clock, with its simple wooden mechanism, is in the Uhrenmuseum (Clock Museum) here; tours in English explain the history of timekeeping from Stonehenge to atomic clocks. Nearby Triberg has the Schwartzwald-Museum (Black Forest Folk Museum) with more clocks, costumes, and an impressive model train; Triberg also boasts Germany's tallest waterfall.

The Triberg area was so beautiful, with lush forests and rushing streams. It really did look like the fairy-tale descriptions in "Hansel and Gretel," "Snow White," and all the other Grimm fairy tales. We picnicked by a beautiful waterfall and enjoyed hiking around in the forest. What incredible views from the mountaintops! The kids had pinecone wars, built little bridges across the streams, and played all sorts of imaginary games in the forest.

—Ellen Manuel, Bellevue, NE

After Triberg, finish your tour of the Black Forest by heading east to Rottweil. It's ironic that such a pretty town has contributed flameless gunpowder and fearsome dogs to the world. Today Rottweil is best known for the architecture and atmosphere of its ancient city center, where many of the houses are painted with beautiful murals. Elaborate costume festivals take place in Rottweil at Carnival (usually in February) and at Corpus Christi (usually in June).

Schauinsland Cable Car (0761–292930; www.bergwelt-schauinsland.de) is located about 10 km southeast of Freiburg. Adults €11.50, children six to fourteen €7.00, families €26.00. Uhrenmuseum (07723–920–2800; www.deutsches-uhrenmuseum.de), in Furtwangen, is open daily 10:00 A.M. to 5:00 P.M., later in summer. Adults €4, kids €3. Schwartzwald-Museum (07722–4434; www.schwarzwaldmuseum.de), Triberg. Open daily 10:00 A.M. to 5:00 P.M. April through October. Adults €4.50, children five to thirteen €2.50.

berlin

Berlin is where it's happening today in Germany. Reunited after the "fall of the wall" in 1989, the city is experiencing a building boom that means construction around every corner as Germany reestablishes its capital here.

It's a great place to bring kids because it has a huge variety of museums, most of which cater to kids with special exhibits. Its art museum (Bodemuseum) and ethnological museum (Völkerkundemuseum), for instance, both have "junior museums" within them, designed to draw kids into the worlds of art and other cultures. Contact the Berlin Tourist Office for their brochure *Fun for Kids with Kids*, or just wander the Web site at www.berlin.de.

We don't make it a habit to recommend specific hotels in this book, but one in Berlin may be worth looking into. It's part of the Familotel group we mentioned in the Hotels chapter. What makes it special are the family theme rooms—a regular double bed for Mom and Dad, with bunk beds for the kids in a castle or an Old West stockade or some other special enclosure in the same room.

Berlin Tourismus (030–25–00–25; www.berlin.de), Am Karlsbad 11, 10785 Berlin. Familotel Wittelsbach (030–864–98–40; www.hotel-pension-wittelsbach.de), Wittelsbacher Straße 22, 10707 Berlin.

berlin zoo

With more species than any other zoo in the world, the 150-year-old Berlin Zoo is renowned—and justifiably so. Bao Bao, the panda, is perhaps the star of the show, but a 1,000-pound Komodo dragon, the world's largest reptile, provides stiff competition. Monkeys, hippos, lions, tigers, elephants, and camels roam in their natural habitats, and there is a huge aquarium and an insectarium.

There are two entrances. The main one is closer to the subway, but the one at Budapesterstraße is more fun: It's called the Elephant Gate and consists of a giant Oriental arch made up of the pudgy pachyderms. The entire zoo covers sixty-four acres, so be prepared to walk (and walk and walk).

The Berlin Zoo (030–25401–0; www.zoo-berlin.de) is located at Hardenbergplatz 8; near the Ku'damm, Berlin's shopping mecca. Take almost any subway line to the Zoologischer Garten station. Open daily 9:00 A.M. to 5:00 P.M., longer hours in summer. Adults €11.00 (€16.50 for zoo/aquarium combi-ticket), children five to fifteen half price.

teknikmuseum (science museum)

Officially called the Deutsches Teknikmuseum Berlin, this is Berlin's science museum. The biggest collection is the trains, but the museum abounds in push-button exhibits on everything from printing to space technology.

A separate building called the "Spectrum" holds hands-on classes and experiments kids can take part in, but an understanding of German is necessary to join in productively.

Teknikmuseum Berlin (030–90–25–40; www.dtmb.de), Trebbiner Straße 9 in the Kreuzberg district. U-Bahn: 1–2 Gleisdreieck. Open Tuesday through Friday 9:00 A.M. to 5:30 P.M., Saturday through Sunday 10:00 A.M. to 6:00 P.M. Adults €4.50, kids €2.50.

world war II

My first visit to Germany was jarring because the only German I had heard before was in war movies, where the language was spoken in snarling tones by Nazi bad guys. For our generation it's hard to separate Germany from its role in the war. But that's all the more reason to visit—to move beyond the stereotypes to a balanced, firsthand picture of Germany. Even as we do so, though, it's important to look back over our shoulders to make sure that the same horrors are never repeated.

We don't recommend that families visit any of the concentration camp sites in Germany or Eastern Europe, as they are simply too much for kids. Instead of the concentrated evil of a single extermination camp, use other opportunities to reach kids at a level they can more readily assimilate. Stop in Paris as you walk along the Seine, and point out the memorial to the deported Jews. Visit Anne Frank's house in Amsterdam. Talk about the courage of the Danes, who protected almost all their Jewish citizens from the Nazi onslaught. Six decades after the end of World War II, it's still not difficult to find plenty of reminders that can provoke good family discussions.

One such option in Berlin is the Kaiser-Wilhelm–Gedächtniskirche at the eastern end of Ku'damm. While the rest of the city has been built up and paved over since the war, this one-hundred-year-old church has been left in ruins. Inside, an exhibit shows what the church looked like before the war and displays photos of Berlin as it lay devastated in 1945.

Kaiser-Wilhelm–Gedächtniskirche (030–218–50–23; www.gedachtniskirche-berlin.de) is at Breitscheidplatz in the Charlottenburg district. U-Bahn: Zoologischer

Garten. Church open 9:00 A.M. to 7:00 P.M. daily; museum open Monday through Saturday 10:00 A.M. to 4:00 P.M.

berlin wall and checkpoint charlie

While Germany's past will long remain a dark smudge on the horizon, more recently the country has been symbolic of peace and hope, with the fall of the Berlin Wall in November 1989. Here's a momentous historic event that happened within older kids' lifetimes and is therefore all the more meaningful.

Within a year after the fall, only remnants of the wall were left. The Web site, www.dailysoft.com/berlinwall, maintains an updated list telling where you can view vestiges of the wall. In 2004 a 140-meter section of wall was relocated near Checkpoint Charlie, one of the original pass-through points (a copy of which has also been rebuilt next to this site). Look also for a double row of paving stones snaking through today's streets, marking the route of the former wall.

You'll get the whole picture if you visit the Haus am Checkpoint Charlie. This small museum shows, with photos and maps, how the wall was put up virtually overnight on August 13, 1961, slicing neighborhoods and even houses in half. The museum also documents heroic escape attempts over the twenty-eight years of the wall's life, with artifacts from both successful and unsuccessful efforts. What would your family have done? What makes someone trust his life to a homemade hot-air balloon or curl up in a car trunk to be free?

Once you leave the museum, travel around Berlin and challenge your kids to note differences between conditions and architecture in the two halves of the reunited city—differences that become more and more subtle by the month. Ponder the work Germany must finish to sew its country back together again, but rejoice that the Cold War standoff has ended.

Haus am Checkpoint Charlie (030–25–37–25–0; www.mauer-museum.com) is located at Friedrichstraße 44. U-Bahn: Kochstraße. Open daily 9:00 A.M. to 10:00 P.M. Adults €9.50, kids €5.50.

austria

Austria's a wonderful mix of cultural influences. It's basically Germany, but with the warm laughter of Italy seeping up from the south and the nothing's-fixed-in-stone attitude of the Middle Eastern bazaars reaching Vienna. A small country today, Austria basks in the memory of the Habsburg Empire, which dominated European politics for more than 200 years and held lands from present-day Hungary to Italy, Spain, and as far away as the Netherlands. Yet the country is made up of strong farmers as well as aristocrats, as our typically Austrian sites show.

vienna: lipizzaner stallions

At the end of World War II, Gen. George S. Patton discovered a disheveled group of horses in a village in Czechoslovakia, where they were working as farm animals. Today the offspring of these noble equines spend their Sundays prancing elegantly in performance, restored to international prominence as the renowned Lipizzaner Stallions.

Those who've seen pictures of the celebrated beasts may not realize that the first Lipizzaners came to Austria from Spain as early as 1560, or that the horses are actually born with brown or mousy-gray hair and only turn white after four to ten years. They may also not realize that it's almost impossible to get tickets for the Sunday performances unless you plan at least six months ahead or have powerful connections.

What to do? If you're in Vienna in the off-season, attend morning exercises held Tuesday through Saturday much of the year. Spectators should purchase tickets at Gate 2 of the Spanische Reitschule (Spanish Riding School) on Josefsplatz on the day they want to attend, starting at about 10:00 A.M. The inevitable line moves along whenever visitors already admitted choose to leave.

The Spanische-Reitschule (0533–90–31; www.spanische-reitschule.com) is in the Hofburg (Imperial Palace). Morning exercises are generally held mid-February to June, September, October, and mid-November 10:00 A.M. to noon, Tuesday through Saturday. Adults €15, kids €8. Check the Web to see the current schedule and fees for training sessions and performances.

innsbruck: tyrolean folk museum

Folk museums crammed full of historic everyday objects are almost always a good bet for family trips. In Innsbruck an especially fine one is the Museum of Tyrolean Folk Art, which displays the rich Austrian tradition of carving and painting everything from toys to tools and buckets to beds.

Four exhibits might prove of special interest to your kids. The first is a collection of brightly painted Nativity sets on the ground floor. Next, on the first floor, is an architectural exhibit with dollhouse-size models of different Tyrolean farmhouses. There are great carved wooden toys here, too.

Once they've seen the outsides of typical homes, let your children walk through the many actual furnished rooms with their richly paneled and carved walls and ceilings. These original rooms, moved here from peasant cottages all over Austria, are on both the first and second floors and were my favorite part of the exhibit. Finally, finish your tour on the second floor by examining the dozens of life-size mannequins sporting Austrian folk costumes.

The Museum of Tyrolean Folk Art (Tiroler Volkskunstmuseum) (0512–584–302; www.tiroler-volkskunstmuseum.at) is in Innsbruck, Austria, on Universitätsstraße between Rennweg and Angerzellgaße. Open Monday through Saturday 9:00 A.M. to 5:00 P.M.; Sunday 10:00 A.M. to 5:00 P.M. Adults €5, children under fourteen €2.

salzburg: the hills—and fountains—are alive

The "Squirt-Gun Castle" is not its real name, but that's how your kids may remember Lustschloss Hellbrunn, 5 km south of Salzburg.

This magnificent pleasure palace was built in the early seventeenth century by Italian architect Santino Solari for Prince-Archbishop Marcus Sitticus, an inveterate practical joker. Secret fountains throughout the grounds in statues, gardens, and even park benches were designed to be activated when the archbishop's guests least expected it. There's even an outdoor table, booby-trapped with water jets in each seat, where the bishop dined with his friends.

Elsewhere on the grounds, water is used to power enchanting figurines: chirping birds, dancing bears, gypsies, and a whole baroque cityscape of tiny water-powered people. Fans of *The Sound of Music* will be delighted to find that the castle is the location of the gazebo where the young lovers met in the rain.

Speaking of *The Sound of Music*, you might also consider a bike tour that hits all the familiar movie locales. The three-hour tour travels 99 percent of its route on bike paths, and since it's all flat cycling except for one hill, it's suitable for any kid who's learned to ride a bike.

The Sound of Music *bike tour was the best adventure of our five-week trip to Europe. The fräulein who took us was dressed as a young Maria. She had three kids and was a delight to talk to. It allowed us to get a little exercise, but was not too difficult for my eight-year-old.*

—Colleen Krause, Keene, NH

Schloss Hellbrunn (0622–82–03–72; www.hellbrunn.at) is on Hellbrunner Allee, just west of the Salzburg-Süd station. Open daily April through October 9:00 A.M. to 4:30 P.M., later in summer. Adults €8.50, children four to eighteen €3.80, families €21.50. Trick fountains only, on summer evenings: adults €8.00, children €3.80.

Fräulein Maria's Bicycle Tour (0676–342–6297; www.mariasbicycletours.com) operates daily at 9:30 A.M. from May 15 through October 8. Meet at the entrance to the Mirabel Gardens, behind the Landestheatre. Fee of €22 includes bike rental. Call ahead to Rupert Riedl if children's bikes or child seats are required.

If you plan to visit several museums in Salzburg, consider a Salzburg Card. In summer it costs €23 for twenty-four hours, €31 for forty-eight hours, and €36 for seventy-two hours, kids seven to fifteen are half price. The card entitles you to free admission at most museums and free public transport. Available at hotels, tourist offices, and some banks; see details at www.salzburg.info.

hallstatt: salt mines

Salzburg, Austria, got its name from the salt trade once so important to the area. Today you can still visit many old salt mines in the Salzkammergut region for a great mix of fun and information.

The world's oldest working salt mine is located in Hallstatt, a name that actually means "salt place." Here your tour starts with a short four-minute trip up the mountain by cable car. Once you arrive at the mine, you'll dress in protective overalls, then descend into the depths on two long wooden slides (the best part of the tour for most kids!). There you'll see a salt lake and learn about the extraction of salt, then travel back up to the light of day on a little train. Other salt mines in the area are located at Hallein, Altaussee, and Bad Ischl, as well as over the border in nearby Germany. But Hallstatt's mine is the best known.

We visited the salt mines near Berchtesgaden, Germany. You get dressed up in miners' clothes: oversize pants, a big white shirt, and a leather "seat" that attaches with a belt. That's so you can slide down wooden slides from one level to the next. Our kids, then twelve and fifteen, liked the beautifully lit salt crystals in the museum at the end. We never realized salt came in so many colors!

—Maya D'Anjou, Morgan Hill, CA

Hallstatt, a charming lakeside village, makes a good base for touring the area. The region abounds with underground attractions, including the Dachstein Ice Caves and the Mammoth and Koppenbrueller Caves. Aboveground water sports and summer concerts are popular. Contact the Hallstatt tourist office (Tourismusverband Hallstatt, A-4830 Hallstatt, Austria; www.hallstatt .net) for a booklet that lists reasonably priced pensions and hostels in and around town.

To reach Hallstatt take the 158 east from Salzburg to Bad Ischl, then the 145 south to Bad Goisern. Turn off on the 166 and follow signs to Hallstatt. Salt mines (06132–200–2400; www.salzwelten.at) are open May through October 9:30 A.M. to 4:30 P.M. (3:00 P.M. in October). Entry to the salt mine costs €15.50 for adults, €9.30 for kids seven to fifteen, and €7.80 for kids four to six, families €32.60 (children under four not permitted in the mines).

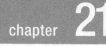
the totally biased guide to italy, spain, greece, gibraltar, and morocco

Spain, Italy, and Greece share the obvious common trait of bordering on the Mediterranean Sea. For traveling families, though, they share an even more significant trait. In all three, children are treated as little adults rather than as a separate alien species.

This means that kids are integrated thoroughly into everyday life; they're welcome everywhere, from neighborhood bars to formal restaurants. But this also means that few museums and other tourist sites make special provisions for children; you will not find nearly as many of the open-air museums, children's museums, and science museums so common in Northern Europe.

But there's still plenty to do. This chapter covers Italy and Spain while sampling Greece, Gibraltar, and Morocco.

italy

Italy is everything you hoped it would be. The food is sublime, the people are friendly—especially to children—and the country itself is rich in history and culture. Other stereotypes are true, too: The overall approach to life is much less structured than American life, so schedules for buses and museum openings can be somewhat whimsical.

But who cares? You're on vacation, the country's beautiful, and if you don't get there today, you might get there tomorrow. (*Hot tip:* If you're an incurable Type A personality, northern Italy and southern Switzerland offer Italy's language, its great food, and its warmth with some of the precision and predictability of Switzerland.)

With history and culture lurking around every corner, Italy—perhaps more than any other country—is a great place to rent a house and simply

italy, spain, greece, and morocco

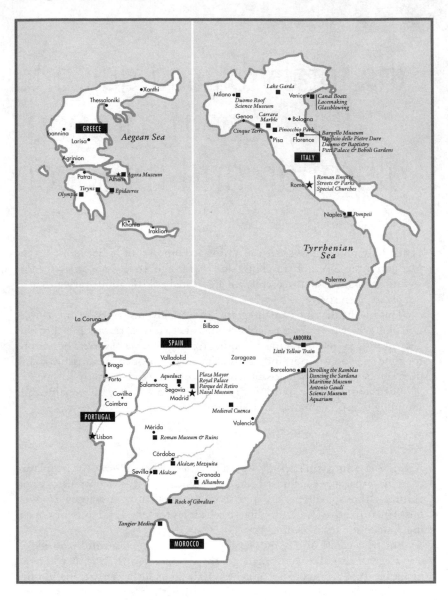

GREECE

Xanthi
Thessaloniki
Ioannina
Larisa
Agrinion
Patrai
Olympia
Tiryns
Athens • Agora Museum
Epidavros
Khania
Iraklion

Aegean Sea

ITALY

Lake Garda
Milano
Duomo Roof
Science Museum
Venice • Canal Boats
Lacemaking
Glassblowing
Genoa
Carrara
Marble
Bologna
Cinque Terre
Pinocchio Park
Pisa
Florence • Bargello Museum
Opificio delle Pietre Dure
Duomo & Baptistry
Pitti Palace & Boboli Gardens
Roma • Roman Empire
Streets & Parks
Special Churches
Naples • Pompeii

Tyrrhenian Sea

Palermo

SPAIN

La Coruña
Bilbao
ANDORRA
Valladolid
Zaragoza
Little Yellow Train
Braga
Barcelona • Strolling the Ramblas
Dancing the Sardana
Maritime Museum
Antonio Gaudí
Science Museum
Aquarium
Porto
Aqueduct
Plaza Mayor
Royal Palace
Parque del Retiro
Naval Museum
Salamanca
Segovia
Covilha
Madrid
Coimbra
Medieval Cuenca
PORTUGAL
Valencia
Mérida
Lisbon
Roman Museum & Ruins
Córdoba
Alcázar, Mezquita
Sevilla • Alcázar
Granada
Alhambra
Rock of Gibraltar
Tangier Medina
MOROCCO

enjoy day-to-day events. Four distinct areas are recommended for homestays: Naples-Sorrento-Capri, Rome, Tuscany, and Milan–Lake Garda. To augment your homestay, definitely get hold of the *Italy Discovery Journal* (details in chapter 22, Resources) and review our suggestions below for a few ideas that only hint at what you can do in Italy.

pompeii

Italy's ancient city of Pompeii is very large, and the weather is often hot. Bring water bottles. Before you go, plan an itinerary using free maps and pamphlets from the local tourist office on Via Sacra across from the Plaza Barolo Longo. With a plan you'll avoid aimless wandering in the heat and crowds—and you won't be surprised by adult sites like the bordello on Vico del Lupanare, with its pornographic paintings in each bed stall.

To start, visit just one or two of the best-preserved villas, such as Casa di Menandro. And stop by the bakery, complete with counters and petrified loaves of bread. Its intact ovens convinced Dan and Wendy's kids that they'd found the original Italian pizza parlor. A small flashlight helps illuminate corners of some of the enclosed buildings.

Older kids will be drawn to the macabre body casts of Vesuvius victims along the western side of the forum. Many younger children are fascinated simply to walk in the streets, following the original chariot-wheel ruts. Be patient while your kids try out the crossing blocks, stepping stones that kept the citizens of Pompeii out of the 18-inch-deep mud in the streets.

Be prepared that the approach to Pompeii is through impoverished areas with high unemployment. Aggressive kids will offer to wash your windshield for a few pennies on the way, and once you arrive, phalanxes of guides will offer their services. Be firm and say "no" if you'd really rather go on your own.

Pompeii (081–861–0744) is located about 30 km southeast of Naples. Open 8:30 A.M. until 7:30 P.M. April through October and 5:00 P.M. off-season. Entry €11 adults, €.5 kids.

rome

The Roman Empire has left more reminders of its existence than perhaps any other empire in the history of the world. Finding these ruins in odd corners of Europe brings home the reality of conquest more vividly than seeing them in Rome, yet a visit to the epicenter of the empire is also an excellent idea. What sort of city would be needed to administer such an extended territory? The answer to that question is not hard to find in today's Rome. Yet the city also has more to offer than just traces of empire.

the roman empire

Start at the Forum, the governmental center of Rome, entering from the Via dei Fori Imperiali across from Via Cavour. This gives you about a half-kilometer walk through the Forum, past the brick Curia, where the Senate once was held; the Comitium Well, where (male) citizens voted; and the Rostra, a pulpit, where any citizen could stand up and express his thoughts. Kids, especially younger ones, may find the Forum a bit hard to visualize. But that's okay; by the time you've bored the kids with their democratic antecedents, you'll have arrived at the end of the Forum for the treat they've earned: the Colosseum.

The Colosseum is a sure winner. The scale of the place is awe inspiring, with seats for 50,000 spectators. The Romans even used to flood the place for mock naval battles! A favorite with children is the maze of tunnels and cages visible on the ground floor, where animals were kept until they were needed for combat. This intriguing maze was once hidden under a floor of solid stone, but Romans over the centuries "mined" the interior marble floors and seats to build other buildings.

If you have any energy left, use it to visit the Pantheon. Originally erected as a temple to all the gods, the Pantheon has survived almost two millennia virtually without change. This alone can be awesome to kids (and to us adults), who expect any ancient Roman artifacts to be crumbling ruins like the Forum and Colosseum. When you go in, look up at the opening in the 143-foot dome. It's the building's only source of light, and when it rains, water pours onto the marble floor below. If the building seems familiar, it was the inspiration for the Jefferson Memorial in Washington, D.C.

The Forum and Colosseum (06–39–96–77–00; visit www.capitolium.org for a great overview) are both open daily 9:00 A.M. to one hour before sunset (Forum closed Sunday). Metro B: Colosseo. Forum: free entry; audioguides €4.50. Colosseum: adults €9, children €3.

The Pantheon (06–689–71–97) is located on the Piazza della Rotonda (follow signs everywhere), is free, and is open Monday through Saturday 8:30 A.M. to 4:00 P.M. (7:30 P.M. in summer). Bus 119. All three of these sites are at www.romaturismo.it; click on "Discovering Rome."

roman street life

Children appreciate the drama of the streets in Rome perhaps better than anywhere. It starts with the fountains: They're everywhere and a constant fascination to kids. Equally captivating are the original Roman drinking fountains from the first century. Challenge your kids to find them. They're little pipes—Augustinian aqueducts—coming out of the walls. To get a drink, simply put your finger on the end of the pipe till water squirts up through the hole. (Be prepared for the kids to aim the stream at their siblings as well as at their own mouths!)

As the day wears on, the human drama competes for your attention. On a single corner Gypsies perform, a man sells birds, and an artist paints impromptu portraits. Romans live on the streets: They eat, they argue, they shop—all in the public eye. Don't worry about visiting any more museums. The real Rome is here on the streets.

Many buildings in Rome stand *on top of* the original buildings of the Roman Empire. The Piazza Navona, in the old part of town not far from the Pantheon, serves as a good example of this. The Piazza was a stadium and horse-racing track in ancient days. Its oval shape is still apparent, though its walls have for the most part been reassembled into other buildings. Stand around the edges of the Piazza and you'll see Roman columns incorporated into modern structures. In the basement of some of these buildings, it's still possible to see the spectator stands, recognizably intact. The Piazza Navona is also a great place to catch street life, packed as it is with street musicians, cafes, and people.

When the day gets hot, follow the Romans to Villa Borghese, Rome's largest park with a perimeter of 6 kilometers. There's a Punch and Judy show nearly every day in the park's Pincio section, and rowboats can be rented from 9:00 A.M. to noon and 2:00 P.M. to sunset, for a ride among the swans and ducks at the Giardino del Lago (around €1 per person, per twenty minutes). You can also rent four-person pedal carts or ride horseback.

The park's zoo, recently spiffed up and rechristened BioParco, covers almost thirty acres and tries to reproduce the animals' natural habitats as much as possible. It includes monkeys, giraffes, deer, seals, elephants, a bird house and a reptile house, and even pygmie hippopotami.

To reach Villa Borghese take Metro A: Flaminio or Spagna for the area nearest BioParco. BioParco (06–360–82–11; www.bioparco.it) is open daily 9:30 A.M. to 5:00 P.M. (6:00 P.M. April through October). Adults €8.50, children €6.50.

For some great exploration suggestions for Rome, visit www.romaturismo .it and select "Discovering Rome" and then "Itineraries."

roman churches

Having recommended you choose street life over buildings, we must add that the Sistine Chapel was a surprising hit with Dan and Wendy's kids. Despite their ages, all three Hallinans were so overcome by the vibrant, colorful images in Michelangelo's newly restored ceiling that they each clamored for a poster to take home. Nat, then twelve, kept the poster on his bedroom wall for ages.

Rome is of course resplendent with churches. They're free and cool, so duck in for a physical and spiritual time-out from Rome's crowded bustle. Three especially neat ones are Santa Maria Maggiore, for wonderful mosaics (Metro A: Termini); Sant'Ignazio, for its trompe l'oeil dome (Piazza di Sant'Ignazio, near the Pantheon); and Santo Stefano Rotondo, for its round shape, wooden rafters, and lovely frescoes (Metro A: San Giovanni).

Santa Maria della Concezione is like no other church. A museum, really, it contains the bones of 4,000 long-departed monks . . . skulls, tibias, spines . . . hung in various artistic arrangements. Not as macabre as it sounds. Certainly a hit with our kids!

—Maureen Parmar, Evansville, IN

A few readers have also recommended Santa Maria della Concezione, not for the church itself but for the crypt beneath it. When the Capuchin monks were forced to move across town in 1631, they dug up their dead and rein-terred them creatively to save space under their new church. The bones are arranged by theme in six rooms and a corridor; the results are fascinating for older kids but definitely too spooky for younger ones.

Sistine Chapel (06–69–88–43–41; www.vatican.va) is at the Vatican Museums, near Piazza San Pedro. Metro A: Ottaviano. Open Monday through Friday 8:45 A.M. to 3:20 P.M. (Saturday 8:45 A.M. to 12:20 P.M.). Closed holy days and most Sundays. Adults €13, children €8.

Santa Maria della Concezione is at the bottom of Via Veneto, Metro A: Barbarini. Open daily 9:00 A.M. to noon and 3:00 to 6:00 P.M. Free.

florence (firenze)

By now you know we advocate smaller towns and villages over city visits with kids. But if you're in Tuscany, of course you'll want to make at least a brief visit to Florence. Here's our plan for a family-friendly day trip to Florence.

art inside and out

Much of Florence's wonderful art is outside, which is great for kids. Start early in the Piazza delle Signoria, where a copy of Michelangelo's David stares across at several other great statues sheltered under a beautiful loggia. Stop for gelato (said to be a Florentine invention), then continue a few blocks to the Bargello Museum.

Of the three major museums in Florence—the Uffizi, the Academia, and the Bargello—we nominate the Bargello as most kid friendly. Younger kids can run around in the lower open courtyard or spend their time looking up at the amazing carved and painted ceilings. With older kids, circle the first floor and list how many different materials (ivory, ceramic, metal, etc.) you can find. Look for statues of roosters, turkeys, and owls—it's not all naked men! Then make a beeline for the third floor with its satisfying armor and ivory saddles.

An alternative choice (open only mornings, like the Bargello) is the Opifi-cio delle Pietre Dure. This small museum showcases and explains the Firenzan art of *pietra dura*, a way of making intricate stone mosaics. You'll see how the artists pick stones with different colors and textures to "paint" complex pic-tures in stone. Challenge your kids to compare these stone jigsaw puzzles with their oil counterparts and find the differences. A fascinating and truly local art.

Go to www.aboutflorence.com to find hotels or rentals, or to book museum tickets in advance. On arrival check bookstores for Florence for Kids, *a graphically engaging English-language guide written on a kid's level.*

Bargello Museum (055–238–8606; www.sbas.firenze.it), Via del Proconsolo 4. Open Tuesday through Saturday 8:15 A.M. to 1:50 P.M. plus some Sundays and Mondays. Long lines, so visit early! Adults €4, children €2.

*Opificio delle Pietre Dure Museum (055–265–111; www.museumsinflorence.com),
Via degli Alfani 78. Open Monday through Saturday 8:15 A.M. to 2:00 P.M. Adults
€2.50, kids free.*

duomo and baptistry

After your museum visit, stop for gelato (are you starting to see a pattern?),
then stroll a few more blocks to the Duomo, Florence's cathedral. Walk
around the unusual green-and-white-striped edifice and tell the kids how
Brunelleschi built sleeping areas, restaurants, and even lavatories inside the
dome during construction so that workers wouldn't waste time going up and
down. Brunelleschi's plan made sense, as you'll see for yourself if you opt to
climb the 400 steps up to the dome. But unlike the workers who had to toil
in the dome, you'll get to relax after your climb and enjoy the panoramic view
from the cupola of the cathedral. If attention spans are lagging, however, skip
the Duomo interior in favor of the adjacent Baptistry, a marvel of gold leaf
and mosaics inside.

By now it's time to sit down and enjoy a pizza, or perhaps visit what our
family calls an "Italian salad bar," an informal restaurant where you check
out prepared pasta salads and other antipasti in a showcase and point to
what you like.

*The Duomo (www.duomofirenze.it) is open 8:30 A.M. to 7:00 P.M. Monday through
Friday and 8:30 A.M. to 5:00 P.M. on Saturday. €6 to climb up the dome. Baptistry,
opposite the Duomo, is open Monday through Saturday noon to 6:30 P.M., Sunday 9:00
A.M. to 1:30 P.M. Admission €3.*

boboli gardens and museums

After lunch let off some steam by romping in the Boboli Gardens across the
Arno, with their wonderful sculptures (look for the god Bacchus riding a tor-
toise!). The Pitti Palace houses three museums—the Silver Museum, the
Porcelain Museum, and the Costume Museum—that may be of interest to
some older kids. They're included in your ticket to the gardens. (Unfortunately the Carriage Museum—the most interesting to kids—had been inex-
plicably closed as of press time. Ask if it's open when you visit!)

*Pitti Palace and Boboli Gardens (055–294–883; www.polomuseale.firenze.it) are
in the Oltrarno district. Open daily 8:30 A.M. to 4:30 P.M., later in summer. Closed first
and last Mondays of the month. Combined ticket: adults €6, kids free.*

collodi: home of pinocchio

If your children enjoy the story of Pinocchio, the wooden puppet whose nose
grew every time he told a lie, take them to visit his "birthplace" in Collodi,
Italy. It was here, in 1881, that Carlo Lorenzini penned his famous story. But
it was not till 1956 that Pinocchio was memorialized with the marvelous
sculpture park that bears his name.

Children entering Parco di Pinocchio start by encountering a giant statue of the puppet, which they are welcome to climb. Then their route explores several episodes in the well-known tale: They'll sneak through the legs of a scolding policeman in the Land of Toys, wander through a maze, and finally climb into the mouth of the Giant Dogfish—complete with a spraying blow-hole. Both you and your kids will get more out of the park if you take the time to read a good complete version of the classic story on the way to Collodi.

Souvenir sellers line the park, and you won't be able to resist your own wooden puppet to take home. The best ones have wooden noses that unscrew, so you can replace them with a longer nose with every lie!

Across the street is the Villa Garzoni, also recommended, with a wonderful garden full of inventive fountains, grottoes, and mazes.

Parco Monumentale di Pinocchio (0572–429342; www.pinocchio.it) is located in Collodi, about 60 km northwest of Florence. From Lucca take route 435 toward Pescia for about 15 km; watch for a small side road to the left. Open daily 8:30 A.M. to 6:00 P.M.; longer in summer. Adults €8.50, kids three to fourteen €6.50. Villa Garzoni (0572–428400) is open daily 8:30 A.M. to dusk. Adults €5.50.

carrara: marble quarries

There's a reason why Carrara is almost synonymous with fine marble: The Italian city is home to more than 500 quarries that have supplied the world with marble since around 200 B.C. and still produce more than 8,000 tons a year.

Quarry tours are sporadic and usually in Italian, so your best bet is a self-guided family tour. One choice is to take the Codena–Bedizzano road about 7 km from Carrara to Colonnata, one of the best-known marble towns and the origin of much of the marble used by Michelangelo in his sculptures.

Follow signs for CAVE, the Italian word for quarry. As you get closer, you'll see that the "snowcapped" peaks are really marble outcroppings, and you'll hear the sound of blasting as great marble blocks are carved out with explosives and thin wires. Numerous quarries are visible from the road, so you can readily see how the enormous blocks of stone dwarf the men and trucks assigned to wrestle them from the earth. Don't forget to stop the car and pick up samples from among the marble scraps lying near every quarry!

Carrara (0585–240063; www.aptmasscarrara.it) is located about 20 km south of La Spezia. (Find Genoa and Pisa on your map, then look for La Spezia halfway between the two.) All three major roads heading into the mountains from Carrara lead to quarries. Look for signs reading COLONNATA, FANTISCRITTI, or RAVACCIONE, or follow suggested itineraries on the Web site.

cinque terre

If your children are seasoned walkers, one good place to savor the spirit of Italy is in the Cinque Terre, five unspoiled villages along the Italian Riviera about 40 km north of Carrara.

If you study your map, you'll find out how these villages have maintained their charm for so long: This is the one section of the coast that's so steep and rocky that the major coastal highway had to head inland and bypass the area. Still, Cinque Terre is well served by train and by foot, so you will *not* be alone during your visit!

You'll start at Monterosso, the largest of the villages. From here a train connects all five villages, burrowing through tunnels along the steep coastal cliffs, then popping out at each town. The train gives you the freedom to walk until the kids get tired, then hop back on the tracks. From Monterosso, for instance, you can hike an hour to Vernazza along a narrow goat path, then a steep hour and a half to Corniglia with its pebbly beach, then continue for another hour to Manarola, famed for its colorfully painted houses. A short hike later you'll arrive at medieval Riomaggiore. Hiking through all five towns covers about 7 km.

We aren't recommending any museums or amusements in these five villages. But if quiet beaches, fresh-air walks, Italian seafood, and charming scenery attract you, the Cinque Terre can't be beat.

The Cinque Terre area is located along the northwest coast of Italy, just north of the city of La Spezia (not technically in Tuscany). Trains leave somewhat hourly from La Spezia to Cinque Terre, for less than two euros. Riomaggiore, Vernazza, and Corniglia have many small guesthouses, while Monterosso has overpriced hotels. Always reserve ahead in summer. Before you go, contact the Monterosso tourist office (0187–817506), Via Fegina 38, Monterosso, for maps and information.

milan

Milan is a vibrant city with some of the craziest traffic anywhere on the Continent. Cars are triple-parked everywhere—one row on the street and two on the sidewalk. Two-lane roads carry three lanes of traffic. Park your car on the outskirts and ride the wonderfully efficient Metropolitana, then walk through the compact city center, where cars are severely restricted.

the duomo

High above the city you'll find a serene respite from Milan's hectic noise—on top of the cathedral, or Duomo. Kids aren't usually enthusiastic about cathedral visits. So instead of going inside, walk around the left-hand side of the building to the back corner. There you'll find an elevator that takes you to the roof of the Duomo.

Imagine: You stoop under buttresses, steal a close-up peek at flamboyant Gothic tracery, eyeball saints and gargoyles, and even walk on the very ridgepole of this immense building. The noise of traffic fades far below, and the view is stunning (all the way to the Alps, if it isn't too smoggy!). Sturdy railings make the trek safe for small children. The 135 marble spires and 2,245 marble statues make it exciting. After you come down, drag the kids inside for a few minutes. The world's third-largest church is wonderfully ornate, and the munchkins may actually enjoy the mosaic floors and jeweled crowns on display.

The Duomo (02–860–358) is open daily 9:00 A.M. to 4:15 P.M. (5:45 P.M. in summer). M1 or M3: Duomo. Round-trip elevator €5.00, stairs €3.50.

celebrate leonardo

Most adults visiting Milan head for the convent of Santa Maria delle Grazie on Via Caradosso to view *The Last Supper,* Leonardo's masterpiece. Don't bother with kids: Lines are long and visitors are rushed through to limit damage to the fragile painting.

Instead, show your appreciation for Leonardo da Vinci by visiting the Museo Nazionale della Scienza e Technica. Here an entire gallery is devoted to wooden models of some of the famous inventor's brainstorms. The rest of the museum is a treat, too, with the usual motors, trains, and space exhibits of great science museums everywhere. Exhibits don't cater to English speakers. Just watch all the little Italian kids and you'll figure out how to run the interactive exhibits and experiments!

Take an unforgettable trip to the roof of Milan's cathedral.

Science Museum (02–485–551; www.museoscienza.org), Via San Vittore 21, off Via Carducci. M2: Sant'Ambrogio. Open daily 9:30 A.M. to 5:00 P.M.; closed Monday. Adults €8, kids €6.

lake garda

Lake Garda, Italy's largest lake (150 square miles), is an overdeveloped zoo at the height of the summer but a delight in late spring and early fall. It's pretty, it's relaxing, and there's just enough history so you won't feel that you're Pinocchio escaping to Pleasure Island.

Head for Sirmione, where your tour starts at Rocca Scaligera, a thirteenth-century turreted castle with a moat and great tower views. When the children begin to flag, stop for a fresh-fruit gelato, then rent a rowboat near the castle bridge or a paddleboat at the public beach near Via Catullo. Sirmione's excellent beaches invite wading with shallow, clear water that's safe even for young children.

If you can interest your offspring in another round of history, visit the splendid ruins of the Grotte di Catullo. Though historians are unsure as to whether the famous poet Catullus actually lived here, his name is attached to this fascinating ruin of a Roman villa with baths.

Sirmione (www.sirmione.com) is located at the end of a 7-km-long peninsula that juts out from the southern end of Lago di Garda (Lake Garda). From Verona take Route 11 west about 31 km to Columbare, then go north up the peninsula. Rocca Scaligera (030–916468) is open daily 8:30 A.M. to 7:00 P.M. Adults €4.50. Grotte di Catullo (030–916157) is open Tuesday through Sunday 9:00 A.M. to 6:00 P.M. Adults €4.50.

venice

What can you say about a city that really does have the world's most beautiful architecture and all those romantic canals? A city that will fulfill every Renaissance fantasy you've ever had? "It's wonderful," report our readers, "but—." Venice's charms are undeniable, but you must know a few tricks to avoid tourist hordes and overly high prices. That said, here are our four top Totally Biased tips for a wonderful stay in Venice.

- Don't bring your car. Venice is a collection of islands connected to the mainland by a 4-km causeway. Cars are banned from almost all of Venice; it's better to park in Mestre on the mainland than to pay exorbitant rates on the islands to garage a car you can't use. Take the train from Mestre to Venice for around one euro each way, then walk or take public transportation (all boats!) everywhere.

- Want to ride a gondola? Tourists officially pay €70 to €80 for a fifty-minute gondola ride, but gondoliers often charge more and cut the time short. Instead, take your kids on the *traghetti,* small public gondolas that cross the canals. These short rides fit short attention spans—and riding standing up is very exciting. The cost? About 40 European cents. While *traghetti* travel across canals, *vaporetti* travel up and down them. *Vaporetti* are really "water buses," not as romantic or cheap as *traghetti* but great for getting around.

- Travel light. Most hotels (like most everything in Venice) are accessible only by foot. You'll be schlepping your luggage across cobblestones and up and down steps, so don't bring more than you can carry.

- Costs escalate in direct proportion to their proximity to Piazza San Marco. Two cups of coffee and a shared dessert might cost you €30 in the middle of the piazza, €22 a block away, and €10 as you get out of the San Marco sestier. Keep this in mind and your savings will be dramatic.

There are no particular must-sees for kids in Venice. Simply wander and soak in the fairy-tale surroundings. Walk in the streets and sit at the cafes. Encourage your kids to find the boat equivalent of transportation they're used to: Can they find a boat "moving van"? A boat UPS "truck"? A boat police "car"?

Venice has a reputation as a tourist rip-off. Yes, it's expensive, but much of that is because everything, from clean laundry to vegetables, must be brought in by boat. Don't buy anything in or near Piazza San Marco and you'll be fine. We've encountered wonderful, warm people, from the musicians we "met" on the Internet who saved us front-row seats at their concert and the cafe owner who remembered, from one day to the next, that I liked apricot juice, to "mama," the elderly proprietress of a trattoria who decided she could choose our meals better than we could. (She was right!)

Don't miss Venice. Come with a full wallet and leave with a full heart.

Traghetti *and* vaporetti *leave from designated stops (*fermate*) all over the city. You pay cash on* traghetti, *and buy* vaporetti *tickets at a little kiosk at the stop. You can also buy one-day (*€15*) or three-day (*€30*) vaporetto *passes at the ticket office at the Piazzale Roma. Validate tickets in the time-stamp machine as you board or there is a fine. Also consider a Venice Card (www.venicecard.com), which gives you discounts on boats and sites.*

murano and burano

While in Venice you might also want to take a boat to the nearby islands of Murano and Burano.

Murano has been famous for glassblowing for more than 700 years, and here you can watch master glassblowers at work, creating colorful swirled vases and goblets from gobs of molten glass. (Look for FORNACE signs for free demos.) There's also a glass museum if your kids get intrigued.

Wandering the streets of Murano, we stumbled upon the private work-shop of Paolo in a tiny courtyard with apartments and homes. Paolo, who has been glassblowing since the age of ten, let us watch him make seashells out of glass. He wanted to practice his English on us, and we really enjoyed getting to know him. It was fascinating to watch him work, and the kids liked asking him questions. (He showed us all the burns on his arms in response to one question.) We bought some of his work, and he even gave the kids some free trinkets. So delightful, compared to the throngs at the publicized factory.

—Ellen Manuel, Bellevue, NE

On neighboring Burano, the craft to watch is lacemaking. Peek into shops all along the main drag, and you'll see old women patiently twisting and tying thin threads. At the Scuola di Merletti di Burano you can see exhibits of old lace and watch lacemakers at work. Just walking around the island is fun, too, as the houses generally sport bright, unexpected colors.

Vaporetto 12 goes to both Burano and Murano for around €4 round-trip. The Murano glass museum (Museo Vetrario Antica di Murano, 041–739586) is at Fonda-menta Giustinian 8. Open Thursday through Tuesday 10:00 A.M. to 5:00 P.M. Adults €4.50. Burano's Scuola di Merletti (041–730034) is on Piazza Galuppi. Open Wednes-day through Monday 10.00 A.M. to 5:00 P.M. Lacemaking from 9:00 A.M. to 1:00 P.M. and 2:30 P.M. to closing. Adults €4.50.

spain

Spain never sleeps, and it lives its boisterous social life in public, which makes it easy for visitors to jump into the party. Join in the *paseo*, an established rit-ual stroll around town at dusk. Sit at a bar, where Spaniards meet their friends. Watch your kids take part in an impromptu soccer game in any park. Dinner's not until 9:00, 10:00, or even 11:00 P.M., so there's plenty of time.

After years of making no special allowances for kids, Spain is now catch-ing up on family attractions; Barcelona recently opened a wonderful new aquarium, for instance. But don't neglect the laid-back enjoyment of simply *living* instead of looking for packaged entertainment!

the pyrenees valley

Park your Castilian Spanish as you cross into Spain from France. On the western edge of the border lies Euskadi, three provinces where Basque, a language unrelated to other European languages, is spoken. On the eastern edge is Catalunya, where Catalán, a Romance language, is the favored tongue. Our brief tour of Spain will start in Catalunya.

Towns nestled in the eastern Pyrenees have long been passed back and forth between France and Spain. Even today the border confusion hasn't been entirely straightened out: One Spanish town, Llivia, was exempted from a 1659 treaty and lives on in modern times completely surrounded by French territory!

Exploring a border area helps your kids realize that people don't follow dotted lines on maps; signs and conversations in mixed languages underscore the overlapping cultures. You can soak in these lessons while riding Le Petit Train Jaune, or little yellow train. Your ride on the Pyrenees' last narrow-gauge railway starts in either Bourg-Madame or La Tour de Carol, both on the French side of the border across from the small Spanish city of Puigcerda. You can ride the entire 63-km round-trip for €34. If you get off to browse or picnic in Mont Louis or in the walled city of Vilafranca (Villefranche de Conflent), Le Petit Train makes a great daylong outing.

The little train rides through mixed French-Spanish border towns.

Check out the Web site at www.trainstouristiques_ter.com/train-jaune.htm for sched-ules, costs, and great photos, or simply present yourself at the station in Bourg-Madame or La Tour de Carol.

barcelona

Barcelona is the capital of bilingual Catalunya, and you'll see and hear the Catalán language all around you here. Almost totally banned during Franco's repressive regime, the language has made a dramatic resurgence as an expression of Catalán pride. Barcelona's citizens have much to be proud of: Theirs is a thriving, lively city, long the economic capital of a Spain that is increasingly following Barcelona's bustling example.

barcelona street life

The Ramblas is the heart of Barcelona street life, a beautiful if touristy boulevard filled with shops, cafes, street musicians, and flamenco dancers. With children a small stretch is plenty. Start at the Plaça de la Boqueria, where beautiful mosaics by Joan Miró brighten the pavement. Nearby is the Mercat de Sant Josep, also known as the Boqueria Market. Housed in an engaging nineteenth-century cast-iron structure, this traditional food market holds candies, fruits, meats, vegetables, breads, and every manner of edibles.

If you're very fortunate you'll be able to dance the *sardana,* the regional dance of Catalunya. It's a simple dance—everyone holds hands and dances in a circle—and it's done in public in Barcelona, making it easy for visitors to join in. Just because you're from someplace else doesn't mean you can't celebrate Catalán unity along with the rest of Barcelona!

Boqueria Market is open all day Monday through Saturday, but many stalls close up by 2:00 or 3:00 P.M. Metro: Boqueria.

Check local papers or www.fed.sardanista.cat for up-to-date information on public sardanas. Look for the word "ballades" denoting join-in opportunities. Common times and places usually include: Plaça San Jaume (Sunday 6.00 P.M.), Plaça Catedral (Saturday noon and 6:00 P.M.). Free and spontaneous.

a seafaring life

So much of Barcelona's past and present is linked to the sea. Now it's time to head toward the port, location of the imposing Monument a Colom (Columbus Monument). Columbus reported his New World discoveries to Ferdinand and Isabella here in Barcelona, earning him this monument. For several years, in fact, a full-scale replica of the *Santa Maria* lay at anchor in Barcelona, but the ship was unfortunately destroyed in 1992.

The glories of the Catalán navy of 500 years ago are preserved in the Museu Marítim, near the monument. One of the best marine museums in the world, this one is full of figureheads, ship models, maps (including one by Amerigo Vespucci, for whom America was named), and a full-size reproduction of the sixteenth-century Spanish galley *Real,* complete with its dozens of slave-powered oars. Lew especially liked a 15-foot-tall fully rigged model, used for the hands-on training of sailors. More recent vessels, including commercial and fishing craft, are also included, but the older ships will likely interest most kids the most. The museum is evocatively located in the half-dozen remaining cathedral-like stone dry docks of Barcelona's old medieval shipyards.

Not far from the Maritime Museum, on the waterfront, is Barcelona's aquarium, the largest in Europe. It features twenty different tanks, each reproducing a different Mediterranean or tropical ecosystem, plus an 80-meter glass tunnel that lets you take an underwater stroll. Sharks and poisonous stonefish—with venom that can kill a person in twenty-seven seconds—as well as eels, seahorses, and coral colonies are among the creatures that kids find most interesting. On the way out, stop at the gift shop, which has a sunken treasure-ship theme and a good selection of underwater-inspired gifts, T-shirts, and CDs.

Monument a Colom (93–302–52–24) has an elevator that takes you to the top for a wonderful view of the city and harbor. Open daily June through September, 9:00 A.M. to 8:30 P.M.; closed for lunch in off-season. Adults €2.20, children €1.20.

Museu Marítim (93–349–99–20; www.museumaritimbarcelona.com) is at Plaça Portal de la Pau 1. Metro: Drassanes. Open daily 10:00 A.M. to 8:00 P.M. Adults €6.50, kids seven to sixteen €3.25.

L'Aquarium (093–221–74–74; www.aquariumbcn.com) is on Moll d'Espanya. Metro: Drassanes. Open daily 9:30 A.M. to 9:00 P.M. (later in summer). Adults €15.50, children €10.50.

antonio gaudí

Mixed in with the inevitable sterile, high-rise towers of a "serious" city, Barcelona celebrates its self-confidence with the undulating architecture of Antonio Gaudí. Kids, charmed by the idea of a grown-up who doesn't follow the rules, are often very drawn to Gaudí's work. You can learn more at www.gaudiclub.com.

Focus on Casa Batlló, which our family dubbed Puff the Magic Dragon's house. Why? The roof looks just like the arched back of a dragon, complete with scales—a salute to St. George, Barcelona's patron saint. The facade of Casa Batlló is scattered with bright tiles that glint in the sunlight and punctuated with marvelous undulating balconies. A tiny tower tops the house, which Gaudí promised his client would be "a vision of paradise."

Inside is just as creative, with a curved staircase repeating the dragon-tail theme, and even furniture that was Gaudí inspired. Casa Batlló was opened to the public for the first time in 2002 as a temporary exhibit, but it has proven so popular that it remains open—and hopefully will still be when you visit. If not, even the exterior is extraordinary.

A short cab ride away is Sagrada Familia, Gaudí's cathedral. Some children have described it as a "drip castle," comparing its towers to those they have created at the beach by dribbling wet sand through their fingers. Gaudí died in 1926, when the cathedral was only partly finished. Today it's still not complete. But that's part of the fascination. How often can you see a cathedral being constructed? Models and exhibits in the cathedral's crypt help you picture Gaudí's complete vision.

If you're energetic, finish your study of Gaudí with a stop at Parc Güell. Originally designed and landscaped as the setting for a housing development, its dwellings were never built. But today it offers a wonderful view over the city and a great place to run around while marveling at Gaudí's snaking mosaic benches and pagoda and large multicolored lizards guarding hidden grottoes.

Casa Batlló (93–488–06–66; www.casabatllo.es), Passeig de Gràcia 43. Open daily 9:00 A.M. to 2:00 P.M. Call to reserve. Metro: Diagonal. Sagrada Familia (93–455–0247) is on Calle Marinara between Calle Mallorca and Calle Provença. Metro: Sagrada Familia. Open 9:00 A.M. to 6:00 P.M. daily year-round; longer hours in summer. Adults €8, kids €5. Parc Güell is on the north edge of Barcelona, about 2 km north of Sagrada Familia. If you skipped the cathedral, you can take Bus 24 directly from Passeig de Gràcia to the park entrance. Otherwise, take the metro to Lesseps station, then walk ten minutes to the park. Open daily 10:00 A.M. to 6:00 P.M., longer hours in summer.

science and folklife in the hills

Two hills overlook Barcelona: Montjuïc and Tibidabo. The views from either are great on one of Barcelona's rare, smog-free days. Or you can come for the museums here.

On Tibidabo you'll find the Museu de Ciéncia, locally known as Cosmo Caixa. This hands-on science museum is in the process of more than tripling its size, constantly adding fascinating exhibits. There's a working model that compresses a day in the life of an Amazon rain forest—complete with lightning, downpours, and a rainbow—into ten minutes. Another exhibit challenges kids to find thirty hidden insects in a seemingly empty vivarium. This museum's interactivity transcends any language barrier.

Montjuïc, Barcelona's other hill, is far more scenic than Tibidabo. The site of the 1992 Olympics, Montjuïc is also home to Poble Espanyol (Spanish Village), which has been described as "Spain in a bottle." One hundred fifteen original and reproduction buildings from all over Spain are arranged on five acres of narrow streets and plazas, mixed in with sixty craft shops, many with artisans demonstrating traditional crafts. Concerts and flamenco dancing take place on some evenings. Poble Espanyol is a staple of the Barcelona tourist scene, built for the 1929 Exhibition. Some of our readers have called Poble Espanyol hokey; others have reported their kids loved it. You be the judge.

Museu de Ciéncia (93–212–60–50), calle Teodor Roviralta 55. Metro: Verdagur. Open daily 10:00 A.M. to 8:00 P.M. Adults €3, children €2.

Poble Espanyol (93–508–63–30; www.poble-espanyol.com) is on Avinguda del Marquès de Comillas. Metro: Espanya. Open daily at least 9:00 A.M. to 8:00 P.M. (as late as 4:00 A.M. summer weekends!). Adults €7.50, children €4.00.

segovia

The aqueduct in Segovia is amazingly well preserved. Its 128 pillars and two tiers of 163 arches were built entirely without mortar—and yet this engineering triumph was carrying water to Segovia's citizens until a few dozen years ago. Even then the aqueduct was retired not because it leaked or malfunctioned but because its water had become polluted.

In the middle of Segovia the aqueduct is huge, towering over the main street of the new city, drawing the eye directly to the old city high above. Our kids decided they had to see *into* the aqueduct to see if there was water in it, so we followed it for several hundred meters, walking uphill away from town until the soaring arches became lower and lower. Finally we could see the inside channel, its stones worn smooth from carrying water for more than 2,000 years.

After our aqueduct adventure, we visited the Alcázar. The obligatory Spanish tour bored Lib and Sam immensely, though later they listened with interest as we retold the tale of Prince Pedro's nurse, who dropped the royal baby from a window, then followed him to his death in the courtyard below. *Our advice:* View this fairy-tale castle from outside, or, if possible, skip the tour and simply climb the tower.

Segovia aqueduct is accessible at all hours; no fee. Alcázar (92–146–0759; www .alcazardesegovia.com). Open daily 10:00 A.M. to 7:00 P.M. (6:00 P.M. in winter). Adults €4.00, children €2.50. Free on Tuesday.

madrid

Madrid is a giant, sprawling city of more than three million people. Yet most of the sites you'll want to see are centered within a relatively compact area—only about a mile wide—between the royal palace and Retiro Park. We recommend you walk around as much of this area as little legs will permit to soak in the vibrant life of Spain's capital.

parque del retiro

Meet most of Madrid in the city's best park, Parque del Retiro. Aside from the usual—flowers, grass, trees—this green haven features a huge pond (El Estanque) with ducks and fish that like to be fed and paddleboats that like to be rented. Three children's playgrounds, puppet shows, Gypsy fortune-tellers, ice-cream stands, and band concerts (on summer Sunday mornings) round out the attractions. You can also see flamenco dancing on occasion in the park. Check the weekly *Guia del Ocio* or the monthly *En Madrid* to get the latest listings of special shows and performances.

Parque del Retiro is like Central Park—so big you can't miss it. It's located on the eastern edge of downtown. Metro: Retiro. Rent paddleboats from 9:30 A.M. to 8:30 P.M. for about €3.50.

museo naval

It's no coincidence that we're recommending marine museums in both Barcelona and Madrid. Madrid was, after all, the capital of the world's greatest empire at one point. And that empire gained its power solely through its well-equipped navy. The Museo Naval features room after room of beautifully intricate ship models, but kids like the reconstructed ships' cabins best. It's hard to believe how cramped and tiny accommodations were for months at sea. Older kids who have studied the European exploration of America (often a focus in sixth grade) will appreciate the enormous map showing Spanish expeditions from the fifteenth to eighteenth centuries.

Museo Naval (92–379–5299; www.museonavalmadrid.com) is on Paseo del Prado 5. Metro: Banco de España. Open Tuesday through Sunday 10:00 A.M. to 2:00 P.M. Closed Monday. Free.

plaza mayor and palacio real

One way to savor the glory of old Spain is to walk from the Plaza Mayor to the Palacio Real, or royal palace. As in any self-respecting Spanish city, Madrid's Plaza Mayor is its heart. A vast open space surrounded by weathered buildings, it was once the site of bullfights and of executions during the Spanish Inquisition. Today it serves as Madrid's living room, where the city gathers in the evening to loll in the cafes and stroll in the square. There's nothing special to see or *do* here. The point is just to *be*.

Head out the northwest corner of the Plaza Mayor, then follow Calle Mayor to Calle de Bailén—or choose to meander through tiny ancient streets toward the royal palace. Don't worry about getting lost: At any point you can smile at passerby and ask, "Palacio Real?" in a quizzical tone, and you'll be set straight. The palace is less than a half mile from the Plaza Mayor.

The royal palace, with 2,800 rooms, was never completed; what stands today is only a part of what was originally planned to dwarf all other royal palaces. When you see it you'll have to admit it's not too shabby, though. The palace was built by the Bourbon kings in the early 1700s and was occupied by Spanish royalty until the Civil War in the 1930s. Today the king and queen call the smaller Zarzuela Palace home but use the Palacio Real for state occasions.

English tours last around two hours; if possible skip the tour and wander on your own. (If they make you take the tour, use our slink-ahead system recommended in chapter 6, Sightseeing Survival.) Kids have told us they especially like the armor collection, filled with helmets, breastplates, and shields. Contrary to what your kids may think, this smallish armor was not for children but for adults, who were simply much smaller, on average, in past centuries. (*One caution:* Be prepared to hustle younger children past a few gruesome torture devices in the collection—and to drag older children away!)

On the grounds children will seek out the playground in the Plaza de Oriente. They'll also enjoy the carriage museum (Museo de Carruages Reales) with its collection of fairy-tale carriages, some still used for royal processions.

Palacio Real (91–454–8800; www.patrimonionacional.es) is located at the end of Calle Mayor, on Calle de Bailén. Metro: Opera. Open Monday through Saturday 9:30 A.M. to 5:00 P.M. (6:00 P.M. in summer), Sunday 9:00 A.M. to 2:00 P.M. (3:00 P.M. in summer), closed when the palace is used for state receptions. Adults €9, children €6. Come early to avoid long lines.

medieval cuenca

About 160 km southeast of Madrid you'll find the city of Cuenca. Modern Cuenca has little to recommend it, but far above today's city, Old Cuenca hangs suspended over a deep river gorge. It's not on the way from anywhere to anywhere else, but sometimes locations like this retain the flavor and mystery of a country better than the well-traveled routes.

It's a definite trip back into the Middle Ages to walk in Cuenca's narrow streets, many of which lead under covered passages. Most enchanting are the *casas colgadas,* or hanging houses. Five to six hundred years old, these houses were built into a cliff and are cantilevered out over the river 60 meters below. A great view of the old town and the new city can be had from the pedestrian suspension bridge not far from the *casas colgadas.* Equally good views can be had from the two roads on either side of the old town, but kids will enjoy the wiggly footbridge best.

Medieval houses cling to the hillsides in Cuenca, Spain.

The town features an archaeological museum and an abstract art museum, but neither has much to recommend itself to the average child. Stay outdoors and enjoy the views and the architecture, and your kids will learn plenty about Spain's history.

Not far from Cuenca is a natural wonder, the Ciudad Encantada, a collection of rock formations carved by eons of erosion. Enjoy a nature hike, and see if your kids can spot the elephant, the dog, and other fanciful forms.

To reach Cuenca take the N111 southeast from Madrid in the direction of Tarancón (81 km), then the N400 about an equal distance to Cuenca.

Ciudad Encantada is 36 km northeast of Cuenca, on a very scenic route passing through Valdecebras.

mérida roman museum and ruins

When Rome was the center of an empire, the city of Augusta Emerita lay near its outer edge. Here a grateful Caesar Augustus pensioned off a group of legionnaires with land, and the old soldiers built a city worthy to be the capital of Lusitania, the Roman province encompassing Portugal and part of Spain.

Remnants of the empire are so extensive that Mérida was declared a UNESCO World Heritage Site in 1993. As you approach, two aqueducts mark the route; inside the city there's a Roman theater (Teatro Romano) that originally seated 6,000 next to an amphitheater that held 14,000. Turn almost any corner and you'll see a Roman temple next to a *supermercado*.

To display Mérida's many archaeological finds, Spain built the Museo Nacional de Arte Romano here, straddling an ancient Roman road. The museum is wonderfully laid out, with ceilings high enough for soaring Corinthian columns, walls that can display an entire mosaic floor, and dozens of little alcoves, each dedicated to a particular theme (lighting devices, coins, jewelry, etc.). In the basement are actual Roman excavations, including the unearthed road that courses through the museum's courtyard. (Sam was overcome by the urge to walk where Roman feet had trod.) Across the square from the museum are extensive Roman ruins you can wander through, including a theater, an amphitheater, and a hippodrome where chariot races once were held.

Mérida is in Spain's Extremadura region, about halfway between Madrid and Lisbon. Roman Museum (92-431-1690; www.museoarteromano.mcu.es) is open Tuesday through Saturday 10:00 A.M. to 2:00 P.M. and 4:00 to 6:00 P.M., Sunday and holidays 10:00 A.M. to 2:00 P.M. Adults €2.40, kids free. Teatro Romano and Anfiteatro (92-431-2530) is open daily 9:30 A.M. to 2:00 P.M. and 4:00 to 6:00 P.M. Adults €9, kids nine to sixteen €5.

moorish spain: córdoba, sevilla, granada

The invasion of Vandals and Visigoths from the north drove the Romans out of Spain, but these groups (who left little evidence of their visit) were, in turn, replaced by invaders from the south: the Moors.

The Islamic occupation left its traces all over Spain and even into southern France. A visit to any of the Moors' three largest cities—Sevilla, Córdoba, and Granada—offers a great way to begin to appreciate the rich culture of the Moors and to open your eyes to an atmosphere unlike that found anyplace else in Europe. Wander along the narrow streets and peek through open doors, and you may catch a glimpse of leafy courtyards and trickling fountains in many of the older houses and hotels.

In Córdoba visit the Mezquita, the world's largest mosque when it was completed in the tenth century. Pink- and blue-marble pillars; red-and-white-striped alabaster arches; and pink, blue, and gold mosaics are in architectural contrast to the sixteenth-century baroque cathedral plunked down in the middle of the Mezquita. Ask your kids to reflect on this strange juxtaposition and on the issues of conquest and cultural change it represents.

All three cities boast *alcázars*, or palaces, with warrens of Arabic-looking rooms with carved wooden ceilings, colorful tiled walls, bulbous archways, and magnificent gardens. Córdoba's Alcázar, built in 1328, almost a century after the Moors were driven out of Córdoba, was inaugurated as the Palace of the Christian Kings. Yet the design clearly shows the Moorish styles still practiced by local craftsmen. Sevilla's Alcázar is the oldest palace in Europe still used by royalty; King Juan Carlos lives here when in Sevilla. Don't miss the hedge maze in its gardens, among lemon trees, fountains, and pools of enormous goldfish.

Granada's Alcázar is the grandest of all and is part of the fortress complex known as the Alhambra. Here, on a hilltop in southern Spain, the Moors held on to their last foothold in the Iberian peninsula until the end of the fifteenth century. Finally the Moorish influence in Spain was ended, but it must be remembered that Granada was once one of the richest and most enlightened cities in Europe.

Córdoba Mezquita (95–747–0512; www.turismodecordoba.org) is open daily 10:00 A.M. to 6:30 P.M. Adults €8, children €4. Córdoba Alcázar (95–742–0151) is open Tuesday through Saturday 10:00 A.M. to 2:00 P.M. and 6:00 to 8:00 P.M. Adults €4, children €2.

Sevilla Alcázar (95–450–23–23; www.patronato-alcazarsevilla.es) is open Tuesday through Saturday 9:30 A.M. to 8:00 P.M. (6:00 P.M. off-season), Sunday 9:30 A.M. to 4:00 P.M. (2:30 P.M. off-season). Adults €5, children free.

Granada Alhambra (95–822–0912; www.alhambradegranada.org) is open daily 8:30 A.M. to 8:00 P.M. (6:00 P.M. off-season); night session also, if your kids are older. Tickets are sold for morning or afternoon, with entry to the Nasrid Palaces in a specified half-hour time slot. Adults €10, kids under eight free. Gardens only €5.

gibraltar

Gibraltar offers evidence of a more recent imperial conquest: the last remnants of the British Empire. This place is a curious community of mixed cultures. Where else can you munch English fish-and-chips that you've ordered in Spanish while listening to a wailing Arab chant over the radio?

Ask your kids what they think of the British owning a little corner of Spain. How would they feel if Japan or Italy or Brazil owned Cape Cod or the

San Francisco peninsula? How would the culture change if all three of these groups invaded in turn?

We visited Gibraltar after three weeks of hearing no one outside our own family group speak more than a few words of English. The little British colony flooded us with unexpected relief—how welcome to have a few hours off from struggling to understand everything around us! For us as adults, the best part was a chance to stock up on English-language paperbacks at the Gibraltar Bookshop on Main Street. Don't be ashamed if you feel this way, too. No matter how eager you are to learn about other cultures and languages, a small respite helps.

While you're there, visit with the "apes of Gibraltar," actually small monkeys. The tailless rock apes are the only simians living wild in Europe. These creatures invaded from North Africa before the Moors and have not been dislodged from the area known as the Ape's Den by Vandals, Moors, Spaniards, or Brits! (Legend has it that the Brits will lose control of the rock when the last monkey is gone, so the creatures are carefully treated.) *Beware:* Libby and Sam were delighted when one monkey jumped up on the hood of our car, then startled when he darted for the open window. We rolled it up just before he jumped in. No wonder signs and leaflets warn women to hold on to their handbags when these aggressive creatures are nearby.

To see the apes take the cable car from Grand Parade at the southern end of Main Street (€12.50 adults, €7.00 kids, round-trip) or drive up Europa Road from the center of town, then take Old Queen's Road past the Ape's Den. For details contact the Gibraltar Tourist Information Center at 749-50; www.gibraltar.gov.gi.

morocco

Okay, it's not Europe. But if you're already in Spain, ponder a side trip to Morocco as one way to introduce your kids to a non-Western culture. The ferry from Algeciras, near Gibraltar, takes only ninety minutes to arrive in Tangier.

We went for a single, fascinating overnight stay. We roamed through the twisting alleys of the Medina, the old section of the city, and bargained for red leather slippers, a wooden whistle, and copper bangles, all at rock-bottom prices (even when you figure we paid at least ten times what the locals would have paid for the same items). We sat in our hotel window and watched men in hooded robes wrestle rascally goats, and veiled women rushing their loaves to community ovens. We walked in the streets in the warm night followed by pitiful little beggar girls.

If you go, be forewarned that all your assumptions—about your "right" to privacy, about what is "fair," about the role of women in life—should be left behind. We were prepared for hustlers who would offer to be our guides, but we weren't prepared for the following:

- Seven taxi drivers who told us our *Let's Go*-recommended hotel had closed down, before the eighth agreed to take us there. (The first seven offered to take us to "the very fine hotel of my brother's wife's uncle," or some such.)

- Men who followed us everywhere, even after we had politely refused their "guide" services, even after we ignored them. We learned later that these men could collect a commission on anything we bought in the shops, simply by claiming to have been with us. No wonder they wouldn't take no for an answer.

- Restaurants serving men only. While women may not have actually been barred from entry, I felt uncomfortable even considering these male bastions as we searched for a possible dinner site.

- The pervasiveness of the *muezzin*'s predawn prayer call that wails on forever, to make sure that all the faithful—and infidels like us—are awakened from sleep in time to pray. It's a vivid reminder of how religion is inalterably woven into everyday life in most Muslim countries.

- The extent of the hunger we all felt in observing the holy month of Ramadan, when Muslims refrain from eating or drinking during daylight hours. Sharing the custom is half courtesy to local practices and half necessity—restaurants aren't open during fast hours. (Take-out food can be bought and eaten behind the doors of your hotel room if you happen into a Muslim country during Ramadan. Ramadan varies according to the Muslim calendar, so check on this before you go.)

- The fellow who offered us 2,000 camels for our daughter. (Sam said, "For *Libby?* He must be joking." I suspect he was.)

These are not complaints. They're simply reactions to an environment so unlike anything we'd experienced anywhere else in our travels. It's startling how lost you can feel when all of your basic tenets and beliefs simply don't apply to the present reality around you. Yet that's what traveling is all about: challenging and questioning the givens of your life.

On reflection Morocco was a great experience, even with this shallow sampling (and even given the fact that Tangier is considered by many a tourist trap and *not* the real Morocco). Still, we could have learned even more and felt less disoriented if we'd gone about a few things differently. If we had it to do again, we'd welcome the first personable guide who approached us and go with the flow instead of judging everything from a hopelessly Western perspective. Privacy is impossible, and getting to know one fellow is far preferable to feeling hassled by dozens.

We'd also feel less challenged by the need to bargain for everything. To many Westerners, bargaining seems like nothing more than a way for vendors to cheat shoppers into paying too much for an item. From the non-Western point of view, though, our custom of set prices may seem barbaric: The customer has *no say* in the cost of an item, and purchases can be made without any human interaction whatsoever.

The sights and sounds of Morocco stayed with us for a long time, integrated into the kids' backseat banter. Weeks later, as we drove through France,

I'd hear Sam's accented voice in the backseat suddenly say, "How many dirham will you give me for this fine cookie?"

Libby would answer immediately, "That cookie is not so fine. I will take it off your hands for 5 dirham."

"This is a very fine cookie," Sam would retort in a hurt tone. "It is entirely handmade in my country. It is worth at least 25 dirham."

And on and on they'd go, making a mutually enjoyable twenty-minute bargaining session out of a simple cookie exchange, with fond memories of Morocco.

Ferries for Tangier leave from Algeciras, a grimy port near Gibraltar, every ninety minutes from 7:00 A.M. to 10:00 P.M. in summer; less frequently in winter. Crossing takes one-and-a-half hours. Adults €24, children under twelve €12.

greece

While Italy is gorgeous and gregarious, it's also chaotic and careless. Greece offers all the pluses of Italy with few of its drawbacks. Run through a mental checklist: Antiquity? In spades. Nice people? Definitely. Familiar food? Well, two out of three isn't bad. Greece, like Italy and Spain, is a country that loves children and is therefore a great destination for a family trip. And it's still reasonably priced, compared to the rest of Europe.

We had not originally planned to include Greece in this book. But Dan and Wendy were so enchanted by their visit there that they insisted. Consider this short section just a sampler to give you the flavor of Greece.

it's greek to me

Many people pass up Greece because of the language barrier. We're including this extra section to convince you not to let language stand in your way. Before you go, take some time to learn the sounds of the different letters of the alphabet. You'll be surprised at how many words you can understand once you are able to sound them out phonetically. A few examples:

κοτολεττα	*kotoleta*	cutlet
σαλατα	*salata*	salad
κροκεττε	*krokette*	croquette
μαρμελαδα	*marmelada*	marmalade, jam
ομελεττα	*omeletta*	omelet
παστα	*pasta*	pastry
σοκολατα	*sokolata*	chocolate

Beyond words like this, which are similar to English, are words that you'll recognize because of the pervasiveness of Greek roots in medicine. Anyone who takes his kids to a pediatrician has a fighting chance of figuring out that *bolmenou gia paidia* (*menu yia pedia*) is "children's menu." And if you studied biology in school, you'll understand that when a boy yells *megalostoma* at his sister, he's calling her big mouth. In any event, many of the signs in Greece are in both Greek and Roman ("normal") letters.

If you're still stuck, you'll find English much more widely spoken in Greece than in Italy. Young people often work for a year or two in America or Australia, so it's not uncommon to be addressed in perfect English by your gas station attendant. Consider Greece!

cultural sites in greece

Greece has recently created a very useful Web site (http://odysseus.culture.gr), where its many ruins, monuments, and museums are described in detail in English. Unfortunately, the individual pages have very long obscure names, and the navigation within the site is awkward.

But the information is fairly good—and in English—so I *do* recommend this site. In place of the usual attraction Web site addresses in this section, we'll give you information for using Odysseus. In all cases, start by going to http://odysseus.culture.gr, and then click on English. Then pick the category (Museums, Monuments, or Archaeological Sites), then choose "Alphabetical Index" and pick the name of the site.

For example, for the Agora, "Odysseus/Museums/Ancient Agora of Athens" means that you pick the category Museums, then find the name Ancient Agora of Athens in the alphabetical listing. Trust me—it's the best way!

athens

The ancient city of Athens *is* every bit as smoggy and crowded as you've heard. Yet it's also a great place to ponder the differences between ancient and modern cultures. Visit Athens at the end of your stay in Greece. Then you'll have a little knowledge of how the language works, a good idea of what foods your family enjoys, and, most important, an understanding of the warmth of the Greek people. Wendy defines this as "the comforting knowledge that in Greece, the default is positive." When in doubt, assume someone's intentions are only the best.

Proof of this came when four-year-old Morghan fell on her head in Athens. Complete strangers helped the Hallinans get to the children's hospital, where the treatment was free, quick, and thoughtful. Five hours later Morghan was certified healthy, and her family was "ready to move to this very humane place." Maybe it's no accident that this culture was the cradle of democracy, a system of government that depends on citizens who respect and care for one another.

Instead of the children's hospital, Dan and Wendy recommend you take your kids to the Agora Museum. The Agora, at the base of the Acropolis, was ancient Athens's original marketplace. Today it features one of the most complete temples in Athens. The museum is housed in the Stoa of Attalos, next to the Agora. Help your kids find the ancient baby bottles and potty chairs, and the voting machine from 400 B.C. Another good bet in Athens is the small Greek Folk Art Museum, much of which is devoted to traditional costumes with awesome embroidery.

The Agora Museum (210–321–0185; Odysseus/Museums/Ancient Agora), Adrianou Street, about 500 yards north of the Acropolis, is open Tuesday through Sunday 8:00 A.M. to 5:00 P.M., Monday 11:00 A.M. to 5:00 P.M. Adults €4, kids free.

The Greek Folk Art Museum (210–322–9031; odysseus/museums/Greek folk art) is on Odos Kidathineon 17. It's open Tuesday through Sunday 8:00 A.M. to 7:00 P.M., Monday noon to 7:00 P.M. Closed off-season. Adults €2, children free.

tiryns and epidavros

The great attraction of Greece for many kids is the opportunity to explore ancient ruins. For this the best approach is to avoid well-known tourist traps and head for obscure locations. Unmarked rubble lines the sides of many roads, especially in the Peloponnesus. Stop for a picnic, and let your kids roam at will. Or seek out some of the lesser-known established sites.

For example, bypass the famous Mycenae unless you can get there good and early; by 10:00 A.M. a name-brand site like this may already have ten buses lined up, disgorging tourists. Instead, continue on to Tiryns, about 20 km farther south toward the sea. Arrive at 8:00 or 9:00 A.M., while the air is cool and the ruins are deserted, and your kids can pretend they're the first ones to discover the ancient Mycenaean fortress and its surrounding buildings.

Dan and Wendy harbor vivid memories of their kids claiming their own bedrooms and trying to find the kitchens and bathrooms—a simple but magical morning spent alongside the invisible children of ancient Greece.

Also in eastern Peloponnesia is Epidavros (Epidaurus). Epidavros is famous for its amphitheater, a 2,300-year-old structure with 14,000 seats in fifty-five tiers. From June to September the amphitheater resounds with traditional Greek dramas by the likes of Euripides and Aristophanes. Pass these by: They're in Greek and are unlikely to interest most kids.

Instead, come into the theater when it's empty, again preferably in the early morning. Its acoustics are legendary: When one kid whispers on the stage, another can hear every word from the highest seats. Once the children tire of this, there are lovely arbors and orchards for picnics. After lunch visit the museum of the sanctuary of Aesculapius. This museum, dedicated to the god of healing, contains a fascinating collection of medical artifacts that will be interesting to older children and adults.

Tiryns (27520–22657; Odysseus/Archaeological/Tiryns) is located about midway between Argos and Návplion. Open daily 8:30 A.M. to 7:00 P.M. (8:30 A.M. to 3:00 P.M. in winter). Adults €3, kids free. Mycenae (27510–76585; Odysseus/Archaeological/ Mycenae) is north of Argos (if the Peloponnesus is a mitten, Argos is located at the base of the thumb). Open daily 8:00 A.M. to 7:00 P.M. (8:00 A.M. to 5:00 P.M. in winter). Adults €3, kids free. Epidavros (0753–22009) is on the other side of the "thumb" from Tiryns. Open Monday noon to 7:00 P.M., Tuesday through Sunday 8:00 A.M. to 7:30 P.M. Adults €8, kids free.

olympia

Whether you think of Olympia as a symbol of the fiercest competitions of gods and men or as a model for proving national prowess on the playing field instead of on the battlefield, the famous mountaintop in Greece merits a visit.

Besides, it's just plain fun for kids. What active child wouldn't like to stand at the starting line of the *stadion,* the original Olympic racetrack? There's plenty left to mark the site where the Olympic games began in 776 B.C. Come prepared to walk, as the ruins of this ancient religious shrine are spread out across several acres.

Besides the athletic facilities like the *stadion* and the wrestling school, make sure to visit the Archaeological Museum. Because Olympus was the dwelling place of the gods, Greek citizens brought the best of everything here as offerings. Many of the pictures you see in school textbooks and art books, in fact, are of objects from Olympia.

You may not be as fortunate as Dan and Wendy, who arrived during a crashing thunderstorm, when the angry gods were easy to imagine. But nonetheless Olympia is definitely a place to bring the family.

One final tip: Start reading Greek myths with your kids when you enter Greece. *D'Aulaire's Book of Greek Myths* is especially good, with plenty of pictures and relatively short versions of the traditional stories. Knowing the major players—especially before you reach Olympia—will help everyone enjoy Greece.

Olympia (26240–22517; Odysseus/Archaeological/Olympia) is in western Peloponnesia, about forty-five minutes from Pirgos. Olympia site and museum is open daily 8:00 A.M. to 7:30 P.M. April to October. Hours vary in off-season. Museum and Olympic site: adults €9, kids free.

resources

In this chapter we've included nearly every publication or organization mentioned in the text of the book. You'll also find several additional resources and a number of great books and bookstores that will lead you to even more resources for your trip.

Note: ISBN numbers are included for the current editions of all books whenever possible so that your local bookstore can order them for you. Be aware that new editions will have different ISBNs, so these numbers may have changed by the time you read this.

airline tickets

Use a good travel agent; try a comparative-fares Web site such as www .expedia.com, www.orbitz.com, www.comparefares.com, or www.bootsnall.com; or call an airline directly:

Air France	(800) 237–2747	www.airfrance.com
Alitalia	(800) 223–5730	www.alitaliausa.com
American	(800) 433–7300	www.aa.com
British Airways	(800) 247–9297	www.british-airways.com
Delta	(800) 241–4141	www.delta.com
Icelandair	(800) 223–5500	www.icelandair.com
Lufthansa	(800) 645–3880	www.lufthansa.com
Northwest-KLM	(800) 225-2525	www.nwa.com
SAS	(800) 221–2350	www.flysas.com
United	(800) 538-2929	www.united.com
US Airways	(800) 428–4322	www.usairways.com
Virgin Atlantic	(800) 821–5438	www.virgin-atlantic.com

books (background)

Children's Books in Print. RR Bowker, annual. Don't buy this one: Your public library should have it. Look up the countries you'll be visiting in the subject index. Then read as many books as you can with your kids before you go!

Clan of the Cave Bear. Auel, Jean. Bantam Books, 1984. ISBN: 0-5532-5042-6. Great background reading for visiting prehistoric caves in France, even though the book is based elsewhere.

Cultural Misunderstandings: The French-American Experience. Carroll, Raymonde. Translated by Carol Volk. University of Chicago Press, 1990. ISBN: 0-2260-9498-7. A fascinating exploration of the differences in social interaction in France and the United States. For adults.

French or Foe? Getting the Most Out of Visiting, Living & Working in France. Platt, Polly. Cultural Crossing, 2003. ISBN: 0-9646-6842-4; www.pollyplatt.com. Covers many of the same issues as Carroll's book, above; equally fascinating to any Francophile.

The History of Art for Young People. Janson, Anthony. Prentice-Hall, 2003. ISBN: 0-1318-3300-6. Expensive but good. Try your library before you go, and let your kids "shop" for masterpieces they'd like to see in Europe.

The New Spaniards. Hooper, John. Penguin Books, 2006. ISBN: 0-1401-1609-4. Wonderful commentary on the vast changes in Spain since Franco. Highly recommended to anyone spending time in Spain. For adults.

Sarum: The Novel of England. Rutherfurd, Edward. Ivy Books, 1992. ISBN: 0-8041-0298-8. Michener-esque historical saga based in Salisbury, England. Too long to read out loud in its entirety, but it gives great background for English history.

books (general guidebooks)

Europe Through the Back Door. Steves, Rick. Avalon Travel, 2006. ISBN: 1-5669-1808-1. If any book is the adult version of *Take Your Kids to Europe*, this is it. Buy it—then get on Rick's mailing list for more good info: P.O. Box 2009, Edmonds, WA 98020; (425) 771–8303; www.ricksteves.com.

Eyewitness Travel Guides. Dorling Kindersley. Wonderfully illustrated European guidebooks with maps, cutaways, and photos.

The Family Travel Guide: An Inspiring Collection of Family-Friendly Vacations. Meyers, Carole Terwilliger, ed. Carousel Press, 1995. ISBN: 0-9171-2014-0. Firsthand family travel accounts from all over the world. Helps you picture your trip—and includes additional suggestions of places to go and things to see.

Let's Go guidebooks. Harvard Student Agencies, St. Martin's Press, annual. Series of excellent budget guidebooks includes Britain & Ireland; France; Germany; Greece; Ireland; Italy; Spain, Portugal, and Morocco; Switzerland and Austria; Western Europe; and Eastern Europe. Sites geared to adults; trustworthy lodging recommendations are updated annually and include triple and quad information. Excerpts from *Let's Go* guides are also now at www.letsgo.com.

Mona Winks. Steves, Rick, and Gene Openshaw. Avalon Travel, 2001. ISBN: 1-5669-1345-4. Guide to all major European art museums. Saves buying museum-specific guides and helps you plan "treasure hunts" for the kids.

The Packing Book: Secrets of the Carry-on Traveler. Gilford, Judith. Ten Speed Press, 1998. ISBN: 1-5800-8021-9. Has sections devoted to traveling with babies, kids, and teens, plus lots of other useful information. Reader recommendation.

Rick Steves' Europe 101: History and Art for the Traveler. Steves, Rick, and Gene Openshaw. Avalon Travel, 2007. ISBN: 1-5669-1516-3. Unstuffy history helps kids (and parents!) better understand how different historic events relate to one another. Review this before you go—suddenly all that high school history will start to fit into place.

books (kids' guidebooks)

Around . . . series. Fodor's. Easily carried minibooks cover sixty-eight things to do in each city. Nearby eats and cautions for parents round out well-written info on sites. No general background info, just a two-page spread on each recommended site.
Around London with Kids. Brown, Jacqueline, 2006. ISBN: 1-4000-1663-0.
Around Paris with Kids. Emerson, Emily, 2003. ISBN: 1-4000-1150-7.
Around Rome with Kids. Prescott, Dana, 2002. ISBN: 0-6769-0188-3.

Découvrir Paris est un Jeu d'Enfant. Calabre, Isabelle, and Orlane Dupont. Editions Parigramme, 2007. ISBN: 2-8409-6414-7. A great guide: Covers museums, parks, zoos, markets—even pick-your-own farms near Paris! In French, from www.amazon.fr.

Florence for Kids. Filipponi, Stefano, and Annalisa Fineschi. Fratelli Palombi Editori, 1998. ISBN: 88-7621-922-6. A thin, colorful guide to Florence written at an upper-elementary level. Only available in Italy.

Guide de la France des Enfants. Bellenger, Marylène. Sélection du Reader's Digest, 2004. ISBN: 2-7098-4885-6. Out of print for several years, this classic has now been rewritten and reissued. In French, from www .amazon.fr.

Ireland for Kids. MacKenzie, Derek. Trafalgar, 2001. ISBN: 1-8401-8304-7. Very comprehensive; includes activities, museums, hotels, and restaurants throughout the Republic and Northern Ireland.

Italy Discovery Journal. Byrne, P. L. This 164-page book is not available in stores. You pay a small fee and download pdf files from www.kidseurope .com. Do it if you're headed to Italy. The book is filled with activities and ideas that will help kids truly interact with and think about Italian language and culture.

Italy with Kids. Pape, Barbara, and Michael Pape. Open Road, 2006. ISBN: 1-5936-0064-X. Real parent-tried advice with sections for Rome, Venice, Verona, Tuscany, Naples and Amalfi, and Milan and Lakes Region.

Kids' London: Dorling Kindersley Travel Guides. Adams, Simon. DK Publishing, 2000. ISBN: 0-7894-5249-9. All the great pictures of a DK guide with kid-level text.

Le Guide de la Science en France. Guides Hachette, 1994. ISBN: 2-0124-2153-9. A wonderful guide to factory visits, nature parks, aquariums, and all things scientific in France. Includes editors' top picks. In French; buy it on arrival or from www.amazon.fr.

Le Guide du Routard Junior . . . Paris et ses environs avec vos enfants. Hachette Livre, 2004. ISBN: 2-0124-4013-3. Exhaustive French guide to Paris activities, restaurants, and shops for kids. In French, from www.amazon.fr. Also look for *Le Guide du Routard France* in the same series.

London for Families. Lain, Larry, and Michael Laine. Interlink Publishing Group, 2004. ISBN: 1-5665-6534-0. A little more anecdotal and personal than the professional tone of *Take the Kids London*—choose the style that suits you, as both are thorough with a diverse choice of activities.

London with Kids. Gwinner, Valerie. Open Road, 2005. ISBN: 1-5936-0037-2. Comprehensive with lots of budget tips. Gwinner is the mother of two and an experienced writer—put them together and you get a helpful, up-to-date guide.

Once Upon a Time in Great Britain: A Travel Guide to the Sights and Settings of Your Favorite Children's Stories. Wentz, Melanie. St. Martin's Griffin, 2002. ISBN: 0-3122-8338-5. Just what the long title suggests: a guide to sights associated with Winnie the Pooh, Mary Poppins, Peter Pan, and all your kids' favorite Brit-based stories.

Paris for Families. Lain, Larry, and Michael Lain. Interlink Publishing Group, 2004. ISBN: 1-5665-6535-9. Very comprehensive; even includes info on short-term apartments and sample letters in French to help you book.

Paris with Kids. Gwinner, Valerie. Open Road, 2003. ISBN: 1-5936-0004-6. A fresh spin on Paris, with all the usual sights, some offbeat ideas, and very useful "side dishes" of kid-friendly restaurants, restrooms, and parks.

Take the Kids series. Cadogan Guides. Series has an attractive layout with maps, pictures, trivia, and comprehensive information on every possible site. Includes some ideas for shopping, restaurants, and hotels. Thorough and recommended. Series includes:
Take the Kids Amsterdam. Bolt, Rodney. ISBN: 1-8601-1990-5.
Take the Kids England. Fullman, Joseph. ISBN: 1-8601-1353-2
Take the Kids Ireland. Corzine, Amy. ISBN: 1-8601-1315-X
Take the Kids London. Fullman, Joseph. ISBN: 1-8601-1311-7
Take the Kids Paris + Disneyland. Truszkowski, Helen. ISBN: 1-8601-1320-6
Take the Kids Short Breaks/London. Fullman, Joseph. ISBN: 1-1861-1876-3.
Take the Kids South of France. Whitehouse, Rosie. ISBN: 1-8601-1111-4.

Take the Kids Travelling. Truszkowski, Helen. Cadogan, 1999. ISBN: 1-8601-1991-3. More geared to U.S. and Europe trips than *Travel with Children* (below). Good selection of U.K. resources not available in the United States.

Travel with Children. Lanigan, Cathy. Lonely Planet, 2002. ISBN: 0-8644-2729-8. Advice for hard-core family travelers, even those heading to third-world countries with infants and toddlers. Useful info for anyone; will make travel in Europe seem like a snap.

Treasure Hunt series. Mouchawar, Ellen, and Marvin Mouchawar. Available at www.kidsgoeurope.com. Small pocket guides written by a traveling family encourage kids (and grown-ups) to engage with the history and culture of each city.
Treasure Hunt Florence. ISBN: 0-9772699-1-4
Treasure Hunt Venice. ISBN: 0-9772699-0-6.

Usborne Book of Europe. Treays, Rebecca. Usborne, 1998. ISBN: 0-8811-0677-1. Comprehensive enough for parents, but written for kids to read, too. Good overview of the Continent.

Usborne Book of London. Butterfield, Moira. EDC Publications, 1987. ISBN: 0-7460-0050-2. The history and landmarks of London with photos and cut-away illustrations. For kids ten and older.

books and gear web sites

www.amazon.com. General travel books. Also check country sites like www.amazon.fr (France) and www.amazon.de (Germany) for foreign guides, if you're multilingual.

www.bookpassage.com. One of the biggest travel-specialty bookstores.

www.globecorner.com. Venerable Boston-based travel specialists, Globe Corner Bookstore.

www.interculturalpress.com. Books aimed at understanding other cultures and on living and working abroad for very extended periods.

www.magellans.com. Sells all sorts of travel gadgets: plug adapters, waterless shampoo, dual-voltage appliances . . . all kinds of cool stuff.

www.travelbookstore.com. Stocks hard-core books like the Thomas Cook train guides.

www.walkabouttravelgear.com. Amazing range of useful travel gear personally tested by dedicated budget travelers.

camping resources

AA Caravan & Camping Europe 2006. AA Publishing. ISBN: 0-7495-4791-X. Campground guide with more than 3,500 campgrounds throughout Europe. More listings, but not all as thoroughly inspected as Alan Rogers's guides. Available at www.amazon.com.

Alan Rogers Good Camps Guides. www.alanrogers.com. For three decades Alan Rogers has been inspecting and reviewing European campsites. Currently there are six volumes: Europe, France, Britain & Ireland, Italy, Spain & Portugal, and Central Europe & Croatia. Great Web site allows you to search for campsites by criteria—location, suitable for toddlers, offer bungalows, etc.—or even book ferries and selected campsites.

Camping Europe. Mickelsen, Carol. Carousel Press, 2001. ISBN: 0-9171-2018-3. Largely anecdotal book on car camping, from an author with twenty-five years' experience. Not geared to kids and families, but it puts you in the mood.

Country-specific camping guides. Most National Tourist Offices in Europe provide excellent, free camping booklets and maps; ask them, using the contact information at the end of this chapter.

Europe by Van & Motorhome. Shore, David, and Patty Campbell. Odyssey Press, 2001. ISBN: 0-9382-9712-0. A comprehensive resource to everything involved with buying, renting, or simply surviving in an RV or camper in Europe.

Family Campers and RVers. (800) 245-9755; www.fcrv.org. Family memberships in this camping organization are $25 and include children under eighteen. For an additional $20, members can purchase an International Camping Carnet.

Guide Officiel Camping/Caravaning. Camping guide from the Fedération Française de Camping et de Caravaning includes almost 9,000 sites in France. Order online or search listings electronically at www.camping france.com. (The Web site has lots of other great info in French.)

Traveler's Guide to European Camping. Church, Mike, and Terri Church. Rolling Homes Press, 2004. ISBN: 0-9652-9688-1. Useful info from experienced travelers. Includes details on more than 350 campgrounds for RVers or tent-campers.

rv rentals

Auto Europe (888-223-5555; www.autoeurope.com). U.S. rental car agency also offers RVs in most European countries.

Barbara Lohmer (www.intercamper.de/logo_e.htm). Camper rentals offered by a German high school principal. She'll pick you up at the airport, stock your fridge, and otherwise hold your hand through your first family camping experience.

MC Rent (www.mcrent.de). German-based company offering a good variety of RV rentals.

car purchase/repurchase plans

Auto France, Inc. (800-572-9655; www.autofrance.net). Purchase/repurchase deals for Peugeots in Europe. Can be cheaper than renting, for leases of seventeen days to six months.

Europe by Car (800-223-1516; www.europebycar.com). Arranges Renault and Peugeot plans; Web site makes it easy to compare.

Renault Eurodrive (800-221-1052; www.renaultusa.com). A program similar to Peugeot's purchase/repurchase deal, available through agents or direct from Renault. All rates include any taxes, insurance, unlimited mileage, and twenty-four-hour roadside emergency service in English.

car rentals

Call for quotes, as no one company always has the lowest rates in all countries.

Alamo	(800) 462–5266	www.alamo.com
Auto Europe	(888) 223–5555	www.autoeurope.com
Avis	(800) 230–4898	www.avis.com
Budget	(800) 527–0700	www.budget.com
Euro Vacations	(877) 471–3876	www.eurovacations.com
Europe by Car	(800) 223–1516	www.europebycar.com
Hertz	(800) 654–3001	www.hertz.com
Kemwel	(877) 820–0668	www.kemwel.com
National	(800) 227–7368	www.nationalcar.com
Sixt (Dollar)	(800) 800–6000	www.dollar.com

driving in europe

American Automobile Association (AAA) (800–AAA–HELP, www.aaa.com). Join AAA and you may enjoy free reciprocal privileges while traveling. AAA is also good for passport photos and international drivers' permits.

Moto-Europa, Bredesen, Eric. Once a printed guide, this book is now available only electronically at www.ideamerge.com/motoeuropa. Pop online and get country-specific driving information on all the stuff you're nervous about (even though you shouldn't worry).

family travel specialists

France for Families (www.france4families.com). This UK-based organization's Web site has a wealth of information resources for families traveling to France. Sure, it's supported by links and ads, but you don't have to buy anything to benefit from its wonderful suggestions.

Idyll, Ltd. (888–868–6871; www.untours.com). Home rentals with hand holding: Idyll arranges apartments (including one in a German castle!) and includes low-key orientation and optional group activities at your destination. A reader recommendation.

Let's Take the Kids (613–594–5633, www.letstakethekidstravel.com). Friendly Canadian agency that can book Center Parc holiday camps on the Continent.

ferries

DFDS Seaways USA (800–533–3755; www.seaeurope.com). DFDS takes reservations for ferries and cruises on North Sea and Baltic routes in Denmark, Sweden, Norway, Finland, England, Germany, and the Netherlands.

Ferry Ticket Company (www.ferryto.co.uk). Convenient Web site where you can check routes, times, and costs for ferries all over Europe.

friendship/meet-the-people groups

CouchSurfing (www.couchsurfing.com). Over 200,000 members in 200 countries. Some can offer overnight accommodations; others could hook you up with local families.

Friends Overseas (www.friendsoverseas.org). A Scandinavian-American friendship program run by retired junior high guidance counselor Larry Eisner. Join for around $25, and Larry will send you the names of several Scandinavians interested in meeting and entertaining visiting Americans. The rest is up to you to establish contact by mail and to make arrangements to visit and learn about local life. Not geared to families, but still a good resource.

SERVAS, U.S. Servas Committee, Inc. (707–825–1714; www.usservas.org). An international cooperative system of carefully screened hosts and travelers established to help build world peace, goodwill, and understanding.

Sister Cities International (202–347–8630; www.sister-cities.org). Check the Web site directory to find existing city pairs or to learn how to set up a sister city program.

World Pen Pals (845–246–7828; www.world-pen-pals.com). Matches kids up with pen pals in another country. Call or check the Web site to request an application.

home exchange

HomeExchange.com (800–877–8723; www.homeexchange.com). About 5,500 members, half in the United States and half elsewhere. You pay $99.95 per year to list your house—but you can seek houses for free without joining. Guaranteed: If no one chooses your house, you get a second year for free. Rentals also listed.

HomeLink USA (800–638–3841; www.homelink.org). The largest and oldest exchange club, with fifty years' experience. Representatives in member countries can help you if problems arise. More than 11,000 listings, about 3,000 in the United States and the rest elsewhere. $75 per year for online database access; $40 extra to receive printed directories.

Intervac U.S. (800–756–HOME; www.intervacus.com). U.S. branch of an association covering more than fifty countries. About 10,000 members, most of them overseas. $95 per year for Web-only membership; $140 for book-Web combo that gets you three directories, with your photo listing in one, plus access to the online database.

The Invented City (415–846–7588; www.invented-city.com). About 1,900 listings, with approximately one-third in Europe. Nonmembers can view abbreviated listings before joining. $50 the first year for online database access, $25 per year renewal.

home rentals (multicountry)

EuroGites (www.eurogites.com). *Gîtes* organizations in twenty-one countries across Eastern and Western Europe have banded together and created an association for rural tourism. Their Web site is an easy portal to country-specific *gîte* rentals.

Homeliday (www.homeliday.com). About 30,000 European listings, about half in France, with another 10,000 split between Italy and Spain. Not an agency—basically a catalog of owner ads; you book directly with the owners.

IHA (www.iha.com). More than 7,000 private rentals in Western Europe, largely in France, Italy, and Spain. Many rent for €250 per week or less, as this is also an owner-based Web site. Not as extensive as Homeliday, but with better interface and prices.

Interhome, Inc. (800–882–6864; www.interhome.com). Nearly 20,000 rental homes in sixteen European countries, from $400 per week. All listings examined, scored, and quality rated with one to five stars. The U.S. reservations office connects to a main-office computer in Switzerland for instant, accurate information on availability with guaranteed U.S. dollar prices.

Novasol (www.novasol.com). One of Europe's larger rental companies, featuring houses for rent in Norway, Sweden, Denmark, Holland, Belgium, Poland, Hungary, Austria, and a few other countries; see Web site for prices, which range from $238 per week off-season to about $800 per week in high season. Online booking in English.

www.countrycottages.com. More than 9,000 listings in England, Scotland, Ireland, and France. You can search by location and number of people, but not by price.

www.holiday-rentals.com. Not an agency but a U.K.-based database that lists more than 22,000 private homes, most with photos, full details, and prices. Pick the one you like, then contact the owners directly.

home rentals by country

belgium

Fédération des Gîtes de Wallonie (011-32-81-311-800; www.gitesde wallonie.net). Belgium also has *gîtes*. You can check details and prices in English online for about 500 furnished rental homes from $200 per week and 250 bed-and-breakfast lodgings in the French-speaking part of Belgium.

Flemish Federation for Farm and Country Tourism. For *gîtes* in the Flemish half of Belgium, you can access a database of more than 200 choices through the main national tourist Web site at www.visitbelgium.com. Select "Where to Stay," then scroll way down to "Farm Stays" and look for the link.

britain

CottageGuide (www.cottageguide.com). Charming collection of 6,000 U.K. rentals.

www.visitbritain.com. Visit the British Tourist Office's outstanding Web site; choose "Accommodation" and you'll get access to a large online database of self-catering rentals.

france

Best bets are IHA and Homeliday. See above.

Maison des Gîtes de France (011 33 1 49 70 75 75; www.gites-de-france.fr). Source for about 55,000 inexpensive, simple, reasonably priced rural rentals and B&Bs in France.

germany

Black Forest Tourist Office (011 49-761-296-2271; www.schwarzwald-tourist-info.de). This regional tourist office has a good selection of rentals, but it's only in German. A much smaller site, www.blackforestfarms.de, is a collaborative effort, in English, of twenty local farmers offering farm holidays.

www.accommodation.de. Copious German rentals (and many elsewhere in Europe) on this German-run Web site. Owners post listings; it's not an agency, so prices tend to be reasonable. Prices are near the top layer of the Web site to make browsing quicker.

www.landtourismus.de. Germany-wide farm vacation database with great detailed English descriptions. Example: Two-bedroom flat on a farm with goats, ponies, rabbits, and covered wagon rides, for $46 per night.

www.vacation-apartments.com. Only about 600 listings, but generally very low prices.

ireland

Irish Cottage Holiday Homes (011-353-1-205-2777; www.irishcottage holidays.com). Good variety of listings from $150 to $750 per week.

Irish National Tourist Board (www.ireland.ie). Select "Where to Stay" then "Self-catering" for a good selection of listings at $100 to $700 per week.

italy

Agriturist Farm Holidays (011-39-564-418051; www.agriturist.it). More farm holiday choices. Web site in Italian.

IHA and Homeliday. See above.

The Parker Company (800-280-2811; www.theparkercompany.com). Hundreds of villas and apartments, most with pools. Rentals start at about $600 per week in the off-season. Can also arrange airfare, cell phones, and other travel needs.

RentVillas.com (800-726-6702; www.rentvillas.com). About 1,000 properties in Italy and five other countries. Starting at $500 to $700 per week in the off-season and running $1,200 to $2,500 in the high season.

Toscana Agriturismo (www.toscana.agriturismo.net). My favorite for apartments and houses in Tuscany—despite the name, it has both country and city locations. Web site in English and Italian with prices right up front. Starting at €300 to €500 per week off-season; €600 and up high season.

www.agritour.net. Italian site with a database of about 2,000 farm holiday sites. Top layers are in English, but many individual listings are in Italian only.

norway

www.bergen-guide.com. The Web site of the Bergen tourist office has a good listing of accommodation links, from in-city apartments to rural cabins.

spain

Casas Cantabricas (011-44-1223-328-721; www.casacantab.co.uk). Rentals in "Green Spain"—Cantabria, Asturias, and Galicia—and in the mountains between Salamanca and Extremadura. Low season starts at about $250 per week, high at about $360. Office is based in England.

TurGalicia (Galicia Tourist Office) (011-34-981-54-25-27; www.turgalicia.es). A good English database of apartments, B&Bs, and rural rentals in Galicia.

www.casaspain.com. Pick English, then click on the map of Spain to choose an area. Once you find a listing you like, you will contact the owners directly. One of the best selections of Spanish listings we've seen.

sweden

Destination Stockholms Skårgård (011-46-8-542-481-00; www.dess.se) Cottages in the Stockholm archipelago, starting at about $250 in the off-season and $350 in midsummer. Book seven to eight months ahead for high season.

Sweden Home Rentals (www.swedenhomerentals.se). A great Web site covering rentals all over Sweden, starting at about $300 per week. Descriptions are almost universally in English.

switzerland

Holiday-Home (www.holiday-home.ch). Hundreds of rentals all over Switzerland and many in other countries, too. Off-season rentals start as low as $400 per week; high season $500 and up.

Schweizer Reisekasse (REKA) (www.reka.ch). Nonprofit devoted to inexpensive family vacations. Web site in French, German, and Italian provides access to 3,000 rentals.

Swiss Holiday Farms Association (011–41–31–329–6633; www.bauernhof-ferien.ch/englisch). Two hundred seventy farm vacations, in cooperation with REKA (above). Most parts of Web site in German only.

hosteling

Country-specific hosteling information. Many national tourist offices in Europe provide excellent free hostel guides or maps. Contact the national tourist offices listed under "Tourist Offices (NTOs)" later in this chapter to obtain them.

The Hostelling International Official Guide. Hostelling International (HI). $18. Location and booking info on all hostels worldwide. Tells whether family rooms are available. Order this book from HI-USA when you get your membership.

Hostelling International–USA (HI-USA) (301–495–1240; www.hiusa.org). Adult memberships $28, under eighteen free. Join HI-USA and stay in European hostels for about $18 per night ($25 to $40 in big cities).

www.guideforeurope.com. This well-done Web site offers a wealth of information about hosteling, including reviews and instructions for making a sheet sack. This is where I found the list of castle hostels.

hotels

Budget chains in Europe include:

Campanile	www.envergure.fr
ETAP	www.etaphotel.com
Fast Hotel	www.fasthotel.com
Formule 1	www.hotelformule1.com
Motel One	www.motel-one.com
Premiere Classe	www.envergure.fr

Hello! series of hotel guides (www.HelloEurope.com). All by Margo Classé, Wilson Publishing. Guides to hotels in most European cities in the range of $50 to $99 (£50 to £99 in Britain), with good-value restaurants and other helpful advice thrown in. Series includes:
Hello Britain and Ireland! ISBN: 0-9653-9449-2
Hello France! ISBN: 0-9653-9440-9
Hello Italy! ISBN: 0-9653-9446-8
Hello Spain! ISBN: 0-9653-9441-7

Logis de France (011–33–1–45–84–70–00; www.logis-de-france.fr). There are 3,000 reasonably priced hotels in France, many of them designated "Logis-Famille" for their special family features.

www.eurapart.com. Great information on budget hotels.

language and translation

ALPs (Accelerated Language Programs), Dartmouth College (603–646–2922; www.dartmouth.edu/~rassias/alps). Perhaps the best intensive language program in the country. Using the world-renowned Rassias Method, students cover the equivalent of a ten-week semester in ten days. Expensive but highly recommended. I learned German at ALPS.

Audio Forum (800–243–1234; www.audioforum.com). Leading producer of audio and video language tapes in more than forty languages, from $20 to $275.

The A–Z of French Food. de Temmerman, Geneviève, and Didier Chedorge. Paris: Scribo Editions, 1998. Fax: 011–33–3–86–88–01–51. The absolute best menu dictionary for French food. Buy it in Paris at W. H. Smith's and you will never be clueless in a French restaurant again.

Berlitz European Menu Reader. Berlitz Travel Guides, 1997. ISBN: 2-8315-6245-7. Compact (4 by 5¾ inches) volume carries useful phrases and common dishes for fifteen European languages, from Swedish to Serbo-Croatian, plus a useful explanation of British food terms. An excellent all-in-one guide for a bargain price.

First Thousand Words in . . . Usborne/EDC Publications. Colorful cartoon illustrations (sort of like a Richard Scarey wordbook) introduce your kids to a few words of language before your trip. Available for French, German, Spanish, Italian, and Russian.

Language flash cards. Visual Education Association (800–243–7070; www.vis-ed.com). One thousand vocabulary cards in the language of your choice.

Marling Menu Masters. Altarinda Books. France, Germany, Italy, or Spain. Pocket-size books of about one hundred pages. Because each country has its own book, the Marling guides are more comprehensive than the all-in-one Berlitz guide.

Language practice CDs. Champs-Elysées, Inc. (800–824–0829; www.champs-elysees.com). Sixty-minute CDs of news and interviews. Great for intermediate students who want to improve their comprehension of native speakers. French or German: monthly, $168 per eleven issues or $97 per five issues. Italian or Spanish: bimonthly, $110 per six issues. Choices include:
Puerta del Sol (Spanish)   *Champs-Elysées* (French)
Schau ins Land (German)   *Acquerello Italiano* (Italian)

Worldwide Gestures. Kavenaugh, James. Waterford Press. If you don't speak a language, universal body language helps bridge the gap. This clever sixteen-panel laminated pocket guide summarizes the world's most universal gestures—and saves you from making unintended insults abroad. At www.amazon.com.

magazines and newsletters

International Living (877–819–4064; www.internationalliving.com). Monthly newsletter covers travel, work, living, and retiring overseas. Good commonsense details and financial information. If you get hooked on overseas life during your trip, this publication will help you run away permanently. $49 per year.

International Travel News (800–486–4968; www.intltravelnews.com). News and tips "for the high-frequency international traveler." Bare-bones newsprint publication, but extremely useful due to very interactive format with lots of reader input. Published monthly, $19 per year.

Transitions Abroad (802–422–4827; www.transitionsabroad.com). Bimonthly magazine encouraging intercultural interaction and travel. Although much of the content focuses on teaching English overseas, the variety of perspectives from contributing writers is always inspiring. $19.95 per year.

tourist offices (ntos)

National tourist offices exist to promote tourism to their countries. Contact them and explain the goals of your trip (family travel, budget deals, stamp collecting—whatever) and you should receive a big packet of brochures and maps in return. Most now have great Web sites, including family-specific tips.

Austrian National Tourist Office, 500 Fifth Avenue, Suite 800, New York, NY 10110; (212) 944-6880; www.austria.info

Belgian Tourist Office, 780 Third Avenue, Suite 1501, New York, NY 10017; (212) 758-8130; www.visitbelgium.com

British Tourist Authority, 551 Fifth Avenue, Seventh Floor, New York, NY 10176; (800) 462-2748; www.visitbritain.com

French Government Tourist Office, 444 Madison Avenue, New York, NY 10022; (410) 286-8310 for brochures; www.franceguide.com

German National Tourist Office, 122 East Forty-second Street, Fifty-second Floor, New York, NY 10168-0072; (800) 651-7010; www.visits-to-germany.com

Greek National Tourist Organization, Olympic Tower, 645 Fifth Avenue, New York, NY 10022; (212) 421-5777; www.greektourism.com

Tourism Ireland, 345 Park Avenue, New York, NY 10154; (800) 223-6470; www.tourismireland.com

Italian Government Travel Office, 630 Fifth Avenue #1565, New York, NY 10111; (212) 245-5618; www.italiantourism.com

Luxembourg National Tourist Office, 17 Beekman Place, New York, NY 10022; (212) 935-8888; www.visitluxembourg.com

Netherlands Board of Tourism, 355 Lexington Avenue, Nineteenth Floor, New York, NY 10017; (888) GO HOLLAND, www.goholland.com

Portuguese Trade and Tourism Office, 590 Fifth Avenue, Fourth Floor, New York, NY 10036; (212) 354-4403; www.portugal.org

Scandinavian Tourist Board (Denmark, Iceland, Finland, Norway, Sweden), 655 Third Avenue #1810, New York, NY 10017; (212) 885-9700; www.go scandinavia.com

Tourist Office of Spain, 666 Fifth Avenue, Thirty-fifth Floor, New York, NY 10103; (212) 265-8822; www.okspain.org

Switzerland Tourism, 608 Fifth Avenue, New York, NY 10020; (877) 794-8037; www.myswitzerland.com

time line

World History Chart. International Timeline Inc. (800-886-4478; www .historychart.com). This 90-by-27-inch time line chart compares simultaneous historic events in fifteen regions around the world. A great help in building a sense of context for history. $34.95 unlaminated, $54.95 laminated (shipping extra).

trains

Each country offers a bewildering array of passes. Get good advice before you go from:

Europe Through the Back Door, 130 Fourth Avenue N, Edmonds, WA 98020; (425) 771-8303; www.ricksteves.com. Excellent source for rail passes, travel books, and just generally trustworthy information. Request Rick's Guide to Rail Passes and his free quarterly newsletter.

Rail Europe (888-382-7245; www.raileurope.com). Comprehensive info on train fares, schedules, special rail passes, etc., in Europe.

Many of the country-specific train Web sites offer schedules and prices for trains throughout Europe, in English. Check out www.bahn.de—it's one of the best.

travel communities

The Internet is a wonderful resource for learning from other families who are eager to share their travel tips. For more in-the-trenches experiences, these are four of our favorite sites:

www.bootsnall.com. Go to "Community" then scroll down to the section labeled "Other Travel Related Stuff," where you'll find the topic "Traveling with Kids."

www.frommers.com. Go to "Travel Talk" then "Lifestyle Boards" then "Family Travel."

www.ricksteves.com. Go to "Graffiti Wall" then "Diverse Travelers" then "Travel with Kids."

www.slowtrav.com. Go to the search box and type in "family."

index